RESEARCHING DIGITAL LIFE

'*Researching Digital Life* is essential reading for anyone interested in investigating and understanding how the digital has become part of our lives. This excellent book offers an incredibly accessible and comprehensive guide to digital methods, and by introducing approaches from the social sciences, arts and computational sciences alongside each other it also delivers the interdisciplinary vision of digital research that all researchers will benefit from.'

Prof. Sarah Pink, Emerging Technologies Research Lab, Monash University

'The pervasive digital mediation of everyday life presents unique epistemological, methodological, ethical and practical challenges for social science researchers. This text offers researchers a thorough and greatly-needed critical review of these issues, along with vital guidance for undertaking studies of digital life.'

Prof. Sarah Elwood, Dept of Geography, University of Washington

'This book represents a pivotal moment in digital social research. By exploring a comprehensive range of questions, methods and means of data generation and analysis, it captures the present and future of social research. Thoughtful, thorough and reflexive, the text insightfully details how to make sense of our digital lives.'

Prof. David Beer, Dept of Sociology, University of York

James Ash • Rob Kitchin • Agnieszka Leszczynski

RESEARCHING DIGITAL LIFE

Orientations, Methods and Practice

1 Oliver's Yard
55 City Road
London EC1Y 1SP

2455 Teller Road
Thousand Oaks
California 91320

Unit No 323-333, Third Floor, F-Block
International Trade Tower, Nehru Place
New Delhi 110 019

8 Marina View Suite 43-053
Asia Square Tower 1
Singapore 018960

Editor: Umeeka Raichura
Assistant editor: Hannah Cavender-Deere
Production editor: Victoria Nicholas
Marketing manager: Ifeoma Uzoka
Cover design: Shaun Mercier
Typeset by: KnowledgeWorks Global Ltd

© James Ash, Rob Kitchin and Agnieszka Leszczynski 2024

Apart from any fair dealing for the purposes of research, private study, or criticism or review, as permitted under the Copyright, Designs and Patents Act, 1988, this publication may not be reproduced, stored or transmitted in any form, or by any means, without the prior permission in writing of the publisher, or in the case of reprographic reproduction, in accordance with the terms of licences issued by the Copyright Licensing Agency. Enquiries concerning reproduction outside those terms should be sent to the publisher.

Library of Congress Control Number: 2023941852

British Library Cataloguing in Publication data

A catalogue record for this book is available from the British Library

ISBN 978-1-5296-0166-4
ISBN 978-1-5296-0165-7 (pbk)

Contents

List of Tables — vii
List of Figures — ix
About the Authors — xi
Acknowledgements — xiii
Preface — xv

Part 1: Orientations — 1

1 Introduction — 3
2 Methodologies, Ontologies and Epistemologies — 15
3 Research Design and Implementation — 29
4 Research Ethics — 47

Part 2: Methods and Approaches — 69

5 Interviews, Surveys, Observation and (Auto)Ethnography — 71
6 Walking Methodologies, Walkthroughs and Audits — 91
7 Arts-based Methods — 109
8 Participatory Methods — 127
9 Historical Methods — 143
10 Data Visualisation and Mapping — 157
11 Data Analytics — 179

Part 3: Methods in Action — 191

12   Interfaces and Apps — 193
13   Social and Locative Media — 205
14   Mobilities — 217
15   Smart Cities — 229
16   Digital Labour — 239

Part 4: Conclusion — 253

17   Final Thoughts — 255

References — 259
Index — 303

List of Tables

3.1	Reasons for undertaking research	31
4.1	Fair information practice principles	54
11.1	Data mining tasks and techniques	183

List of Figures

3.1	An example of a Gantt chart	32
10.1	Quantitative data visualisation techniques	165
10.2	Qualitative data visualisation techniques	168
10.3	Percentage of the local area population who are internet users in England, Scotland and Wales	172
10.4	Cartographic techniques, including for mapping enumerated thematic data (a to c) and for aggregatting individual-level data (d and e)	174
16.1	Online labour demand: within-country share of demand by occupation	245
16.2	Online labour demand: global market share of demand for digital work by occupation	245

About the Authors

James Ash is a Reader in technology, space and society at Newcastle University. His work investigates the cultures, economies and politics of digital interfaces and the role that digital technologies play in transforming everyday life. He is the author of *Phase Media: Space, Time and the Politics of Smart Objects* (Bloomsbury, 2017) and *The Interface Envelope: Gaming, Technology, Power* (Bloomsbury, 2015). He also co-edited the collection *Digital Geographies* (Sage, 2018) with Rob Kitchin and Agnieszka Leszczynski.

Rob Kitchin is a Professor in Maynooth University, Social Sciences Institute and Department of Geography. He was a European Research Council Advanced Investigator for the Programmable City project (2013–18) and Data Stories project (2022–27), and a principal investigator for the Digital Repository of Ireland (2009–17). He is author, co-author, editor or co-editor of thirty-four other academic books, and author or co-author of more than 200 articles and book chapters. He has been an editor of *Dialogues in Human Geography, Progress in Human Geography* and *Social and Cultural Geography*, and was the co-editor-in-chief of the *International Encyclopedia of Human Geography*. He is a recipient of the Royal Irish Academy's Gold Medal for the Social Sciences.

Agnieszka Leszczynski is an Associate Professor in the Department of Geography and Environment at Western University in Canada. Her work is broadly situated in the field of digital geographies, with a particular focus on intensifying intersections of digitality and cities. She is a former co-editor of *Big Data & Society*, and a current editor of *Dialogues in Human Geography* and *Environment and Planning F: Philosophy, Theory, Models, Methods and Practice*.

Acknowledgements

As all authors are aware, writing a book is an individual and a collective endeavour. While the writer crafts the text, it is informed and shaped through numerous interactions with others. *Researching Digital Life* is infused with the practical and conceptual knowledge and experiences we have each gained through working on numerous projects with multiple collaborators over many years, alongside feedback we have received when presenting our research at various events or through referee comments. It would be foolhardy to try to list all those that have helped shape our thought and praxes, as no doubt such a list would be very long and risk many omissions. Rather, it is simpler to extend a universal thanks to all those who have generously provided constructive feedback and observations on how to conduct productive and insightful research in general, and in particular with respect to making sense of the effects of digital technologies on society.

In addition, we would like to thank all the various staff at Sage who have shepherded *Researching Digital Life* to publication. Jai Seaman helped shape the original proposal and guided the book through its opening phases. Umeeka Raichura took on the baton and guided the text to completion and into the production process. They were aided by Rhiannon Holt and Hannah Cavender-Deere. Victoria Nicholas and Sarah Meaney aided the manuscript through production at Sage and we are thankful for their diligence.

A number of the figures in Chapter 10 were prepared by Karen Van Kerkoerle at Western University, and we are very grateful for her contributions. Figure 10.3 is reproduced from Blank et al. (2018) under terms of CC BY 4.0 licence. Figure 10.4 uses Tatauranga Aotearoa/Stats NZ Geographic Data Service data licensed for reuse under the CC BY 4.0 licence. Figures 16.1 and 16.2 are reproduced from Stephany et al. (n.d.) under terms of CC BY 4.0 licence. Chapter 11 draws in part on a chapter on data analytics in the second edition of *The Data Revolution*; the material used has been reworked and extended.

Preface

Since the birth of digital computing in the 1950s, how society operates and is managed, and the ways in which social relations take place, have become ever more entwined with the digital. In particular, from the 1990s on, the digital has become a progressively pervasive presence and force in social life, underwritten by the adoption of personal computing, the exponential growth of the internet, the proliferation of suites of software, the digital mediation of existing systems and infrastructures, and a plethora of new digital technologies and platforms. We now live in a present where networked digital technologies, systems and infrastructures are thoroughly interwoven into home, work, governance, consumption, travel and play. We routinely interact with and co-produce the digital, so much so that everyday life has become 'digital life'. Given the centrality of the digital to the spaces and practices of everyday life, it has become a core focus of interest in the social sciences. Over the past decade this centrality has been marked by the formalisation of numerous sub-disciplines, including digital sociology (Lupton, 2014), digital anthropology (Horst and Miller, 2012) and digital geography (Ash et al., 2018a).

These substantive 'digital turns' in social sciences scholarship have been paralleled by the flourishing of innovative methods and methodologies for researching – and researching with – digital phenomena. This has led to a number of methods texts detailing the use of digital tools in social sciences research, as well as volumes that examine how digital phenomena have permutated established social sciences methodologies such as ethnography. However, less attention has been given to how to research the digital in the broader sense of a phenomenon that permeates the spaces and practices of everyday life for which traditional social science research methods, such as conducting surveys and interviews, are not always appropriate or sufficient. The aim of this book, therefore, is to provide an interdisciplinary introduction to the key methodological orientations and approaches to researching digital life, extending considerations of the digital beyond the remit of human life to include researching the lives of data, smart and connected objects (the IoT, or Internet of Things), and spaces from the scale of the smart home to that of the smart city, providing grounded, well-illustrated advice as to how to conduct such research. As such, our ambition has been to provide a guide to researching and making sense of our thoroughly digitally mediated world, introducing the reader to key ideas, issues, debates and methods for researching digital life, and to demonstrate how these have been applied in practice within existing studies.

To perform this work, the book is structured into three main parts. **Part 1** provides an initial orientation with respect to the theoretical aspects of framing and approaching research on digital life and how this relates to the methodology and methods adopted, along with a discussion of the practical and technical, and political and ethical, issues of conducting research on the digital. **Part 2** details a number of related methods and approaches for researching digital life. Both traditional and digital methods are profiled, detailing how the methods are applied in practice, and their pros and cons. **Part 3** provides illustrative examples of how the array of methods and methodologies profiled in **Part 2** have been successfully mobilised across a number of empirical studies to research five facets of digital life: interfaces and apps; social and locative media; mobilities; smart cities; and digital labour. The book concludes by reflecting briefly on the challenges of undertaking research on digital life. While this structure provides a fairly linear path through the material, it also facilitates the reader to dip selectively into the material most pertinent to their research project. We advise reading the whole of **Part 1** before elements of **Part 2** or **3**, as the chapters discuss issues that are relevant for all research relating to digital life.

In writing each chapter, we have sought to provide clear pedagogic supports including:

- a chapter overview and summary of key ideas at the start and end of each chapter;
- a clearly written narrative that ensures that the conceptual material is explained in an accessible way, using examples to illustrate how an idea works in practice;
- plenty of case material, grounding the discussion in ideas, praxis, and findings from real-world research projects;
- clear signposting of how to navigate and make optimal use of the text, and cross-referencing to guide readers to other relevant material in the book;
- a selection of references that point the reader to relevant key works; and
- a short guide to further reading and resources at the end of each chapter.

Throughout the text we have sought to highlight diversity, equity and inclusion issues, including case study material relating to a spectrum of marginalised communities broadly conceived (i.e., along lines of gender, race, sexuality, disability, etc.). We also discuss methods and approaches that seek to be more inclusive in their conception and application, such as participatory methods and decolonial approaches, as well as issues such as the politics of research, reflexivity, positionality and ethics.

Our central assertions are two-fold. First, everyday life has become digital life and this demands sustained critical and empirical attention. Second, making sense of digital phenomena and the difference they make requires moving beyond traditional social science and humanities approaches and methods. Our hope is that this book provides a valuable resource for making sense of our digital world, that it inspires its readers to undertake innovative, rigorous and robust research, and that it helps to inform and strengthen those research endeavours.

Part I
Orientations

1
Introduction

Overview

This chapter:

- offers definitions of key terms used in the book, including 'digital', 'technology' and 'digital life';
- provides an overview of the kinds of phenomena that are studied when researching digital life, including technologies, practices, mediations and space-times;
- identifies the need for engaging with questions of method when embarking on research about digital life, and specifies how methods are engaged in this book; and
- outlines the structure of the book and the different methods that can be used to study digital life.

Introduction

Everyday life is digital life. This claim speaks to how the mundane routines and rhythms of moving and making it through the day as a human in the world – including the quotidian aspects of work, social reproduction, leisure, mobility, sociality, education and civic engagement – are now pervasively inflected by digitality (Leszczynski, 2020a; Pink et al., 2017). It also captures how we have come to take digital phenomena as entirely ordinary, at times unremarkable, yet expected presences in the space-times of our daily lives. Simultaneously, everyday life is the context in which digital phenomena become meaningful and assume significance, and in which they are negotiated, contested and remade by any number of actors, be they human, non-human or more-than-human (Pink et al., 2017). Digital life, then, refers to these recursive, 'co-generative dynamics' (Rodgers and Moore, 2018: n.p.) between everyday life and digitality. In this way, 'digital life' constitutes a synonym for all aspects of scholarly interest and activity in and across a number of social science fields that recognise and engage with the importance of 'the digital', including but not limited to digital geography, digital sociology, digital anthropology and digital communication and (new) media studies.

This rise in academic and social science interest in understanding and studying digital phenomena is cause for celebration for the potential digital researcher, but it has also brought with it a number of issues. Principle among these is the emergence of a novel set of challenges related to *how* to go about researching the myriad ways in which digitality is (re)shaping ways of being, thinking and doing that mediate how people live with and relate to other things and beings in the context of intensifying intersections between digitality and the everyday. While there are now a number of methods for using digital tools (e.g., software, platforms, archives) in social sciences research, as well as work that contends with how digital phenomena have permuted established social sciences methodologies such as ethnography, less attention has been given to how to research the digital in the broader sense of phenomena that permeate the spaces, practices, relationalities and temporalities of everyday life for which traditional social science research methods, such as conducting surveys and interviews, are not always appropriate or sufficient. That is to say, to date, insufficient attention has been paid to how to account for digital life in social sciences research.

The rest of this introductory chapter is structured as follows. The next section provides definitions of key terms used throughout the book, including 'digital' and 'digital life', as well as of key concepts that represent subjects and objects of study about digital life, including 'digital mediation', 'digital practices' and 'space-times'. The chapter then outlines our engagement with method and argues for an irreductionist approach to researching digital life. The chapter concludes with an outline of the structure and content of the book.

Definitional Matters

Digital

In this book, we espouse a multifaceted definition of 'digitality' that we have previously advanced elsewhere (Ash et al., 2018a, 2018b). Specifically, we define digitality as comprising an expansive universe of objects, aesthetics, logics, discourses and genres of production that implicate and are implicated by the architectures and systems of digital computing, yet which are irreducible to them. At the most immediate level, 'digital' designates the translation of computational 'inputs and outputs into binary' digits of '0s and 1s, which can be stored, transferred, or manipulated at the level of numbers' (Lunenfeld, 1999: xv). This is true even where we do not encounter, experience or interact with digital phenomena as strings of 1s and 0s *per se*, but rather as, for instance, seamless streams of videos, music, audio, imagery and feeds of content posted to social media that we access and consume through digital screens and interfaces.

When we refer to digital objects, we are designating material digital phenomena, including digital devices (such as smartphones, tablets and computers used to access, generate and interact with digital content), data (digitally encoded information), media, code, software, algorithms, interfaces and various elements of digital infrastructure (e.g., fibre optic cables, Wi-Fi routers and 5G cells). These objects are often colloquially referred to as digital technologies: phenomena that draw on the power of binary computation to encode, process and act on data at speed and in huge volume. In this sense of objects, then, digitality is rooted in technical enablement and enactment, an essentialised property of computational systems that has also been referred to as technicity (Kitchin and Dodge, 2011): the inherent power of digital objects to make things happen independently of humans, whether they have been designed explicitly by humans or not (such as the recent advent of 'generative AI'). Like other non-human entities, such as animals, objects and tools, digital technologies have an autonomy and capacity to perturb and influence humans and other non-humans in ways that exceed or confound human intention.

Beyond objects, digital technologies have themselves 'recoded multiple other' phenomena (Ash et al., 2018b: 26). As such, digitality is:

> also an aesthetics, capturing the pervasiveness of digital technologies and shaping how we understand and experience space and spatiality as always-already 'marked by circuits of digitality' that are themselves irreducible to digital systems (Murray, 2008: 40). As we adopt and ubiquitously embed networked digital technologies across physical landscapes, they come to enact progressively routine orderings of quotidian … interactions, opportunities, … configurations, and flows (Franklin, 2015) … To this we [also] add … digital discourses which actively promote, enable, secure, and materially sustain the increasing reach of digital technologies. (Ash et al., 2018b: 26).

Holistically, then, we use 'the digital' 'to make reference to material technologies characterized by binary computing architectures; the genre of socio-techno-cultural productions, artefacts, and orderings of everyday life that result from our … engagement with digital mediums; and the logics that both structure these ordering practices as well as their effects' in and for everyday life (Ash et al., 2018b: 26). Importantly, these aspects of digitality are not mutually exclusive but rather implicate and are implicated by each other. When researching digital life, scholars engage with digitality in one, or multiple, of these senses of the term. Yet in addition to studying the digital technologies, aesthetics, logics and discourses of digitality, scholars digital life also closely engage with additional concepts that likewise are the foci of research about digital life. These include digital *practices*, *mediation* and *space-times*.

Practices

By practices, we refer to what people do with digital things. This involves people who create and work with digital hardware and software, as well as those that are involved with these products and objects as end users, either in terms of consumers or those who have to engage with them as part of their work. Schatzki et al. (2001: 11) usefully define practices as 'the skills, or tacit knowledges and presuppositions, that underpin activities'. How practices are conceptually understood, however, varies across theoretical and philosophical traditions, with different conceptualisations emerging from feminism (Ahmed, 2006), non-representational theory (Anderson and Harrison, 2012) and pragmatist philosophy (Dreyfus, 1991). For example, feminism might cast practices as sites where gendered forms of difference come into being, whereas non-representational theory might consider practices as productive sites of the making and un-making of subjectivity, while pragmatism might consider practices as the basis of embodied intelligence and being-in-the-world. While there are important differences in emphasis within and between these traditions, we take three points of agreement as key to why studying practices matter for researching digital phenomena.

As arrays or fields of activity, practices with other humans and non-humans are key sites at which: a) bodily habits are generated and reinforced; b) societal norms are formed and stabilised; and c) power relations are established (Pedwell, 2016). How these three modes of practices relate to one another can be illustrated with respect to social media. The use of images and image memes create new habits of checking, swiping and sharing that involve distinct bodily gestures and ways of seeing and feeling (Ash, 2015; Pedwell, 2017). These digital media also form new societal norms about what is appropriate to share with others (Wagner, A., 2018), and further establish power relations between social media platforms, government regulators and the general public in terms of who decides what can be shared, how and when (Rochefort, 2020). What unites different approaches to understanding digital practices is a recognition that practices can be both discursive and non-discursive, conscious and unconscious, tacit and implicit, as well as overt and explicit. In many cases, practices are so powerful because those enacting them are not even aware of how their norms, habits, and power relations are affecting them, or other enmeshed humans and non-humans, even when they are discursive, conscious, overt and explicit.

Mediation

The concept of 'mediation' is long established and debated within media theory. As Mitchell and Hansen (2010) argue, the concept of mediation takes many forms, from common sense understandings of mediation as a means of communication that enables a message to be transmitted, to Marxist definitions of mediation as labour, where work connects humans to the non-human world through the acquisition, modification and transformation of 'natural' and 'raw' materials. While we recognise that there are multiple definitions of mediation, in this book we adhere to Kember and Zylinska's (2012: 40) definition that casts mediation as a 'multiagential force that incorporates humans and [digital] technologies … in an ongoing process' of world-making. Kember and Zylinska's (2012) theory of mediation is particularly significant for our efforts to engage with methods, approaches and orientations for researching digital life for two reasons. First, because it is non-humanist in its articulation (i.e., it does not privilege or centre humans), it is ontologically neutral regarding who – and what – has the capacity to participate in digital-social life (see **Chapter 2**). And second, it refuses false separations, or binaries, between digitality and society.

Instead of mediation constituting an intervening factor that explains recursive relationships between sociality and digitality, Kember and Zylinska (2012) argue that mediation itself is an 'intrinsic condition of being-in … the [digital] world' (p. 1), in which humans and digital, 'technological, social, economic, geographical, and other influences … well beyond those controlled by the human' 'become-with' together (p. 9). In other words, any number or entities – including humans and the vast array of digital phenomena – co-generate the everyday contexts, rhythms and space-times of everyday life. In claiming that 'we have always been mediated', Kember and Zylinska (2012) are saying that mediation describes and captures how technology (and now more recently digitality), sociality and humanity are co-constitutive of each other. As a force of these dynamics, mediation works to fix or stabilise these processes of digital-social becoming and being-with in ways that make them appear legible and tractable to us (as humans), rendering digital life as something that we can actually research and study. Yet importantly, mediation is simultaneously lively, full of the 'possibility of the emergence of forms always new or [of the] potentiality to generate unprecedented connections and unexpected events' (Kember and Zylinska, 2012: 24). This liveliness attunes us as scholars to contending with the ever-shifting, evolving, and undetermined nature of digital life and of methods and approaches for studying it.

Space-times

By 'space-times' we refer to the spaces/places and temporalities that digital technologies, logics, aesthetics, discourses, practices and mediations are linked to. This includes considerations of when and where these phenomena and forces are enmeshed (e.g., pre-existing space-times), as well as the spaces and temporalities that they can alter or generate (e.g., the space-times that digital technologies can produce, which can interact with or alter pre-existing space-times). Here, we are thinking of space-times as diverse as cities, smart homes, interfaces and video games. Like the concepts of technology, practices and mediation, the concept of space-time is not without diverse conceptualisation (May and Thrift, 2001). In this book, when we refer to space-time we are influenced by feminist thinkers of space-time such as Doreen Massey (2005). She forwards a productive and relational definition in which space-time is neither a container in which things unfold over time nor simply a set of relations between things, but rather spatial and temporal relations are actively produced by and through the relations between phenomena, where many of these relations undergird or exceed particular phenomena themselves. For example, we could say that using an on-demand delivery app on a smartphone, such as Uber Eats to order a prepared meal, does not simply connect a delivery vehicle (e.g., bicycle), courier, restaurant and customer across a pre-given space of a city (e.g., the route from the food preparation location to the location of the consumer). Rather, as Lizzie Richardson (2020) argues, the app arranges the space-time relations of the city by creating a sense of near and far, now and the future, based on how the interface of the app displays the courier's location relative to the restaurant *and* to the customer, and the estimated time of delivery of the meal. In this way, the Uber Eats app creates the space-times of the city that alter how consumers and couriers sense and understand the city around them, remaking the city space in ongoing processes of translation and transformation.

Digital Life

Through the forces of mediation, digital technologies, logics, aesthetics, discourses and practices are together generative of digital life. In the same way that the term 'digital' needs interrogation and definition, so does the term 'life'. Otherwise, the term 'digital life' could itself become a kind of black box. We recognise this risk and in particular acknowledge the long and complex philosophical debates over what constitutes life and the living within multiple academic disciplines, including biology and the medical sciences, as well as sociology, philosophy, and the humanities and social sciences more broadly (Thacker, 2010). Within many social sciences, the question of what constitutes life and the living has been recently cast in terms of a 'vital materialism'. From a vital or new materialist perspective (Bennett, 2009; Coole and Frost, 2010), life is not reducible to biological processes of growth and reproduction most usually associated with humans, animals and plants. Rather, vital materialism posits a kind of general affectivity to all things, living and dead, animate and inanimate, and organic and inorganic.

In this book, we wish to take life in this general sense: as a kind of general affectivity that crosses between what has been traditionally thought of as alive and dead. Yet unlike strong forms of vital materialism that emphasise a difference in degree rather than kind between traditionally distinct realms of living and non-living being (such as animal or human, or human and technical) (e.g., Roberts, 2014), we believe that differences in kind between entities can be identified and usefully posited to aid analysis of different phenomena and issues about digital life. However, we make this claim with two considerable caveats.

The first caveat is that there is a recognition that any differences in kind identified between digital phenomena are not absolute and may always be thought otherwise. The second caveat, built on the first, is that differences in kind may be established only once key research questions, theoretical positions and methods have been established and reflected on by the researcher. As decades of feminist scholarship has carefully shown (Haraway, 1988; Rose, 1997), research questions, theoretical positions and methods, like all forms of knowledge and techniques of knowledge production, are not value-free and do not emerge from nowhere; rather, they are produced by situated human knowers and the sum of their experiences, pedagogies and implicit and overt biases (i.e., they are value-laden) (see **Chapter 2**). Having integrity as a researcher is not about attempting to overcome these assumptions to produce a truly objective account of digital life. Rather, it is about reflecting on and recognising how our assumptions affect the methods and approaches that we choose to use to study digital life, and how different methods will bring different aspects of digital life to light.

With the above definitions of digitality and an irreductionist approach to life established, digital life can be understood as an ongoing transformation of ways of being, thinking and doing that inform how people live with, and relate to, other humans and non-humans who mediate (co-generate) the digital-social worlds that comprise the spaces and times of our everyday lives. In this sense, we also advance digital life in a second, very general meaning as a synonym or umbrella term for all aspects of enquiry about digitality in the social sciences and corollary disciplines, including in the fields of digital geography, digital sociology and digital anthropology, among others. This conceptual approach to digital life directly informs how we think about methods (specific techniques of data collection and analysis) and the appropriate deployment of methods (methodologies and research designs). (See **Chapters 2 and 3**).

Studying Digital Life

Taking an irreductionist approach to conceptualising digital life seriously, we espouse an equally irreductionist perspective on the actual study of digital life. For this reason, this book presents an expansive cross-section of methodological orientations and specific techniques for collecting, sourcing and analysing data about digital life. By data, we do not refer only to digital capta (digitally encoded information), but also use this term to encompass the wealth of different kinds of evidence that social scientists gather and produce that may also be analogue in nature (e.g., handwritten notes in a field journal or log) that are *about* aspects of digital life. As with our definition of digital life, here too we stipulate two caveats pertaining to how methodologies and methods for researching digital life are covered in this book. First, the range of approaches engaged are non-exhaustive in the sense that while we have grouped methods and methodologies thematically, we have not endeavoured to cover all methods that have ever been used to study digital life in the social sciences and corollary disciplines. If a method is not included, this does not mean that it should be discounted for use in your research project. Instead, as an orienting text, this book is intended to constitute a starting point for *some* methods of researching digital life. Indeed, we suggest a tactical approach to mobilising methods (selecting the best methods for the purpose of a research project), and as such we hope this book inspires further exploration and careful evaluation of alternative methods. Furthermore, the rapidly evolving landscape of digital life – in which phenomena such as AI are making increasingly quotidian and intense incursions – both necessitates and inspires continuous methodological innovation, including the modification of existing methods and the development of entirely new research approaches and techniques.

The second caveat concerns the nature of methodological developments for researching digital life to date. In researching this book, we have found that much of the methodological innovation and development concerns the advancement of techniques for the collection of both qualitative and quantitative data about digital life, and in techniques for the analysis of quantitative digital data (see **Chapter 11**). On the side of qualitatively oriented research designs (see **Chapters 2 and 3**), however, methodological developments have largely concerned innovations in techniques for data collection – as seen in, for instance, the development of virtual and digital ethnography, and methods and platforms for conducting digital and virtual interviews and focus groups (see **Chapter 5**). Yet when it comes to analysing qualitative data collected through these new techniques, social scientists continue to rely largely on stalwart social science methods. These include, but are not limited to:

- *Qualitative coding and content analysis*, which designates a range of approaches centred on an iterative, recursive process of segmenting, categorising and labelling, and re-assembling qualitative data (e.g., interview transcripts, images) around key categories, usually referred to as 'themes', that reflect patterns in the data (Braun and Clarke, 2021; Cope and Kurtz, 2016);

- *Discourse, narrative and conversational analysis*, which seeks to identify how meaning and stories are constructed and conveyed within texts and non-verbal communication, and how people relate to and engage with one another (Grbich, 2013);
- *Semiotic analysis*, which identifies and interprets phenomena (e.g., body language, written texts and image elements) that function as signs that denote (directly signify) and connote (signify associations with) cultural and social meanings (Aiello and Parry 2020; Harrison, 2003); and
- *Visual methodologies* for analysing visual artefacts (e.g., still and moving images), encompassing content (analysis of what appears), compositional (analysis of how things appear, including in relation to other image elements) and semiotic analysis techniques (analysis of meaning) (Rose, 2022).

Because these qualitative analysis methods are so established, they have been covered extensively elsewhere, including in a plethora of texts dedicated to social science and qualitative research. For this reason – and because these methods may already be familiar to a number of readers – we do not delve into the specifics of qualitative analysis. Instead, the book attends to orienting readers to those aspects of the doing of research of digital life that have been most inflected by spirited methodological innovation and development.

Structure of the Book

With the above points in mind, the rest of the book is organised in three parts. Part I, 'Orientations', is composed of four chapters that provide a methodological introduction to key orientations and debates in digital social sciences research. Chapter 2 offers an overview of the methodological, ontological and epistemological positions and commitments that underwrite a range of orientations to digital phenomena in social sciences and humanities research. Chapter 3 discusses a range of concerns related to the operational and practical issues in researching digital life. These concerns include research design, as well as sourcing data and sampling issues of data quality and ecological fallacies, and producing data management plans. Chapter 4 examines the politics and ethics of conducting research concerning digital life, including ethics frameworks, researcher positionality and situatedness, and identity politics and power in the research process.

Part II, 'Methods and Approaches', provides a set of chapters that each examine a number of related methods and approaches for researching digital life. Both traditional and digital methods are profiled, detailing how the methods are applied in practice, and their pros and cons. Chapter 5 focuses on methods of interviews, focus groups, surveys, observation and (auto)ethnography for studying digital phenomena and how these methods are increasingly digitally mediated, taking place online or facilitated by digital media. Walking and walkthrough method/ologies are discussed in Chapter 6, which details a range of methods that mobilise walking as both a physical practice and a metaphor for approaches that systematically trace digital practices and unpack the black boxes of digital technologies, such as app walkthroughs and audits. Chapter 7 details the turn towards arts-based methods for both undertaking and communicating research on digital life, including the use of creative writing, artistic methods, creative non-fiction, film and exhibitions. Participatory and action research, where research is undertaken with and by a community rather than about and for them, is outlined in Chapter 8. A range of participatory approaches are detailed, including various forms of citizen science such as participatory sensing, crowdsourcing and hackathons, citizen engagement approaches – including public participation GIS (Geographic Information Systems), online participation tools and serious games – and participatory action research – including counter-data actions, community and counter-archiving, and civic hacking. Chapter 9 discusses historical methods, including the digitisation and archiving of data, the production of primary historical data through oral interviews, discovering and collating materials, examining or surveying artefacts and sites, and undertaking historical analysis using digital tools and techniques. Chapter 10 provides an overview of methods for visualising digital data for a range of purposes, including interpreting, communicating, spatialising and expressing the aesthetics of digital datasets. Methodological frameworks covered include digital mapping, cultural analytics, and other techniques for visualizing qualitative and quantitative data. An overview of data analytics used to make sense of big data is detailed in Chapter 11. Methods discussed include data mining and pattern recognition used to identify associations within datasets; network analysis to identify and analyse the structure of digital infrastructure, websites, social media and relations in big data; statistical techniques for testing the salience of relationships between phenomena; and the use of modelling and simulation techniques designed to understand how systems presently function and are likely to perform in the future under various conditions.

The third part of the book, 'Methods in Action', illustrates how specific methods have been put into practice to research digital life across a range of themes. Chapter 12 outlines how interfaces and apps have been researched across a select number of empirical studies that successfully mobilise the techniques and methodologies of app walkthroughs, tracking algorithms and code, interface ethnographies and data visualization and mapping methods. Chapter 13 discusses how social and locative media have been studied using interviews and ethnographic methods, and how social and locative data are being used as a key data source for understanding a wide range of phenomena through the application of data analytics, mapping and visualisation. How different forms of digitally mediated mobilities have been studied through a variety of digital methods including digital ethnography, audits and modelling is detailed in Chapter 14. Chapter 15 outlines how the smart city has been researched using walking methodologies, visualisation (cultural analytics), and sensory prototyping and participatory sensing. Finally, Chapter 16 profiles how interviews and ethnography, data visualisation and digital mapping, and participatory and action research have been used to research the reconfiguration of work by digital technologies, and the rise of digital forms of labour in what has been termed the 'gig economy'.

Understood in relation to practices, mediations and space-times, digital life is a complex set of phenomena. On finishing the book, we hope readers are sensitised to this complexity and have developed an appreciation of the ontological and epistemological implications of different methods and how they might be employed to study different digital issues. In doing so, we hope that both students and researchers new to the field will be enlivened to explore and study the highly uneven nature of digital life, drawing on pre-existing concepts and methods. At the same time, we hope that the principles outlined throughout the book – where digital life is taken as multiple and irreducible – emboldens and empowers students and researchers to develop new methods and concepts to explore digital life as it continues to shift into the twenty-first century and beyond.

Summary

- 'Digitality' can be defined as an expansive universe of objects, aesthetics, logics, discourses and genres of production that implicate and are implicated by the architectures and systems of digital computing, yet are irreducible to them.
- 'Digital life' can be understood as an ongoing transformation of ways of being, thinking and doing that inform how people live with, and relate to, other humans and non-humans who mediate (co-generate) digital-social worlds that comprise the spaces and times of our everyday lives.
- There are multiple methods for studying digital phenomena and researchers can take a tactical approach, mobilising particular methods to suit the research problem at hand.

Recommended Reading

Ash, J., Kitchin, R., and Leszczynski, A. (2018) 'Digital turn, digital geographies?', *Progress in Human Geography*, 42(1): 25–43.
A discussion of the multifaceted nature of digitality and how the empirical focus, concepts and practices of a discipline are being reshaped by a turn towards the digital.

Housley, W., Edwards, A., Beneito-Montagut, R., and Fitzgerald, R. (eds) (2022) *The Sage Handbook of Digital Society*. Sage, London.
A collection of essays that provide a broad overview of contemporary issues concerning digital life.

Kitchin, R. (2022) *The Data Revolution: A Critical Analysis of Big Data, Open Data and Data Infrastructures*. 2nd edn. Sage, London.
An updated introduction on how digital technologies have changed how data is understood, collected and used in the world.

Lunenfeld, P. (1999) *The Digital Dialectic: New Essays on New Media*. MIT Press, Cambridge, MA.
A classic set of essays that theorises the nature of the digital and its consequences.

McLean, J. (2020) *Changing Digital Geographies: Technologies, Environments and People*. Palgrave Macmillan, London.
A powerful account of digital technologies and their relationship with non-humans.

2
Methodologies, Ontologies and Epistemologies

Overview

Chapter 2 examines:

- concepts of methodology, ontology and epistemology, and the linkages between them;
- realist, constructivist, critical realist and non-Western social ontologies, and how these underpin different conceptualisations of digital-social reality;
- the ontological statuses of digital phenomena in digital-social relations;
- positivism and feminist epistemologies, and how these inform knowledge about digital life; and
- why methodological, ontological and epistemological questions are important considerations in researching digital life.

Introduction

To research digital life, social scientists have used a range of scholarly approaches and methods. The purpose of this chapter is to help guide selection from among this range of approaches and methods by providing an overview of three concepts and the linkages between them: methodology, ontology and epistemology. All methods are underwritten by commitments to a particular understanding of social and digital worlds (ontology) and a theory of how we may legitimately claim to know something about those worlds (epistemology). This chapter introduces a non-exhaustive range of different social ontologies, and discusses the status and role of digital phenomena in conceptualisations of digital-social reality. It furthermore establishes connections between these ontologies and specific epistemologies. This serves to identify which epistemologies align with generating knowledge about digital life within different ontological paradigms, and how different epistemologies open onto different ontologies of digital life and of digital phenomena. First, however, it is important to understand why ontologies, epistemologies and methods work together in the context of research studies. This is accounted for by the concept of methodologies.

Methodologies

The term 'methodology' is sometimes used interchangeably with the concept of *research design* (see **Chapter 3**) to refer to a plan for how, and in which order, particular methods for data collection and analysis are deployed in the course of a research project or study. It is also frequently associated with the concept of a *scientific paradigm*, which describes an accepted way of doing things within a scientific community of practice, field or discipline (Kuhn, 1962). But methodologies are distinct from, and are more robust and expansive, than research designs and scientific paradigms. As defined by Smith et al. (2016: 140), a *methodology* is a framework that 'forms the interpretive link between the ways in which knowledge is defined and understood and the practices of inquiry that are used by those who research and conduct scholarship' in a given disciplinary, philosophical or theoretical tradition. Research methodologies 'provide the rationale for research questions and legitimate critical concepts, and they justify the use of [specific] methods' in the generation of knowledge (Smith et al., 2016: 132). This justification for methods and the development and mobilisation of concepts is informed by often taken-for-granted commitments to 'ontological and epistemological positions' (Scotland, 2012: 10). Methodologies accordingly involve considerations about *what* is studied (a question of ontology), including what merits or warrants scholarly attention as a subject/object of research; *how* it is studied, including both the accepted ways in which the subjects/objects of study may be known (a question of epistemology); and which *methods* may justifiably be used to collect and analyse research data about those subjects/objects of study.

In the natural and physical sciences, methodology is often implied, adopting what is popularly called the 'scientific method'. The scientific method almost always involves elements of *empirical* (directly discernible by human senses) observation, *quantitative* (numerical) data collection through measurement, and the statistical testing of hypotheses through a process of *deduction* (research that starts from theory, in this case usually expressed as a hypothesis). While some social scientists do mobilise deductive, quantitative approaches to questions of digital life, others work within methodological orientations that may be described as *qualitative* (centred on the collection and analysis of non-numerical data) and *inductive* (research starts from the data and builds theory through analysis rather than starting from and testing a theory). Examples of qualitative (non-numerical) data include, but are not limited to, the written word, audio, video, still imagery, artistic performance, bodily gestures, signs and symbols. Non-numerical forms of evidence are sometimes described and referred to as a 'texts'.

Furthermore, in social science research, 'theory' may mean different things. In the context of deductively oriented quantitative studies, theory is a hypothesis – an informed 'hunch' about a relationship between phenomena – that may be tested using statistical methods (see **Chapter 12**). Conversely, in qualitative studies, the term theory may refer to either 'high' or 'low' theory. 'High' theory is a framework that provides an internally consistent explanation of social phenomena deployable across a range of research studies (e.g., Marxist theory, feminist theory, postcolonial theory), whereas 'low' theory is constituted by 'small or emergent conceptual arguments' or interpretations that provides an explanation of phenomena advanced within the context of a single study or intervention (which may or may not be couched within the framework of 'high' theory) (Cope and Kurtz, 2016: 655).

The reason for methodological differences in approaches to researching digital life arises from three factors. First, there are multiple worldviews, rooted in different disciplines and traditions, that are concerned with questions about digital life, each of which have entrenched views concerning the appropriateness of particular methodologies for generating knowledge. Relatedly, scholars have varied pedagogical backgrounds and thus different methods training. And third, methodological differences arise from divergences in scholars' preconceived ideas about what digital-social worlds are like – in other words, differences in social ontologies and epistemologies. Differences in these commitments 'often lead to different research approaches', including 'towards the same phenomen[a]' (Scotland, 2012: 10).

Ontologies

An ontology is an axiomatic (pre-existing, taken-for-granted and unfalsifiable) belief about what the world is like. It is a meta-account 'of all the phenomena' – material, conceptual and social – 'that are seen to validly exist in the world' (Leszczynski, 2017a: n.p.). Importantly, because ontologies are axiomatic, they are not a theory of what the world is like. Ontologies are distinct from theories in the sense of a scholarly framework that provides explanation for phenomena, including research findings, in ways that are internally consistent. Instead, an ontology 'specifies what it is possible for reality to be', which 'involves not only objects and qualities in the world, but also their legitimacy' (Leszczynski, 2017a: n.p.). By extension, a *social ontology* is a claim about the nature of society and of social reality – and about who and/or what is considered a legitimate social actor, which includes digital technologies and differences among scholars regarding whether they are accorded status as social actors in and of themselves.

In the Western philosophical tradition, there are three main social ontologies: *realist*, *constructivist* and *critical*.

Realist, Constructivist and Critical Social Ontologies

A realist social ontology conceives of society and social reality as existing independently of social actors (people), all of whom are granted direct access to social reality through the physical senses (sight, hearing, etc.). This gives all members of a society access to the same social reality, which is empirically confirmable. Human behaviour is understood to be directly observable, verifiable and measurable independently of the observer and of the means of measurement. Observations of human behaviour are unaffected by the geographical locations, life experiences, and/or subject positionalities of people because the social world is equally externally knowable to everyone. The realist view also holds that certain social relations are natural, inevitable and logical. For instance, the notion of 'survival of the fittest' (problematically) holds that some members of society will 'naturally' outcompete others, justifiably achieving higher social and economic status, better health, etc. Furthermore, from the realist perspective, the internal life of humans (i.e., their consciousness) is not important, nor is the significance that people ascribe to social interactions, practices and events, as meaning is understood to reside solely in objects (Scotland, 2012).

A constructivist social ontology is the view that social realities are constructed, or made, by social actors themselves (Searle, 1995, 2010), often in the process of social interaction (as per the framework of symbolic interactionism; see Meltzer et al., 1975). Because social realities are seen as being constructed and specific to the actors who construct them, reality is understood not as being external to people, but instead as 'subjective [to them] and differ[ing] from person to person' (Scotland, 2012: 11). This commitment to subjective reality is related (though not identical) to the ontological position of relativism. Because social reality is seen as being continuously (re)made, this rules out the possibility of universal 'laws' that can be used to predict human behaviour, since behaviours and practices are emergent and socially, temporally and spatially contingent. So are people's motivations, which are unique to them and subject to change over time. This means that motivations are not directly observable and may remain hidden – even to social actors themselves – alongside the significance that people attach to words, signs, actions, gestures, etc.

There is an intermediary ontological position known as critical realism that represents a straddling of the ontological claims of both realism and constructivism. Associated with the philosophy of Roy Bhaskar (e.g., 1989, 2007), critical realism affirms an independent, external reality, but accepts that this reality may never be fully known outside of social actors' subjective experiences of it. Critical realism avoids the polemics of the descent into relativism associated with the (purely) constructivist social ontology by asserting that the same external phenomena present themselves to researchers, but it is how they are known – and the conclusions drawn about them – that differ (Amaturo and Aragona, 2022). Critical realism is, however, distinct from the ontological position described solely as 'critical'. A critical social ontology sees social reality to be the historical outcome of unequal social power relations and values – including those of gender, race/ethnicity and class – that have crystallised over time. Reality is still understood as (socially) constructed, but rather than reality being continuously reproduced, social actors 'inherit a world in which meaning has already been made'; this world is one that is 'stratified' along axes of social difference and saturated by inequality (Scotland, 2012: 13). Scholarship within critical ontological paradigms works to render these inequalities apparent, as well as to contribute to their undoing. A number of scholarly traditions, including Marxist and decolonial methodologies, adhere to a critical social ontology, using 'historical hindsight to explain patterns of power that shape our intellectual, political, economic, and social world' (Mohamed et al., 2020: 659). Marxist and decolonial scholarly traditions are both 'critical' in their ontological orientations in that they 'attack' unequal social realities, refusing to accept inequality as the natural, necessary, or inevitable order of reality (Scotland, 2012: 13).

What differs between critical traditions is what they emphasise as the origins of social inequality. Marxist approaches direct such efforts towards unequal class relations between capital and labour; for instance, those between gig workers and digital platforms (see **Chapter 16**). Decolonial and decolonising approaches conversely '[centre] vulnerable peoples who continue to bear the brunt of' ongoing processes and legacies of colonisation, including the 'negative impacts of [digital] innovation and [techno-]scientific progress' (Mohamed et al., 2020: 659). A further distinguishing factor is that Marxism is a Western scholarly tradition, whereas decolonising methodologies work to actively decentre the self-positioning of Western philosophy and science as superior bases for what counts as reality, research and knowledge (Smith, 2012; Smith et al. 2016: 141). Foregrounding and critiquing Western scientific imperialism's central role in practices, projects, legacies and contemporary lived relations of colonisation, decolonising methodologies assert non-Western ontologies, ways of knowing, and modes of research production – namely, Indigenous Knowledges – in service of 'the repatriation of Indigenous land and life' (Smith, 2012; Tuck and Yang, 2012: 1).

Indigenous Knowledges

As defined by Smith et al. (2016), Indigenous Knowledges are 'theories, practices and protocols for being in the world [and] ideas about what it means to know something' (p. 134–5) that 'have had meaning for generations, that have evolved over generations[,] and that are still applied and adapted to contemporary conditions and have meaning for [Indigenous] communities' (p. 137). As discussed by Smith et al. (2016), Indigenous Knowledges are 'not so easily mapped onto science and traditional academic based methods' (Smith et al., 2016: 135), 'travers[ing W]estern philosophical concepts of … ontolog[y] and epistemolog[y]' (p. 134). For example, for Māori, the Indigenous peoples of Aotearoa New Zealand, 'what is real' is informed by a core ethos – a way of being in the world – defined by:

> the collective (*whanaungatanga*) interdependence between and among humankind (*kotahitanga*), a sacred relationship to the 'gods' and the cosmos (*wairuatanga*), and acknowledgement that humans are guardians of the environment (*kaitiakitanga*), combining in the inter-connection between mind, body and spirit. (Henry and Pene, 2001: 235)

This relational-ethical cosmology not only informs 'traditional *Maori* ontology and assumptions about human nature' (Henry and Pene, 2001: 235), but also defines the purpose of knowledge, which is to 'uphold the *mana*' – 'the spiritual power and authority that can be applied to people, their words and acts' (p. 235) – 'of the community' (p. 236). Māori knowledge (*mātauranga Māori*) 'emphasizes interdependence and spirituality as a fundamental component of intellectual endeavour', and 'is implicitly founded on collective consciousness and historical and cultural concepts that are not necessarily reflected in qualitative-quantitative [methodological] … positivist-interpretivist-critical' epistemological, or realist-constructivist ontological splits (Henry and Pene, 2001: 238).

Indigenous Knowledges are important to acknowledge in the context of this chapter's discussion, which neatly differentiates between ontological and epistemological questions in the Western philosophical tradition by discussing these as separate though often intimately bound constructs. The purpose of this discussion of ontology outside of the context of Western philosophical hegemony is to foreground that not only are ontological orientations not universal, but also that the treatment of ontologies and epistemologies as distinct questions is itself not universal. It is also important to acknowledge that Indigenous Knowledges are plural, reflecting the diversity and plurality of Indigenous peoples around the world (Smith et al., 2016), while sharing in the endeavour of 'affirm[ing] and sustain[ing] relationality and reciprocity with human and non-human worlds' (Rivera, 2023: 13). The plurality of Indigenous Knowledges opens onto multiple ontological claims about digital phenomena, as well as phenomena that implicate concepts and notions of digitality, such as 'data', which in our present moment, likely makes us think of *digital capta* (Kitchin, 2014a): the discrete, machine-readable units that represent (stand in for) aspects, features, parameters, traces, and records of a multitude of phenomena, including digital communications, everyday movement trajectories, our biometrics, air quality, real-time traffic flows, and the ever-expanding universe of digital content. For example, Duarte et al. (2019: 166) identify multiple ontological statuses accorded to data by 'Indigenous and [d]ecolonial scholars', including ontological assertions of data as: *story* (a 'crafting of narrative of the world through data'); an *object* (a 'set of scientific observations ... shorthand for datasets'); *property* (a 'set of information that an authorized community of users recognizes as IK [Indigenous knowledge], TK [traditional knowledge, or] TEK [traditional ecological knowledge]; as *proprietary*, commensurate with intellectual property and private property'); and *kinship* (a 'mapping of ways [I]ndigenous peoples and nations relate to one another; genetic information; genealogy'), among others.

Ontologies and Digital Phenomena

The ontological statuses of digital phenomena – including their qualities, roles, and capacities – are important to consider because they have implications for claims about the nature of social reality and of where knowledge comes from. In social ontologies, the status of digital phenomena refers to whether digital technologies (hardware, software, data, algorithms and code) are accorded status (i.e., recognised) as having sociality and/or as participating in social relations. This has implications for our understandings of social life because it tells us something about who and/or what plays an active role within the sphere of digital life, which is an ontological claim about the nature of digital-social worlds, and who/what is seen as legitimately taking part in them. Where digital phenomena are seen as being generative of and/or contributing to social realities, then concerns over ontological status also pertain to what kinds of relations these phenomena may participate in, and indeed with whom and/or what. Here, considerations of the ontological status of digital phenomena need to be differentiated from the three Western ontological paradigms already discussed (objectivism, constructivism and historical materialism), which we may consider 'Ontologies' with a capital 'O'. Conversely, assertions about the ontological status of digital phenomena *within* social ontologies constitute ontological claims with a lower case 'o', and these latter claims are not unique to, nor do they necessarily neatly map onto, identified and established social 'O'ntologies.

Depending on their methodological, theoretical and philosophical positions, some scholars consider digital objects to be merely artefacts of social relations; that is, objects that are the products of human social relations and practices (e.g., digital, technological, scientific research innovation and development; marketing, lobbying and advertising; practices of their adoption, etc.). These objects and artefacts may also be seen as representing concretisations of unequal power relations in society, reflecting a critical ontological stance. For instance, training data, machine learning algorithms, and artificial intelligence (AI) have emerged as technologies of racial profiling and discrimination under a digital carceral regime that Ruha Benjamin (2019) has termed 'the New Jim Code' (in reference to the pre-digital 'Jim Crow' era of racial segregation in the American South). Furthermore, these objects may be understood as exerting influence over digital and social ontologies themselves. For instance, software systems and interfaces may '[define] the functioning of digital objects' in ways that have 'a structuring and modeling effect on which data to collect, which to consider important, and which to keep for ... analysis' (Amatura and Aragona, 2022: 3; see also Manovich, 2013). This latter ontological claim asserts that digital objects themselves have the capacity to define 'what exists', the qualities of what exists, and how phenomena come into being in digital-social worlds.

Elsewhere, and by contrast, other scholars claim digital phenomena to constitute social actors in and of themselves, which means that they are axiomatically ascribed or accorded capacities to broker, mediate, dis/assemble and otherwise participate in social relations (see **Chapter 1**). Depending on philosophical and theoretical traditions and frameworks, where they are recognised as social agents, digital phenomena may be referred to as 'actants' (based on Actor-Network Theory; see, e.g., Baron and Gomez, 2016); 'lively' or 'vibrant' matter (in materialist and new materialist philosophy; see, e.g., Bennett, 2009); and 'technics' that possess and express capacities of technicity (see Ash, 2012 for discussion). Among researchers who accord ontological status to digital technologies as social agents, they differ in how they position these phenomena as participating in the socialities of digital life. For some, digital phenomena are ontologically claimed to participate in social relations only in the context of social relations with other humans (sociality as encompassing digital technologies *and* humans; see, for instance, Watson et al., 2021). For other scholars, digital phenomena are seen to have autonomous sociality independent of our social relations and interactions with them, even where these autonomous socialities have implications for people (see e.g., Ash, 2017).

Epistemologies

Ontology answers the rhetorical questions: What is the nature of digital-social reality? Who/what participates in it? In what ways do they take part? But how do we as researchers of digital life *know* that digital social worlds are the way we assume and claim they are? This is a question of epistemology. An epistemology is a theory of knowledge. More specifically, it accounts for the genesis of knowledge (where knowledge comes from) and how it is generated. Stated in simpler terms, an epistemology 'is the lens through which we view reality' (Schuurman, 2020: n.p.). Following Schuurman (2020):

> [t]he easiest way to think of epistemology is to imagine a series of filters laid over [reality]. What we perceive depends on our filter. Different scientific traditions, different cultures and different humans use different filters. The trouble with descriptions – whether they be … in text or through photographs – is that they often claim to be the *truth* about the world. But they are ontological entities that result from specific epistemologies. (n.p.)

These filters (epistemologies) are normative as they axiomatically assert not only how knowledge *is* created, but also about how it *should* be created. This chapter considers two philosophies of knowledge – and their related epistemologies – for knowing digital life: positivism and feminist epistemologies.

Positivism

Positivism is a philosophy of knowledge associated with the epistemological claims of objectivism and empiricism. Objectivism is the claim that scientists 'go forth in the world impartially, discovering absolute knowledge about' objective facts that exist in the external world, commensurate with a realist position (Scotland, 2012: 10). Empiricism holds that direct sensory observation of phenomena is sufficient for knowledge. Positivism is the application of these scientific epistemologies – and more specifically the scientific method – to the study of social phenomena. Positivism contends that by objectively collecting and analysing data regarding society, we can determine laws to predict and explain social relations (Kitchin 2015). It rejects asking normative (what should be) and metaphysical (concerning being and beliefs) questions because they cannot be answered scientifically (they are issues of faith, values, opinions and judgements rather than facts). It has its roots in the early nineteenth century and the ideas of Auguste Comte, who advocated for methods of data collection that could be replicated and for the formulation of theories that could be tested, leading to the identification of laws that would explain human behaviour. The development of logical positivism, a philosophy that prioritises verification (testing whether hypotheses hold true by establishing the strength of relationships between variables) developed by the Vienna Circle in the 1920s and 1930s, and critical rationalism, which centres falsification (testing whether a hypothesis can be falsified) as forwarded by Karl Popper, helped to further establish the use of quantitative data analysis in social research (Kitchin, 2015).

Positivism remains a key epistemology of computational social science approaches to researching digital life, which largely rely on methods of data analytics (see **Chapter 11**). However, this does not mean that all quantitative and data-centric research engagements with questions about digital life are epistemologically positivist and thereby realist in their ontological position. Many researchers using scientific and quantitative methods now adopt critical realist and critical positions, which may be underwritten with any number of other, non-positivist epistemologies, including feminist epistemologies.

Feminist Epistemologies

Feminist epistemology is a philosophy of knowledge associated with the epistemologies of subjectivism and interpretivism. Subjectivism is the epistemological claim that knowledge is produced through people's subjective experiences of the world – including those that are affective, sensory, emotional and embodied – and that these experiences may only be 'understood from the standpoint of the individuals' participating in a subjective social reality (i.e., a constructivist social ontology) (Scotland, 2012: 12). While social reality may only be understood from the perspective of subjects, researchers can come to know these social realities by interpreting the meanings and significance that people attach to their behaviours, practices, interactions, motivations, etc. These meanings and significances are understood to be latent, residing in the things people do and say, as well as how they do and say them. Yet these meanings may be hidden even to subjects themselves – in which case, they may be uncovered or identified through interpretivism, which is the epistemological claim that knowledge is produced through the interpretation of meaning. Importantly, many critical-interpretivist approaches are also interventionist, characterised by a lack of separation between knowing the world as unequal and simultaneously 'engaging in social action' to challenge those inequalities (Scotland, 2012: 13). This is evidenced in some approaches to researching digital labour (see **Chapter 16**).

Feminist epistemologies accept that knowledge is subjective, but also go beyond subjectivism by claiming that knowledge is situated. Situated knowledges, famously advanced by Donna Haraway (1988), asserts that knowledge is contingent on, particular to, and reflects the intersectional social positionalities (gender, race/ethnicity, class, etc.), life experiences and values/biases of human knowers. This is a direct critique of objectivist and positivist epistemological claims that all knowledge is value-free (i.e., unaffected by knowers' positionalities, biases, pedagogies, etc.) by virtue of the fact that social reality is presumed to be universally shared by all. By contrast, feminist epistemologies hold that knowledge production can never be objective and neutral in its execution as its formulation and practice are value-laden (informed by people's views, implicit and explicit biases, experiences and subject positionalities). Situated knowledges furthermore point to the plurality of knowledges that are possible. Feminist epistemologies do not privilege any one suite of research methods, orientations (e.g., quantitative versus qualitative) or approaches (e.g., inductive versus deductive), but rather call for *reflexivity* – the acknowledgement of one's own subject positionality – as a central tenet of research ethics (see **Chapter 4**).

In *Data Feminism*, Catherine D'Ignazio and Lauren Klein (2020) mobilise a feminist epistemology for studying digital data, which they term 'feminist data science'. Returning to Schuurman's (2020) analogy of epistemology as a set of filters, one of the filters that feminist epistemologies lay over reality is a concern with embodiment, which may be understood as the social and cultural condition and experience of having and living in a physical body. Applying this filter of embodiment to the study of digital data makes us appreciate that digital data are the product of embodied human labour, in turn rendering apparent who is doing the work of datafication. Following D'Ignazio and Klein (2020), this includes the ways in which Github, a software development and versioning platform, makes the work of collaborative coding visible, as well as the embodied subjectivities of workers scanning Google Books, who are 'disproportionately women and people of color' (p. 181). A feminist data epistemology may further be mobilised within practices of data visualisation (see **Chapter 10**).

Conclusion

Before beginning designing and carrying out a research project or study, we need a clear idea of what we believe to be the nature of social reality and digital life (ontology), and the bases on which our convictions lie (epistemology). Our pre-existing conceptualisations of what comprises our social worlds and the role and status of digital phenomena in these realities, as well as the entry points that we see as being available to us for investigating them, will implicate certain methodologies (quantitative versus qualitative, deductive versus inductive) and specific methods as being suitable and appropriate for our research purposes. The use of specific methods will confirm and shore up particular ontologies (conceptualisations of social reality) and epistemologies (our understandings of how that reality may be known by us). Simultaneously, understanding the epistemologies of different methodological approaches to researching digital life, and of different methods practices, is important because it allows us to evaluate the ontological claims that underpin certain approaches and what they purport to reveal – or not – about digital life.

Our ontological and epistemological convictions should directly inform our choices of methods as well as the forms of evidence (research data) that we need to collect, analyse and enrol in our research studies. Some methods and forms of evidence will confirm these ontological and epistemological positionalities, whereas others will contradict and indeed undermine them. This is important to understand because it highlights that ontologies, epistemologies and methodologies cannot be combined at random. For instance, one could not reasonably claim to be a social constructionist while choosing to mobilise a positivist research design, as methods associated with positivism seek to inform the derivation of 'laws', or analytic findings that are taken at face value as being replicable across all social contexts – a direct violation of the tenets of social constructivism. Furthermore, while scholars may evolve in their ontological and epistemological positionalities over time (e.g., moving from espousing a purely constructivist to more of a critical realist stance), they do not abruptly switch between ontologies, epistemologies and methodologies from one study to the next, proclaiming themselves to be qualitative feminists one week and quantitative positivists the next. Again, the operationalisation of different methodologies and adherence to ontological and epistemological positions are informed by personal conviction, but also by pedagogical training and what is considered an accepted way of producing knowledge within a discipline or scholarly community of practice. For these reasons, questions of ontologies, epistemologies, methodologies and their consistency relative to each other are core considerations in any research design, which is taken up in the next chapter.

Summary

- Ontology and epistemology are axiomatic claims about the nature of reality and about how those realities are known, respectively. They cohere alongside methods (specific instruments and techniques of data collection and analysis) within research frameworks referred to as methodologies.
- A realist ontology conceptualises of an objective, universally shared social reality that is knowable through direct sensory observation and verification via the application of methods and techniques of the natural and physical sciences to the study of society.
- The constructivist – also known as relativist – ontological position understands social reality to be constructed (made) by social actors, and therefore specific

to the social actors who make and participate in a social world. These social realities may only be known from the positionalities of the subjects themselves (an epistemology of subjectivism), which may be accessed and uncovered by researchers via epistemological interpretivism).
- Critical social ontologies understand social reality to be marked by inequalities that are inherited, having solidified over time. Epistemologically, critical methodologies are subjectivist, but knowing the world as unequal is also inseparable from intervening against those inequalities.
- Feminist epistemologies understand knowledge to be situated in the social positionalities of human knowers and require reflexivity (self-positioning) in the advancement of knowledge claims.

Recommended Reading

Amaturo, A., and Aragona, B. (2022) 'Epistemology of the digital', in Punziano, G., and Delli, P.A. (eds) *Handbook of Research on Advances Research Methodologies for a Digital Society*. IGI Global, Hershey, PA, pp. 1–10.
A Western account of epistemological approaches to engaging with and producing knowledge about digitality.

Carroll, S.R., Herczog, E., Hudson, M., Russell, K., and Stall, S. (2021) 'Operationalizing the CARE and FAIR Principles for Indigenous data futures', *Nature: Scientific Data*, 8: 108.
An illustrative example of how Indigenous epistemologies open onto different ontological understandings of data within Indigenous research.

D'Ignazio, C., and Klein, L. (2020) *Data Feminism*. MIT Press, Cambridge, MA.
Demonstrates the mobilisation of feminist epistemologies to the study of digital data and data visualisation.

Haraway, D. (1988) 'Situated knowledges: The science question in feminism and the privileges of partial perspective', *Feminist Studies*, 14(3): 575–99.
A classic and still highly influential feminist critique of scientific rationality and its claims to epistemological objectivity and argument for knowledge as situated and embodied.

Scotland, J. (2012) 'Exploring the philosophical underpinnings of research: Relating ontology and epistemology to the methodology and methods of the scientific, interpretive, and critical research paradigms', *English Language Teaching*, 5(9): 9–16.
A clear introduction of ontologies and epistemologies in the Western philosophical tradition, and a discussion of the strengths and limitations of different ontological and epistemological positionalities.

3
Research Design and Implementation

Overview

Chapter 3 examines:

- the construction of a robust research design;
- various approaches to sourcing data for research;
- issues of data quality and the problem of ecological fallacies in undertaking data analysis and interpreting results; and
- the construction of data management plans.

Introduction

Alongside conceptual concerns regarding the ontological and epistemological framing used to make sense of digital life discussed in **Chapter 2**, a number of operational, practical and technical issues need to be considered in researching digital matters. This chapter details a number of these issues, which are vital in terms of formulating and operationalising a viable research design that will deliver the data and analysis necessary to understand and explain a phenomenon. Much of what is covered is standard fare in the methods literatures, applicable to all forms of research, and is discussed in brief to provide a rudimentary introduction to core considerations, with pointers to sources that detail a more in-depth explanation. Other aspects are more specific to researching digital life, such as generating data utilising digital methods (e.g., web scraping or accessing data via official application programming interfaces (APIs) or digital ethnographies), engaging with online communities or undertaking research on algorithms that are typically 'black-boxed'. This chapter opens with a brief outline of the fundamentals of research design. The following section considers how to select an appropriate means to source data for understanding digital life. The generation of primary data, including issues of sampling, coverage, representativeness and access to cases and populations are discussed, as well as utilising secondary, tertiary, derived and simulated data. Next, issues relating to data quality and ecological fallacies are detailed, which are vital in aiding analysis and assuring validity in interpretation. The final section details the formulation of data management plans for archiving, sharing and re-using generated data. These are becoming an increasingly common expectation for funded research projects.

Research Design

Research design is the means by which research questions are formulated and operationalised within a framework that aligns with a set of underlying philosophical assumptions (see **Chapter 2**). A research design details how the empirical research will proceed in practice; it is the equivalent to a construction plan of a building that sets out the organisation, materials, processes and timelines for a successful completion (Cresswell and Cresswell, 2018). The plan includes decisions about the specific research objectives and questions, what methods to use for data generation and analysis, and project management. Increasingly, it also includes the formulation of research ethics (see **Chapter 4**) and data management plans. To a large degree, the key tenets for undertaking research on digital life are the same as with other research endeavours, though there are specific characteristics of the digital that need particular consideration, especially when conducting the research within or through digital media (such as various forms of internet communities and social media) or using digital methods.

The general starting point for research design is the motivation driving its undertaking. There are many reasons for conducting research, with seven common motivations detailed in **Table 3.1**. Along with the theoretical framing, these motivations shape the formulation of research questions and the plan for answering them appropriately. As discussed in the previous chapter, the research process consists of an intimate binding of philosophy, theory, methodology and practice. Ontological, epistemological and ideological positions directly inform ways of knowing, asking, interpreting, writing and acting; how an empirical study is designed, the questions examined, the research is conducted and its intended purpose. While some might approach research in what they perceive to be a common-sense manner, this in itself is an epistemological and ideological position (i.e., that there is an accepted, taken-for-granted approach with a set of commonly agreed tenets). However, as we demonstrate in **Part 3**, there are

Table 3.1 Reasons for undertaking research.

Aim	Reason
Exploration	To get a sense of a little-understood phenomenon and generate specific questions for further examination.
Documentation and description	To chart the characteristics of a phenomenon.
Understanding	To comprehend a phenomenon in a broad, holistic sense.
Explanation	To identify in specific cause-and-effect terms why and how a phenomenon occurs and its consequences.
Evaluation	To assess the efficacy of an approach to a phenomenon.
Prediction	To forecast future outcomes relating to a phenomenon.
Provoke, unsettle, intervene and change	To use research to challenge the *status quo* in relation to a phenomena.

Source: Compiled from Marshall and Rossman, 1995; Leavy, 2017.

many ways of framing, approaching and making sense of phenomenon, and a research design needs to be reflective of these.

Likewise, we need to be cognisant of how our research and questions relate to 'low theory' (see **Chapter 2**); that is, theories about specific phenomenon (e.g., theories about what produces a successful smart city (see **Chapter 15**), or why certain digital platforms grow while other stagnate). Here, theory is a means of explaining why and how a situation, process or activity occurs. Whenever research takes place, it usually seeks to assess the validity of an existing or proposed theory (using a deductive approach) or to construct a new theory from the data and findings (using an inductive approach). In each case, the research does not take place in an empirical and conceptual vacuum; rather, it is informed by the wider literature and the historical body of reported research and established theoretical knowledge. The research questions formulated seek to enable theory testing and making. Research questions should then be carefully formulated to meet the research aims and objectives of a study, and to produce useful and valid insights. In general, most projects seek to answer a small suite of interrelated questions. As a rule, questions should be clear and unambiguous, and where multiple questions are posed, these should be logically linked.

Research questions are answered through the use of carefully selected research methods framed within a chosen methodology (see **Chapter 2**). Methods might relate to the generation, handling, processing, analysing, visualising and storing data. There are suites of specific techniques for undertaking all of these tasks (see **Part 2**), each designed to work in different ways based on conceptual assumptions, the characteristics of the data, access to appropriate equipment, and what outcome is being sought. Selecting methods and formulating how they will be deployed in practice is then an important aspect of research design. While some researchers may favour qualitative or quantitative methods for generating and analysing data, a method should be ideally selected because it is the most suitable means of answering a question. In many cases a suite of complementary methods are used, each designed to reveal different facets of insight and compensate for the limitations of specific methods used in isolation. This includes a mixed methods approach in which both qualitative and quantitative methods are employed (Cresswell and Cresswell, 2018; Leavy, 2017).

In addition to conceptual and methodological concerns, a research design must take account of practical constraints concerning resourcing, costs, access to data, consumables and equipment, case and field sites, and time availability. Effort spent on carefully planning a project's execution is well invested, as allowing the research to unfold in an ad hoc manner will almost certainly lead to headaches throughout the project and possibly a failure to produce valid and useful insights (Blaikie, 2000; Cresswell and Cresswell, 2018). If the project is fairly sizeable – perhaps seeking to answer several related questions and involving a number of researchers working together – then the operational aspects of the research design might be divided into separate work packages, with each work package having its own plan of organisation and action. These work packages need to work in concert and, through a process of synthesis, add up to more than the sum of their parts. Part of the planning phase might involve preliminary or exploratory research, including pilot testing of favoured methodologies to ensure that the design is robust and will meet research objectives. Indeed, pilot studies are an important, iterative means of assessing and refining a research design and avoiding

Figure 3.1 An example of a Gantt chart.

Phase	Tasks	Week									
		1	2	3	4	5	6	7	8	9	10
1	Identify and recruit interviewees										
	Meet with key stakeholders										
	Produce and test data audit tool										
2	Conduct interviews										
	Conduct data audit										
	Construct data dictionary and data workflow										
	Assess level of standardisation across organisations										
3	Follow-up clarification meetings with interviewees										
	Draft final report										
	Present research to stakeholders										

costly mistakes in the main execution phase. Another useful element of the planning phase might be to formulate a guiding conceptual framework – usually expressed in a diagram or table – that details the logic of how a project is organised to ensure that the research objectives are met and questions answered. These are often useful to include in funding applications because they demonstrate to reviewers the rationale and salience of the research design. Likewise, the production of a Gantt chart, that visually displays the timelines and milestones of research activities across the lifetime of a project (see **Figure 3.1**), and a detailed budget of anticipated expenses (to include all salary, travel, equipment, consumables, and dissemination costs) is valuable for ensuring the viable delivery of a project.

Sourcing Data

Taking into account the chosen epistemological and methodological framing, a key decision in research design is the means by which data are to be sourced. There are four principal means of gathering data for answering research questions: generating *primary data*, using *secondary data*, producing *derived data*, and employing *simulated data*.

Primary Data

Primary data are those generated by the researcher using their chosen methods. Here, the researcher designs, constructs and implements the means of generating data, tailoring well established methods (such as surveys, interviews, focus groups) for specific deployment or developing new methods to produce suitable data. Generally, generating primary data is viewed as the most preferable means of sourcing data. This is because the researcher has control over how a technique is configured and administered, being able to tailor the method to answer the research question(s). Primary data can be generated under experimental conditions in a controlled environment (such as a lab) or in real-world conditions. In many cases, primary data generation is now digitally mediated, either wholly or in part (e.g., surveys are administered through webpages, interviews are recorded with digital devices, measurements are made with digital sensors, and images are captured using digital cameras). In cases where the media and practices under investigation are digital in nature, they might only be captured using digital methods. Rogers (2013) defines digital methods as techniques that use and repurpose digital media and technologies to produce digital data. In other words, digital methods are those where the mechanism and process of generating data are entirely digital in design and execution.

A key concern in generating primary data is to determine the study/case sites and populations to be examined. This always involves decisions regarding breadth and depth of investigation. One could seek to do a global analysis of some aspect of a platform (e.g., edits in Wikipedia or number of nodes in OpenStreetMap or location of users of GitHub; Graham et al., 2015), but that provides no in-depth understanding of the nature of those edits, nodes or users, or the reasons for their existence or usage. The latter requires concentrated attention on a selection of cases (e.g., a particular city or user community). And within any selected cases, it is unlikely that every single instance can be examined, such that choices are required about which elements (e.g., users, contributions, posts, edits, etc.) will be included. Without a time-series of data, one will only get a snapshot of a phenomenon at a particular moment. Attention then needs to be paid to issues of coverage, sampling and representativeness. Are the cases selected appropriate to the question being investigated? Do they encompass sufficient populations, territory and times? Will the data produced be representative of the wider community? Even with big data, which might claim to be exhaustive, it is important to remember that the data are a sample and not fully representative of a population (e.g., not everyone uses a platform or system; Kitchin, 2014a).

There needs to be a clear rationale for why cases were chosen for a study and how they fit into the research design. For example, one might investigate a particular community (e.g., teenagers) in three locations (which might be different geographic sites or different digital platforms) that share the same kind of profile, or have quite different profiles, to see whether the same outcomes are produced across place and why they might vary. If we were interested in whether class influenced a phenomenon, the profiles of those teenagers might vary in terms of the socio-economic characteristics of their families. Within each case, a means of sampling teenagers from the whole population needs to be devised. In statistical analyses carried out within deductively oriented quantitative research designs, a desirable sample is free of bias and representative of the larger population. A representative sample may only be drawn using a probabilistic sampling method. Probability sampling methods include *random sampling* (elements selected randomly), *stratified random sampling* (population is stratified into groups, with random selection within groups) and *multi-stage random sampling* (population is stratified into groups, with a random selection of which groups to include, and then random selection within those groups) (Bryman and Bell, 2019). Generally, the more random the selection, the more representative it is likely to be. Typically, probability sampling aims to generate a sample size sufficiently large that the findings derived from the data can be confidently accepted as representative.

There are usually good reasons why non-probabilistic sampling methods are used. These include difficulties in accessing potential participants or because the research is more purposeful in orientation, seeking to focus on specific rather than representative populations. Non-probabilistic sampling methods include *quota* (e.g., the first thirty encountered), *systematic* (e.g., every tenth case), *purposeful* (selected because they have particular characteristics or knowledge and skills or belong to a particular community), *judgemental* (sample selected based on the knowledge and contacts of researcher), *convenience* (selected based on ease and availability) and *referral* (members of initial selected sample suggest others to be included) sampling. Much qualitative research is intentionally non-probabilistic in its sampling strategy, and is typically purposeful in application, selecting specific elements (participants, cases) to include on the basis that these individuals and/or instances will inform greater insight about a phenomenon. For example, if one is seeking to research how a specific digital policy was formulated or a digital platform was created then it is vital to talk to the set of actors involved, not a representative sample of all policy actors or software developers. Referral sampling is often used to supplement a purposeful sampling method in cases where sourcing participants proves difficult. In qualitative research, the sample size might be quite small. This may be because the population being examined is inherently small or because a saturation point in the information being gathered is quickly met. Saturation is said to be achieved in a sample when no new insights are being gleaned from the addition of new data. In a systematic review of empirical studies, Hennink and Kaiser (2022) found that saturation might be achieved with as few as nine to seventeen interviews or four to eight focus groups when the sample population is quite homogenous. In comparative studies, or those involving more diverse populations, the saturation point might be much higher. In general, data generation in qualitative studies proceeds until a state of saturation has been reached.

Recruitment for both probabilistic and non-probabilistic studies can be difficult as participants need to agree to take part in the study and perform the chosen method. It is not uncommon to have a sampling rate of less than twenty percent of those asked to participate. Yet, if one cannot get individuals or institutions to co-operate with a project, or gain access to necessary sites or technologies, then the research will flounder. Recruitment then is a vital activity. For probabilistic sampling, this means being prepared to contact an ever-larger population to generate a decent sample size. For non-probabilistic sampling, it might mean persuading a community gatekeeper of the project's merits. In both cases, incentives such as payment for participation, or in-kind incentives such as access to resources or the resultant datasets or findings, might need to be considered and offered. A range of recruitment techniques might also need to be adopted, such as attending events, placing adverts in newspapers or posting notices on social media platforms. In Dattani's (2022) study of online dating apps, she recruited participants by creating a dating profile in which she stated she was a researcher seeking to interview the apps' users. Gaining access to digital communities is different to in-place communities, in that communication is digitally mediated; pseudonyms and anonymity might be prevalent; and social norms, expectations and obligations might work differently. Gaining trust and access might involve a lot of preparatory work and time. In researching other aspects of the digital, the media itself might provide additional access challenges. For instance, examining the workings, politics and praxes of algorithms is difficult because they are usually black-boxed and closed to scrutiny, as are the sites of their production, particularly if created by companies or states (Kitchin, 2017; see **Chapter 6**). This does not mean that black-boxed algorithms are impossible to study, but rather that gaining access might be tricky and necessitate techniques to reverse engineer their rule set and how they operate (Diakopoulos, 2013; Seaver, 2013), or involve following public debates about how an algorithm works or interviewing those that seek to game them (Bucher, 2012).

Secondary, Tertiary, Derived and Simulated Data

In many cases, generating primary data might not be possible due to the scale of the task or the time frame being examined (e.g., historical data is required) and secondary, tertiary, derived and simulated data are the only means of examining a phenomenon. Alternatively, the use of non-primary data may be preferable due to the additional value contained within the dataset. Secondary data consists of datasets that have been produced by a third party. The benefit of such data is that they are already generated, saving time and expense. The downside is that they were generated for someone else's interest and agenda, and there is no ability to tailor how the data are produced. This is particularly the case for commercial data that has not been produced with academic research in mind, and which might be treated as 'exhaust' or 'data fumes', the by-product of a system rather than a purposeful resource (Thatcher, 2014). Secondary data are usually sourced from archives and repositories (see **Chapter 9**). These archives might exist in a physical form, with paper records and other artefacts (e.g., tapes, devices) held in storage that must be visited to access the sources, or they may be digital in nature, accessible via the internet. In the case of digital repositories, the data might consist of previously analogue data (e.g., scans of paper documents or printed photos) or be born-digital data. While much research on digital life utilises secondary digital data, it might be necessary to access physical archives and analogue records, particularly for historical research on the development and use of digital media when organisations were still largely paper-based.

There has been an enormous growth in digital archives and repositories over the past two decades, driven by mass datafication, advances in archiving technologies (such as cloud computing) and the open science and open data agenda (Borgman, 2015; Kitchin, 2014a). However, publicly accessible datasets are produced largely by the state and academia, with commercial data much less likely to be open access, though some might be available through an application programming interface (API), a piece of code that allows users to gain access to and collect data through an external software application or interface (rapidapi.com provides access to hundreds of APIs that can scrape data from commercial sites such as TikTok, Instagram and Google). Beyond using an API, there are two main means to accessing commercially held data: first, to form a working relationship with the company; and second, to script an API to web scrape data from a company site. It can be difficult to form industry partnerships as companies generally want to protect their intellectual property and commercial advantage, and many will only work with academics if they can see the value proposition of doing so (and even then, they might insist on non-disclosure agreements or licensing that limits data use and publication). It is possible to capture some commercial data in a non-digital way (e.g., interviewing social media users in person), but born-digital data (e.g., the text, emojis, links, photos, gifs, videos and sound files contained within social media posts) are best captured and compiled using digital techniques. Similarly, while captured data can be printed out and manually coded, or coded using data management and analysis software such as MaxQDA or NVivo, the volume of records is best dealt with by using big data analytics such as automated content or sentiment analysis techniques that can quickly process and run calculations on large volumes of data (see **Chapter 11**).

Some secondary data are only made available as tertiary data, a form of derived data that masks individual records, typically using aggregation, for reasons of privacy and confidentiality. Data released by state bodies are typically tertiary data. Derived data are data that have been produced through some form of transformation or analysis performed on the original generated data. For example, counts might be transformed into percentage share, or be aggregated into attribute, temporal or spatial categories. Or the data might be combined in some fashion with other data to produce a new derived dataset; for example, a social index combining a number of variables through a weighted formula to produce a derived value. Or primary data might be entered into a model, with predicted or simulated data (such as projected counts at different times, or under different conditions) being the output. The simulated data might then be combined with other data and a new round of analysis conducted. Derived data are generally produced to comply with fair information practice principles (FIPPs) that detail how data can be legally shared and used (Minelli et al., 2013; OECD, 1980; see **Table 4.1**), or to add value by producing more useful and meaningful data. Simulated data might be used where there are gaps in a dataset, where data does not exist for particular conditions or scenarios, or where data needs to be extrapolated to provide necessary characteristics. For example, in agent-based models, where there might be thousands of agents that need attributes that shape their behaviour in the model, those attributes are simulated based on training datasets (see **Chapters 11** and **14**).

Data Quality and Ecological Fallacies

Data quality is imperative in undertaking research because it directly affects the extent to which one can trust the resultant findings, interpretation and conclusions. The maxim 'garbage in produces garbage out' holds: poor quality data leads to research with weak validity and veracity. Producing high quality data, or establishing the veracity of secondary data, is therefore an important task. Data quality is multifaceted in nature. With respect to quantitative data, data quality is concerned with how clean (error and gap free), untainted (bias free) and consistent (few discrepancies) the data are, and the extent to which they accurately (precision) and faithfully (fidelity) represent what they are meant to (McArdle and Kitchin, 2016; Shi et al., 2003).

Error is the difference between a measured and real value, and can include mistakes (such as misreading or miscoding), absences (missing data) and deliberate faking or gaming of data (e.g., in order to 'juke the stats').

Bias occurs when there is a consistent pattern of error within a dataset, usually caused by the method, instrument or sampling technique used unduly influencing data generation (Kitchin, 1996). This might happen inadvertently or be shaped by inherent ideological views of the researcher. Most datasets include some degree of error that is either tolerated or attempts are made to address it through calibration and modelling (Garnett, 2016).

Completeness of data concerns the extent to which there is the necessary coverage in terms of required attributes and spatial and temporal extent, or whether there are gaps and missing values (Shi et al., 2003). Sampling inherently erodes completeness since it generates data from only a portion of the population being examined at a particular snapshot in time. Within a sample, however, one would seek to capture the necessary attributes and minimise gaps. With respect to metadata, completeness refers to the extent to which all necessary metadata information is available for the dataset (UNECE, 2014).

Consistency is stability in methods and processes that ensures that the produced data maintain their characteristics over time, and thus their direct comparability. Changes in techniques, equipment or data practices have the potential to disrupt data consistency, and such effects are usually compensated for by maintaining compliance with established data standards (Gal and Rubinfeld, 2019).

Cleanliness refers to the extent to which data needs to be cleaned and wrangled to make it into serviceable data for analysis, storage and sharing. This might include having to perform error-checking and fixing, calibration or modelling to address bias or gaps; transformation or restructuring to address formatting issues; or some form of matching to link together related data (McArdle and Kitchin, 2016).

Representativeness relates to the extent to which the data sufficiently signifi a phenomenon, and a sample of data represents an overall population. As measures of a phenomenon captured through some instrument (e.g., thoughts through words), data are inherently representational. With respect to social media posts, do the poster's words, emojis, uploaded images and photos really denote a person's views, or are they performatively staged to create a particular impression (Manovich, 2011)? In datasets that consist of aggregated data, are the values really representative of a population given that any internal variance is being masked (Kitchin and Fotheringham, 1997)?

Timeliness refers to data being generated in a timely manner, either during or shortly after an activity or matching a designated schedule of data collection (such as hourly, weekly, monthly, quarterly, etc.), and that data are shared in a timely fashion (Shi et al., 2003). Long delays in generating data or misalignment with a schedule weakens validity and disrupts a time-series. Delays in sharing data can create a disjuncture between the dataset (which has become historical data) and present conditions, and reduces their utility for timely applied use.

Relevance concerns whether the data are fit for the purpose for which they are being used (OECD, 2011). The data might have little error or bias, but if they are being misapplied to reveal insights about something that they are at best tangentially related to, then any conclusions will be invalid and a more applicable data should be sourced.

Reliability concerns the repeatability and reproducibility of data generation and analysis. Quixotic reliability is achieved when a single method of observation continually yields an unvarying measurement; diachronic reliability refers to the stability of an observation through time; and synchronic reliability is a consistency of observations within the same period across cases (Golledge and Stimson, 1997). Poor levels of reliability suggest that the means of measurement or analysis is flawed, thus undermining confidence in the findings and conclusions drawn from them.

Metadata is an important means of being able to assess the quality and veracity of a dataset. Metadata are data about data and refer to both the data content and the dataset as a whole (NISO, 2004). Content metadata provides details about specific fields and data definitions that help a user understand the data, aiding use, interpretation and linking datasets together. Dataset metadata provides information about its constitution (e.g., description of its contents, language), method of generation and processing (e.g., instruments and techniques used, sampling framework, transformations), organisation and coverage (e.g., attributes, structure, formats) and its provenance and lineage (e.g., author, publisher, rights). Without this information it is difficult to make sense of a dataset, judge and make informed choices about its use (Marsden, 2019). As such, the absence of metadata inherently raises a flag that suggests that the dataset should be treated with caution.

Despite the efforts of those that produce data, and the development of various guidelines and standards, there are very few quantitative datasets that are free of data quality issues related to either the data or associated metadata. Even if a dataset is clean of error and bias, and is complete and consistent in content, there might be concerns related to representativeness that might not be simple to resolve. In some cases, the quality issues are viewed as an inherent feature of the dataset. For example, poor or undocumented levels of data quality is a known issue for many big data datasets. Social media data is quickly transitioning, varied and unstructured in nature, with issues of gamed and faked content. Sensor data often contain a fair degree of noise in readings and their accuracy is dependent on the sensor sensitivity and calibration (McArdle and Kitchin, 2016). Likewise, crowdsourced and citizen science data are produced largely by an unrepresentative cadre of amateur contributors and can be uneven in coverage and inconsistent in content and metadata (Carr, 2007). Many big datasets, especially those produced by companies, have little public metadata or methodological transparency, making it difficult to assess their veracity (Kitchin and Stehle, 2021). Some analysts have made the case that poorer data quality in big data is not necessarily a major hindrance to analysis and interpretation because the exhaustive nature of datasets removes sampling biases and nullifies the effects of any errors, gaps, biases and inconsistencies (Mayer-Schonberger and Cukier, 2013). In other words, the scope and volume of the dataset compensates for any flaws it might have. The problem with such a view is that regardless of the scale and coverage of a dataset, systemic, widespread flaws weaken veracity and undermine confidence (Kitchin, 2014a).

Issues such as error, bias, representativeness, reliability and relevance are also concerns with respect to the quality of qualitative data. One wants to be sure that what was said in an interview is accurately transcribed, that it reflects the views of the interviewee, that if a person were interviewed again the same views would be expressed, and that the data are relevant to the questions being examined. Yet, since qualitative data are generally purposeful and often reflect personal values, beliefs and opinions (that may be inherently biased), a different set of quality measures are also considered (Lemon and Hayes, 2020; Patton, 1999). For instance, one can seek to assess the credibility of the source and their trustworthiness in providing an honest account of their views and actions. *Credibility* might be judged by considering the experience, track record, status and training of a source, and the degree to which others trust them

(Patton, 1999); and *trustworthiness* by seeking to establish any documented cases of presenting conflicting positions or misleading information. Alternatively, one can seek to establish the dependability, transferability and confirmability of information relating to a dataset. *Dependability* might be judged by assessing the internal consistency of views within a dataset; *transferability* by considering the extent to which the data are reflective of other contexts and places; and *confirmability* by triangulating data against other sources to determine consistency across accounts or to fact-check statements by cross-referencing with established trustworthy sources such as official documents or newspapers of record (Lemon and Hayes, 2020).

Critically, data quality issues can exacerbate ecological validity concerns, which also arise from poor choices in data analysis and flawed reasoning in interpretation. Selecting an inappropriate method of analysis is likely to produce invalid findings. For example, using non-parametric tests designed to analyse nominal or ordinal data on interval or ratio data will produce nonsensical outputs. Similarly, how data are presented in graph or map form can lead to misinterpretation through misleading scaling, categorisation and visual organisation. Ecological fallacies consist of drawing conclusions that are not supported by the data, despite appearing to be valid on first sight. Several forms of ecological fallacy exist, including:

- *sampling bias*: 'drawing conclusions from a set of data that isn't representative of the population' under investigation;
- *false causality*: 'falsely assuming when two events appear related that one must have caused the other';
- *gerrymandering*: changes to geographical boundaries and scales altering the results;
- *over/underfitting*: the results are too sensitive to noise rather than the general trend/the results do not capture the underlying structure of a dataset;
- *cherry picking*: 'selecting results that fit [a] ... claim and excluding those that don't';
- *observer effect*: 'the act of monitoring someone can affect that person's behaviour';
- *aggregation effect*: aggregation removes variance within a dataset and hides underlying patterns, and can also lead to conclusions about a population that are not supported by individual-level data;
- *Simpson's paradox*: 'A phenomenon in which a trend appears in different groups of data but disappears or reverses when the groups are combined'; and
- *data dredging*: repeatedly analysing a dataset to find statistical significant results rather than testing a hypothesis.

(List from Kitchin, 2022; quotes from Geckoboard, 2020, which details other ecological fallacies)

A number of these ecological fallacies are evident with respect to studies that use big data, where it has been demonstrated that some techniques create false causality (identifying relationships in datasets that are not significant) or apophenia (seeing patterns that are in fact random), or are an effect of overfitting (the analysis is overly influenced by the training data used in machine learning techniques (see **Chapter 11**), meaning that it is trained to identify certain relationships and ignore others that might be present) (boyd and Crawford, 2012; Silver, 2012). Indeed, Taleb (2013) contends that the curse of big data is that as the size of a dataset increases, the number of false positives multiplies to the point where almost every relationship between data appears to be statistically significant, with the effect of hiding actual relationships. Outputs can also be overly sensitive to the assumptions, parameters and weightings within models, meaning that slight tweaks to a method can lead to different findings and conclusions (Silver, 2012). Approaches such as ensemble testing, whereby several techniques or models are used to analyse the same dataset can be seen as a form of data dredging, which can lead to cherry picking the desired answer (Siegel, 2013). Care must be taken not to fall into the trap of making such fallacious claims and not to inadvertently 'lie with statistics' (Huff, 1993; Spiegelhalter, 2019) or 'lie with maps' (Monmonier, 1996).

Data Management

It is rarely the case that data generated or sourced from others can be analysed directly with little to no data management. Instead, active data management is required in order to prepare data for analysis and to make them available for re-use. Managing data consists of several related processes, including data handling, cleaning, wrangling, transformation, merging, restructuring and storage. Each requires choices and decisions to be made about formats, technologies, practices, protocols and standards. *Data cleaning and wrangling* involves dealing with issues of data quality – such as gaps, errors and biases – and collating and structuring data so that it is amenable to the preferred mode of analysis. *Data transformation* consists of altering the data in some fashion, such as calibrating values, aggregating into classes or producing derived data. Data might be restructured to enable them be stored within a database and to facilitate datasets to be joined, enriching the data and opening them up to additional analysis in the process. These tasks are a normal, routine aspect of conducting research, so much so that they often receive little overt reflection and planning. This has started to change in recent years with many funding agencies now requiring a *data management plan* (DMP) to be submitted as part of a project proposal. In many cases, the expected DMP is concerned principally with data sharing on project completion; however, a DMP should have a wider remit (Williams et al., 2017).

A data management plan is defined by the Data Management Association as 'the business function that develops and executes plans, policies, practices and projects that acquire, control, protect, deliver and enhance the value of data and information' (cited in Williams et al., 2017: 131). A DMP sets out in formal terms how data will be generated, handled and stored, what the data will be used for, how data practices will comply with research ethics and legal requirements concerning privacy, copyright and data security (e.g., the General Data Protection Regulations of the European Union), and who will have access to the data during and after the project's lifetime. The initial DMP is drafted during the project planning phase and usually stipulates:

- how the data will be organised and formatted, the production of derived data (and if it will be treated differently from 'raw' data);
- data ownership and intellectual property rights;
- quality control procedures and the use of data and metadata standards;
- how data will be anonymised and encrypted;
- how the data will be stored during the project and archived for re-use;
- anticipated rules around sharing and citation; and
- necessary resourcing required, as well as roles and responsibilities for plan delivery.

(Digital Curation Centre, 2013; University of California Curation Centre, 2022)

Once a project starts, the DMP remains a live document, updated throughout the project's life cycle as the project evolves and the procedures and institutional arrangements are put in place. The final DMP is produced at the project end and documents the data management performed during the research (including workflows and equipment/software used) that will provide insight into data quality and enable reproducibility (without details of any cleaning, wrangling or transformations other researchers provided with the same dataset will produce findings that vary to some degree), and the post-project archiving arrangements related to curation, discoverability and conditions for sharing and re-use (e.g., access and use-case permissions) (Williams et al., 2017). In general, research agencies expect the data produced through their funding to be open in nature and meet the FAIR principles (findable, accessible, interoperable and reusable) (Wilkinson et al., 2016). The Global Indigenous Data Alliance has recently complemented FAIR principles with collective benefit, authority to control, responsibility and ethics (CARE) principles that seek to take account of issues of Indigenous data sovereignty, data ethics and data justice (Carroll et al., 2021; GIDA, 2019). Where relevant, the DMP will set out the reasons why data cannot be shared or re-used in their original form, needing to be transformed into tertiary data, or why they cannot be shared at all, for reasons of privacy and confidentiality, as well as details of data disposal at the end of a project life cycle. Where data are to be shared, a key decision will be to decide on a suitable data repository (usually either an institutional or disciplinary specific repository), recognising that the project will need to comply with the chosen repository's own procedures and rules. A number of tools are available that can help in the preparation of a DMP, such as DMPtool.org or www.dcc.ac.uk/dmponline, and a register of research data repositories can be found at re3data.org. While a DMP is often seen as a compliance chore by researchers, it has intrinsic value in terms of forcing active reflection and planning on data management that improves research design and operational matters (Donnelly, 2012). It should therefore be a key consideration in the initial project design and planning and remain a core task in on-going project management.

Summary

- This chapter has detailed a number of operational and practical issues central to the successful undertaking of a research project. If these issues are ignored then it heightens the chances that a project will produce few, if any, meaningful insights.
- It is vital that research is appropriately framed and designed in relation to the epistemological and ideological views of the researcher, with the questions posed and the methods adopted aligned with these views, as well as being informed by established knowledge evident in the literature.
- Every study requires a well-planned research design that, on the one hand, aims to investigate rigorously the research questions, and on the other hand, takes account of practical constraints such as access, costs and time. Failure to plan adequately a project's design and execution is likely to cause on-going problems and weaken the veracity of a study.
- Data can be sourced by generating primary data, using secondary data, producing derived data or employing simulated data. Generating primary data requires careful consideration of access, sampling frame and representativeness. There is a wide variety of secondary and tertiary data available for re-use for research through archives and repositories, although it might not have been generated to answer the specific questions of a research project.
- It is imperative that data quality is sufficient to produce meaningful insights and ensure trust in the veracity of a study. There are several different components of data quality and a number of means to assess and address them. Poor quality data can exacerbate ecological fallacy concerns in which data are presented or analysed in ways that provide false impressions.
- Data are a vital ingredient for research and it is essential to manage them appropriately. Data management plans formalise the process by which data are handled, cleaned, prepared for analysis and stored for re-use.

Recommended Reading

Blaikie, N., and Priest, J. (2019) *Designing Social Research*, 3rd edn. Polity Books, Cambridge.
A clear discussion of the principles and practices of research design, including the generation and sourcing of data.

Burkholder, G.J., Cox, K.A., Crawford, L.M., and Hitchcock, J.H. (eds). (2019) *Research Design and Methods: An Applied Guide for the Scholar-Practitioner.* Sage, London.
An overview of research design for different methodological approaches and a range of epistemological positions.

Corti, L., van den Eynden, V., Bishop, L., and Woollard, M. (2021) *Managing and Sharing Research Data: A Guide to Good Practice*, 2nd edn. Sage, London.
An overview of managing different forms of data before, during and after conducting a research project.

Cresswell, J.W., and Cresswell, J.D. (2018) *Research Design: Qualitative, Quantitative, and Mixed Methods Approaches*, 5th edn. Sage, London.
A comprehensive discussion of all aspects of research design and planning research projects.

4
Research Ethics

Overview

Chapter 4 examines:

- the central principles of research ethics;
- ethics frameworks and a situational and reflexive approach to research ethics;
- researching vulnerable communities and sensitive issues, and power relations in research;
- the ethics of using 'found data' produced by others; and
- ethical considerations in producing data using digital media.

Introduction

Research ethics is centrally concerned with ensuring that research is conducted in a manner that adheres to moral principles and societal norms and expectations, and is fair, transparent and non-discriminatory. It recognises that the decisions and practices of conducting research can involve questionable practices that have potentially negative consequences for participants (who are engaged directly in a study), data subjects (those whose data is being used for research without their knowledge) and the communities to which they belong, as well as the researchers themselves, and actively encourages research designs and their implementation that seeks to minimise these. Kidder (1981) notes a number of questionable research practices, including:

- involving people in research without their knowledge or consent;
- coercing them to participate;
- withholding information about the true nature of the research;
- otherwise deceiving participants;
- inducing them to commit acts diminishing their self-esteem;
- violating rights of self-determination;

- exposing participants to physical or mental stress;
- invading participants' privacy;
- withholding benefits from some participants;
- not treating participants fairly, with consideration or respect; and
- failing to protect a participant's confidentiality or anonymity.

Four general principles have been central to the development of research ethics (Markham and Buchanan, 2015; Salganik, 2018):

- *respect for people*, in which individuals are treated as autonomous beings who can choose whether to participate, and those with diminished autonomy have additional protections;
- *justice*, in which everyone is treated equally and no group is denied access to, or the benefits from, research;
- *beneficence*, in which all risks and potential harms are minimised and benefits are maximised; and
- *respect for law and public interest*, in which research complies with law, regulations and rules; is transparent and accountable; and aims not to damage communities or undermine public interest and trust.

A related concern is research integrity and the extent to which the research is undertaken in good faith and in line with scientific expectations (e.g., that there is no misconduct such as fraud, fabrication of data or plagiarism).

Formulating appropriate research ethics in research design and application involves a risk/benefit analysis that calculates the probability and potential severity of adverse events, and weighs these up against the potential benefits of the research to the participating community and society in general (Salganik, 2018). In other words, an assessment is made as to whether the research might cause undue stress on participant well-being or cause psychological trauma, or whether the research findings might negatively impact on an individual or community by producing stigma, differential treatment or disinvestment. Such harms might be caused through insensitive or invasive questioning, breaching confidentiality and the disclosure of private information, misuse of data generated (e.g., using information collected for one purpose for a different purpose without the participant's consent) and ill-judged interpretation and communication that might harm a participant's reputation or provides a false impression. The research design of a study needs to anticipate and plan to mitigate against such risks and harms in advance of an empirical study taking place to prevent or limit their occurrence, and to consider possible mitigating procedures in case they do. Ethical uncertainty – where participants and stakeholders have partial information, or are not convinced that suitable protocols and safeguards are in place – can have a chilling effect in terms of securing and maintaining involvement (Salganik, 2018). Practising weak ethics can lead to reputational damage, potential legal action and blacklisting from funding opportunities.

This chapter examines ethics with respect to researching digital life. It starts by detailing key aspects of research ethics in a general sense, discussing ethics frameworks, the concept of contextual integrity, researching vulnerable communities and sensitive issues, power relations in conducting research, the work of institutional review boards, and the value of adopting a situational and reflexive approach to ethics. It next considers specific issues related to digital research, divided into two primary sections. First, the ethics of using 'found data' (secondary data available on the internet) are discussed, including privacy, consent, data minimisation, and analysing scraped, hacked and historical data. Second, the ethics associated with creating data using digital media are considered, including lurking, covert participation, using commercial crowdsourcing and panel companies, applying data analytics, sharing data and working with the state and businesses.

Key Aspects of Research Ethics

Before considering ethics specifically relating to researching digital life, it is important to be cognisant of broadly applicable issues relating to moral philosophy and ethical practices in conducting research. These include the adoption of an ethical position that guides how ethical decisions in research are made; practising contextual integrity wherein ethical practices are sensitive to context and emerging issues; being aware of particular issues in researching vulnerable communities and sensitive issues, and how power relations within the research process need to be actively managed; considering how researchers themselves also need to be protected from potential risks and harms in conducting research; understanding the role of institutional review boards in overseeing ethical conduct; and a researcher being reflexive and open about their ethical conduct.

Ethics Frameworks

There is no one size fits all, purely instrumental approach to practising research ethics. Indeed, a number of ethical positions and frameworks exist across cultural and disciplinary contexts (Vaughan, 2014). *Deontological* approaches to ethics prioritise action and following agreed-upon rules concerning what is right or wrong over consequences. *Consequentialism* holds that right or wrong should be judged in relation to the consequences of actions, not on whether they comply with rules. *Virtue ethics* places the emphasis on seeking to do the right thing, rather than on following rules and consequences. A feminist *ethics of care* is founded on reciprocity and treating people as one would want to be treated. In each case, ethics is rooted in a different aspect of producing and using knowledge: action, consequence, intent and reciprocity (Vaughan, 2014). Scandinavian countries tend to adopt a deontological approach to research ethics, prioritising the protection of rights for all participants and emphasising dignity, autonomy, equality, and trust (franzke et al., 2020). In contrast, the United States and the United Kingdom are more utilitarian and consequentialist in outlook, willing to consider risking the rights of a few taking part in research for the sake of the greater good. Western ethics tends to focus on individual rights, whereas in non-Western and Indigenous cultures, communal and group rights might be prioritised (franzke et al., 2020). Researchers need to be aware of the prevalent ethical views in the jurisdictions in which their institutions are based and in which fieldwork is to be conducted, and to balance this with their own personal values regarding ethics so far as possible within an institutional review board (IRB) framework (noting that at all times the research needs to be legally compliant). It also means being sensitive to such differences and context when judging the research of others, and being aware that more than one ethically defensible position can be adopted in relation to specific issues (franzke et al., 2020).

Contextual Integrity

Regardless of the ethical framework adopted, in recent years it has been recognised that it is 'impossible to standardize or universalize what constitutes the ethically correct actions in ... research contexts, not least because we cannot predict what will happen as a result of our choices' (Markham et al., 2018: 3). Instead, ethicists contend that researchers need to assess carefully, on a case-by-case basis, the specific methods and research design being adopted, and the cultural, regulatory and legal context in which the research is taking place (Hewson, 2016; Lomberg, 2019). In other words, an expectations-based framework for ethical reasoning is applied to consider whether a proposed research design and its possible harms and risks are appropriate within a given context; that is, whether the research design has *contextual integrity*. Contextual integrity is a concept first developed by Helen Nissenbaum (2010) with respect to privacy. She notes that what different communities expect in different circumstances varies, and a one-size-fits-all model of ethical limits calibrated to the highest level of protections that takes no account of context can place unnecessary restrictions on research and curtail valuable studies. As Lomberg (2019: 106) notes, '[t]he principle of contextual integrity invites researchers to dwell on the possible ethical consequences' of their research, and to devise an ethical framing appropriate to the focus, context and vulnerabilities and expectations of participants.

Researching Vulnerable Communities and Sensitive Issues

Many of the ethical concerns pertaining to research relate to protecting the rights of marginalised and vulnerable people, and approaching culturally and politically sensitive issues in an appropriate manner (Markham and Buchanan, 2015). The research ethics literature provides dozens of examples of research projects that have perpetrated deliberate harm on communities in order to observe effects (such as denying essential medical treatment), or else have unintentionally created harm through a lack of planning and foresight (such as causing further mental trauma to victims of abuse through the research design) (Israel and Hay, 2006). It is these studies that have prompted more institutional and regulatory attention being paid to research ethics and the establishment of IRBs by universities. Research in relation to marginalised communities, usually distinguished by social markers such as gender, race, class, disability, sexuality and ethnicity, is often considered sensitive in nature because it potentially has social, political and legal implications, or is considered taboo, sacred or private, or it is actively managed by subjects to limit stigmatisation and negative consequences. Many marginalised communities have a justifiable fear of authority. For example, members of the LGBTQ+ community might wish to remain anonymous due to the potential effects of being outed, especially in countries where homosexuality remains illegal, and any research conducted with them must limit any potential threat and protect their identity. Children are a specific class of potentially vulnerable research subjects who have less ability to understand and evaluate participation in research, and weaker autonomy to make decisions regarding consent (Alderson and Morrow, 2020). In many jurisdictions, research involving children requires enhanced ethical controls, consent of parents and/or guardians, and police vetting (Monaghan et al., 2013).

Power Relations in Undertaking Research

Related to the issue of researching marginalised communities and sensitive issues is the question of power relations within the research process. Researchers are generally well educated and possess a reasonable degree of social status and cultural capital. They are the ones deciding on a research agenda and formulating a research design. Consequently, there is an asymmetrical power relationship between researchers and those being researched. Such asymmetry can create tensions, particularly if it results in decisions that might cause harm in some way or it alienates research participants where they feel they are not being listened to or are being exploited. England (1994) notes two problematic issues that arise from these power asymmetries: *research tourism* (also referred to as 'academic voyeurism') and *appropriation*. In the case of research tourism, a researcher who does not belong to a social group can act as a voyeur of a marginalised group from a dominant position. The researchers construct the marginalised group's story for them, yet enjoy the privilege of returning to their ordinary life without obligation or responsibility for any consequences of the research that may affect the participants. The marginalised might gain visibility, but not on their terms.

This raises the issue of appropriation; that is, taking a group's knowledge, experiences and skills and materially benefitting from them. Appropriation has been the subject of live debate in fields such as disability studies, queer studies, Black studies, Indigenous studies, decolonial and postcolonial studies, and development studies for several decades. For example, in disability studies, there is a long-standing debate concerning whether research should be conducted on, with or by disabled people, and about the role, actions, motives and consequences of non-disabled researchers undertaking research on disability issues (Burke and Byrne, 2021; Kitchin, 2000). Some have suggested that the traditional 'expert' model of research, wherein non-disabled researchers study disabled people, represents an extractive model of research whereby disabled peoples' knowledge and experiences are appropriated for academic gain (Oliver, 1992). In many cases, this research, however well-meaning, perpetuates the stigmatisation and marginalisation of disabled people. Similar arguments have been made in relation to research and data systems concerning Indigenous communities. As Indigenous scholars have argued, Indigenous communities have experienced centuries of data extraction by non-Indigenous researchers without prior and informed consent, using biased or flawed methodologies, or have been deliberately omitted from official data sources for ends that have rarely benefitted Indigenous peoples (Kukutai and Taylor, 2016; Rainie et al., 2019). Consequently, Indigenous scholars and communities have called for greater data sovereignty; that is, the right to determine and govern how data related to them are generated, analysed, documented, owned, stored, shared and used (Mann and Daly, 2019). In so doing, Indigenous communities are calling for decolonial research methodologies and practices, and for existing data generation systems (such as the production of official statistics) to be decolonised (Pool, 2016; see **Chapter 2**).

Similarly, many social scientists researching communities to which they do not belong favour a research design that seeks to be more inclusive, rebalances power and is sensitive to the concerns of participants. This includes researchers adopting a role that is empathetic and rooted in mutual respect, devolving some aspects of research design and decision-making to research participants, and adopting more participatory approaches in which research is undertaken with and by a community rather than on and about them (England, 1994; Kindon et al., 2007; see **Chapter 8**). As Elwood and Leszczynski (2018) note, digital scholarship has been relatively slow to consider and address the ways in which it is saturated with and (un)consciously reproduces power.

Protecting Researchers

In addition to protecting research subjects from risks and harms, there is an ethical imperative to do likewise for researchers. In the social media age, undertaking research on certain issues (such as exploitation, discrimination and geopolitics) can provoke strong ideological reactions and expose researchers to online abuse, harassment, doxing (publishing private information about the researcher) and even death threats (franzke et al., 2020). Researching issues such as online hate acts, pornography, criminal activity, terrorism and war can expose researchers to images and first-person accounts that can elicit emotional and psychological reactions and long-term trauma (Roberts, 2019). Principal investigators on projects have a duty of care to their research staff and themselves to consider their safety and psychological well-being, and to put in place suitable procedures to protect staff and deal with any short and long-term issues (franzke et al., 2020).

Institutional Review Boards

A formalised means of assessing the ethics of research is the use of IRBs that aim to ensure compliance with a set of defined acceptable ethical practices. As Hutchinson et al. (2017: 59) note, '[e]thics reviews are a procedural guarantee that normative principles of research integrity have been considered and codified in the research methodology'. Meeting IRB expectations is often the minimum requirement for those researching digital life. The heart of many IRB principles is the FIPPs, developed and adopted by the Organisation for Economic Co-operation and Development (OECD) in 1980. These principles have subsequently underpinned privacy legislation and data protection measures in OECD countries, including the General Data Protection Regulation (GDPR) in Europe. All researchers in the OECD are expected to comply with FIPPs, which set out eight principles of good practice concerning the generation, use, disclosure and sharing of personal data (see **Table 4.1**), as well as the obligations of data controllers (those who determine the purposes for and the manner in which any personal data are processed) and data processors (those who hold or process data given to them by the data controller) (Solove, 2013). A researcher generating and storing data is a data controller; one who is using secondary or tertiary data is a data processor. Each role has obligations and responsibilities with respect to data subjects and the law.

Table 4.1 Fair information practice principles.

General principle	General description	Original OECD principle and description
Notice	Individuals are informed that data are being generated and the purpose to which the data will be put.	*Purpose specification principle* – The purposes for which personal data are collected should be specified not later than at the time of data collection and the subsequent use limited to the fulfilment of those purposes or such others as are not incompatible with those purposes and as are specified on each occasion of change of purpose.
Choice	Individuals have the choice to opt-in or opt-out as to whether and how their data will be used or disclosed.	*Openness principle* – There should be a general policy of openness about developments, practices and policies with respect to personal data. Means should be readily available for establishing the existence and nature of personal data, and the main purposes of their use, as well as the identity and usual residence of the data controller.
Consent	Data are generated and disclosed only with the consent of individuals.	*Collection limitation principle* – There should be limits to the collection of personal data and any such data should be obtained by lawful and fair means and, where appropriate, with the knowledge or consent of the data subject.
Security	Data are protected from loss, misuse, unauthorised access, disclosure, alteration and destruction.	*Security safeguards principle* – Personal data should be protected by reasonable security safeguards against such risks as loss or unauthorised access, destruction, use, modification or disclosure of data.
Integrity	Data are reliable, accurate, complete and current.	*Data quality principle* – Personal data should be relevant to the purposes for which they are to be used, and, to the extent necessary for those purposes, should be accurate, complete and kept up to date.
Access	Individuals can access, check and verify data about themselves.	*Individual participation principle* – An individual should have the right to: 1. obtain from a data controller, or otherwise, confirmation of whether the data controller has data relating to him or her; 2. have communicated to him or her, data relating to him or her within a reasonable time; at a charge, if any, that is not excessive; in a reasonable manner; and in a form that is readily intelligible to him or her; 3. be given reasons if a request made under subparagraphs(a) and (b) is denied, and to be able to challenge such denial; and 4. challenge data relating to him or her, and if the challenge is successful to have the data erased, rectified, completed or amended.

Table 4.1 Fair information practice principles. (Continued)

General principle	General description	Original OECD principle and description
Use	Data are used only for the purpose for which they are generated and individuals are informed of each change of purpose.	*Use limitation principle* – Personal data should not be disclosed, made available or otherwise used for purposes other than those specified within the notice, except with the consent of the data subject or by the authority of law.
Accountability	The data holder is accountable for ensuring the above principles and has mechanisms in place to assure compliance.	*Accountability principle* – A data controller should be accountable for complying with measures that give effect to the principles stated above.

Sources: compiled from OECD (1980) and Minelli et al. (2013)

IRBs can be tricky for social scientists to negotiate for two reasons. First, their foundational principles can often be rooted in medical and health ethics, which are then mapped onto social research with little adaptation or flexibility. Framed around malpractice and potential litigation, bioethics are not well suited to deal with situations 'where normative ethical strategies are unworkable and may threaten academic freedom or participant rights' (Hutchinson et al., 2017: 63). For example, it is unreasonable to seek consent for researching the online activities of a terrorist organisation such as ISIS, or to expect the research strategy or results to be shared with them (Hutchinson et al., 2017). Second, many IRBs fail to acknowledge the variety of ethical frameworks that can be adopted, or permit contextual integrity, being overly rigid and cautious (franzke et al., 2020; Monaghan et al., 2013). One-size fits all assessments can be unhelpful, even if they are well intentioned. Consequently, many social scientists find themselves negotiating with IRBs to persuade them that not only have ethical issues been considered, but the approach being proposed is the most appropriate.

Situational Ethics and Reflexivity

Research ethics is often practised as a set of compliance rules: a set of procedures and practices that are followed in order to meet expected professional conduct demanded by IRBs. For some they are seen as a nuisance to be adhered to rather than as the minimum, basic moral standards concerning how research is conducted. This is particularly the case in research that frames itself as being scientific, objective, detached, value-free and impartial. For others, research ethics as delineated by IRBs do not go far enough in addressing the politics and power operating within and arising from research. Instead, they advocate for a thorough consideration of ethics and politics at all stages of a project and for the practice of *situational ethics* (Markham et al., 2018). Such an approach involves continually questioning the politics of the research design (in terms of what might be silenced, excluded or privileged through the choices made), the validity of analysis and interpretation, and whose agenda it might be serving. Such views are often grounded in feminist critiques of science that question its supposed objectivity, neutrality and representativeness.

Donna Haraway (1988, 1991) criticises the dominant epistemology of science for employing what she terms a 'god trick'; that is, claiming to measure and understand the world in a disembodied, emotionless, apolitical view from nowhere that applies to everywhere. Somehow, the researcher is detached from the context and processes of research, the instruments used are in no way reflective of the values of their creators and serve no purpose other than generating objective 'raw' data, and the knowledge produced are representations of reality that are valid outside of cultural interpretation (Propen, 2009). The power of the 'god trick' is that it 'denies the partiality of the knower, erases subjectivities and ignores the power relations involved in all forms of knowledge production' (Kwan, 2007: 24). Moreover, science practised in this way typically privileges those in power and reproduces hegemonic relations and status quo, subjugating, silencing or erasing other perspectives. Instead, Haraway (1988) advocates for an epistemology of partial perspective that she terms *situated knowledges* (see **Chapter 2**), which calls for transparency and reflexivity in the framing and execution of research projects.

Reflexivity is a key element of a situated approach to knowledge production. To be reflexive is to be self-aware of the politics of choices and decisions being taken, to understand them in context and to consider what the implications of them might be (England, 1994; Rose, 1997). A researcher reflects deeply on epistemology and methodology assumptions, how a project is operationalised, its ethical aspects and consequences for knowledge produced, their positionality, and situated action and interpretation. Reflexivity also involves researchers considering their relational position within the field sites in which they are working (including digital media and platforms), their interactions and asymmetric power relationships with those being researched, how these inflect and mediate the research process, and how the research might affect participants (e.g., negative impacts on their everyday life through the research process itself; or downstream through the introduction of new policies, programmes, regulations, etc.) (Whitson, 2017). In other words, reflexivity involves 'self-critical introspection' and 'self-conscious analytical scrutiny of the self as researcher' *and* the research endeavour (England, 1994: 244), and it recognises that researchers do not 'parachute into the field with empty heads' (England, 1994: 248) but rather arrive with learned knowledge, values, opinions, beliefs, assumptions and 'feelings, failings, and moods' (Stanley and Wise, 1993: 157).

Ethics in Researching Digital Life

Ethical considerations for researching digital life mirror those of non-digital research, but also have a number of specificities and novel aspects (Markham and Buchanan, 2015; Tiidenberg, 2018). For example, given that the internet is scaled globally, which national or international ethical standards should apply to data or subjects that are transnational in character? What are the obligations and legal requirements relating to privacy and data re-purposing for subjects who are engaging in 'public' activities such as posting on social media? How should subjects who are anonymous or may be posing as someone else be treated? How should research on minors be conducted via digital media, and how should consent for participation be sought and verified? What is the legal and ethical status of scraped or hacked data? Do app developers and the owners of platforms have the right to conduct mass experiments on the users of their systems? Moreover, the digital realm raises the question, what counts as a human? Should an avatar in a virtual world or game qualify for ethical protections? Should a robot or a machine that displays some level of autonomy in decision-making be afforded some moral rights (Gunkel, 2018)? In complex systems, such as IoT deployments that might include a number of technologies and stakeholders bound together in complex technical, economic and legal relations, where do responsibilities and consent lie? Similarly, in multi-participant data science (see **Chapter 11**), who is responsible and accountable for practices and outputs (Leonelli, 2016)? The remainder of the section divides the discussion into two related sections, using a distinction between *found data* (exhaust and secondary data accessible online, generated and held by others) and *made data* (produced directly by a researcher and research subjects) (Jensen, 2012). A number of ethical issues and dilemmas are detailed, some of which (such as privacy, consent and working with companies) span both digital and non-digital research.

Ethics and 'Found Data'

Vast quantities of information relating to people, organisations, businesses and their activities are stored as digital data online, which are a potential source of evidence for research. People leave all kinds of data footprints (produced by them) and data shadows (captured by others) through interactions with digital systems, including traces and records of their activities, purchases, location and movement (Kitchin, 2014a). Moreover, they share an enormous amount of information online that in previous generations might have been shared with only a handful of people (family, close friends, employers): CVs or résumés, personal and family stories, family photographs and videos, and personal preferences and thoughts. Digital devices and apps are designed to continuously generate fine-grained data, and digital platforms and infrastructures are *de facto* mass surveillance systems (Zuboff, 2019). These data comprise 'found data': data that are generated, not for the purposes of academic research, but rather for operational, regulatory and optimisation reasons by public, non-profit, business, institutional and other private entities. For instance, users shopping online and posting on social media are engaged in business transactions and social interactions, and do not anticipate their data being repurposed for academic studies.

Found big data are highly relational, being indexical (uniquely tagged to a person, object, location or transaction) and exhaustive (data is generated for all entities in a system rather than being sampled) in nature. What this means is that big datasets contain extensive, fine-grained information about people's digital and digitally mediated interactions with systems, platforms, algorithms, apps, and interfaces. For example, a social media company has information on all posts, shares, likes, and social graphs for all its users; a supermarket chain has detailed time-series purchase records for customers across all its stores; and a telecoms provider has records of all customer activity across its networks. Such records contain a wealth of sensitive information about consumption, interactions, social connections, and beliefs and values. There are clearly ethical issues regarding access to, as well as the handling, analysis, and sharing of, such 'found data'. These include concerns relating to consent, data minimisation, privacy and confidentiality, and uses of scraped or hacked data (see below).

Privacy and Confidentiality

Given the extensive, fine-grained, personal and relational nature of big data, there are clearly issues involving privacy and confidentiality related to how much of the data are publicly accessible or open to scraping, hacking, leaking and analysis. When used in research, found data carry the potential of creating privacy harms (e.g., revealing confidential information) by extending the insights that can be extracted from them through exposure, linkage and analysis, even where the data are publicly available. For example, 'publishing verbatim quotes from a public online discussion forum could lead to them being traced back to source, viewed in context, and individual authors being identified, posing a serious potential threat to participant confidentiality' (Hewson, 2016: 213). High-profile cases that breach privacy include AOL releasing for research more than 20 million search queries from 658,000 users that could be re-identified; a Danish researcher who published the data for 70,000 OKCupid users (a dating site); and 173 million New York taxi journeys being released as open data that were not fully de-identified (Metcalf and Crawford, 2016; Tiidenberg, 2018; Zimmer, 2018). A means to try to mitigate against such harms is to fully de-identify the data and to implement a data management plan (see **Chapter 3**) that takes data protection and security seriously. De-identifcation can be achieved through several techniques, including anonymisation using pseudonyms, aggregating data, removing selected fields, reducing precision through generalisation, or adding 'noise' (false data) to remove or mask identities (Green et al., 2017). Even when data are de-identified, there may be group privacy issues that need consideration. Group privacy refers to protecting individuals within communities of shared characteristics (such as ethnicity, religion, class, gender, age, health condition, location or occupation) from profiling and differential treatment based on their membership of a group (Rainie et al., 2019; Taylor et al., 2017). Additional means of safeguarding against privacy harms include restricting access to people who can be trusted with data (e.g., people who have undergone ethical training); and storing data on computers with appropriate physical (e.g., locked room) and software (e.g., password protection, encryption) protections (Salganik, 2018).

Consent and Data Minimisation

A central concern with respect to 'found data' is consent, a cornerstone of FIPPs. *Consent* involves securing research subjects' direct permission to participate in a study, and to analyse and share generated data and analysis (Solove, 2013). Most big datasets have not been generated for the purposes of research, and consent to re-use the data has not been sought. Consequently, if their data are re-used, data subjects remain unaware and have no ability to object or withdraw their data from re-use. This was the case in relation to the AOL, OKCupid and New York taxi data mentioned above. In the case of social media or other platform data, some will contend that the data are publicly accessible and therefore are in the public domain and thus open to re-use (Markham and Buchanan, 2015). Here, it is often assumed that any publicly viewable data or data accessible via an API *de facto* has user consent. In such views, there is also a tendency to treat the data as being independent from their subjects, and since humans are not directly involved in the study to believe that the ethical concerns of the research are diminished (Markham et al., 2018). For example, it is not uncommon for data scientists to argue that their research does not require ethical review as it does not involve direct interaction with human subjects (Salganik, 2018).

However, the data are publicly viewable on platforms because their display are essential for their operation; they are not open data, posted so that they can be freely shared and re-used. Moreover, the individuals to which the data refers remain 'data subjects' who have data protection and privacy rights (Buchanan, 2017) and re-use also breaks the data minimisation principle of FIPPs and legislation such as the European Union's GDPR. Data minimisation stipulates that data controllers and processors should only generate data necessary to perform a particular task, that the data are retained for only as long as they are required to perform that task (or as long as legal requirements dictate), and that the data generated should be used only for this task (Tene and Polonetsky, 2012). That is, data should not be re-purposed without consent. Re-using found data that has no research mandate clearly breaks the data minimisation principle. Seeking consent in practice is difficult to achieve given that the data might refer to hundreds of thousands of people and tracking them all down to seek permission is generally impossible. One way that researchers seek to skirt around consent and data minimisation issues is to de-identify the data so that it cannot be traced back to specific individuals. This often involves creating new derived data through generalisation techniques (such as categorisation) that are not subject to the data minimisation principle. This is a less than perfect solution and the ethics of using found data without consent remains a live issue.

Ethics of Using Scraped or Hacked Data

Platforms are commercial enterprises that generate income through the monetisation of their data. While some platforms provide researchers with access to selected data via their APIs (such as TikTok, Meta or YouTube with certain restrictions; Lurie, 2023), most do not openly share their data, although some may enter into specific data-sharing contracts with researchers. However, given that data are publicly accessible as an essential feature of many platforms, they are viewable and amenable to capture through scraping, where a bespoke piece of software (an API) is used to automatically capture data from a platform. An example of scraped data used for research is that collected by Inside Airbnb, which has produced a longitudinal database of scraped short-term rental data from Airbnb for cities across the globe (Scassa, 2019). Data published on government sites are also open to scraping and use in research. For example, Brown (2021) scraped data from the Irish Refugee Appeals Tribunal Archive to assess the practices used by the Irish state to determine asylum in Ireland. The key question with respect to scraping is its legal status. As Scassa (2019) details, while the use of scraped data research often has public interest value, there are uncertainties regarding their ownership, sharing, derivation, intellectual property rights and rights to control data use, as well as how the law views scraping as an activity (e.g., as trespass or theft). Scraped data lacks consent and breaks the data minimisation principle. In using scraped data, or conducting their own scraping, researchers should be mindful of these issues and their possible consequences in terms of legal challenge. Similar concerns relate to the use of hacked data, where non-publicly accessible data have been illegally accessed, copied and shared (Poor, 2017). Such data can be of enormous public value, such as the Snowdon files, Wikileaks and Panama Papers. There are clearly ethical questions in using hacked data in research projects, even when they shed important light on the illegal activities of others. To a large degree, the use of such data is a personal moral decision, though IRBs might seek to block or put limits on such research.

Ethics Relating to Historical Data

Data archives and infrastructures hold vast quantities of historical data, much of it digitised from analogue formats. Much of these data are quite old, episodic and patchy in content, and the individuals to whom the data refer are no longer alive, so issues of consent and privacy dissipate. In countries such as the United Kingdom and Ireland, government data relating to individuals are kept confidential for 100 years before being transferred to national archives, and data relating to government decision-making during key events might be kept confidential for thirty to fifty years. Digital scans of these documents will likewise be kept confidential for the same period. Recent historical data, particularly born digital data, are by comparison more systematic, granular, and indexical; are easier to search and cross-reference; and make it easier for individuals to be found and viewed (Lomberg, 2019). Moreover, whereas ordinary people are less likely to be included in an identifiable form in older historical datasets, they are well represented in big data, such as data generated via social media platforms, even where these data may have been posted by users many years earlier. In addition, what may have previously been considered an unnoticed, niche, private, safe space on the fringes of the web can persist, over time becoming part of the public record in ways unanticipated by former users (Lomberg, 2019). Further, the temporal distance with the present is small as it concerns recent historical data (e.g., a ten-year-old post to a web forum) and any issues may potentially still be live (e.g., a debate and event such as Brexit might unfold over several years and older posts can be easily resurfaced to defend positions or re-ignite flashpoint issues). Consequently, historical data from the recent past containing personally identifiable data need to be subject to ethical practice in similar ways to contemporary data since the same potential harms persist; that is, the principles of respect for people, law and public interest, beneficence and justice still hold. Given time lapses, however, it may be difficult to trace individuals to gain consent, particularly if individuals are no longer active or have left platforms (e.g., deactivated their accounts).

Ethics and 'Made Data'

In contrast to research utilising found data are studies that generate their own data (also known as 'made data'). Here, researchers use prescribed methods to create data. In social science projects, this may involve interactions with people in some fashion;

for example, through observation, interviews, surveys and focus groups. In the case of researching digital life, these interactions may be digitally mediated and occur at a distance rather than in person. For example, ethnographies and interviews can be conducted via digital platforms and mobile devices, including messaging apps, email, video conferencing software, online forums and social media (see **Chapter 5**). While the ethics of such research often mirrors traditional methodologies, this digital mediation does produce some unique challenges, which are discussed below.

Consent

Informed consent is required in all cases where research subjects are knowingly taking part in a research study, and participants must be able to withdraw at any time. In many cases, this is easily dealt with by sending respondents an information sheet and a consent form in advance of a video or email interview, or as the first stage in an app survey. However, the non-proximate nature of the research means that ensuring and verifying that participants have read and understood the information and the nature of their consent, and that they are eligible to take part in terms of age and qualifying criteria (especially when participants are anonymous), is trickier (Hewson, 2016). It is also more difficult to implement effective withdrawal and debriefing procedures, especially when the data generation takes place without researcher presence and involves anonymous subjects with no means of tracing or contacting them (Hewson, 2016). In such scenarios, care must be taken to make consent as effective and meaningful as possible; for example, by using double confirmation (re-confirming the initial consent) or continuous consent (seeking consent at each stage of the research process – pre-fieldwork, fieldwork and post-fieldwork phases) and making sure that information is publicly accessible beyond the interaction (e.g., available on a website) (Klykken, 2022). Continuous consent might have particular salience in studies that involve vulnerable populations and sensitive topics. For example, in her study of sexy selfies on social media, Tiidenberg (2018) re-sought consent each time the research shifted phases to ensure that participants continued to be comfortable with the work being undertaken.

Ethics of Lurking, Covert Participation and Researching Closed Groups

Consent is a particular issue in projects where a primary means of generating data is to observe an online community or platform. In general, this takes the form of lurking in which a researcher is virtually present but does not interact with other participants, simply observing and recording activity. Lurking is seen as an attractive method because it observes naturalistic, everyday online interactions, with a reduced risk of the participants changing their behaviour because they know they are being studied (Hine, 2000).

This presents a number of related ethical issues. Online communities and platforms can be populated with tens of thousands of participants, many of whom may be anonymous and transitory users, making obtaining individual consent all but impossible. One route is to seek consent from the administrators or owners of a site, group or medium (e.g., a forum or a Facebook page) and to announce publicly that research is underway. However, individual consent will still be absent, and an announcement may not be seen or understood by all. Another approach is to observe covertly, not seeking to gain any form of consent. This, however, challenges the ethical guidelines of many IRBs (Grincheva, 2017). Yet there may be good reasons for using such an approach; for example, the activity is of public interest but is transgressive or illegal, and the research would be impossible to conduct if it were announced; or gaining consent and undertaking the research might fundamentally influence and transform what is being studied. To gain approval from an IRB, researchers must provide strong justification for the covert nature of the study. Similarly, researching a closed group, such as an online support group where membership is by approval only, requires careful handling. The group is closed to protect privacy, and many closed groups are safe havens where members can share their experiences and feelings without being judged (Hård af Segerstad et al., 2017). This may be at odds with the goals of much research, which endeavours to throw light on and examine issues. If a community feels its space, values and trust have been compromised, then significant harm has been inflicted by a study. Care is required in how such groups are approached and consent sought, and how the research data are analysed and disseminated.

Ethics of Using Commercial Crowdsourcing and Panel Companies

Sourcing participants to take part in research studies can be an arduous task. Many academic and commercial researchers have sought to lessen this burden by using third-party platforms and companies to recruit subjects, who then perform the research task online. There are a number of platforms for crowdsourcing research participants, including Mechanical Turk, Prolific Academic, ClickWorker and CrowdFlower (Pittman and Sheehan, 2017). Members of these platforms are offered the opportunity to take part in a study for a fee, usually set per task or unit of time. Crowdsourced participants generally have little screening or sampling controls and are recruited from a general pool. In contrast, research panel companies provide pre-screened, demographically balanced panels of participants who match *a priori* sample criteria and who have usually also agreed to participate in future research, thus providing participant continuity. Panel companies are usually more expensive to employ. Ethical issues relating to the use of crowdsourced platforms and research panels include: fair payment for labour, given that workers receive relatively low wages (often below minimum-wage rates); whether payment enables undue inducement and coercion, encouraging participants to disclose information that they would not otherwise; ensuring effective consent and that principles such as participants can exit at any time are met; and a lack of transparency, since the identity of the researchers commissioning third-party platforms are generally withheld from participants, meaning they cannot evaluate their reputation or trustworthiness (Pittman and Sheehan, 2017). There is live debate concerning whether participants should be paid; the effects of payment on the quality and integrity of research conducted; and issues such as mutual respect, trust and accountability (Grady, 2019; Head, 2009). Some argue that interested volunteers are a better source of research subjects than paid participants, who may feel exploited and care little for study outcomes. Others would favour fair payment to address this issue (Pittman and Sheehan, 2017).

Ethics of Using Data Analytics

Immense computational power and new analytical techniques are now available to merge datasets from disparate sources together, and to sort and sift through datasets and identify patterns and relationships (see **Chapter 12**). This raises ethical questions concerning the use of data analytics to reveal relations that would otherwise remain hidden, and to act on the findings in ways that might cause harm. In cases where the research is using algorithms and machine learning, there are specific concerns relating to, on the one hand, issues of bias within the learning methods and analytic methods and dependence on third-party datasets (see **Chapter 6**), and on the other, transparency, review and accountability (Bechmann and Zevenbergen, 2020; Pasquale, 2015). The mobilisation of data analytics in research may produce a false and unfair view of particular populations through a flawed and black-boxed methodology. This might be exacerbated by a reliance on algorithms to interpret and act on data, with an absence of contextual meaning making by domain experts (Markham et al., 2018). There are also questions concerning how the models produced might be used, whether they could be deployed maliciously, and to what extent researchers are responsible for the downstream effects of models if used inappropriately (Bechmann and Zevenbergen, 2020). In such cases, it is incumbent on researchers to consider how their work might be made open, reproducible (when re-analysed using the same methods, the same data will produce the same results) and replicable (when the same methods are applied to new data the same results are produced demonstrating the original study is valid and reliable), in part to help allay ethical concerns (NASEM, 2019).

Ethics of Sharing Data

A predominate trend in academia is for research data to be archived and shared for re-use to facilitate the extraction of additional value and insights. While this is a commendable goal, there are potential ethical issues in sharing research data relating to privacy, confidentiality, data minimisation and potential harms arising from re-use (Corti et al., 2014). In the first instance, care must be taken to ensure that consent covers re-use, particularly as it can be tricky to track down participants later to seek new terms and conditions regarding their data. If data re-use has been consented to, then it is important to ensure that the shared dataset is compliant with privacy and data protection legislation, such as GDPR. This means ensuring that the data are fully de-identified. Qualitative data, such as interview transcripts, can be trickier to de-identify as several elements of non-personal data in the narrative can often be linked to re-identify the interviewee. Solutions include redacting information or converting material into more vague descriptors (Corti et al., 2014). If the sound file is also being deposited, then personal identifiable material should be bleeped out and the voice can be disguised by altering the pitch and tone; similarly, faces in photos or videos can be pixilated. It may also be necessary to implement tiered access (e.g., limiting access to authorised users); embargos (e.g., data are only released after a set period of time); or stipulations that the data only be used for particular purposes, such as replication and reproducibility, but not for others, such as being enrolled into commercial databases and monetised in some way. Implementing all these techniques can be time consuming and expensive.

Ethics of Working with States and Companies

Much research concerning digital life focuses on the work of states and businesses and how they use digital technologies to regulate and manage society and to produce profit. This research is often critical in nature, detailing how these entities' actions (re)produce structural relations, and questioning their logics and practices. Unsurprisingly, then, there are concerns about academics working with such actors. Indeed, there is a long-running debate in the social sciences concerning the independence and purpose of academic research (see Fuller and Kitchin, 2004). On one side are those who believe that academic research should necessarily maintain a separation from state and industry to ensure critical distance and scientific autonomy, and to avoid being co-opted into and legitimising state and industry actions (Allen, 2011). On the other side are those who believe that academia should work with state and industry to tackle societal and fundamental problems by pooling knowledge, expertise and resources (Bastow et al., 2014). It is a personal choice to work with state or business partners, but if one does choose to collaborate with these entities, there are a number of issues to keep in mind. Agreements concerning ethics might operate solely at the level of compliance with legal requirements, as achieving an alignment with respect to moral philosophy might be difficult and partners might have quite different ambitions regarding research outcomes and how they will be applied in practice. Moreover, industry partners might not operate in alignment with the IRB structures demanded by universities or funding agencies, and lack independent oversight mechanisms (Hoffman and Jonas, 2017). They may also demand the signing of non-disclosure agreements that prevent academic researchers from being fully transparent and from voicing their concerns about aspects of a study. However, it might well be that the only way to examine the platforms and services of digital technology companies is to enter into a working arrangement with them, meaning that a compromise of usual ethical standards enables important access to hidden assets, practices and outcomes. While potentially of benefit, a danger here is the partnership enacts a form of ethics washing (Wagner, B., 2018), with the university collaboration legitimatising problematic practices.

Summary

- This chapter has detailed the various ethical issues that need to be negotiated in researching digital life. In particular, it has examined specific ethical issues related to using 'found' and 'made' data.
- A number of general issues, such as privacy, consent, data minimisation and working with state and business partners, need to be considered in designing and implementing a project, as well as issues that are more specific to researching digital life, such as using scraped or hacked data, lurking or crowdsourcing.
- All research is saturated with ethics and politics in its formulation, execution and outcomes and careful attention must be paid to the power relations at play within a project and the various harms that undertaking research might have on participants and communities. This is particularly the case for researching vulnerable communities and sensitive issues.
- Researchers might seek to ensure that their research practices are conducted in a neutral, detached, objective manner that minimise harms to people and systems under investigation, but striving for such a goal involves active, reflexive attention to ethics throughout the *lifetime* of a project as circumstances change.
- At a minimum, a project should comply with IRB principles. Better still, a thoroughly moral, reflexive and situated approach to conducting research and ethics should be adopted that aims to minimise detrimental practices and harmful effects to participants while producing insightful and useful knowledge.

Recommended Reading

franzke, a.s., Bechmann, A., Zimmer, M., Ess, C., and the Association of Internet Researchers (2020) *Internet Research: Ethical Guidelines 3.0*, https://aoir.org/reports/ethics3.pdf (accessed 16 August 2023).
This report details a comprehensive set of ethical issues in conducting digital research and how to approach them.

Markham, A. N., and Buchanan, E. (2015) 'Ethical considerations in digital research contexts', in Wright, J.D. (ed.), *Encyclopedia for Social & Behavioral Sciences*. Elsevier, Waltham, MA, pp. 606–13.
A clear, concise introduction to research ethics in internet and big data research.

Utrecht Data School (n.d.) *Data Ethics Decision Aid for Researchers*, https://deda.dataschool.nl/en/ (accessed 5 Sept 2023).
A useful tool for prompting critical thought on the ethics of a project.

Zimmer, M., and Kinder-Kurlanda, K. (eds) (2017) *Internet Research Ethics for the Social Age: New Challenges, Cases, and Contexts*. Peter Lang, New York.
Provides a wide-ranging discussion of ethics in conducting research using social media platforms and digital methods, including detailed case studies.

Zimmer, M. (2018) 'Addressing conceptual gaps in big data research ethics: An application of contextual integrity', *Social Media + Society*, 4(3): 1–11.
Provides a useful heuristic for thinking through the potential ethical issues of big data research.

Part 2
Methods and Approaches

5
Interviews, Surveys, Observation and (Auto)Ethnography

Overview

Chapter 5 examines:

- how different digital mediums can be used to conduct interviews and focus groups;
- online surveys and questionnaires using social media, and web-based and app-based tools;
- observation, ethnography and autoethnography, and how they can be used to study digital life; and
- the advantages and challenges in undertaking digitally mediated interviews, focus groups, surveys, questionnaires, observations and (auto)ethnography.

Introduction

Interviews, focus groups, surveys, questionnaires, observation and (auto)ethnography encompass a broad range of research methods for directly engaging with and observing people's digital and digitally mediated behaviours and practices. These methods are long established within the social sciences but have been transformed by the advent of digital tools that re-mediate their use and create new methodological opportunities and challenges for researching the phenomena of digital life. Such re-mediation has been necessary, in part, to enable the investigation of new digital media and platforms in everyday life, where the application of traditional iterations of these methods have more limited utility. This chapter opens by examining interviews and focus groups as longstanding methods of social science enquiry, as well as how the use of digital tools has altered their form, implementation and outcomes. The focus next turns to surveys and questionnaires, with a particular focus on how web-based tools provide researchers with new means of engaging previously difficult to access groups of people. Subsequently, observation methods and (auto)ethnography – and how they are being remediated and applied to the study of digital phenomena – are discussed. In each section, attention is paid to the benefits and challenges of using these methods to make sense of digital life.

Interviews

Interviews have a long history as a social science research method. Most simply, interviews are a form of conversational exchange wherein an interviewer (researcher) seeks to understand the experiences, thoughts and feelings, and/or values and attitudes of an interviewee (study participant), usually in relation to a specific topic or phenomenon (Valentine, 1997). There are three general types of interviews commonly used by researchers.

Structured interviews have a set sequence of questions that every interviewee is asked, often in the same order, and are often weighted towards 'closed' (interviewees select from a predetermined range of possible responses) over 'open-ended' questions. There is usually little opportunity for either the interviewer or interviewee to deviate from the prescribed structure of the interview. The benefit of such a format is the consistent application of questions and standardised responses across interviewees, ensuring that equivalent information is captured across the entire sample, thus facilitating direct comparison and quantification. The structured interview format is equivalent to that used in survey questionnaires (see the next section).

Semi-structured interviews involve a comparatively more open conversation between interviewer and informant. While the interviewer relies on a guide, or list, of open format questions (including follow-up questions) to pose to informants, the questions do not need to necessarily be asked in the same order, and the conversation is allowed to head in different directions, especially if the informant raises interesting points the researcher had not anticipated. However, the interviewer is still taking a guided approach, seeking to ensure that a predetermined set of topics and questions are asked over the course of the interview. The benefit of adopting a semi-structured approach is that the interview is more conversational in tone and interesting answers can be explored further, yet none of the key research questions are omitted to ensure comparability across interviewees.

Finally, *unstructured interviews* consist of a completely open conversation, where the interviewer has a topic or theme they want to explore, but there is no set of specific questions to be asked with questions arising from the unfolding conversation (Alshenqeeti, 2014). An unstructured interview often begins with a single conversational prompt or question posed by the interviewer but is then largely directed by the informant. This format is informal in nature and more like a typical conversation, enabling the informant to more fully express their views and the interviewer to further probe the most interesting answers. Interviews can be conducted in-person or over the telephone, and these are still very common modes of interview. More recently, walk-along and walkthrough interviews have become more popular (see **Chapter 6**). Importantly, interviewing has been remediated by the advent of digital tools, wherein interviews can be conducted online through video calls, message boards, chat apps, social media and email. Digital interviews may be conducted either synchronously or asynchronously (O'Connor and Madge, 2023).

Synchronous online interviews involve the researcher and participant being simultaneously present on a platform and interacting in real time. Here, a researcher might interview a participant through Voice over Internet Protocol (VoIP) (Tomás and Bidet, 2023) or video conferencing platforms, such as Zoom (Howlett, 2022) or Skype (Longhurst, 2013). Alternatively, researchers might interview participants using a text interface on a messaging platform, such as WhatsApp (Gibson, 2022) or Instagram (Willcox and Hickey-Moody, 2020), with the participant actively responding to questions as they arise. Interviews over VoIP are effectively the same as conducting telephone interviews, though the medium does enable recording of the conversation and in some cases auto-transcription (Hay-Gibson, 2009). More recently, VoIP has been largely replaced by the use of video conferencing software, enabling a digital equivalent of face-to-face interviews. This is useful, as Howlett (2022: 390) suggests, in as much as '[t]he real-time nature of the exchanges can resemble the "honesty" of onsite interviews'. Furthermore, 'the dynamic environments prevent participants from overthinking their answers or considering the most socially desirable responses. Video calling also allows researchers to access verbal and nonverbal cues, providing an equally authentic experience to in-person interviews' (Howlett, 2022: 390). Alternatively, researchers can engage with synchronous text-based interviews through online word processing software, such as Google Docs (Opara et al., 2021). The researcher and interviewee can chat in real time using text, based on a structured, semi-structured or unstructured question sheet. This method is particularly useful as the document automatically saves and the interview is transcribed as it takes place.

Asynchronous online interviews refer to interviews where the researcher and interviewee do not meet in 'real time'. Instead, the researcher might send questions to an interviewee via email or through discussion or message boards, wait for their responses to be returned and then send further follow up questions (Schiek and Ullrich, 2017). Researchers may also send pre-interview questions to participants in order to build rapport and identify key areas that might guide the interview, where a semi-structured or unstructured interview format is used. In Linabary and Hamel's (2017) study using asynchronous email interviews, the interview was organised around four main question sets that were composed of two to four questions, followed by a fifth set of questions, where participants could review all their interview responses. Linabary and Hamel suggested that participants complete one set of questions a week, with participants sent one question at a time, so that interviews were conducted over a five-week period, offering participants the opportunity to reflect on their answers.

Other forms of interview use digital tools to incorporate aspects of both asynchronous and synchronous approaches. These can involve the use of messaging services such as WhatsApp, which allow real-time immediate feedback, but that take place over much longer durations than synchronous VoIP or video-conferencing interviews (e.g., exchanges of messages over weeks or months). For example, mobile instant messaging interviews (MIMI) is a form of hybrid interview that involves a blend of a diary method and 'mobile experience sampling' (Consolvo et al., 2017), where apps or links to surveys on mobile devices are used to prompt participants to document their thoughts and feelings in their everyday lives. In particular, MIMI can be utilised through messaging platforms (Kaufmann and Peil, 2020). Researchers using the MIMI method can recruit participants who agree to respond to researchers' questions across a set time frame (such as a day, a week or a month). Researchers then send questions to interviewees at different time points (perhaps every hour) and invite the interviewee to respond in whatever way they wish, using text, images, emojis or video. In Kaufmann and Peil's study, messages were sent at random times in order to gain insight into what respondents were doing in their everyday lives, and to discourage the interviewee from staging their activities.

Both synchronous and asynchronous digital interviews offer a number of advantages over face-to-face interviewing. The most obvious is that digital interviews are more cost effective than travelling to meet participants (Cater, 2011), and interviews can be more easily conducted with remote groups across national and international boundaries (Deakin and Wakefield, 2014). Furthermore, both synchronous and asynchronous interviews allow interviewees to be interviewed in comfortable spaces they are already familiar with, such as their home, which can increase a sense of ease and thus the quality of discussion (Gray et al., 2020; Janghorban et al., 2014). A clear advantage of asynchronous methods in particular is that participants have time to reflect on their answers before responding, and those with verbal impairments or other disabilities may be able to more fully take part in the interview (Ison, 2009). An advantage of utilising text-based interviews is that the conversation is already transcribed. In synchronous interviews via video conferencing, depending on the software or platform used, there may be auto-transcription functionality and recordings can be saved to cloud systems, which can save a significant amount of time in resources compared to transcribing audio recordings (although be aware of data management issues) (Richardson et al., 2021).

Although they allow access to geographically distant groups and offer cost savings, digital interviews can also create a range of cross-cultural communication issues and affect the quality of data generated. For example, participants may be limited to what they feel they can say due to potential internet monitoring and censorship by governments, which may limit the ability of participants to freely discuss politically contentious or sensitive topics (Lawrence, 2022). Moreover, some researchers have found that conducting synchronous interviews through video-conferencing apps can create a situation in which they were unable 'to read body language and nonverbal cues' of their interviewees, which generated a 'loss of intimacy' (Seitz, 2016: 229), even when researchers were interviewing people from the same national and cultural context. Synchronous digital interviews on Skype and other video platforms have also been shown to produce shorter transcripts compared to those of in-person interviews, and fewer 'conversational turns' (Johnson et al., 2021: 1148), where back and forth discussion between researcher and participant is more limited compared to the 'gold standard' of in-person interviews (Johnson et al., 2021: 1142). Researchers interested in utilising synchronous digital interviews should therefore work hard to establish rapport with the interviewee (Weller, 2017), and perhaps increase the amount of conversational acknowledgement and affirmation, such as nodding and using other forms of gestural communication to ensure that the interviewee feels like they are part of a conversation, rather than a container of answers. Practically, while synchronous interviews conducted via video-conferencing platforms might produce auto-transcription, this auto-transcription will almost certainly require reworking to reflect an accurate record of the conversation. This may require additional traditional transcription on top of, or alongside, machine-generated transcripts. As such, it is important for researchers to recognise that while convenient, the digital platform used to conduct interviews will alter the interactions that they have with their participants and in turn, the data that is generated through these interactions (Sullivan, 2012; Van Zeeland et al., 2021).

The ability to interview people digitally, either asynchronously or synchronously, also raises the question of recruitment. Traditionally, recruitment for in-person interviews might take place through posters on message boards, flyers through letter boxes and on-street selection. Researchers can still use these techniques to help identify informants to be interviewed digitally, and may also post recruitment calls on email lists, workplace website homepages, and social media sites such as Twitter/X and Facebook

(Janghorban et al., 2014). However, there is a need to think carefully about privacy and ethics in recruiting through social media sites (see **Chapter 4**), even when the data posted by participants appears to be open and public. For instance, many groups on Facebook are open, meaning that anyone with a Facebook account can view the group, what is posted on the group page, and who is a member of the group. If this is the case, then it may be possible to use the group as a recruitment tool for digital interviews as long as the researchers are 'transparent, respectful and sympathetic' to the members of the group (Gelinas et al., 2017: 7). Where groups are closed or moderated, it is then a case of negotiating with the gatekeepers of these groups, such as moderators, drawing on the same ethos of transparency and respect. Alternatively, researchers can work with external partners, such as charities and other third sector organisations, to reach particular groups, who may have their own social media channels and have already built trust with these groups (Benedict et al., 2019).

Focus Groups

A focus group is a kind of group interview, in which a group of people are brought together by a researcher to discuss a particular issue or topic, through which a set of common themes, issues, norms or beliefs shared by the group might emerge (Parker and Tritter, 2006). Focus groups are usually facilitated and moderated by the researchers, and tend to be either semi-structured or unstructured in format as the goal is to allow group participants to explore the topics/issues of interest, and to prod and challenge each others views and opinions. In traditional social science research, focus groups take place in person or, more unusually, over the telephone. As with interviews, synchronous and asynchronous 'online' focus groups are now common (Stewart and Shamdasani, 2017).

An online synchronous focus group holds many of the same qualities as a traditional focus group, in the sense that it takes place at a set time, with multiple co-present participants. However, the meeting is mediated by a video-conferencing platform such as Skype or Zoom, or through message board webpages such as Google Groups (Lobe, 2017). Tuttas (2015) suggests that using video conferencing is advantageous in that it enables the bringing together of geographically dispersed groups, while also reducing barriers to access such as literacy and ability to type at speed. A good example of synchronous focus groups using video conferencing is Willemsen et al.'s (2022) work on FitKnip, an eHealth project in the Netherlands. Seven focus groups were conducted using the online video platform Jitsi, with between three and five participants per group. Separate focus groups were created for both stakeholders in the eHealth field and for health care professionals. Groups discussed the acceptability, feasibility and usability of FitKnip, as well as the design of the FitKnip platform and their satisfaction with the offered applications (Willemsen et al., 2022: 3). Willemsen et al. (2022) point to the importance of setting house rules when engaging in online focus groups, such as instructing participants to keep their mics muted when not talking, and if they do wish to speak, to use the 'raise hand' function to avoid participants talking over one another. In addition to visual video channels, text-based media might be used. For instance, Fox et al. (2007) opted for a text-based synchronous focus group, using their own university software. Seeking to understand young people's experiences of chronic skin conditions, the focus groups aimed to include a minimum of five respondents, with a researcher mediating discussion. Given the topic of the research and its visible nature, Fox et al. (2007) suggest that textual communication might enable more open and frank discussion between the participants than utilising a synchronous video method.

As with interviews, it is possible to conduct asynchronous focus groups. Here, a researcher might invite people to a message board such as Google Groups or to a thread on an open-source discussion platform such as Discourse.org (MacNamara et al., 2021) or a messaging platform such as WhatsApp (Estrada-Jaramillo et al., 2022). As people respond to the thread, the researcher can act as a moderator and post prompts such as images, text or video to elicit discussion (Gordon et al., 2021). A number of different versions of this approach are possible, which utilise different ways of grouping participants (Hallam, 2022) and different forms of exercise and prompts given to participants during the focus groups (Gordon et al., 2021). These groups can last varying lengths of time, from hours to months, and participants can be anonymous or openly identifiable (Zwaanswijk and van Dulmen, 2014). The evidence for ideal group sizes within these focus groups are mixed, with some studies showing the ideal group size to be ten to thirteen, whereas other suggested smaller groups were more effective (Gordon et al., 2021).

An example of how an anonymous asynchronous focus group can be run digitally is Gordon et al.'s (2021) study of body image and health among transgender and gender diverse young adults, utilising the Discourse.org platform. The focus groups took place over four days with participants given two distinct prompts, consisting of one to four questions that were posted each day in the morning and afternoon. Participants created an anonymous username to encourage involvement by protecting their identity. The multi-media nature of the Discourse.org platform enabled two forms of activity: a social identity mapping activity and a digital image board activity. These activities allowed participants to identify where they felt their social identity lay on a graphical social identity wheel, which they could then post to the group to elicit discussion. In turn, 'participants were asked to use an interactive online "whiteboard" tool (www.webwhiteboard.com) to curate text, photographs, drawings or other images depicting and narrating some of the appearance-related messages they experience online or in other parts of life' (Gordon et al., 2021: 6). In turn, participants could also share their images from the whiteboard to encourage discussion. In this example, the anonymous focus group enabled a vulnerable group to discuss sensitive issues in a complex way, aiding the researchers' understandings of body image amongst transgender and gender diverse young adults.

It should also be noted that emerging methods seek to blur the boundaries between synchronous and asynchronous forms of focus group. For example, Colom (2022) used a closed WhatsApp group to engage in-group discussion with activists from western Kenya. The focus groups were designed to last for a day and work with participants' activities and schedules. Colom had seven total topics for discussion, which were posted through the day to enable both instant synchronous responses, as well as asynchronous discussion among the members of the group. Topics were posted between 8.30 a.m. and 2 p.m., and then at 2 p.m. and 7.30 p.m. By providing gaps between posting topics, this enabled participants to reflect on the discussion and allowed people who could not answer the discussion when it was initially posted to respond. Furthermore, Colom was sure to let participants know that the gaps between topics was normal and that the conversation had not ended. Colom's method (and the MIMI method discussed in the Interviews section) points to the way that digital platforms are themselves changing what methods are and can be, and perhaps suggest that the distinction between synchronous and asynchronous interviews and focus groups will become less important in the future.

Online focus groups share a number of advantages with traditional focus groups. Unlike individual interviews, the researchers can work to identify shared norms and beliefs. In turn, online focus groups can also create unexpected events and moments that reveal new things to researchers they had not been able to elicit through a one-on-one interview (Wilkinson, 1998). Some studies also show that respondents may be more likely to share sensitive and personal issues in an anonymous online focus group setting compared to an in-person interview or focus group (Guest et al., 2017), although this may be dependent on the groups involved in the research (Kruger et al., 2019). There are also some added benefits to online focus groups. In particular, online focus groups can allow participation from sometimes hard to reach populations, including those unable to physically attend focus groups, such as those with disabilities or living in remote areas, although these groups may still favour in-person focus groups if possible (Nicholas et al., 2010).

This being said, different types of online focus group also introduce their own challenges. In terms of synchronous groups that interact through the medium of message boards, those who are less capable typists can become less involved in the discussion. In terms of asynchronous focus groups, moderation may not be immediate and it may be difficult to keep participants actively involved (Gill and Baillie, 2018). Researchers will also have to be aware of the issues attached to traditional forms of face-to-face focus group and how they might be amplified in a digital setting (Ranieri et al., 2019). For example, as moderators, researchers will need to work to ensure the possibility of equal involvement of participants (Reisner et al., 2018). There is also the question of how to analyse discussion and how to present results, especially within virtual (online) settings. For instance, how might the movement of avatars be analysed and presented in relation to the use of quotes and contextualisation within conversation? Ethically, focus groups have always raised issues regarding the power dynamics between participants. Within digital settings, researchers should be mindful of pre-existing power relations, and also ensure that participants understand participant confidentiality. This is especially the case when participants might screen record or take screenshots and post them outside of the focus group setting.

Questionnaires and Surveys

A questionnaire consists of a pre-defined set of questions arranged in a specific sequence. Questionnaires generally seek factual information, generated in a way that is standardised across all respondents. For example, a census form is a type of questionnaire. Questionnaires may be self-administered (i.e., filled in directly by a respondent), or delivered using the format of a structured interview (where participants' responses are recorded by a researcher who has verbalised the question and response items). Generally, questionnaires consist of closed-format questions, which a respondent answers by choosing from a number of pre-designated response items. But questionnaires can also include more open-ended questions, though these are usually factual in orientation and are used to allow respondents to provide answers or additional information not covered by the range of pre-populated response items. Questions can take the form of stating facts, selecting from lists, and rating or ranking criteria on scales (for instance, to express degrees of agreement or disagreement).

Questionnaires are often utilised as part of surveys. As defined by Guthrie (2010: 77):

> [t]he survey method selects a sample that is representative of a larger population and uses the results to generalise about that population as a whole. Its strengths are in collecting demographic and socio-economic data, and in describing people's general perceptions and attitudes.

There are three types of survey: exploratory, descriptive and explanatory (Jann and Hinz, 2016). *Exploratory* or *pilot surveys* involve gaining some general or initial insight into a phenomenon. This might then be followed up with more representative descriptive or explanatory surveys. *Descriptive surveys* seek to understand some general trend or aspect of a particular population. *Explanatory surveys* work to explore relationships between different variables within a population and try to establish correlations between these variables. The relatively short nature of a questionnaire (compared to other methods, such as qualitative interviews) and the ability for it to be completed by the participant remotely, means that questionnaires are often used to gather large amounts of data necessary for representative surveys (of either a particular population or group, or of a population as a whole) (Guthrie, 2010). Before the advent of the internet, questionnaires were mostly delivered via the post or conducted over the telephone. Now, it is much more common for questionnaires to be conducted electronically via the internet.

Email questionnaires are perhaps the oldest form of digital questionnaire. Here, researchers send out questions via specific email lists, list-servs, workplaces or organisations, and ask for respondents to fill in and return them via email (e.g., Dibb et al., 2001; Hovhannisyan and Sougari, 2014; Jones and Pitt, 1999). If choosing to conduct an email questionnaire, it is important to think carefully about whether the questions are presented in plain text in the body of the email or attached as a separate document. Michaelidou and Dibb (2006) also recommend that anonymity and privacy in email interview responses are assured. In particular, if emailing groups of people, it is important to blind carbon copy (BCC) respondents, in order to avoid all the respondents being able to identify and/or contact one another.

A number of free digital tools are available to set up and run a digital questionnaire that can be filled in via web browser software. The most popular of these include SurveyMonkey (e.g., Merolli et al., 2014; Waclawski, 2012) and Google Forms (e.g., Arafat et al., 2020; Kumar and Naik, 2016). The advantage of web-based questionnaires over email questionnaires is that the technological affordances of the web-based platform can both mimic familiar forms of paper-based questionnaires, as well as incorporate more responsive digital elements (Mondal et al., 2018). As Regmi et al. (2016: 641) suggest:

> [s]imilar to the paper-based survey; online questionnaire surveys are capable of question diversity (e.g. dichotomous questions, multiple-choice questions, scales), skip irrelevant questions for sub-groups in the sample (i.e. no pregnancy questions for men) and even collect ... open-ended questions (qualitative data) through a free text box. Similarly, the construction of the online questionnaire can also be built to help better response rate for each item; for example, respondents must answer a question before advancing to the next question. This, however, might create an unfavourable situation to some research participants if they do not want to answer sensitive questions such as sexual behaviours or drug use.

Furthermore, once written, hyperlinks to the digital questionnaire can be easily sent through other digital platforms such as WhatsApp, which helps to easily further disseminate calls for participation (Cotrin et al., 2020). However, as Regmi et al. (2016) also point out, completely open web-based questionnaires can lead to multiple responses from the same user, which can undermine the validity of results. As such, they recommend registration of interested participants via email prior to the completion of the online questionnaire, which provides a unique participant number and personalised access (e.g., via a unique link). Also, it is important to note that the free versions of web tools such as SurveyMonkey and Google Form often have limited functionality, such as a cap on the total amount of questions that can be asked or the total number of respondents.

The development of digital tools such as email, web browser software, social media platforms, and apps allows questionnaires to be distributed much more widely and without the costs associated with traditional forms of questionnaire. However, conducting questionnaires using email, web, social media and app-based tools raise a number of issues around sampling. Two key types of sampling are important to mention here: probability sampling and non-probability sampling (see **Chapter 3**). In probability sampling, sampling is random, meaning all members of the population have an equal likelihood of being surveyed, which is necessary for obtaining a representative sample. In non-probability sampling, sampling is purposive or intentional rather than random, meaning that some members of a population are more likely to be surveyed.

As Andrade (2020) points out, online questionnaires are highly unlikely to be completed by a truly random sample, meaning their results are unlikely to be representative of either the population under study or a population in general. This can be for a number of reasons. For example, people who are part of the population under study might not have internet access, an email address, or be part of the social media site through which the researcher is recruiting participants, which means that they are excluded from the sample. Furthermore, the distribution of calls to engage in email or web-based questionnaires via listservs can lead to significant self-selection bias, where volunteers in social research might only take part because they already have a strong opinion or interest in the subject matter (Vehovar and Manfreda, 2017). As such, Van Selm and Janowski (2006) argue that online questionnaires necessarily involve non-probabilistic samples. Researchers should be aware of the limitations that come with this form of sampling; namely, that the results of these surveys are non-representative and therefore non-generalisable to a group (or the population at large).

Another concern is the ease with which digital surveys and questionnaires can be set up and run. This can create a false sense of the difficulty involved in constructing a good questionnaire, such as avoiding bias or leading questions and ensuring that the questionnaire is the right length to maximise completion rates (Dewaele, 2018). Indeed, researchers should be aware of the low response rates of online questionnaires, which can be as little as 11 per cent (Evans and Mathur, 2018). It is also important to note that some studies show that recruitment to complete questionnaires via email is far lower than through social media apps. For instance, Moraes et al.'s (2021) study, which recruited dentists in Brazil to complete a web-based questionnaire, showed that five times as many participants responded to a request to complete the questionnaire through an Instagram post than through targeted emailing. In this regard, researchers might think about the multiple ways participation in their questionnaires can be advertised on social media (for more examples, see Amon et al., 2014; Guillory et al., 2018) and how effective email questionnaires may be as compared to web questionnaires. In other words, while these methods might appear to be convenient, they require careful planning and considerable follow up work in terms of reminding participants to complete the questionnaire, as well as care in developing conclusions from the data that is collected.

Observations, Ethnography and (Auto)Ethnography

The relationship between the methods of observation, ethnography and autoethnography are complex, and there are some shared characteristics between them, which can make clear distinctions between them difficult (Abidin and Seta, 2020). These methods differ from interviews, focus groups, surveys and questionnaires in that they require the researcher to work within the setting they are studying and to observe what goes on within it. In doing so, researchers often seek to uncover the everyday practices, behaviours and social structures that take place in and shape each particular setting, such as a public space, a business, or in the case of ethnography, a sub-culture or society.

At its broadest, observation can be defined as an organised and intentional engagement with a particular setting or phenomena to understand how they work. There are three sub-types of observation: participant observation, non-participant observation and indirect observation (Ciesielska et al., 2018). In *participant observation*, a researcher works to become immersed in a particular setting for a significant length of time, actively engaging in the activities taking place, with the aim of gaining insight into the setting and activities. Partially distinct from this, *non-participant observation* involves being present in a setting and observing what happens, but not actively becoming involved in the practices or situation that the researcher is observing. Finally, *indirect observation* is a method through which the researcher draws on observation performed by others (such as a research assistant), or observes and analyses the objects or artefacts that make up the setting under study (rather than the people active in the setting) in order to infer their social use (such as studying a piece of digital editing software to understand practices of digital film editing).

Observation and its different forms are both part of, and distinct from, ethnography. *Ethnography* is a research design based on the longitudinal immersion of researchers as active participants in a sub-culture, community or society, famously described by anthropologist Clifford Geertz (1998: 69) as a scholarly process of 'deep hanging out'. Ethnography seeks to '[uncover] the processes and meanings that undergird sociospatial life' to generate 'thick' (i.e., detailed) descriptions of the 'take[n] for granted … structures that provide the blueprint for social action' among a collective or community (Herbert, 2000: 551). *Thick descriptions* are generated via observing and interacting with social groups being studied over time. As such, doing ethnographic research involves both a social interaction component and an observational component (and may also involve the use of interviews with key informants).

Whereas observation as a standalone method might be focused on a particular individual or setting, 'ethnography deals with people in the collective sense, not with individuals. As such, it is a way of studying people in organised enduring groups, which may be referred to as communities or societies' (Angrosino, 2007: 1). Like observation, there are multiple forms of ethnography, including covert, non-covert and autoethnography. In a *covert ethnography*, the researcher does not reveal the fact they are a researcher to the group they are studying. In a *non-covert ethnography*, the researcher does reveal that they are a researcher and may explicitly seek permission as a researcher to engage with the group. *Autoethnography* is a form of ethnography that begins from the self-narration of the researcher, where they use a reflection on their own involvement in a situation to 'understand or represent some worldly phenomenon' (Butz and Besio, 2009: 1660). In relation to researching digital life, observation and (auto)ethnography can be used in at least three ways. First, observation and (auto) ethnography can be used to study digital phenomena such as online video games as kinds of worlds or communities in and of themselves (known as virtual ethnography). Second, observation and (auto)ethnography can be used to study how people engage with digital devices and technologies (digital ethnography). And third, digital tools can be utilised in the practice of observation and (auto)ethnography to gain new or novel insights into other social issues.

Virtual Ethnography

Ethnography can be used to study particular virtual worlds, such as online games like *World of Warcraft* (Nardi, 2010), *Everquest* (Rowlands, 2012) and *Second Life* (Boellstorff, 2015). Here, ethnography can be employed to understand what is often pitched as a strange new kind of world. *Virtual ethnography* is thus a matter of dwelling within an online environment to understand the 'patterns of behaviour' that may be observed there (Carter, 2005: 150). Practically, researchers interested in engaging in virtual ethnography can choose a game or virtual world and begin to spend time there by 'hanging out' (perhaps even assuming an avatar), learning how to engage with the in-game systems and developing relationships in game through a form of virtual participant observation. The researcher might keep diaries of their engagements and interactions, and save chat logs with other users (Collister, 2014). Furthermore, researchers can utilise other qualitative methods including semi-structured interviews with other users within the game and also through other synchronous and asynchronous methods, both digitally and in-person (Boellstorff et al., 2012).

An advantage of virtual ethnography is that if the researcher spends enough time in these virtual worlds, they can gain a deep appreciation of how they work and the kinds of social relations that emerge there. However, one potential issue with virtual ethnography is that it positions virtual and cyber spaces as somehow outside of, or distinct from, everyday life. In the same way that early Western anthropologists used ethnographic methods to go and study 'unknown', 'exotic' cultures or spaces (Carter 2004, 2005), graphical, avatar based virtual worlds such as *Second Life* can be presented as strange foreign lands that require charting, mapping and interpreting (Boellstorff, 2015). However, in doing so, the embodied engagement and technological affordances that enable users to engage with these worlds can be underplayed and an overly strong distinction between 'offline' and 'online' life can be maintained.

Digital Ethnography

At least partially distinct from virtual ethnographies, *digital ethnography* seeks to understand how people engage with digital technologies and tools within practices of everyday life, rather than seeing digital technologies as producing distinct virtual spaces, experiences and identities (Bluteau, 2021). Digital ethnography therefore considers how 'digital media are part of people's everyday worlds', and so it 'might focus specifically on those domains of activity in which digital media are used rather than on the characteristics or use of media' (Pink et al., 2015: n.p.). Digital ethnography often focuses on embodied and sensory experiences in relation to digital life, with methods to study these experiences taking many forms, including both digital and non-digital techniques (Murthy, 2008). These methods are as diverse as video tours (Pink and Mackley, 2012), video re-enactments (Pink et al., 2016), digital go-along interviews (Anderson et al., 2020) and close observations of smartphone use *in situ* (Tacchi and Chandola, 2015), among many others. As Pink et al. (2015: n.p.) put it, in utilising digital ethnography:

[w]e might be watching what people do by digitally tracking them, or asking them to invite us into their social media practices. Listening may involve reading, or it might involve sensing and communicating in other ways. Ethnographic writing might be replaced by video, photography or blogging.

A notable form of digital ethnography includes the filming and re-enactment of digital practices. Utilising ethnographic interviewing, researchers can ask participants to perform everyday tasks with digital things and video record what they are doing (Pink et al., 2017). For example, Pink et al. (2016) video recorded people's hands as they demonstrated to researchers how they worked with their smartphones. These forms of re-enactment can work to disclose 'embodied ways of knowing' (Pink et al. 2016: 242) to the researcher, which even the participant may not be aware of. 'Digital go-along' (Anderson et al., 2020) methods can also be used within ethnographic interviews, where participants can re-enact particular events of media use, without video recording. Instead, the researcher asks the interviewee to talk about what they are doing as they engage with a digital device or service, which can provide a way of understanding how embodied, unconscious practices can help inform how people make decisions through digital devices, such as deciding to apply for a loan online. A related though more formalised and structured approach to studying people's interactions with digital interfaces and apps is the app walkthrough method profiled in **Chapter 6**.

Researchers also might wish to 'interview' digital technologies using an 'ethnographic sensibility' (Maalsen, 2020). For example, a researcher can ask questions of voice assistants such as Alexa or Siri to try to analyse the underlying logic of their responses or to understand how these devices fit into and alter different settings, such as the home or work environment. Pushing this perspective further, digital devices can be enrolled as 'co-ethnographers' in the study of digital life (Maalsen, 2023). Here, the specific capacities of digital devices are employed to provide another point of view on things. For instance, a digital ethnographer can utilise camera-enabled devices on mundane objects such as a kettle to gain new insights into how spaces of the home (e.g., kitchens) are used (Giaccardi et al., 2016).

Another form of 'interviewing digital objects' can involve a process whereby a researcher reflects on how they relate to different digital devices utilising what Adams and Thompson (2016) term 'heuristic devices'. For them, a heuristic is a kind of 'invention or approach hoping to discover, uncover or find out something new' (Adams and Thompson, 2016: 19). By applying a range of heuristics, Adams and Thompson suggest that it is possible to observe digital devices in a new way and so understand how they operate in the world. Their first heuristic, for example, termed 'gathering anecdotes', invites researchers to 'describe how the object or thing appeared, showed up or was given in professional practice or everyday life' (2016: 24). This might involve beginning with anecdotes from the researcher's own experience. For example, an anecdote might be the writing of an uncanny experience of verbally talking with a friend about an obscure or previously undiscussed subject, and then having items associated with this subject appear as adverts or promoted posts on one's Facebook feed. This initial anecdote might then be examined with a subsequent heuristic such as 'following the actors' (Adams and Thompson 2016: 33), where the researcher may decide that they are interested in discovering whether Facebook is listening to them through the speaker of their smartphone and using this data to feed them content and adverts. With this focus in mind, researchers can go about identifying the digital actors that may be involved in such a possible outcome. These actants might include the Facebook privacy agreement, available as text via the Facebook app menu, particular privacy settings in the Facebook menus, the smartphone operating system's privacy settings, and even individual smart phone components, such as the microphone used. The goal here is not to produce a total or exhaustive list of actants, but rather to have a practical starting point from which to follow actants wherever they lead. Perhaps looking at the privacy agreement leads the researcher to an awareness of how the Facebook API is communicating with other apps on the phone or the phone's browser. In this case, through the course of following the actors, new actors appear, which also invite further tailing and investigation. Like digital ethnography, this heuristic method is keen to explore the sensuous experience of the digital world, but also to expand that sensuousness to the non-human digital realm. In doing so, Adams and Thompson (2016) suggest that new ways of knowing digital life become possible.

In some cases, digital ethnography also refers to methods that use digital tools to study other social issues that are not explicitly digital. On a practical level, digital smartphones can be an important tool in ethnographic research, enabling researchers to take photos and videos, record interviews and keep notes (Duggan, 2017; van Doorn, 2013). Digital apps and platforms accessed on smartphones can also be used as tools for producing research diaries as part of an ethnography. For example, Datta and Thomas (2021) developed a closed WhatsApp group and invited twelve women to post daily messages about their experiences of navigating gender-based exclusion from urban space in India over a period of six months. The women were recruited from an earlier research study and instructed to document their day-to-day experiences in Delhi and could send text, emojis, as well as images and videos to the group. This form of 'WhatsApp ethnography' was useful in enabling participants to update researchers on their experiences as they happened, and the multi-media nature of their messages also helped provoke discussion and provide insight to the researchers. Datta and Thomas (2021: 239) also note that this method was effective in helping afford 'a modicum of equalising space in self-authorship', where the participants were perhaps more able to express themselves with greater ease, as compared to formal spaces of discussion such as face-to-face interviews. Furthermore, the WhatsApp group meant that when participants did meet in face-to-face research workshops there was more shared experience to draw on, which aided discussion in these workshops.

Specific research-based apps for smartphones can also be produced to investigate social issues. These can operate to collect data in the form of video, research diaries including text and images, as well as location and tracking data. The Football Research in an Enlarged Europe (FREE) project, for instance, used a modified commercial app to provide football fans in the United Kingdom with a means to record how football played a role in their everyday lives (García et al., 2016). Specifically, the app enabled participants to upload photos to an album as well as record an audio diary. The interface of the app allowed respondents to tag photos using pre-set tags created by the researchers, and to score images out of ten in relation to how important the photo was to the respondents. A positive of the app was that participants could upload their thoughts and feelings as they happened, rather than recalling them later in an interview or focus group session. Less positively, the app was expensive to develop for the research purpose and had some technical limitations, such as no back button that would allow participants to return to their previous screen. With these issues in mind, researchers should think carefully about whether they need a dedicated app to engage in digital ethnography, or whether they can mobilise similar functionality in pre-existing platforms and software.

Digital Autoethnographies

Remembering that autoethnography is a form of ethnography that begins from the self-narration of the researcher, whereby they use a reflection on their own involvement in a situation to examine some issue or phenomenon that exceeds themselves, *digital autoethnography* can be understood as practices through which researchers reflect on their entanglements with digital technology and how this might relate to broader trends in digital life. One way of performing a digital autoethnography is for the researcher to scrutinise their own digital practices. Following Fraser (2019: 196):

> a useful approach is to identify and reflect upon flashpoints – critical junctures, turning points, frustrations, or repeated moments when actions take a certain direction, rather than another. Like the work of a researcher who asks respondents why they acted in a particular way at a certain crucial moment, considerable value can accrue when the autoethnographer focuses on these occurrences.

For Fraser, digital autoethnography involved keeping a research diary on the Google Keep app on his smartphone. Over the course of a year, Fraser recorded and reflected on his daily practices with his phone and other digital devices in order to identify how his own subjective experience and position might feed into, or be part of, wider trends and features of digital life. Through this reflective process, it became clear to Fraser that, without realising it, his digital practices were ultimately a matter of data curation.

Other modes of digital autoethnography can include reflections on how smart devices and digital technologies are used in the home and other environments. Indicative in this regard is Speed and Luger's (2019) discussion of the privacy implications of a self-developed smart toilet-roll holder, which measured when and how much toilet roll was used in the researcher's domestic bathroom. In this case, digital autoethnography was a matter of installing the device and then recording thoughts and feelings about the device on an *ad hoc* basis. Rather than a matter of personal opinion alone, the autoethnographic method of Speed and Luger, like Fraser, allows the researchers to reflect on broader societal issues in relation to digital life. In the smart toilet-roll holder example, the broader issues examined were privacy and consent. For instance, while the toilet roll holder did not record who was using the toilet directly, it could tell how much toilet roll was being removed from the holder, which could be used to indirectly identify changes in the number of people in the house, or what was happening on the toilet. Drawing on anecdotes from the researcher's family experience of the toilet-roll holder in turn led to an analysis of the concept of consent in relation to smart devices and how data from these devices might inadvertently reveal more than users had actively consented to.

Digital (auto)ethnographic methods thus offer a powerful means to understand experiences of digital life and for generating data about other social issues too. At the same time, there are limitations to these methods (Kaur-Gill and Dutta, 2017). As time and resource intensive forms of intervention, digital (auto)ethnographies are often small scale and so researchers need to be careful about the generality of the claims they make. Furthermore, the specificity of the research sites and modes of data collection might make studies very difficult to reproduce in order to verify results or seek to understand how distinct variables might affect the findings of the research.

Summary

- Digital tools such as email, messaging and video platforms enable both synchronous and asynchronous mediums to conduct interviews and focus groups. While offering a convenient way to engage with remote participants, researchers should be aware that these tools affect the type and quality of data collected.

- In a similar manner, a range of digital tools now enable surveys and questionnaires to be conducted and distributed with relative ease. However, digital surveys raise issues around sampling and researchers still need to be very attentive to a range of issues in order to carry out a successful digital questionnaire.
- There are a variety of forms of observation and ethnography that can be used to study digital life, and many of these overlap one another. Virtual ethnographies provide a way of focusing on engagement with online spaces, whereas digital ethnography and autoethnography can allow insight into how digital technologies impact on and shape people's everyday lives and understandings.

Recommended Reading

Boellstorff, T. (2015) *Coming of Age in Second Life: An Anthropologist Explores the Virtually Human*. Princeton University Press, Princeton, NJ.
Offers a good example of how to conduct a virtual ethnography of an online world.

Colom, A. (2022) 'Using WhatsApp for focus group discussions: ecological validity, inclusion and deliberation', *Qualitative Research*, 22(3): 452–67.
A useful paper that provides a method for using messaging platforms to conduct focus groups.

Fraser, A. (2019) 'Curating digital geographies in an era of data colonialism', *Geoforum*, 104: 193–200.
An example of digital autoethnography and how the method can be used to identify trends in digital life.

Johnson, D.R., Scheitle, C.P., and Ecklund, E.H. (2021) 'Beyond the in-person interview? How interview quality varies across in-person, telephone, and skype Interviews', *Social Science Computer Review*, 39(6): 1142–58.
Offers reflection on how digitally mediated interviews affect the quality and type of interview data collected.

Pink, S., Horst, H., Postil, J., et al. (2015) *Digital Ethnography: Principles and Practice*. Sage, London.
An important overview that discusses the multiple methods involved in practising digital ethnography.

6
Walking Methodologies, Walkthroughs and Audits

Overview

Chapter 6 examines:

- a collection of research practices centred on movement, both physical and processual, distinguishing between:
  - walking methodologies as a group of kinaesthetic methods that pursue intentional sensory encounters with digital phenomena – including data, platforms and digital discards – through physical acts of bodily movement through material spaces such as cities;
  - walking as a metaphor for a systematic, processual (step-by-step) methodology known as a 'walkthrough' that may be used to examine everyday practices with, and interactions modulated by, app and platform interfaces; and
  - audits as approaches for identifying discrimination in digital and digitally mediated processes, practices and systems.

Introduction

For those of us privileged to be able-bodied, walking likely strikes us as a mundane, taken-for-granted activity that we simply 'do' every day. When we do think about walking, it may be as fulfilling a largely utilitarian function – a means of getting from point A to point B over a range of distances, from the very short (from the couch to the fridge to grab a snack), through to the intermediate (from our residence to the train station and back) and the long (distances over several kilometres). We may also think of walking as a form of exercise (getting our daily steps in) and, relatedly, as a form of pleasure (an opportunity to spend quality time with our dog, for example). Yet walking is also an established social science methodology in its own right (O'Neill and Roberts, 2020; Springgay and Truman, 2018). It comprises an exciting set of techniques for researching digital mediations of the spaces, practices and encounters of everyday life. This chapter engages with walking as both a kinaesthetic (bodily) and processual set of research approaches for studying digital life.

As a collection of kinaesthetic (embodied, physical) practices of being in motion, walking methodologies centre acts of pedestrian mobility (footfall) as an approach for pursuing intentional sensory (visual, aural, haptic, olfactory) encounters with a variety of phenomena in real-world settings, including land, elements of nature (rivers, forests, geological formations), features of built environments, social and institutional settings (e.g., schools), sound, as well as digital and digitally mediated spaces (Springgay and Truman, 2018). Encounters with digital phenomena may be pursued through the mobilisation of a number of specific techniques that involve humans moving into, through and across material environments on foot – and other mobility modes, such as wheelchairs and electrified scooters – for purposes of data collection, ground truthing, exploration and knowledge generation.

Alongside this obvious understanding of walking methodologies as research techniques operationalised in the course of physically placing one foot in front of the other, 'walking' also serves as a metaphor for a group of approaches known as walkthroughs in which researchers follow a sequence of steps to 'walk through' a digital or digitally mediated phenomenon. Walkthroughs involve the systematic examination and evaluation of digital objects, their affordances, uses, cultural discourses, biases and intended outcomes, including as they pertain to software, platforms, interfaces and apps (Troeger and Bock, 2022). Sociotechnical walkthroughs may be used to understand how apps and platforms' intended uses are negotiated by users; how apps and platforms themselves modulate particular kinds of user interaction; and how within-app/platform practices leverage cultural referents. A second type of walkthrough method known as an audit may also be used to evaluate digital technologies as well as digitally mediated processes, practices and services for discriminatory outcomes or effects.

This chapter opens with an overview of walking methodologies centred on acts of physical movement through and across space, and identifies their utility for researching aspects of digital life. Next, sociotechnical walkthroughs are discussed, with an emphasis on how they may be used to study digital apps and interfaces via the app walkthrough method. Lastly, audits are introduced as methods for researching digital and digitally mediated instances, processes and systems of discrimination.

Walking Methodologies

Walking methodologies involve physical bodily movement through real-world spaces as a mode of data collection and knowledge generation. This physical movement may be directional, following a predetermined trajectory between points A and B, but it may equally be indeterminate and not tied to any destination, inclusive of 'wandering, strolling and sitting, dallying' and lingering in spaces and paces (Dickinson and Aiello, 2016: 1298; Springgay and Truman, 2018). Where underpinned by commitments to 'sense-making' (making sense of the world through our senses) and ontogenesis (the idea that social realities are emergent), these physical acts of walking themselves are seen to comprise an epistemological practice. Rather than knowledge of the world being informed mainly by historical processes or social discourses (see **Chapter 2**), walking methodologies centre the idea that knowledge of things comes about in the actual process of bodies moving through spaces, which themselves are understood as environments in motion (constantly shifting/changing) (Dickinson and Aiello, 2016; Middleton, 2011; Springgay and Truman, 2018).

Walking methodologies privilege embodied sensory encounters with things (i.e., engaging with phenomena through our senses of sight, smell, touch, taste and hearing) in the real-world contexts in which phenomena of interest to researchers are actually encountered (O'Neill and Roberts, 2020; Springgay and Truman 2018). Sensory reactions and responses are positioned as reliable empirical bases for identifying, examining and understanding the world around us. As explained by Dickinson and Aiello (2016: 1298), '[t]he human body investigates the world as [constituted by] constantly varying and interrelated objects. We produce, perform, and perceive [the world] through our own sensorimotor skills, skills that respond to and anticipate the environment's constant change'. Our knowledge of things and environments – including cities, wilderness and institutional settings – is understood to come about in the process of sensorily encountering things in the course of physically moving our bodies through material environments. As such, walking methodologies are particularly well suited for researching two aspects of digital life:

1. the spatial materialities of digital life, which concerns how and where digital phenomena – including code, data, algorithms, AI and digital devices – appear within and across the spaces and practices of everyday life, as well as the social, political, economic and cultural significance of these patterns; and
2. our emplaced sensory experiences of digital and digitally mediated phenomena, as well as how digital technologies shape our interactions, mobility patterns and experiences of place.

A number of methods may be used to investigate research topics on questions in either of these two areas. Below, four specific methods – all versions of an approach known as a 'walking tour' – are identified: *datawalking*; the *data walkshop*; *data walking*; and *walking interviews*. The discussion of each of these methods pays particular attention to how these techniques may be mobilised as part of scholarly examinations of digital spatialities, and of emplaced uses and sensory experiences of digital phenomena.

Walking Tours

A walking tour is an organised exploration of a particular spatial environment (Pink, 2015), carried out on foot or via a mode of mobility that may be used along surfaces amenable to pedestrian movement. A tour may be organised in that it is prescriptive of a plan or trajectory of travel, anticipating that participants will move through an environment along specific corridors (e.g., designated streets or marked nature trails) in a predetermined order or direction. At the looser end of the spectrum of organisation, what may make a tour a 'tour' is that it is specific to a designated area – such as a neighbourhood, a nature reserve or a country – rather than having a fixed route.

The purpose of a walking tour is to enable data collection about the phenomena being studied as they are situated, occur and are encountered by subjects in the course of moving through real-world environments. Walking tours are an exploratory method in that they do not determine beforehand *what* may be encountered, *how* things will be encountered, nor *where* phenomena may be encountered along a walk. Data collection along a walking tour is likely to focus on recording observations about the phenomena of interest to a research project. It is, however, more than merely a survey technique for compiling a spatial inventory (listing where things are). Observations collected on a walk may include:

- the context of data collection and/or encounters with the phenomena being studied;
- participants' sensory responses (what things look, smell, sound and feel like) to both the phenomena and their surrounding environments;
- positive and negative affective and emotional reactions experienced in place;
- where the walk involves more than just a solo researcher, conversations and exchanges between researchers and/or participants provoked by phenomena encountered along the way; and
- intellectual, conceptual and theoretical reflections, such as connections made to key scholarly works, frameworks and debates in the process of walking
 (based on O'Neill and Roberts, 2020; Ramsden, 2017; Springgay and Truman, 2018).

Such observations may be recorded either *in situ* along the walk or after returning from the tour, and may be captured via an array of media, including photography (Fink, 2012), video (Pink, 2007), digital/analogue notes and diaries (Middleton, 2010), and audio recordings (Pink, 2015). These observational data are also usually associated with place/space, be it through descriptions, maps or geotags (spatial co-ordinates attached to observations captured as digital data). Researchers interested in using walking tours as part of their examination of relationships between digitality and cities may find the similarly named but differently formulated *datawalking*, *data walkshop* and *data walking* methods particularly generative.

Datawalking

Datawalking 'combine[s] purposive physical walks through the (urban) landscape with being specifically attuned to observe and reflect on the variety of processes and infrastructures of datafication [that are] situated in time and space' (van Es and de Lange, 2020: 279). 'Datafication' describes the ways in which all aspects of everyday practices – the quotidian things that we do on an everyday or semi-regular basis, from clicking, tapping and scrolling on digital screens, to travelling on public transit and ordering delivered meals – are increasingly captured and 'transform[ed] … into online quantified data' (van Dijck, 2014: 198). By 'infrastructures of datafication' van Es and de Lange (2020) are referring to the observable, physical forms that processes of datafication assume in real-world environments, such as cities. Examples of infrastructures of datafication include everything from e-bikes and e-scooters, which (usually) require use of a mobile app to rent and ride a shared vehicle; transit card readers, which log data about individuals' public transit journeys; e-commerce locker hubs, which require a unique one-time digital code to retrieve parcels; digital surveillance cameras; automated delivery bots rolling along sidewalks or pavements; urban data centres; co-working spaces; and the offices of digital technology companies.

Much like walking tours, datawalking is not a standalone method, but likewise involves putting other, extant social science research methods – such as observation and photography – into motion along a walk (van Es and de Lange, 2020). Together, these techniques 'offer a[n] anchoring for understanding data' and processes of datafication 'as materially [and spatially] situated' and constituted by our embodied experiences of datafication infrastructures (van Es and de Lange, 2020: 279). In so doing, datawalking challenges narratives of the opaqueness and immateriality of data and the cloud by making the spatialities and materialities of infrastructures of datafication visible; provides context for where, and how, processes of datafication occur; and highlights how social inequalities inform and structure uneven, differential access to datafied materialities across spaces (on questions of inequality specifically, see Jarke, 2019).

van Es and de Lange (2020) give the example of a datawalk of a railway station, which could commence with securing entrance to the station via tapping or swiping a chip card. Researchers could then reflect, and collect observations about, how this process of checking-in to the railway station made them 'feel [and] how … it produce[d] and aid[ed] in performing certain situated subjectivities, for example, as a commuter, a legitimate traveller, a traceable monitored body' (p. 280–1). Continuing with this example, observed reactions could be subsequently connected to reflections about 'underlying infrastructural considerations (e.g., where does the data go, who owns the data, what algorithmic calculations are executed, for how long is the transaction stored, how are spatio-temporal urban infrastructures such as mobility reconfigured through data)' (p. 281). Observational data collected on this datawalk could be recorded as notes, voice memos and/or video, photographs of the digitally mediated objects (e.g., the card reader), any digital security cameras monitoring travellers entering the station, and any other significant phenomena.

The Data Walkshop

A participatory (see **Chapter 8**), community-based version of datawalking, known as the 'data walkshop', has been developed by Alison Powell (2018a; 2018b). A data walkshop involves breaking up a collective of participants into smaller groups. These smaller groups traverse different portions of a cityscape using visual sensory observation, photography and mapping to identify, inventory, record the material forms that data assume in urban built environments, and engage in conversations about the questions, reactions and reflections that are provoked for group members by encountering these material traces of data in the urban landscape. Observational notes, photographs and other artefacts are then brought back by the small groups to the larger collective for a discussion about the questions and sensory and affective responses that were provoked for group members along their walks. The collective then works together to respond to these questions and concerns in a number of ways, including proposed policy interventions, community action plans or speculative ideas for (re)design (Data-Walking.org, n.d., n.p.).

Data Walking

It important here to differentiate between datawalking and the data walkshop methods from a similarly named methodology, 'data walking'. Data walking, as developed by Hunter (2019), is a type of citizen sensing methodology (see **Chapter 8**) that involves practices of walking with GPS-enabled environmental sensors (e.g., temperature gauges, air quality sensors, noise meters, etc.) to collect data about a place or area. These data may then be analysed and visualised to create 'dataspaces' comprised of multi-layered (multiple datasets recorded using different sensors) representations of an area. Whereas datawalking and data walkshops employ walking as part of a methodology for gathering qualitative data about experiences of everyday life in digitally mediated and mediatised spaces, data walking involves walking as a method of using sensors to capture quantitative data used to build visualisations of specific places. While it is a generative approach to understanding real-world environments through the visualisation of sensing data, data walking does not support interpretations of the significances and meanings of digital materialities and situated affective, sensory and relational responses to these phenomena and the spaces in which we encounter them.

Walking Interviews

Another useful approach for answering questions about how research participants experience, sensorily encounter and emotionally respond to digital and digitally mediated materialities in space – and to digitally mediated spaces themselves – involves the use of walking interviews. A walking interview is an interview technique that involves researchers 'walking and talking' with study participants and informants (Anderson, 2004; Clark and Emmel, 2010). In other words, it is an approach to conducting interviews in the course of walking (Anderson, 2004; Clark and Emmel, 2010). Walking interviews can mobilise a variety of forms of interviewing, including unstructured conversations that unfold 'naturally' over the course of a walk (Anderson, 2004) and 'walk-along' interviews, which involves 'researchers accompanying individual informants on outings in their familiar environments, such as a neighbourhood or larger local area' and asking them about their walking practices, where and how they walk in the course of routine activities, and their reasons for doing so (Carpiano, 2009: 264). Similarly, mobilisations of walking interviews differ between those where walking is participant-directed (the interviewees determine the walking route) and where the walking routes are researcher-directed. Furthermore, the walks themselves may consist of wandering that is not directed towards any one destination; or, at the other end of the spectrum, may be comprised of 'highly structured tours that are designed to elicit responses to specific, predetermined places' (Evans and Jones, 2011: 849).

As with datawalking and data walkshops – as well as walking tours more generally – walking interviews may be used in tandem with other data collection instruments, including observation, photography, audio-recording, etc. Indeed, walking interviews can be used as an integral part of a datawalk. Referring back to van Es and de Lange's (2020) example of gaining entry to a railway station, rather than a researcher recording their own (auto-ethnographic) observations and reflections about encountering infrastructures of datafication, a researcher could instead accompany a study participant as *they* encounter, respond to and experience digitally mediated materialities (such as infrastructures that support data capture) *in situ* (in the spatial setting in which these materialities exist).

However a researcher chooses to organise and conduct a walking interview, they are seen as having several advantages over 'sedentary' interviews (Evans and Jones, 2011), particularly in the context of research that is interested in how participants experience digital phenomena in and across real-world environments. Specifically, walking methodologies allow researchers to:

- uncover participants' attachments and/or aversions to specific places, and to things that exist in those spaces (Evans and Jones, 2011);
- allow for serendipity in the interviewing, walking and observation process, which provides room for researchers to ask participants about things (their practices, reactions, responses, comments) that may not have been anticipated in research instruments (conversation prompts, semi-structured interview guides, predetermined stops along a walking route) in advance of setting off on a walk (Clark and Emmel, 2010);
- 'prompt' participants to recollect knowledge, information and experiences (Anderson, 2004: 254);
- provoke sensory responses to phenomena (such as a digital card reader at a railway station);
- observe participants' 'experiences, interpretations, and practices' within the real-world environments in which they occur (Carpiano, 2009: 264); and
- interpret observational data and assign meanings to analytic findings in ways that remain 'firmly grounded in the lived experiences' of participants as they actually unfold in and across real-world contexts (Carpiano, 2009: 263).

Walking interviews may also be used to examine other aspects of everyday digital life beyond encounters with the infrastructures of datafication. This may include research questions about how people feel about being exposed to various kinds of digital content in different places (e.g., private versus public space), as well as specific places where people may use or not use certain kinds of digital devices.

Walkthrough Methodologies

Questions about *how* people use digital devices – and, more specifically, applications and services that run on those devices – require a different methodological approach to ones that involve physical acts of walking. Walkthrough methodologies are research approaches where 'walking' is a metaphor for the step-by-step nature of the methodology, involving researchers and/or participants 'walking' through the operation or utilisation of a digital technology, digitally mediated service or practice in a processual (sequential) manner. Walkthrough methodologies include the sociotechnical walkthrough, a method that originates in software development and interface design, where it has been used to pre-empt defects ('bugs') in commercial software (e.g., Fagan, 1986) and to evaluate interface useability (e.g., Polson et al., 1992). In both of these antecedents, walkthroughs involve researchers assuming various research personae (roles as designers/developers, reviewers, moderators, testers, consumers, end users, etc.) and 'step[ping]' through a series of 'actions' in a digital environment (software code, app interface, digital platform environment) in a largely predetermined sequence (Polson et al., 1992: 742). Sociotechnical walkthroughs are useful for answering questions about *how* digital technologies, objects and artefacts are used and interacted with in the course of everyday life practices. More recently, the sociotechnical walkthrough has been developed for the study of contemporary digital phenomena, including apps and platforms. Perhaps the most significant and impactful of these newer methods is the app walkthrough method.

App Walkthroughs

Developed by Light et al. (2018: 882), the app walkthrough method is an approach for 'engaging directly with an app's interface to examine its technological mechanisms and embedded cultural references to understand how it guides users and shapes their experiences'. This method was designed to answer research questions about two interlinked phenomena specific to digital interfaces:

- how interface design structures user interaction; and
- questions about the broader contexts of how and why users adopt, leave (discontinue use of) and use apps in specific ways.

In the first scenario, where researchers are interested in using the method to understand how digital interface design structures user interaction (i.e., incentivising, modulating and/or encouraging particular kinds of interactions and in-app activities), researchers assume the role of an imaginary end user who interacts with an app through phases of:

- *registration and entry*, including details about how to sign up for or sign into the app, accept terms and conditions of use, and grant permissions for other device functionalities (e.g., location, contacts);

- *everyday use*, which pertains to engaging in activities that ordinary, real-world users would perform within the app by interacting with the app's features (e.g., menus, icons, in-app purchases) and affordances on a regular basis; and
- *app suspension, closure and leaving*, involving identifying how the app may be uninstalled, how accounts may be deleted or paused, etc.

In the second scenario, involving examinations of how real-world users adopt, use or interact with and leave apps, researchers engage with subjects to study how these real-world users actually interact with apps in their everyday lives, while using the app interface itself as an elicitation device. Here, the intent is to understand how real-world users themselves effectively 'walk through' (i.e., navigate, engage in specific interaction sequences and conduct in-app activities) the interfaces of apps, and potentially their motivations and rationales for doing so.

In both scenarios, researchers pay particular attention to specificities of the app interfaces, including:

- *user interface arrangement* – how the app guides users through or to particular kinds of interaction via the placement of buttons and menus;
- *functions and features* – how interface elements, such as pop-up windows and menus, either enable or necessitate particular kinds of interaction, such as providing personal information or linking accounts;
- *textual content and tone* – 'text embedded in user interfaces, such as the order of drop-down menu options or the categories available' (e.g., identity categories such as sexual orientation or gender) 'and their discursive power to shape use' (Light et al., 2018: 892); and
- *symbolic representation* – the 'look' and 'feel' of the app, including the use of symbols, imagery, colour, font, branding, etc., and how this mobilises cultural referents *vis-à-vis* a target user group and imagined scenarios of use.

As with walking methodologies, the app walkthrough method is used alongside additional data collection techniques and opens onto a range of analytic approaches. To collect data about specifics of an app, researchers can use participant observation, interviews (largely unstructured), video and audio recording (including for capturing thoughts and reflections while conducting the app walkthrough), detailed field notes, observational logs, as well as data capture techniques specific to digital screens such as screenshots and screen recording. Depending on the specific research questions, these data may then be analysed using an array of analysis techniques, including content and compositional analysis, qualitative coding and interpretation, and visual semiotic analysis. While designed for the study of app interfaces, the walkthrough method as developed by Light et al. (2018) may also be used for the study of digital platform interfaces (see e.g., Troeger and Bock, 2022; Yang et al., 2022).

Audits

An additional set of methodologies that can adopt a walkthrough approach are audits, which have been specifically designed to identify discrimination (Brown, 2019; Cherry and Bendick, 2018; Gaddis, 2018b). In the context of researching digital life, audits are used to evaluate whether and how digital and digitally mediated phenomena discriminate along social axes of difference, including gender, race and ethnicity, and age, among others. Audits 'walk', or process, a set of intentionally selected research inputs – such as a dataset or a group of individuals with varying characteristics – through the operational logistics of a digital or digitally mediated system, procedure, service or practice in a sequential, step-by-step manner. The outputs or outcomes of the processes in question are then examined to determine if discrimination or bias are present. If any one set of inputs with defined characteristics is observed to give rise to differential outcomes, then an audit may determine that the phenomenon in question is discriminatory. The outputs and outcomes of an audit may be assessed for discrimination and bias against criteria for fairness, equity, equality, objectivity (lack of bias), trustworthiness and/or transparency (Akkerman et al., 2008; Gaddis, 2018a).

Two types of audit are relevant for the study of digital life: *audit studies* and *algorithmic audits*.

Audit Studies

Audit studies are research designs for identifying discrimination in real-world social processes, including but not limited to discrimination in access to housing, education, employment and credit and lending (Brown, 2019; Cherry and Bendick, 2018; Gaddis, 2018b; Sandvig et al., 2014). They are a type of field experiment in which 'a researcher randomizes one or more characteristics' – age, racial or ethnic identity, gender, etc. – of real or hypothetical (imagined) individuals who participate in a study as 'auditors' or 'testers' of a social phenomenon, service, process or practice (Gaddis, 2018b: 5). While these characteristics of participants are diversified, other details about these real or imagined auditors – such as their employment or rental history, educational background – are held constant. This allows for the field experiment to 'control' for these variables, such that the only meaningful differences between testers are the characteristics that researchers have reasonably hypothesised are the basis of differential treatment and outcomes experienced by auditors. Auditors (real individuals or fictionalised profiles) are then sent or released into 'actual economic or social settings to measure how otherwise identical people are treated on the basis of their' perceived or inferred characteristics, such as their 'gender, race, or ethnicity' (Brown, 2019a: 3).

There are two types of audit study designs. *In-person audits* 'rely on trained assistants [auditors] to conduct the experiment' in real-world settings, such as job fairs, rental apartment showings and real estate open houses (Gaddis, 2018b: 6; Sandvig et al., 2014). *Correspondence audits*, also referred to as 'correspondence tests', involve the construction of hypothetical subjects whose profiles match the context of the audit study, with these subjects' fictional profiles submitted as vying for access to or equal treatment in the context of some kind of social good or service, such as a rental apartment, employment position or medical diagnosis and treatment (Gaddis, 2018b; Sandvig et al., 2014).

For example, racial and ethnic discrimination in hiring, including in digital technology sectors of the economy (Noble and Roberts, 2019; Park, 1999), is a well-documented and troublingly persistent phenomenon, one that has been repeatedly established by numerous audit studies using both in-person and correspondence methods (Quillian et al., 2017). As described by Quillian et al. (2017: 10870), in-person experiments auditing hiring practices for racial and ethnic discrimination involve pairs of trained auditors who are externally perceived as being racially dissimilar but who are otherwise 'matched' (equal) in terms of their employment histories and educational backgrounds dispatched to apply in-person for the same job openings. Correspondence approaches to auditing the same phenomenon involve 'fictionalized resumes with distinct racial names' submitted for job openings 'online or [historically] by mail' (Quillian et al., 2017: 10870). In both of these audit study designs, researchers then assess whether there is a difference in the perceived (in-person) or inferred (correspondence) racial identities of the testers (real persons, fictional resumes) who received versus those who did not receive invitations for interviews from real-world employers. Both in-person and correspondence style audits could be used to assess discrimination across an array of digital and digitally mediated social processes, including aforementioned racial and ethnic as well as gender bias in hiring practices in high technology sectors of the digital economy.

Yet multiple social and economic processes and practices are increasingly mediated, and in some instances fully automated, by algorithms and artificial intelligence (AI). This means that decisions about access to social and economic goods, services and opportunities are being made not by humans (alone), but (also) by digital technologies. As identified by the White House Office of Science and Technology Policy (2022a), '[a]lgorithmic discrimination occurs when automated systems contribute to unjustified different treatment or impacts disfavoring people based on their race, color, ethnicity, sex[,] religion, age, national origin, disability, veteran status, [or] genetic information' (n.p.). This includes recorded instances of gender discrimination in the use of algorithmic screening practices and hiring decisions at big technology firms (Crawford, 2021), but also extends beyond employment to many other facets of everyday life, such as racial discrimination in mortgage approvals and rates (e.g., Martinez and Kirchner, 2021); racial discrimination in automated criminal sentencing (Angwin et al., 2016); and racial and ethnic discrimination in secondary school admissions (Lecher and Varner, 2021). This nascent reality – in which automated systems represent novel vectors of decision making and discrimination – necessitates audit-based methods designed for identifying discrimination in specifically digital systems, including algorithms and AI.

Algorithmic Audits

Algorithms are objects of computer code that specify rules for how various kinds of digital inputs – image data, numerical inputs or other pieces of information – are to be processed, and what the output of this processing should be (be this a number, a label, a model or a decision). As such, algorithms consist of 'sets of defined steps structured to process instructions/data to produce an output' (Kitchin, 2017: 14). Examples include search engine algorithms that determine what content is returned in response to a search query, as well as the order in which that content appears in the results chain; video and music streaming platform recommendation algorithms that suggest movies, TV shows, songs, and artists to stream based on users' consumption patterns and the patterns of other users consuming similar content; and algorithms that match ride-hail drivers with riders and dispatch on-demand delivery couriers to pick-up locations and then onwards to customers. Algorithms are critical components of automated systems, which describe 'any system, software, or process that uses computation as whole or part of a system to determine outcomes, make or aid decisions, inform policy implementation, collect data or observations, or otherwise interact with individuals and/or communities' (White House Office of Science and Technology Policy, 2022b: 10).

As per Sandvig et al. (2014), algorithms require bespoke audit methods because unlike in audit study field experiments where identified instances of discrimination may be extrapolated to the general population at large, the discrimination enacted by a machine learning (ML) model (an implementation of AI) or a platform's algorithm is specific to the platform or the model and the results cannot be generalised beyond the automated system itself. Additionally, because algorithms and AIs are unique and differ from instance to instance, audit apparatuses and protocols need to be designed (or at least fine-tuned) to fit the specific parameters and context of the automated system being audited (Sandvig et al., 2014). Moreover, algorithms and AIs are often proprietary and many are 'black boxed' behind platform, app and software interfaces, meaning that their code is often unavailable for direct examination and scrutiny by researchers.

Sandvig et al. (2014) identify five different designs for auditing the algorithms of digital platforms:

1 *Code audits*, which involve direct examinations of algorithms' code. Code audits are possible only where an algorithm's code has been disclosed and/or published as open source.
2 *Non-invasive user audits*, wherein users share a non-invasive selection of their real-world interactions with an algorithm, including their inputs (e.g., a search engine query) and the corresponding outputs (e.g., search engine results chain), from which researchers infer how the black-boxed algorithm operates. In this algorithmic audit design, the users and their queries must be sampled to 'exhibit enough variation on the dimensions of interest' and they must 'provide a useful test of a platform's harmful discrimination along those axes' (p. 11).
3 *Scraping audits*, which involve researchers interacting with algorithms in highly scripted, largely unnaturalistic ways (in contrast to non-invasive user audits described above). This could involve testing directly for discrimination by, for instance, formulating search queries using terms and expressions that users themselves would be unlikely to make (or which may represent a low frequency of actual interactions). This design is called a scraping audit because researchers may be directly accessing a platform via its API; in which case, researchers need to be mindful of a platform's terms of service (which may prohibit scraping) and respect the legality of such practices in their jurisdiction (see **Chapter 4**).
4 *Sock puppet audits*, which resemble the 'field experiment' nature of correspondence audit studies. In this design, researchers create a number of fictitious ('sock puppet') accounts which are 'injected' into an automated system to observe how they are interacted with by other users and/or processed by algorithms (p. 13). As with scraping audits, this practice is illegal in several jurisdictions (representing a form of fraudulent behaviour), and it is the responsibility of researchers to determine the legality and ethics of this algorithmic audit design as they pertain to them in their jurisdiction and/or institution.
5 *Crowdsourced and collaborative audits*. Crowdsourced audits are similar to sock puppet audits, with the difference being that the auditor is a real person (recruited, remunerated tester, such as a digital microworker; see **Chapter 16**) rather than a fictitious account. In collaborative audits, the auditors are stakeholder volunteers rather than remunerated testers.

Beyond platforms, algorithms also play a key role in AI. An AI is a type of automated system that is:

capable of influencing the environment by producing an output (predictions, recommendations or decisions) for a given set of objectives. It uses machine and/or human-based data and inputs to (i) perceive real and/or virtual environments; (ii) abstract these perceptions into models through analysis in an automated manner (e.g., with machine learning), or manually; and (iii) use model inference to formulate options for outcomes. (OECD, 2019: n.p.)

Many AIs 'learn' to make decisions, predictions and/or recommendations by identifying patterns in an initial set of inputs known as 'training data'. Once trained, AIs are then operationalised to make decisions, predictions and recommendations in real-world settings, scenarios and contexts. One example is the use of automated facial recognition (AFR) in the criminal justice system, where this type of AI has been shown to be both unreliable and prejudicial in its (mis)identification of suspects, leading to numerous reported instances of false arrests, particularly of males of colour (e.g., Crawford, 2021; Crockford, 2020; Hill, 2020; Johnson, 2023). One of the sources of discrimination in the misidentification of persons of colour by AFR systems is that the training data has been shown to be biased because in these datasets, images of white (Caucasian) faces are overrepresented as compared to images of people of colour (Boulamwini and Gebru, 2018). By virtue of being trained on these biased datasets, AFR AIs 'learn' to perform identification matching on predominantly white faces, with the result that they end up being more accurate in classifying/identifying characteristics of white faces than the faces of people of colour, who are accordingly more likely to be misclassified and misidentified in real-world applications of these AIs. These biases become embedded in any automated decision-making systems (Boulamwini and Gebru, 2018).

The racial and ethnic biases of image training data have been established through the use of an algorithmic audit design known as *benchmarking*. Benchmarking is an experimental design for 'comparing [machine] learners or algorithms with respect to a certain performance measure' (Eugster, 2011: n.p.), such as how accurately an algorithm identifies the gender of persons with different skin tones in image data (Boulamwini and Gebru, 2018). The experimental design of a benchmarking study may take one of two forms. One approach involves processing established research and industry-standard benchmark datasets (the data used as inputs in benchmarking studies) through a number of ML models and algorithms to audit their performance (e.g., to see which model more accurately identifies the gender of persons across differences in skin tone). A second approach to benchmarking involves auditing the data themselves, which makes it useful for identifying the kinds of biases in training data described above. This can take the form of curating (putting together) a bespoke benchmark dataset (e.g., one with equal representation of faces across different skin tones) and running it and industry/research-standard benchmark datasets (in which white faces are overrepresented) through the same model or models, to see whether different benchmark datasets elicit more accurate results. Both approaches may also be combined together in a single benchmarking study, as they are in Boulamwini and Gebru's (2018) audit of how accurately commercial facial recognition algorithms classify the gender of image data depicting faces of persons with varying skin tones. Their audit evaluated three benchmark datasets – two existing, and one of their own design – against three commercial image classification algorithms. The results of Boulamwini and Gebru's audit (2018) found that racial bias in gender classification was systemic across the automated image classifiers, with the algorithms most accurate in correctly classifying the gender of images of lighter-skinned males, and least accurate in correctly classifying the gender of images of darker-skinned females.

Summary

- Walking methodologies (based on physical bodily movement) and walkthroughs (based on walking as a metaphor for sequentially navigating digital interfaces, social processes and automated systems) may be used to study the space-times, practices and artefacts media of digital life.
- Walking methodologies and walkthroughs do not represent standalone methods. Rather, they often rely on and involve additional methods, many of them established in the social sciences, such as interviews, observation, ethnography, and audio and video recording. What distinguishes walking and walkthrough methodologies from more traditional conceptions of, for instance, sensory ethnography or interviews, is that walking methodologies and walkthroughs effectively put these other techniques 'into motion', both physically and metaphorically.
- While walking methodologies and walkthroughs represent means of organising and/or approaching data collection, they are not prescriptive of analytic techniques. In other words, depending on their own ontological and epistemological orientations and how these inform the goals of any specific project, researchers have wide latitude in deciding on how to analyse the data once it has been collected.
- Walking methodologies and walkthroughs are furthermore versatile in that they can be used to study digital and digitally mediated objects in and of themselves (e.g., app and platform interfaces, or networks of bike-sharing stations in a city), as well as research participants' (i.e., other subjects') perceptions and experiences of, interactions with, and responses to these phenomena.

- Audits are methods designed for identifying discrimination in digitally mediated social and economic processes and practices (correspondence and in-person audit studies), as well as in automated systems (algorithmic audits).

Recommended Reading

Boulamwini, J., and Gebru, T. (2018) 'Gender shades: Intersectional accuracy in disparities in commercial gender classification', *Proceedings of Machine Learning Research*, 81(1): 1–15.
A now classic example of an algorithmic benchmarking audit of racial bias in the automated classification of gender in image data.

Gaddis, M.S. (ed.) (2018) *Audit Studies: Behind the Scenes with Theory, Method, and Nuance*. Springer, Cham.
A definitive collection on the use of audit studies in the social sciences. Contributions do not engage digital phenomena, technologies, or systems, but the collection provides a foundation for confidently using correspondence and in-person audit study designs in researching digital life.

Light, B., Burgess, J., and Duguay, S. (2018) 'The walkthrough method: An approach to the study of apps', *New Media & Society*, 20(3): 881–900.
This paper introduces the app walkthrough method and provides a 'how to' for doing a walkthrough of digital interfaces, supported by empirical examples.

Sandvig, C., Hamilton, K., Karahalios, K., and Langbort, C. (2014) 'Auditing algorithms: research methods for detecting discrimination on Internet platforms', paper presented at the *Data and Discrimination: Converting Critical Concerns into Productive Inquiry* workshop, 22 May 2014, Seattle, WA. https://websites.umich.edu/~csandvig/research/Auditing Algorithms -- Sandvig -- ICA 2014 Data and Discrimination Preconference.pdf (accessed 5 Sept 2023).
A primer on auditing algorithmic discrimination, including different algorithmic audit designs.

Van Es, K., and de Lange, M. (2020) 'Data with its boots on the ground: Datawalking as research method', *European Journal of Communication*, 35(3): 278–289.
An overview of the interdisciplinary, ontological and epistemological, and multimodal and multisensory foundations of datawalking as a method for researching digital life. Synergies with other social science methods are also identified.

7
Arts-based Methods

Overview

Chapter 7 examines:

- the use of arts-based methods in undertaking research;
- the approach of research-creation in which research is conducted through the use of arts-based methods;
- specific arts-based methods used in research-creation: creative writing, artistic methods and creative data stories;
- creative means of disseminating research undertaken using traditional social science methods: creative non-fiction and fiction, film and exhibitions; and
- critiques of using creative approaches.

Introduction

Over the past two decades, there has been a turn towards using creative and experimental practices within social sciences research as a means to examine the materialised, embodied, emplaced and experiential nature of the relationship between digital technologies and society. Utilising various forms of creative writing (e.g., speculative fiction, digital poetry, short stories and creative non-fiction), art and craft practices (e.g., painting, photography, sculpture, textiles) and performance (e.g., theatre, film-making, music), arts-based methods have been utilised to research and make sense of digital life and to communicate research findings to various audiences (Hawkins, 2021; Kara, 2015). The turn to arts-based methods does not deny that there is much creativity and inventiveness in the design and use of traditional social science and humanities methods. Rather, arts-based methods utilise their affordances to ask and explore the same questions in alternative ways, which might provide answers that are more illuminating or more effectively engage audiences. This chapter is centrally concerned with these affordances and the use of arts-based methods for undertaking and disseminating research.

The first section details the rationale of research-creation; that is, using creative practices as a means to conduct research. This is followed by a discussion of how research-creation is being undertaken in practice, and the specific methods being used. The next section documents how research conducted using traditional social science methods can be disseminated using creative media. The final section details some concerns regarding the use of arts-based methods and their efficacy.

Research-Creation

Typically, the use of arts-based methods in academic research occurs near the conclusion of a project as a means of communicating findings to non-academic audiences using media (e.g., creative non-fiction, film, artwork, exhibitions, podcasts) that employ significantly different forms and composition to tradition academic outputs (e.g., journal papers and books). Research-creation, however, is different in that it utilises creative practices and media throughout the entire research process, with its logics and methods permeating research design and implementation. As such, research-creation 'is not the creative presentation of, nor artistic experimentation with, pre-existing 'data' harvested through traditional ... methods' (Truman, 2021: xx). Rather, the framing and process of conducting research is realised by employing artistic practices alongside the use of social science and humanities theory and methods to examine social matters (Loveless, 2019; Truman, 2021). The aim is not necessarily to produce data that will then be analysed in a subsequent process, or to test a hypothesis or theory (Borgdorff 2020). Rather the process of research-creation is the means of insight creation for participants and of producing knowledge. Research-creation can be practised by a scholar-artist working alone, but more typically is collaborative in nature involving a scholar and an artist working together, often with other participants such as stakeholders or community members (Szanto and Sicotte, 2022).

Research-creation, its advocates contend, enables new ways of knowing, representing and intervening in the world. The process opens up new questions, fresh insights, alternative ways to think through issues, and novel and engaging ways to represent and communicate with audiences. This is because artistic practices re-orient the attention and perception of its practitioners (Hawkins, 2015). By utilising a creative register, research-creation enacts a sense of *estrangement* (pushing a person outside of what they comfortably know) and *defamiliarisation* (making the familiar strange) that generates a distancing mirror and prompts critical reflection (Loveless, 2019). It enables the charting of knowledge that is not easily expressed with words or in a formal engagement and allows the exploration of experiences which might otherwise be silenced (Tarr et al., 2018). Undertaken collaboratively, it fosters dialogue and interaction between participants that is less encumbered by hierarchal and formal relations that is usual in communal and workplace settings. Lupton and Watson (2021: 466) contend that research-creation, as an embodied, experiential set of practices that engage directly with discursive, symbolic and imagined meanings, help to 'surface unexpected ... less taken-for-granted' and hidden views, as well as affective affordances, and expose 'practices, habits, routines, tactics [and] sensory engagements'.

The critical reflection inherent in its practices, Foley (2021: 34) argues, 'can help us to become more aware, more conscious and conscientious' about the way we make the world. The creative process prompts participants to question their epistemological and ontological viewpoints, the assumptions and values of their working practices, and the institutional structures and contextual framing of their work; and to consider ways to re-make and re-organise these in productive and just ways. Indeed, the approach has its roots in feminist, queer, decolonial and social justice praxes (see **Chapters 2** and **8**) to trouble established epistemologies and power relations within the academic research process (Loveless, 2019; Truman, 2021). As such, it is often action-oriented, not only as a means to understand an issue in a fresh way, but also a potential means to intervene in and transform the issue itself (Hawkins, 2015). The key outcome then might not be an artwork or short story, but rather a shift in viewpoint and priorities of the participants, including those who initiated the project; that they come to understand an issue in a different way, which might transform how they subsequently think and act. In this sense, research-creation 'invites us to pause and "step-away" from our current path, to reconsider and apperceive our existing conditions and predicaments'; it is 'a process that serves to open up inquiry, raise questions and discover problems, more so than solve them' (Foley, 2021: 34). It casts critical light on the taken for granted and prompts alternative ways to know and act. Later, the creative endeavour and the artistic products might be reflected on, additional discernments deduced and further outputs composed, with the artistic work and successive insights shared through various media (e.g., papers, books, websites, social media and exhibitions).

Traditional social science and humanities research design and methods are typically staid and formalised. They are carefully determined in advance of entering the field and engaging respondents. The approach and methods chosen are usually well tried and tested. Once implemented, the research procedure and tools remain fixed throughout data generation to ensure continuity and equivalence of data across a sample. In some cases, there might be some degree of improvisation, such as with unstructured interviews, though these usually employ some scaffolding and choreography to ensure that the same kind of information is gathered across respondents. In contrast, research-creation is an approach that is inventive, lively and speculative (Tarr et al., 2018). It will utilise methods with little track record, or adapt or devise new ones. It can use multiple methods in combination, and the approach and methods can evolve and mutate as the research takes place. Indeed, the approach encourages exploration, experimentation, play and improvisation (Kara, 2015; Szanto and Sicotte, 2022). There is then a liveness to the process, rather than a bracketing or bordering as with more traditional methods, which is reflective of the relationality, contingency, context and 'ongoingness' of everyday life (Tarr et al., 2018). The process is also lively in the sense that it seeks to be provocative and stimulating, and to evoke a new understanding of the world (Tarr et al., 2018).

That said, research-creation is not an 'anything goes', entirely unstructured undertaking (Truman, 2021). Like all research, it requires a planning stage that provides a framing and some conditions, and there are limitations and protocols to the process, even though the endeavour itself might not be fully decided and be open to improvisation on inception. Planning includes the formulation of 'ethics protocols, coordination with participants, and curation of materials' (Truman, 2021: 14). Nor is research-creation an unskilled process that can be undertaken effectively by anybody. Indeed, some practitioners make the case that people who wish to undertake research-creation should be as skilled in the arts and crafts being utilised as they are in research techniques (Piirto, 2009, cited in Kara, 2015). Moreover, they should be aware of the context and nuances of creative practices; that is, have some domain knowledge about concepts, methods, techniques and application. Just as a scholar would be wary of an artist with no training in sociological methods or disciplinary knowledge saying they are going to undertake a sociological study, we should be sceptical of a sociologist with no formal training undertaking an artistic project (Marston and DeLeeuw, 2013). Others argue that this is an exclusive and exclusionary position as what is important is the process rather than the creative product (Kara, 2015). Anyone can attempt to produce a story, poem, picture or photograph, and engage in meaningful critical reflection while doing so. Moreover, collaboration can bring together people with varying skill sets that can complement one another and enhance the process.

Approaches to Research-Creation

Research-creation is a relatively new methodological approach within the social sciences. As yet, there are no well-established standardised research designs, with its practitioners experimenting with ways to operationalise research-creation in practice. In this section, three initial methodological approaches are described in brief: inreach, braiding and bricolage.

Inreach Method

Between 2013 and 2020, Jessica Foley ran more than forty research-creation workshops through her Engineering Fictions, Stranger Fictions and Data Stories projects, using a range of improvisational writing exercises, such as the creation of short stories, poems, sonnets, mindmaps, lyrics and manuals, to generate reflection and insight on a range of issues (Foley, 2016, 2019). These workshops used a research design that she terms *inreach* (the opposite of outreach; i.e., for a group to look and engage inwards), describing it as a choreographic process that is catalytic and supportive of transversality (that is, communication and productive collaboration between participants) (Foley, 2016; see Foley 2019, 2021 for accounts of the process and outcomes). Each workshop has a *foil*, a person who oversees the research-creation process, co-designs the workshops, sources materials, directs the activities, and acts as the workshop facilitator. The foil works with a *catalyst*, who is a member of the community taking part in the workshop, and who has a desire to examine an idea, question, proposition or provocation. The foil and catalyst co-develop a *seed* for the workshop – the issue that is to be explored – and co-design the methods to be used and associated instructions and constraints. The catalyst is the person who introduces the seed to the community using whatever medium they wish (e.g., through story, slideshow, music or performance). Each workshop has five basic stages:

- *Attuning*, in which people gather, socialise and are introduced to one another.
- *Seeding*, in which the seed is revealed.
- *Conversing*, in which the seed is discussed collectively.
- *Writing* (although this could equally be any creative activity), in which the prepared exercises are undertaken.
- *Sharing*, in which the creative outputs are shared, discussed and reflected upon.

Typically, Foley has sought to organise workshops in a short sequence, inviting attendees to return to further explore an issue using a different seed, which might be co-developed with a new catalyst.

Braided Method

While the sequence and praxis of Foley's inreach workshops tends to develop and unfold in a somewhat *ad hoc* manner, Ash Watson (2020: 68) instead advocates for a *braided approach* in which 'multiple methods are simultaneously employed across distinct research phases, with equal significance and attention given to each method in all phases'. A mix of creative and traditional qualitative and quantitative methods are employed, with two or more in use at the same time and preferably for the same duration.

Every method has its strengths and disadvantages and using more than one enables the vantage points of each to be gained and to ameliorate in part their limitations (Watson, 2020). The research design has a number of phases, with each phase consisting of a period of data generation followed by a period of review before re-entering the same field site to conduct the next phase. Importantly, each strand (application of method) of the braid is seen as distinct and undertaken as a separate exercise, though they are chosen to complement each other, with the findings woven together to produce a braid of shared understanding. The aim is not to use the methods as a means to triangulate data and findings, with those that are not corroborated across methods being discarded. Instead, any differences revealed are reflexively examined in the review periods to consider why divergences and contradictions might exist. The review also considers which methods are appropriate to employ in the next phase to extend the braid and deepen the insights it reveals. In this way, knowledge is produced iteratively, reflexively and synergistically.

Remix Method

Rather than producing a braid, Annette Markham (2013) advocates for creating a *bricolage* using a remix methodology. She describes bricolage as 'the process and product of using what is ready at hand to get the job done', borrowing and adapting philosophy, concepts, methods and techniques as needed (Markham, 2018: 44). She draws inspiration for her approach from remix culture, in which ideas, techniques, media and materials are spliced together in creative ways to produce new entities (such as sampled music, mashup videos, memes, remixed fashion, open source code, fab/maker products). Markham (2018) frames bricolage as an epistemology, action and product. Bricolage, she contends, is a way of knowing that mirrors how we come to know the world by piecing together the moments, fragments and glimpses that we encounter daily (e.g., conversations, overheard gossip, social media posts, news stories). Bricolage seeks to draw together those discoveries and relationalities to jerry-rig through assembling and layering some kind of understanding of their complexity and meaning (Markham, 2018). Bricolage as an action consists of making sense of a situation or solving a problem with the available resources, recognising that this action is contingent and partially incidental and accidental. Bricolage as a product is the resultant coalesced knowledge ('the unique collage, montage, composite, fragmented, or layered account that comes out of the process of … inquiry') or the artistic output produced through action (Markham, 2018: 50). Bricolage as an approach, then, contrasts markedly with the framing and structures of traditional social science research and its formalised research design aligned with theories and hypotheses. Markham (2013, 2018) enacts bricolage through her *remix methodology*. This methodology uses various methods – usually including arts-based methods – in combination, and plays with perspectives to see what results. She identifies five activities of remix enquiry, which she has applied in workshops to explore phenomena:

- *Generate* – the assembly of ideas and data, including all the workings and supports such as notes, early drafts, mindmaps, uncoded and coded transcripts.
- *Play* – the process of exploring and experimenting with the generated material through playful, improvised and inventive combinations.
- *Borrow* – the finding and bringing together of ideas, concepts and techniques to cast new light and help make sense of the remixed material.
- *Move* – continuing to develop and evolve sense-making by revisiting the materials and charting the shifting perspectives and transformations in questions and meaning making.
- *Interrogate* – reflexively questioning the research process, positionality and situatedness, ethics, the phenomenon being examined and the knowledge produced.

These activities aim to produce a bricolage that deciphers meaning from the diverse materials generated and encountered throughout the research process and is simultaneously mindful of the politics of producing such a bricolage.

Research-Creation in Action

A variety of arts-based methods can be utilised within research-creation projects, such as the use of creative writing (including short stories, speculative fiction, improvisation and word play, poetry, screenplays, cartoons), producing artworks (including visual, performance and installation art), making data stories (including interactive media, data art, data physicalisation), photography, dance, film-making, creating games, sound and music, and theatre production. As way of illustration, this section discusses the first three. In each case, the process of research-creation can be undertaken by the researcher independently or collaborating with a writer or artist, or working in partnership with a community of interest usually through workshops.

Creative Writing in Research-Creation

Creative writing as a means to conduct research uses techniques such as word play and storytelling to explore phenomena, experiences and the relations between people, places and things. It enables its practitioners to blend facts and the imagination, to consider scenarios and to speculate, to be inventive and playful, to surface and explore connections and meanings, and use expository and lyrical modes of expression (Loveless, 2019; Singer, 2013). Jessica Foley and Ash Watson specialise in using creative writing as a means of performing research-creation, and both have extensive experience of undertaking their own creative practice. As noted above, in her series of Engineering Fiction workshops, Foley (2016, 2019) asked workshop participants to use a range of improvisational writing exercises and forms (e.g., fiction and creative non-fiction). These provided a rich set of creative writing about particular phenomena, which the group could then further explore through discussion. Watson (2020) used her braided approach to entwine autoethnography, discourse and narrative analysis of literature and fiction writing to produce a sociological novel, iteratively crafting the work through a number of phases. In subsequent work with Deborah Lupton, she used creative writing prompts in two workshops with community members to explore the socio-material and affective dimensions of personal digital data (Lupton and Watson, 2021). In a third workshop, participants worked with art paper, magazines, excerpts from scholarly research, and their own initial writings and mappings to produce a collaborative zine in which collage, creative writing and illustration are layered together (a visual mini-book).

Truman (2021) details a number of research-creation projects utilising creative writing. 'Intratextual entanglements' was a collaborative mail project in which thirty-four participants were sent a scanned text and invited to write observations in the margins or engage with the text however they wished. The returned texts were then sent to another participant, inviting them to annotate the annotations. In another project, she conducted a set of writing and walking exercises with school children:

> exploring rhythm and movement in literature through walking-writing, thinking about place through movement and video poems, walking and writing about speculative versions of the city, describing more-than-human entanglements through Tanka poetry, highlighting social injustices experienced by walking through narrative, creating linguistic maps of affective environments, composing synesthetic verses, and making a dérive map of the school.
> (Truman, 2021: 72)

Another project consisted of creating a Twitter bot, entitled the 'PostQual Diffractor Bot', which composes tweets based on a dictionary and rule-set that parodies post-qualitative literature by auto-generating paper titles that might sound genuine. To explore how social credit scoring in China is being perceived, Lee (2019) employed a scenario-based story completion method, inviting twenty-two participants to react to a scenario and extrapolate a possible future from it. Given the political sensitivities around social credit scoring and surveillance, using a creative method rather than an interview allowed participants to express views in a less formal way. Kitchin (2021) used short stories, along with biographical essays, as a means to explore the politics and praxes of data lifecycles and how data shape everyday lives. The book project 'How to Run a City Like Amazon, and Other Fables' invited participants to use speculative fiction to reveal the desires of smart city proponents by illustrating how cities might function if they were run on the business models of numerous companies (Graham et al., 2019).

Artistic Methods in Research-Creation

Research-creation using artistic media aims to use the process of creating an artwork, and the artwork itself, as a means to generate insights about a phenomenon. Here, there is an attentiveness to the art practices employed, as well as the 'finished' object, recognising that art is constantly in the process of becoming, formed through its creation and its engagement by audiences, and art acts as a site through which knowledge, meaning and identity are reflected on and recast by its practitioners and audience. In this sense, art is 'an ensemble of practices, performances, experiences and artefacts' (Hawkins, 2011: 465), and research-creation capitalises on these qualities to explore issues and views that might not be so easily expressed through traditional social science methods.

Jeremy Wood and Pip Thornton have used artistic practices to explore digital life through their own creative endeavours. Wood (2022) is an artist and mapmaker who has been exploring personal cartographies and location tracking by GPS-enabled devices since the early 2000s. Through a series of art works, in which he traces his own movements, he has examined the authority of maps and issues of accuracy and trust in locative media (Ferdinand, 2018; Lauriault and Wood, 2009; see also **Chapter 13**). Thornton is an academic who engages in artistic practice as a means to conduct research. Interested in what she terms 'linguistic capitalism', and the value of all words in Google AdWords and how their auctioning dictates the ordering of search results on the platform, she devised an artistic intervention, {poem}.py (Thornton 2018). {poem}.py works by feeding poetry into the Google AdWords keyword planner using a python script to ascertain the suggested bid price for each word, then printing the poem using a receipt printer, one word and its bid cost per line, along with the overall cost. In this way, she exposes the hidden inner workings of Google's most profitable business using a technology familiar to all.

Webster (2021) and Osborne et al. (2019) detail collaborations between academics and an artist. Like Thornton, Dan Webster's collaboration with the artist Michael Hanna engaged with Google AdWords, in their case exploring how the marketing system works in practice by placing ads and seeing how users engaged with search links to sixteen art works connected to a 0.1 km radius areas in Belfast and Milan. Those that clicked on the ads and were presented with the artworks were invited to engage in an email conversation with their creators. In this way, creating and placing the artwork revealed the inner workings of Google AdWords and also became the means of sourcing feedback. The Make/Shift/Space project examined social media data related to specific places using performance art (Osborne et al., 2019). The performances were undertaken by artist and researcher, Emily Warner. The project first extracted geotagged photos and associated text from Flickr, posted between 2009 and 2016, which were sited within a bounding box around the city of Birmingham. Examining the areas of Balsall Heath and Digbeth, twenty-four sites were then selected based on the clustering and density of posts. At these sites, Warner set up a stand and produced small artistic products such as annotated photographs or sculptures made of everyday objects or undertook brief performances that engaged with the Flickr data, the local setting and interactions with the people present, also sharing the events online via Twitter and Periscope. In this way, the project examined the relationship between people and the material, virtual and imagined qualities of space.

The Make/Shift/Space project involved some engagement with local citizens. Likewise, artist and designer Christian Nold has engaged more than 2,000 people in twenty-five cities as part of his biosensing community mapping project. Participants explore their local area wearing a sensor device that measures galvanic skin response, which provides a simple indicator of their emotional arousal (Nold, 2009). The data were used to create emotion maps, revealing those places and local issues participants most strongly felt about. Participants then annotated the maps to explain their reactions. Combining maps provided a communal view, which Nold has published in a variety of formats for different cities, including in 3D. Similarly, the 'Everyone's East Lake' project deployed research-creation using a participatory art performance to engage citizens about a land grab by developers of a state-listed ecological scenic area in Wuhan City, China (Lin, 2013). Organised by an architect and artist, citizens were asked to produce an artwork along the lakeshore to voice their concerns over environmental degradation and state and corporate power, with sixty pieces of work being produced by fifty-four participants. Some of these works involved producing physical and online maps. For example, the 'Strolling with 200 mu' (33 acres) was a performative mapping in which an interactive tool was added to Google Maps that enabled users to place a polygon sized to 33 acres over any portion of the globe (Lin, 2013). In this way, they could get a sense of the scale of lake in-fill being proposed. In turn, the art works provoked wider discussion and resistance to the illegal development.

Creative Data Stories

A core resource for research are data from which information and insights are derived. Research-creation has been used to throw critical light on the politics and praxes of generating data and how it is used to communicate information; in other words, to tell stories about data. As an alternative to conventional data visualisations, a number of projects have produced data physicalisations; that is, creating physical forms 'whose geometry or material properties encode data' (Jansen et al., 2015: 2; Offenhuber, 2020). Such physicalisations create tactile as well as visual artefacts, produced through crafts such as knitting, felting, quilting, weaving, potting, sculpting and jewellery-making (Lupton and Watson, 2021). For example, Weinberg (n.d.) has encoded climate data from the National Oceanic and Atmospheric Administration into climate datascapes of woven tapestries and coiled sculptures, providing a more tangible artefact than a table or graph. As summarised by Lupton and Watson (2021), other creative data physicalisations include the production of data souvenirs (Petrelli et al., 2017), data patinas (Lee et al., 2016), digital ceramics (Desjardins and Tihanyi, 2019) and even custom-shaped chocolates and flavoured drinks enabling consumers to taste the data (Khot et al., 2015). Data physicalisations can be supplemented by additional data being map-projected onto models and sculptures, and augmented with tangible interfaces that enable a degree of interactivity and response (Jansen et al., 2015). Other forms of interactive data stories can be entirely digital and shared online. This has included the creation of data art. For example, as part of the Building City Dashboards project, three artists were given real-time data relating to the cities of Dublin and Cork in Ireland, which they then utilised in the creation of three artworks: a twenty-four hour sound mapping of traffic data, an interactive locative media augmented reality app, and a virtual reality environment of word clouds linked to library loans (BCD, 2018). In the same project, Jeneen Naji produced 'The River Poem' in which parts of James Joyce's novel *Finnegan's Wake* were map-projected onto a 3D printed model of Dublin, the words travelling along the length of the River Liffey (Rzeszewski and Naji, 2022). These research-creation projects create what Stark (2014, n.p.) terms 'data visceralizations'; that is, data that we 'see, hear, feel, breathe, ingest', which stimulates a visceral physical or emotional response rather than just critical reflection.

Creative Means of Dissemination

> What if the most powerful way to communicate the research embodied within a certain 'chapter' is not to write about it on a page, but to 'write' it through video? Or in a multimedia installation? Or with a live performance event? Or through an art-activist intervention? (Loveless, 2019: 41)

In research-creation, the act of producing the creative work is the means through which the research is conducted. It is also possible to use artistic media to communicate the findings of research undertaken using traditional methods as an alternative or supplement to academic papers and books, and to reach and engage wider audiences. As Loveless (2019) notes, artistic media might be the most powerful way to communicate research findings. Their use is also being fuelled by calls for research to have greater impact beyond the academy. These calls are being driven by governments seeking to translate their investment in research into applied outcomes and to demonstrate the societal value of research (Bastow et al., 2014), and by social movements who want to ensure that knowledge does not get trapped in ivory towers and speak only to intellectuals, but is opened up for all to consider and apply (Fuller and Kitchin, 2004; Nagar, 2013). As such, there is increasing interest in communicating ideas and analysis using artistic media, such as various forms of creative writing, interactive digital media, infographics, virtual reality, artworks, exhibitions, theatre, podcasts, documentaries and films, as well as through social and traditional media (newspapers, radio, television).

Creative Non-fiction and Fiction

Creative writing is seen as an attractive means of conveying research findings because it provides a different, more accessible and playful, register to 'sterile, jargon-filled, and formulaic' academic writing (Leavy, 2015: 1). For Singer (2013: 141), creative writing enables a toggling back and forth between fact and imagination, between expository and lyric narrative, and to blend together 'scene, description, mediation, raw fact, speculation and reportage' and to cast off 'neutral third person invisibility'. Creative writing opens up new possibilities to be inventive in form, such as producing creative non-fiction, interactive multimedia narratives, short stories, poetry, memoirs and narrative journalism. Creative non-fiction seeks to convey facts and insights gleaned from a project through a more engaging text. This includes essays that eschew formalised academic narrative for a more personalised, reflexive voice that utilises personal experience and viewpoints to explore subjects from different angles (Philips and Kara, 2021). For some, creative non-fiction, while rooted in facts, reads more like fiction, 'shar[ing] with fiction the elements of detail, image, description, dialogue, and scene' and striving to 'show, not tell' and to 'bring the reader on a journey of discovery' (Singer and Walker, 2013a: 3). A number of techniques can be used to convey ideas and interpretation, including 'montage, juxtaposition, toggling, fragmentation, white space, etymological exegesis, the weave, the tangent, and the digression' (Singer and Walker, 2013b: 139). Through digital mediation, creative non-fiction can be quite experimental. Monson (2013) added glyphs to his book, *Vanishing Point*, to denote words that can be typed into a website to unlock new content. Another essay can only be read fully if the HTML code is viewed as additional text is hidden in the comment fields. Monson's aim is to create a text that is 'mutable, updatable, and potentially multilayered, and to offer the reader another avenue of exploration' (Monson, 2013: 84). Also utilising the multimedia and interactive qualities of the internet, the Art/Data/Health project created an online, multimedia story about the COVID-19 lockdown in Brighton, UK, that combines text, live-action video clips, animated infographics and first-person testimonies (Fotopoulou and Beavon, 2020). Others have used fiction as a way of conveying the essence of their research, such as the novel produced by Watson (2020). Her novel is part of the Social Fictions book series, which publishes social research in the form of novels and plays (Philips and Kara, 2021). Several different forms of writing can be used to convey the same material to different audiences. For example, Kitchin (2014c) details how a range of writing praxes, including fiction, blog posts, policy briefs, newspaper op-eds, academic papers and grant applications were used to disseminate on-going research.

Film

Producing films and audio-visual outputs, such as animation, for communicating research has become more common in recent years due to the affordability of equipment, access to open source editing tools and an ability to share the outputs widely via the internet. Films enable the presentation of audio-visual content and, in particular, movement, multisensory interaction and the stream of experiential unfolding rather than static snapshots (Ernwein, 2020; Garrett, 2011). Documentary making was a key output of a project that examined the digital lives of residents of high-rise apartments on the periphery of Toronto. This project used a combination of surveys and non-fiction storytelling to explore the uneven and unequal distribution and access to digital technologies and infrastructures and how these are experienced in everyday life (Cowen et al., 2020). As a means of communicating the findings, the researchers worked with local residents to produce an interactive online documentary, 'Universe Within: Digital Lives in the Global Highrise' (Cizek, 2015). The Building City Dashboards project produced a set of eight short videos to showcase the project's work as part of an online exhibition (BCD, 2020). Given the highly visual and interactive nature of the produced work (e.g., 3D spatial media), the videos give a much stronger representation of the outcomes than the written word or static 2D images. The videos were produced because COVID-19 restrictions led to the cancellation of two public exhibitions, but they have the advantage of remaining online for as long as desired and are accessible to a much larger audience. Instead of a documentary, Sava Saheli Singh (2022), working with screenwriters, has produced a set of four short films as part of her 'Screening Surveillance' project. Each story explores issues related to the highly intrusive surveillance enabled by networked digital technologies. For example, '#tresdancing' speculates on how surveillance and control through new educational technologies will reshape schooling and students' everyday lives, and 'Blaxites' considers how surveillance of social media might affect access to health care (Singh, 2022). The films reveal the power and potential consequences of new surveillance technologies, and prompt critical reflection in relation to the viewer's own lives, through storytelling that is relatable to the public.

Exhibitions

Another means to communicate with the public is through exhibitions of artistic media. This might be the display of artwork, data visualisations, infographics and audio-visual displays, and may include installations and interactive media, such as touchscreens or the use of virtual reality. An exhibition can also act as a site of experimentation and further research (Kullman, 2013). Here, visitors to the exhibition are observed as to their behaviour and interactions, or are surveyed and interviewed to gauge their views and experience. In 'The Museum of Random Memory' participants were invited to take part in performative installations where they engaged in interactive analogue and digital memory-making activities, including donating a personal memory to the system, to prompt critical reflection on how datafication and automated data-related processes shape their lives and their personal and cultural memories (Markham and Pereira, 2019a, 2019b). A series of eight exhibitions were held, with the installations varying in each case as the researchers experimented with the creative media they had developed, e.g., testing the effects of changing layouts, formats, space, prompts and technical assemblages (Markham and Pereira, 2019a). #AanaJaana was a month-long public exhibition in 2019 in one of New Delhi's busiest metro stations that presented WhatsApp diary entries made over a six-month period by young women living in an area of informal dwelling resettlement on the periphery of the city (Datta and Thomas, 2022). The project explored 'what happens when women "see" and "speak" with their phone', their digital and spatial marginalisation, and the expression of power over women's bodies and their experiences of place. The WhatsApp entries were used to create a set of large billboard posters that explored issues identified by the women, including sexual harassment when commuting and inclusion and omission from the emerging smart city, with viewers invited to reflect on the issues and to change their behaviour (Datta and Thomas, 2022).

Critiques of Creative Approaches

While research-creation and the use of artistic media for dissemination have much to offer in terms of exploring research questions in ways that produce new insights and share the knowledge produced with diverse audiences, they have not been universally welcomed. There are concerns as to whether arts-based methods are a valid means to produce academic knowledge (Baldacchino, 2012). Qualitative methods and approaches have long been critiqued for lacking rigour, objectivity and reproducibility due to their openness, lack of standardisation, and unrepresentative samples. This critique is magnified for research-creation, where not only does the research process vary with each undertaking, but no process is repeatable due to its liveness (Tarr et al., 2018). Moreover, the experience of taking part in the process is important to being able to interpret what took place (Tarr et al., 2018). Further, research-creation is not practised in a detached, neutral and objective manner, but rather it is implicitly, and most often overtly, political, seeking to change the world in some way through its praxes (Borgdorff, 2020). As such, research-creation fails the central ambition of the scientific method; that is, to produce data that others can re-analyse and knowledge that is consistent, reproducible and generalisable. This places a question mark against its integrity, reliability, credibility, trustworthiness and accountability for the knowledge produced. Research-creation might be evocative and generative, but its detractors argue it is also too open-ended and confrontational, and does not produce conclusive, defensible findings or arguments (Loveless, 2019).

As with research-creation, there are some concerns about using creative means of dissemination. Creative writing, film-making and producing artwork and crafts to a standard that is effective at communicating research requires skill. Those that do this kind of work for a living have usually undertaken professional training over several years. Researchers, in contrast, have been trained to write non-fiction, academic narratives. It is naïve to think that academics can leap from novices to experts across any media of expression and communication. The danger of trying to do so without collaborating with experts is the production of amateur works that fail in their ambition. Even for professionally produced works, there are some concerns that creative media can lack clarity and intelligibility of meaning and suffer from subjectivity in messaging (Kara, 2015). That is, unlike an academic paper – which tries to unambiguously state how the research was undertaken, what was found and the conclusions drawn – artistic media are more open to interpretation. Moreover, as Singer (2013: 141) notes: '[i]f a piece of nonfiction reads like fiction or poetry, how can you tell it's true?' Others have critiqued what they see as the cynical use of creative media by the academy to comply with the impact agenda of government and funding agencies (Loveless, 2019). Here, creative media are not employed because they are viewed as the most appropriate means of communication but to fulfil a criteria. This has led De Leeuw et al. (2017: 6) to argue that the users of artistic media need to 'remain sufficiently vigilant and critically aware to ensure they do not become a parody of themselves, something wholly corruptible and able to be put to use in exactly the opposite ways as those for which they were intended'.

For practitioners, these critiques judge creative approaches on the terms of the detractors, failing to understand the inherent benefits to creative endeavours and that they are explicitly a challenge to the epistemologies of traditional approaches. What others see as weaknesses, practitioners often view as strengths. These weaknesses though do mean that persuading people to participate in research-creation projects can be a challenge, as there is often a scepticism concerning the utility, integrity and validity of the process. This was evident among the police and state surveillance workers that Foley (2021) engaged, and with the engineers she had worked with previously, who felt the research design unscientific. However, she notes that those who took part found the process and the critical reflection it engendered useful and even asked for follow-on sessions as the workshops had prompted new questions and ways of thinking that they found productive. Interestingly, though the participants were wary of creative enquiry and critical reflection, they paradoxically expressed a desire for such endeavours to support their work. A key issue then is overcoming any initial scepticism and convincing individuals to participate, a task that might require help from a group insider along with a clear articulation of the purpose, process and potential benefits.

Summary

- This chapter has examined the use of arts-based methods across the research life cycle from generating data to sharing findings. It has argued that arts-based methods offer a different set of affordances to traditional social science methods, which enable alternative, productive ways to ask and explore questions and engage audiences. In particular, arts-based methods encourage exploration, experimentation, play, improvisation and reflection.
- Research-creation utilises creative practices and media as the means of conducting research. Importantly, the creative process is an essential aspect of producing insight and knowledge, rather than just generating data that is subsequently analysed.
- While research-creation is generative, inventive and lively, it is not unstructured and *ad hoc* in its implementation. Rather it is a considered and planned endeavour that requires a structured research design that guides its implementation.

- Several different creative practices can be used in research-creation projects, including creative writing, painting, sculpture, media art, photography, dance, filmmaking, games, music and theatre production. Each has its own affordances that enable and mediate how questions are explored and the production of knowledge.
- These creative practices can also be used to transform the findings of traditional social science research into new registers to aid the communication of research to audiences. This can be particularly useful for presenting research to non-academic audiences.

Recommended Reading

Kara, H. (2015) *Creative Research Methods in the Social Sciences*. Policy Press, Bristol.
This book provides a general introduction to using arts-based methods for undertaking research.

Loveless, N. (2019) *How to Make Art at the End of the World: A Manifesto for Research-Creation*. Duke University Press, Durham NC.
This book makes the case for using research-creation and provides a critically reflexive analysis of the approach.

Lupton, D., and Watson, A. (2021) 'Towards more-than-human digital data studies: developing research-creation methods', *Qualitative Research*, 21(4): 463–80.
This paper details the use of research-creation in case studies related to the production of digital personal data.

Markham, A., and Pereira, G. (2019a) 'Analyzing public interventions through the lens of experimentalism: The case of the Museum of Random Memory', *Digital Creativity*, 30(4): 235–56.
This paper provides an analysis of several research-creation experiments related to mass datafication conducted through public exhibitions.

Truman, S. (2021) *Feminist Speculations and the Practice of Research-Creation: Writing Pedagogies and Intertextual Affects*. Routledge, London.
This book details the use of research-creation across a number of projects.

8
Participatory Methods

Overview

This chapter examines:

- participatory approaches for conducting research on digital life;
- citizen science approaches, including participatory sensing, the crowdsourcing of spatial data (known as 'volunteered geographic information') and hackathons;
- citizen engagement approaches, including public participation geographic information system (PPGIS), online participation tools and serious games;
- participatory action research, including counter-data actions, community and counter-archiving, and civic hacking; and
- challenges in conducting digitally mediated participatory research, including initiation and recruitment, retention and managing relationships, resourcing and time commitments, and scientific integrity.

Introduction

Most research projects are conceived and undertaken by a trained researcher, who makes all the operational decisions and performs the research tasks. If others are involved in a project, it is usually as research subjects and their role is passive. Participatory research, in contrast, seeks to involve citizens as active research actors in some way; for example, as data gatherers, analysts or interpreters. Rather than the research being *about* or *for* a community, it is conducted *with* or *by* community members. In this sense, participatory research challenges the usual epistemological framing and methodological norms in conducting research. As such, it is not universally welcomed and many professional researchers would be wary of adopting a participatory approach for fear of undermining the integrity and veracity of a study by involving 'amateur' actors. For advocates, however, citizen participation in research endeavours provides benefits that more than compensate for any shortcomings, such as widening the number of active data generators; ensuring the inclusion of grounded, lived expertise; and making sure that research serves the desires and ambitions of a local community. These advocates have developed a number of participatory approaches that vary in their form, the extent to which citizens have a say in the design and implementation of a project (e.g., they perform a designated role or control the design and implementation), what an initiative is seeking to achieve (e.g., a neutral contribution to scientific understanding or aiming to transform society) and the time horizon of engagement (e.g., short term, one-off events or long-term, sustained collaboration).

This chapter examines a number of these participatory approaches for understanding digital life and discusses how digital media and tools are transforming how participatory research is being conducted. In so doing, it details a number of models for including participants as researchers to study digital life rather than detailing specific methods used within such research, which are discussed in the other chapters in Part 2. It is divided into three main sections: citizen science (including participatory sensing, volunteered geographic information, and hackathons); civic engagement (including public participation GIS, online participatory tools and serious games); and participatory action research (including counter-data actions, community and counter-archiving, and civic hacking). In some accounts, these approaches are conflated and are also referred to using different terms, such as 'digital participatory research', 'community-based research', 'science 2.0', 'open science' and 'amateur science' (Eitzel et al., 2017). This chapter is designed to untangle and differentiate these approaches, teasing apart participatory research oriented to fundamental and discovery science, engaged and policy research, and community-oriented research. Nonetheless, overlaps remain between these concepts, and one should be mindful of varying, intersecting designations and interpretations. A final section considers cautionary issues in adopting a participatory approach.

Citizen Science

Citizen science is '[s]cientific work undertaken by members of the general public, often in collaboration with or under the direction of professional scientists and scientific institutions' (OED, 2022). While this definition is broadly applicable, a number of different understandings as to what constitutes citizen science exist across practitioners. These different conceptions can be grouped into two main strands: participatory citizen science and democratic citizen science. Participatory citizen science refers to the inclusion of the public as actors in research (e.g., as data collectors or analysts) under the supervision of professional researchers (Eitzel et al., 2017). Democratic citizen science repositions the public away from being directed actors to research collaborators or co-creators. As collaborators, citizens can inform the research design and contribute to decision-making, whereas as co-creators they are actively involved in most or all steps of the research process, including leadership roles (Bonney et al., 2009; Haklay, 2013). In some cases, citizens might collegially undertake their own research and communicate their findings without the involvement of professional researchers (Shirk et al., 2012).

Participatory citizen science has a relatively long history and can be traced back to the nineteenth century and the inclusion of amateur scientists in scientific research, especially as data recorders (Silvertown, 2009). Examples include amateur meteorologists observing and sharing measurements from local weather stations with national meteorological bodies, and hobbyist astronomers recording and sharing their observations of the night sky. These citizen scientists were useful because they were geographically distributed and embedded in place through time (which would be difficult and costly to co-ordinate using professional research staff) and they increased sampling rates. However, such citizen science was a minority activity because it was dependent on a fair degree of skill and knowledge, access to expensive specialised equipment (such as a good-quality telescope), as well as strong motivation for maintaining an ongoing commitment (Goodchild, 2007). These constraints have been nullified to a great degree in the digital age (Wynn, 2017). In general, citizens have a stronger knowledge base; can access necessary educational resources and affordable, good quality scientific equipment; and they can share data and analysis easily via the internet, often in automated ways (Silvertown, 2009). In particular, much larger pools of participants can be recruited globally through various social media platforms for little overhead, with their contributions crowdsourced.

Crowdsourcing is the collective, co-ordinated and voluntary generation of data, code and analysis across a common platform (Dodge and Kitchin, 2013). The common platform provides a necessary shared infrastructure and works towards ensuring consistency in data formats, data standards and metadata, and its volunteered nature makes the endeavour cost efficient. The platform can also keep volunteers motivated with respect to contributing data and ensuring data quality by providing instant access to uploaded data, analytic tools to make sense of them, and feedback on their performance in relation to other participants. Citizens might take an active role in generating data (e.g., recording their global positioning system (GPS) traces), classifying or annotating data (e.g., identifying features in images), or transforming or transcribing data (e.g., typed text from handwritten historical documents). A well-known crowdsourced knowledge resource is Wikipedia, in which encyclopaedia entries are written and edited by volunteer writers. Many scientific projects are now utilising crowdsourcing as a means to generate and analyse larger pools of data. The Zooniverse provides a portal to a range of 'people-powered research' projects from across the arts, social sciences, sciences and medicine, enabling citizens to contribute to them (see www.zooniverse.org). In some cases, participants do not need to contribute labour, but rather their spare computing power, downloading and installing software on their home computer that is then used to process scientific data or run simulations (Curtis, 2018). These digitally mediated citizen projects can be long-term initiatives, running for many years, or short-term endeavours addressing specific questions or issues, and can be quite localised (e.g., within a neighbourhood) or operate at a global scale (Hecker et al., 2018).

Here, we discuss three forms of participatory citizen science: *participatory sensing*, *volunteered geographic information* and *hackathons*. Unlike participatory action research initiatives, discussed later in this chapter, it is still largely the case that professional researchers set the agenda and design the research endeavours, even if citizens are consulted about their opinions. Nonetheless, in some cases, these endeavours might be practised as democratic citizen science wherein citizens have some level of ownership and control of the project. Such democratisation is seen as being important for ensuring that research tackles the issues important to citizens, encouraging citizens to use research as a means to address local to global issues and restoring public trust in science (Irwin, 1995; Strasser et al., 2019).

Participatory Sensing

Participatory sensing research aims to leverage sensing capacity through mobilising sensors that citizens possess (e.g., through the digital devices they own), as well as sensors supplied by researchers, to generate and share data for research (Burke et al., 2006; Reddy et al., 2010). Smartphones, smart watches and health-monitoring devices have a number of embedded sensors that measure aspects of their use and the world around them. For example, an iPhone includes a three-axis gyroscope; GPS chip; barometer/altitude sensor; accelerometer/motion sensor; sensors for proximity to screen surface, ambient light, moisture and temperature; along with touch ID, Face ID, a camera and microphone; and Wi-Fi and radio receivers, which can easily interface with other sensors via Bluetooth or wired connections (Costello, 2020; Kanhere, 2013). In addition, smartphones support the installation of specialist monitoring apps that can automate data generation and sharing. Citizens can also be recruited to deploy additional sensors in their habitats (e.g., small sensor arrays that are placed in a home or garden or added to a bike or rucksack) to measure environmental conditions or to capture some aspect of their health or behaviour (e.g., sports activity). In some cases, citizens might work together to undertake their own participatory sensing project to generate data and analysis about an issue that affects them (e.g., measuring noise or pollution levels in their neighbourhood or sharing their health data with their quantified-self community), sometimes in collaboration with professional researchers (Coulson et al., 2018a; Gabrys et al., 2016). Participatory sensing can provide a range of useful data (e.g., data readings, images, audio and location) to researchers, and since a very large percentage of the population possess sensing devices, they potentially offer an extensive, multi-modal sample for relatively little overhead (either in terms of cost or expertise to contribute) (Kanhere, 2013). Since the data are streamed back to a server in real-time, they can be automatically processed, aggregated, analysed and displayed via interactive dashboards and maps, made available to the community who produced them, and potentially enable immediate response (Coulson et al., 2018a). As such, participatory sensing enables timely, fine-grained (individual sensor) and scaled (city-wide, regional, national) views of unfolding phenomena that can be placed in historical context through time-series analysis.

Volunteered Geographic Information

Participatory sensing, along with Web 2.0 technologies, such as locative social media, web mapping platforms, and map mashups have enabled an enormous growth in what Goodchild (2007) termed 'volunteered geographic information' (VGI). VGI describes citizen crowdsourced spatial data such as GPS traces, additions and edits to base map data, and the tagging of place-based information on maps to collaborative projects (Sui et al., 2013). The best-known example of VGI is perhaps OpenStreetMap, an initiative to collectively produce a highly detailed map at the global scale that matches the content and quality of maps produced by national mapping agencies, but is free to use. OpenStreetMap has been produced by tens of thousands of people around the world who contribute content via uploading GPS traces or digitising features from aerial/satellite imagery and adding attribute and metadata (as well as contributions sourced from mapping agencies and logistics and platform companies). Similarly, individuals might augment Google Maps by adding place markers or uploading and overlaying datasets, or contribute information to online maps as part of a public planning consultation (e.g., suggesting the location of new bike stations) (Williams, 2016). In these cases, contributors are aware that they are contributing to a mapping initiative. In other instances, users are passively generating a VGI source of spatial data for researchers, who use a platform's API to gain access to georeferenced data, such as locative social media data (Graham et al., 2015). Given its scope and ease of access, VGI has become an important resource for academic researchers conducting spatial analysis, and also for citizens interested in making sense of their neighbourhoods.

Hackathons

While participatory sensing or VGI projects are often long-term endeavours, hackathons are usually short-term interventions. A hackathon involves bringing together community members over a short period – usually one to three days – to use their knowledge and skills to scope out, formulate and build a solution to a perceived real-world issue. Typically, the solution involves making sense of and utilising data, often involving the creation of an app to undertake analysis and guide action in an automated fashion. Hackathons are usually organised by public or civil society sector bodies, or by business organisations, often in collaboration with academics. Their themes are diverse, ranging from addressing social and environmental issues to creating new commercial products (Irani, 2015). Participants are given access to datasets, mentoring and software and hardware, and are expected to research and develop a project idea, build and test a prototype, and formulate a summary of the approach taken and its potential value (Perng et al., 2018). Those taking part are divided into teams who compete to create workable solutions to real-world problems, with a judging panel deciding on the most effective or promising solution. A number of academic projects have used hackathons to conduct participatory research. For example, at a civic hackathon in Los Angeles, organised by academics and local stakeholders, city residents were invited to analyse police-involved homicide data, create data visualisations and find ways to generate new data by sourcing deaths absent from official sources (Currie et al., 2016). DiSalvo and Anderson (2016) used a twenty-four-hour hackathon to conduct a design experiment and to prototype services for an in-progress civic IoT system, inviting participants to create a mapping application to monitor sensors across a city. A number of other smart city hackathons have been organised, with participants invited to consider how various forms of real-time and administrative data might be leveraged to more effectively deliver city services or to build devices to solve urban problems (Perng et al., 2018).

Civic Engagement

Citizen science focuses mainly on using participatory approaches to tackle fundamental and discovery research, although it may also be applied in orientation. Civic engagement forms of participatory research are centrally focused on the production of engaged and policy research. Such civic engagement research might be conducted by academics interested in contributing to how society is organised and operates, as well as by government (at various levels from local to national to supranational) and civil society organisations seeking citizen input and feedback on existing and potential programmes and policies. Increasingly, this form of research is mediated by various forms of *civic tech*, which enable citizens to express their views and opinions and to contribute to unfolding public debate about the delivery of services and future plans. Here, we discuss three forms of digitally mediated civic engagement research: *PPGIS*, *online participatory tools* and *serious games*.

Public Participation Geographic Information Systems

Geographic information systems (GISs) are software platforms for mapping and managing spatial data, and are a core technology for planning and managing the assets of a locale. PPGISs seek to involve members of the public in the practices of developing and using a GIS. From the late 1990s, PPGIS has been promoted as an approach for engaging with local communities to address issues in their neighbourhoods and territories and to practise collaborative spatial planning regarding future developments (Elwood and Ghose, 2001). At the same time, PPGIS seek to make 'spatial decision-making tools available and accessible to all those with a stake in official decisions' through GIS skills transfer from academic researchers to citizens as part of the engagement (Schroeder, 1996; cited in Williams, 2016: 171). PPGIS practitioners, who are often academics committed to undertaking engaged research, utilise GISs to present data and scenarios to communities, while also encouraging and facilitating citizens to add their own generated data and undertake their own analysis and scenario building, and to formulate potential policy responses and decision-making (Sieber, 2006). PPGISs thus provide insights into how communities understand their locales as well as the social, economic and environmental issues that they perceive as challenges and what they view as viable responses, while enabling participants to take an active collaborative role in policy and place making. At the same time, community members learn a new set of skills, such as research design, data literacy and mapping skills that can be re-used in their future activism and advocacy work (Williams, 2016). In this sense, PPGISs are promoted as being an empowering research methodology, albeit one that often needs a specialist intermediary given the level of technical literacy required to use a GIS effectively (Hein et al., 2008). While PPGISs initially used standalone, desktop GISs, it is now more commonly practised online using web-based and open source mapping and spatial data generation platforms, widening the potential base of collaborators and reducing operating costs (Rzeszewski and Kotus, 2019).

Online Participatory Tools

Online participatory tools (OPTs) provide a means of consulting target populations about an issue, using the resultant views to inform a programme, policy or plan.

Until relatively recently, populations were surveyed about their views and opinions using paper-based questionnaires, in-person focus groups, town hall meetings and requests for written submissions. The internet has enabled the adoption of digital platforms that support similar kinds of information gathering, but in a form that facilitates diverse channels of engagement and data collection (Gordon and Mihailidis, 2016). This could involve email and social media interactions, but is increasingly performed through specialist OPT platforms such as MySideWalk, PlaceSpeak, CitySourced, Crowdbrite and Decidem (Afzalan et al., 2017). In some contexts, such as urban and regional planning, specialist platforms that provide domain specific functionality (such as viewing 3D city models) may be used to support consultative and participatory planning (Anttiroiko, 2021). These platforms are seen to add value to the consultative process by encouraging more people to take an active role in shaping government and civic work relating to their communities, and in part help democratise decision-making. Platforms can be used by diverse communities at a time and place of the participant's choosing. They can allow anonymous engagement, encourage peer-to-peer interactions and consensus building, and facilitate access to key materials and resources and enable social learning (Afzalan et al., 2017). And because the data stream seamlessly into a data architecture, they can be easily analysed, including in a real-time fashion that allows for results to be fed back into an on-going conversation. These tools can be used and repurposed by researchers to engage with communities, or the data from OPTs can provide researchers with detailed views about an issue. For example, it is possible to obtain publicly available information on participatory processes, assemblies, proposals, comments and user interactions enacted in Decidim through its API or by downloading its CSV data files (Chamorro-Padial et al., 2023), and to use these to research its use in debates on smart city deployments (Smith and Martin, 2021).

Serious Games

An alternative means of engaging citizens and gaining insights into a community's views on a particular issue is to have them play what are termed 'serious games'. These are games designed to elicit responses to – and prompt players to be reflexive about – various scenarios, while also being entertaining (Curtis, 2018). In other words, through their game play, researchers can observe players' opinions and behaviour choices with respect to an issue, such as data ethics, local development plans or climate change. To be effective, games seek to mimic or simulate real world complexities, while gamifying how players navigate and make decisions that affect outcomes (Gugerell et al., 2019). Gamification is thought to increase engagement, motivation and retention of players and thus provide a strong stream of high-utility data. An example relating to urban planning was Community PlanIt, a public dialogue game designed to allow community members to consider and suggest the future planning of their neighbourhoods (Gordon and Walter, 2016). Each running of the game attracted more than 1,000 participants and enabled a form of mass collaborative planning. In some cases, games might also be designed to educate and nudge players into thinking and acting about an issue in a different way. The iAdapt game aims to 'empower young people to understand and engage with the complexities, uncertainties and processes of climate adaptation planning' by presenting them with scientifically validated predictions and examples of adaptive interventions, and asking them to make decisions that have political, social and economic outcomes, as well as environmental ones (Hugel and Davies, 2022: 306). The Dérive app, created by architect Eduardo Cachucho, recreates the dérive task devised by Guy Debord in the 1950s to prompt people to explore a city in new ways (Coleman, 2016). In this case, the Dérive app is made up of a deck of sixty-four cards that provide an instruction for moving and interacting with an environment in ways that deviate from expected routes and behaviours. In other cases, game-like elements are embedded into apps to try to shift behaviours. For example, a number of the research projects funded by the European Innovation Partnership for Smart Cities and Communities have sought to build apps that use gaming features such as quizzes, competitions, challenges and rewards to nudge actions (e.g., reducing energy consumption) (Cardullo and Kitchin, 2019b).

Participatory Action Research

Kindon et al. (2007) define participatory action research (PAR) as:

> a collaborative process of research, education, and action explicitly oriented toward social change. PAR involves academic researchers (usually full-time and paid) and non-academic co-researchers and participants (usually part-time on the project and not paid) working together to examine a problematic situation in order to change it for the better on participants' own terms.

What differentiates PAR from citizen science (including democratic forms of citizen science) is the notion that PAR is undertaken on the participants' own terms. While they might be working with professional researchers – who might initiate a project and provide resourcing – it is the community members taking part in PAR projects who define the focus and purpose of the research and guide the research design and activities. The public, then, takes an active part in all aspects of the research from its framing to its implementation and its dissemination. The research is co-designed and co-produced, guided by the community's agenda. Importantly, PAR approaches do not simply study a phenomena, but also seek to transform it: they are action-oriented and interventionist, aiming to tackle an issue and enact change. Here, we discuss three digitally oriented versions of PAR: *counter-data actions, community and counter-archiving* and *civic hacking*.

Counter-data Actions

The aim of data activism is to identify, challenge and reconfigure the data relations and data power that create and perpetuate inequalities and discriminate against different communities (Milan and van der Velden, 2016). Data activist research seeks to support such aims, working with communities to resist dominant data regimes, and to generate and use data on their terms to demand and produce change (Gutiérrez, 2018). As a form of PAR, data activist research enacts what Currie et al. (2016) term counter-data actions, which might involve producing alternative data analysis, data-informed narratives or policy proposals; or improving the data literacy of local citizens to understand how data are being used to shape their lives. The open data movement has been a key enabler of data activism by providing access to government data, which the community can then use in their counter-data actions (Davies et al., 2019). In other cases, the community might generate its own data via participatory sensing or surveys. In Detroit, academics from local universities have worked with community organisations, such as the Detroit Digital Justice Coalition (DDJC) and Detroit Community Technology Project (DCTP), to co-create a series of counter-data actions, including running workshops to build community-owned internet infrastructure, improve data literacy and inform residents of data rights. They have also co-run projects, including those focused on mapping neighbourhoods at risk of eviction and foreclosure (DCTP, n.d.; DDJC, n.d.; Petty et al., 2016; Urban Praxis, 2017). In Canada, First Nations groups have successfully used counter-data actions to assert their land ownership claims (Kidd, 2019). In Argentina, the #NiUnaMenos ('Not One Woman Less') movement has produced the *Índice nacional de violencia machista* ('National Index of Male Violence') to document gender-based abuse to inform public debate and policy interventions (Chenou and Cepeda-Másmela, 2019). In Atlanta, Black housing activists analysed official datasets, as well as creating their own, to campaign for housing rights and affordable housing (Meng and DiSalvo, 2018: 6). And in South Africa, community organisations have examined the datafication of informal settlements, created counter-narratives and sought to produce their own datasets (Cinnamon, 2020). In each case, researchers worked closely with communities to help them use scholarship to achieve their social and political aims.

Community and Counter-archiving

Community run and focused archives seek to provide a more locally focused curation of materials that are meaningful to a community, foster the collective memories of a community's shared pasts and reveal history from the bottom-up (Cifor et al., 2018). They are often run by volunteers from the community, aided by academics, professional archivists and local historians. They might be constituted as charities, seek funding from foundations or government grants, have some professional staff and have formal governance arrangements such as management and advisory boards. Typically, community archives provide a collection of materials that complement and/or act as a counterpoint to the authority of state archives by curating a more diverse evidence base relating to ordinary and marginalised lives rather than those in power (Burgum, 2022; Caswell et al., 2017). Such archives might relate to a specific place (such as a neighbourhood) or identity group (such as people of colour or disabled people), or to a particular event of local interest (or a mixture of all three). In many cases, community archives might act as counter-archiving endeavours, designed to unsettle and challenge mainstream histories and address silences and misrepresentations (Burgum, 2022). In some cases, counter-archiving seeks to provide an alternative archive of the same archival material, or to make material available that is held in relatively inaccessible infrastructures. For example, some researchers have sought to scrape platforms such as Facebook, Twitter/X or Airbnb to produce archives of data that can be used by other researchers (Ben-David, 2020; Inside Airbnb, n.d.; Zook and Poorthuis, 2015). Likewise, they might scrape government databases that have been published in formats that limit their use and republish the data in a more usable form, such as Brown's (2021) scraping of judgements in asylum seeker cases in Ireland. Counter-archiving can also challenge how archives are produced and run, having a different ethos and procedures from formal archives. For example, the archives created by the Occupy Movement utilised a non-hierarchical approach to archiving in which there was no centralised control over records, mirroring how the wider movement operated (Erde, 2014). They can also act as educational resources, with groups such as the Activist Archivists in New York and the Resistance Project in London running courses to teach community members how to create and maintain archives (Burgum, 2022; Erde, 2014). Community archives are a potentially very useful source of data for researching digital life, and a productive means of conducting participatory research on collective memory making, data infrastructures and archiving.

Civic Hacking

Rather than concentrating on data, civic hacking focuses on analytics and software, often producing community developed apps (sometimes termed 'civic media') that seek to address societal issues from their perspective and serve their interests (Schrock, 2016). Unlike hackathons, civic hacking initiatives usually last months rather than being one-off events, and the agenda is set by the community rather than researchers (Schrock, 2018). A form of civic hacking is the open source movement, in which many individuals work collectively to produce free and open software, including operating systems (e.g., Linux), platforms (e.g., Mastodon) and apps (e.g., Libra office suite). In these cases, those working on the initiative are usually geographically dispersed, collaborating across the internet. Civic hacking can also be applied to specific issues, such as projects that collate and present data on gun violence, mass shootings and police-involved homicides in the United States (e.g., Gun Violence Archive, KilledBy-Police, Fatal Encounters; Currie et al., 2016); apply data science to try to improve the lives of people of colour (e.g., Data for Black Lives; https://d4bl.org/); or address local issues. An example of the latter are Code for America meetups, in which citizens in a city gather regularly (usually once a month) to develop apps that seek to solve issues of concern, either using open municipal data or generating their own (Schrock, 2016). Code for America also runs an internship programme in which students with specialist skills and knowledge are assigned to work with a community stakeholder to help co-develop an app. Such placements can be used by researchers as a means of examining civic hacking itself. For example, Sung-Yueh Perng worked as an embedded researcher on a Code for Ireland project to develop an app to aid immigrants applying for work visas in Dublin (Perng and Kitchin, 2018). In some cases, civic hacking is organised or sponsored by state bodies, co-designing and co-developing apps with citizens (e.g., some of the projects initiated by the New Urban Mechanics unit of the City of Boston; Crawford and Walters, 2013). Other forms of civic hacking have focused on infrastructure and hardware; for example, initiatives that seek to build community-owned and run internet infrastructure (Cardullo, 2017; Powell, 2008), or FabLabs in which citizens can build their own or repair devices (Walter-Herrmann and Buching, 2013).

Challenges in Conducting Digitally Mediated Participatory Research

While conducting participatory research with communities can be very productive and rewarding, there are a number of issues that make its undertaking a challenge. These issues are instrumental, technical, social and ethical in nature, and require careful reflection and planning. It is fair to say that participatory research involves commitments, obligations and responsibilities that extend beyond the usual researcher-participant relations in research, and it should not be attempted lightly. That said, it is incredibly rewarding, insightful and impactful if researchers are willing to invest in the process and relationships required.

Initiation and Recruitment

Participatory research is often initiated by a researcher interested in working with a community to understand a particular issue. Yet without a commitment by a community to participate, the project cannot proceed. A relationship founded on trust must be developed for a collaborative working relationship to be formed, especially for projects involving co-creation and co-development (Coulson et al., 2018b). This might take some time and involve a series of social meetings or collaboration on other initiatives to build confidence in progressing with a partnership. For both short-term projects (such as hackathons) and longer-term projects that require shallower relations (such as some citizen science projects), there is the challenge of recruitment and persuading people to sign-up and take an active role. Recruitment can be undertaken through social media, general public appeals, stakeholder groups and panels, and referral sampling.

Retention and Managing Relationships

Once community members are enrolled into a project, the challenge is to retain their on-going involvement. It is widely reported that while citizen science projects might have thousands of registered participants, only a small percentage contribute regularly (Curtis, 2018). Similarly, on more intimate, local projects, there is often a tailing-off of involvement over time as participants tire and lose interest. It is important then to consider mechanisms and incentives to maintain involvement, such as competitions to stoke motivation, financial rewards, feedback on performance and access to the data produced (Restuccia et al., 2016). An important component of retention is maintaining good working relationships. This is not always easy as those participating have different expectations regarding leadership, decision-making and workloads, as well as varying personalities and styles of interacting with others (Philips and Kara, 2021). In co-creation projects, it is often difficult for researchers to cede control of the objectives and research design, especially if it is moving the initiative away from their core motivations and interests. For community members it is frustrating if they feel that their views and opinions are being ignored. Building consensus on how best to proceed can take time and energy and might lead to compromised outcomes that satisfy no one. Any long-term research relationship then needs active management if it is going to survive and thrive.

Resourcing and Time Commitments

All research projects require adequate resourcing in terms of equipment, consumables, expenses, personnel and time. Long-term projects must be able to sustain the necessary resourcing over an extended period. Researchers and community members need to be able to spend adequate time working on the initiative. Maintaining commitments is difficult given competing demands on resourcing and time, and the need to source on-going finance when research funding is typically for a fixed period rather than being multi-annual and non-cyclical. There are several ways in which long-term projects seek to make themselves financially sustainable, though all of them, with the exception of core government funding, have issues that reduce their reliability (see Kitchin et al., 2015 for a discussion of several funding models).

Scientific Integrity and Ethics

A number of commentators have questioned the data quality and representativeness of participatory projects. There is a concern that community members are amateur scientists that are diversely skilled and motivated, are potentially using scientific equipment of differing quality or have been supplied with low-cost equipment with lower thresholds of accuracy, meaning that data quality is also potentially highly variable, as is ancillary data such as metadata (Carr, 2007; Kanhere, 2013). In projects involving interpretation, participants can also have varying levels of data and statistical literacy (Rzeszewski and Kotus, 2019). In addition, those actively participating in projects are small in number and are rarely diverse enough to be representative of the wider population (Crutcher and Zook, 2009). For example, those attending hackathons are usually men aged in their twenties who work in the tech sector (Perng et al., 2018). Of Wikipedia contributors, 0.003 per cent produce two-thirds of the content, with the majority of volunteers producing very little (Haklay, 2018). Similarly, the vast bulk of OpenStreetMap data is generated by a small subsection of contributors (Dodge and Kitchin, 2013). Those taking part in participatory projects might be misplaced in their ambition, or their relevant knowledge may be limited. For example, those attending hackathons are often motivated by socialising, networking and learning new skills, rather than tackling a community issue, and they possess little domain knowledge about the issue for which they are developing solutions (Perng et al., 2018). In some cases, such as participatory sensing and the use of OPTs, citizens might be cautious about revealing their identity (through device identification) or sharing their views because they are worried about potential organisational and social threats that might arise, and so do not take part as a result (Afzalan et al., 2017). Potential participants might also be concerned about being exploited by researchers, who they may perceive as serving their own interests rather than those of the community, and be cautious about fully engaging or sharing experiences and knowledge. Indeed, there are a number of ethical issues in working closely with communities in terms of responsibilities and obligations to do no harm (see **Chapter 4**). Collectively, these issues mean it can be difficult to establish levels of data quality and degrees of reliability across a dataset, reducing their trustworthiness in use. For Carr (2007), this means that participatory research is best employed to check and edit datasets to improve them, rather than create them. Others counter that the participatory process is just as important, or more so, than the product because it leaves a lasting trace in terms of social learning and outcomes for those that take part and their communities (DeLyser and Sui, 2014).

Summary

- Participatory approaches to research are those in which citizens are not simply a data source or the recipients of research outcomes, but are rather active actors within the research process. In other words, a project is undertaken with or by community members to some degree (as data generators, analysts, interpreters or leaders).
- Participatory research can be practised in a number of ways, with a range of digital tools mediating how the research is conducted. These practices include various forms of citizen science, civic engagement and participatory action research.
- The chapter discussed a number of these forms and their application. None are straightforward to implement because they involve negotiation, collaboration and an investment of time and resources. They have significant benefits however, not just in relation to extending the scope and depth of knowledge of studies but also in providing research of direct benefit to communities.
- A number of challenges to conducting digitally mediated participatory research exist, including recruiting participants and maintaining their involvement, resourcing and managing the process, and ensuring that the quality of research undertaken by participants is of sufficient integrity. These can be addressed through a strong research design and active project management.

Recommended Reading

Curtis, V. (2018) *Online Citizen Science and the Widening of Academia: Distributed Engagement with Research and Knowledge Production*. Palgrave Macmillan, Cham.
Provides an overview of conducting citizen science online with a discussion of case studies.

Gordon, E., and Mihailidis, P. (eds) (2016) *Civic Media: Technology, Design and Practice*. MIT Press, Cambridge, MA.
A wide-ranging collection of essays that discuss different approaches to creating social technologies with citizens.

Hecker, S., Haklay, M., Bowser, A., Makuch, Z., Vogel, J., and Bonn, A. (eds) (2018) *Citizen Science: Innovation in Open Science, Society and Policy*. UCL Press, London.
A state-of-the-art overview of the practices of citizen science and issues in its implementation.

Sui, D.Z., Elwood, S., and Goodchild, M.F. (eds) (2013) *Crowdsourcing Geographic Knowledge: Volunteered Geographic Information (VGI) in Theory and Practice*. Springer, Berlin.
A comprehensive overview of VGI and its implications for geographic and social research.

Wynn, J. (2017) *Citizen Science in the Digital Age: Rhetoric, Science and Public Engagement*. University of Alabama Press, Tuscaloosa, AL.
Provides critical analysis and reflection on the objectives and practices of citizen science mediated by digital technologies.

9
Historical Methods

Overview

Chapter 9 examines:

- historical research about digital technologies and digital life;
- how the digital is transforming historiography (i.e., the epistemological and methodological practices of conducting historical research);
- the creation of digital archives and data infrastructures and the sourcing of digital data;
- the production of primary historical data through oral interviews, discovering and collating materials, and examining or surveying artefacts and sites;
- undertaking historical analysis using digital tools and techniques; and
- issues in digital history research, including access, loss of analogue sources, data quality and provenance, and epistemological concerns.

Introduction

The digital era is relatively recent, yet the transformation in technologies and their effects on everyday life has been swift and deep. There is much to be gained from a historical analysis of the unfolding of digital life that traces out the evolutions in digital technologies, systems and infrastructures and how these have altered cultural, social, economic and political relations. At the same time, digitality has transformed historiography; that is, the study and methodologies of history making (Galgano et al., 2008; Graham et al., 2015). The digitisation of analogue records and artefacts, and the creation of online digital archives and repositories, has opened up a rich array of data sources to a wider research constituency. In addition, digital technologies and systems have created vast quantities of born-digital data that can be used as historical source material. Novel digital tools and methods have enabled new ways of asking about and making sense of the past, including the recent past.

This chapter opens with a brief overview of historical analyses of the digital. The remainder details how these histories are being undertaken and how the digital has transformed historiography. The discussion is divided into three main subsections: sourcing historical data; producing historical data; and undertaking historical analysis. While the focus is principally on researching the histories of digital life, it also serves as a guide to how history, heritage and memory studies research are being conducted in the digital era. Indeed, as Graham et al. (2015: 46) note, one does 'not have to be a self-declared Digital Historian [an advocate of computational approaches to historical research] to be a digital historian. Indeed, almost all historians are digital today'. The internet is an indispensable tool for historical research, enabling search and discovery, accessing archives and literature, sharing information and analysis via websites and blogs, and discussing issues on social media. The drafting and editing of historical narrative is undertaken predominately using word processing software, and a range of digital tools are used for data management and analysis. In other words, conducting digitally mediated historical research is no longer a choice, but an everyday practice that is difficult to avoid (Brügger, 2018).

Histories of the Digital

Most analyses of digital life are prefaced with some brief historical analysis of the phenomena under examination as a means of framing a contemporary study. This usually consists of a short, partial account of the genesis and evolution of a digital technology and its evolving effects on a particular activity or community. For others, this historical development is the key focus of analysis, seeking to map out in detail the various histories of the digital. The temporal scope of this work generally spans the 1930s to the present but can extend back to the nineteenth century and tracing out of the pre-cursor developments of the digital age. For example, the genesis of the digital computer is often traced back to the analytical machine of Babbage and Lovelace; programming to the work of human computers who performed analogue calculations; and digital network infrastructure to the development of the telegraph (Abbate, 1999; Haigh, 2019). Early mainframe computers, the internet (infrastructure and services) and personal computing have received the most attention, given their centrality to the digital revolution (see Abbate, 1999; Balbi and Magaudda, 2018; Ceruzzi, 1998). There have also been a number of studies detailing web histories, in part because there have been concerted efforts since the 1990s to archive webpages, which provides a wealth of source material (Brügger and Milligan, 2019; Brügger and Schroeder, 2017).

These studies have been complemented by a smattering of historical work focused on particular practices, domains and businesses, such as the software industry (Campbell-Kelly, 2003), the development of digital currencies (Mullan, 2016), public administration (Agar, 2003), digital games (Williams, 2017), digital music cultures (Collins et al., 2013), blogging (Highfield, 2017), advertising (Crain, 2019), memes (McGrath, 2019), pornography (Paasonen, 2019), the work of individual companies or systems (Bashe et al., 1985; Redmond and Smith, 2000) and issues such as the role of women in the development of the computer industry (Abbate, 2012). This work is supported by dedicated book series, such as MIT Press's *History of Computing* series, as well as specialised academic journals (e.g., *Annals of the History of Computing*; *Internet Histories*), and is complemented by the work of a number of museums (e.g., the National Museum of Computing in the United Kingdom, and the Computer Museum of America). Despite the work underway, there remain large gaps in the histories of the digital, in particular relating to contexts beyond Anglo-America (e.g., Africa, Asia, Latin America, Eastern Europe), and the development, adoption and effects of digital technologies and infrastructures within particular domains (e.g., households, work, consumption, mobility and administration) (Goggin and McLelland, 2017). More recent technologies, such as mobile and smartphones, have also received relatively little concentrated attention to date.

It is also fair to say that depending on disciplinary background, the focus and framing of the historical analysis undertaken varies somewhat in character. For instance, scholars within the discipline of history are likely to focus on key events, individual biographies and technological advances. In comparison, scholars within media and communication studies, science and technology studies, and other social sciences are more likely to situate their analysis with broader political-economic contexts (Haigh, 2019), seek to identify trends and patterns that are generalisable beyond particular cases (Sewell, 2005) and employ their own conceptual and methodological approaches such as media archaeology (Huhtamo and Parikka, 2011). Whereas historians tend to leave their theory implicit, social scientists are more likely to use their historical analysis to develop and test theory (Pollitt, 2008). As discussed below, some scholars have retained interpretative approaches to historical analysis, whereas others have embraced new epistemologies. An example of the latter is the digital humanities, which favours computational approaches including the use of visual analytics, mapping, statistical analysis and modelling. Indeed, a part of charting the history of the digital is considering how the digital has transformed historiography – the epistemological and methodological practices of conducting historical research – over time, as the next section examines in more depth.

Digitally Mediated History

Digital technologies and digitally mediated techniques have profoundly altered the practices of history-making from the 1960s onwards, transforming how historical data are retained and shared, how data about the past are produced and how historical analysis is undertaken.

Sourcing Historical Data

Researching the past, especially that beyond living memory, is heavily reliant on the ability to source relevant materials (e.g., texts, maps, pictures, objects, artefacts) produced in the period and place of interest. Archives are a means of accessing such materials and are a key resource for historians. Archives are formal, institutionalised collections of curated materials that have been designated as worthy of being preserved for future generations (e.g., official records, legal documents, letters and diaries of notable figures, books and journals) (Bowker, 2005). Materials within archives are formally organised and catalogued, and there are governance arrangements with respect to preservation and access (Lauriault et al., 2007). There is a long history of archives being created and maintained by a range of actors, such as the state, businesses, philanthropic organisations, universities and civic organisations. The reason for preserving records varies across these actors, and accessing an archive is not necessarily straightforward depending on the extent to which the material is guarded. While the archives of state bodies have generally been quite open to public access, they might still require permission to enter, and many sensitive records might be restricted to particular groups. Private archives, such as those maintained by companies or family estates, are often closed except to a small number of approved researchers. Even with access rights, individuals need to spend time at an analogue archive's location to sift and search through the material, which requires specialist knowledge to navigate the archive and evaluate what is found.

Archives have been transformed by the application of digital technologies, particularly post-millennium. Initially, converting catalogues from card indexes to digital databases enabled a malleability in (re)organising metadata ontologies. It also represented a step-change in the speed and forms of search (allowing it to be performed in new ways through combination and exclusion of terms), permitting new avenues of exploration (Berry, 2017). Subsequently, the digitisation of millions of archival records and artefacts and their associated metadata, along with the construction of digital archival infrastructure, has enabled rapid retrieval of digital copies of source information (Bowker, 2005). Importantly, connecting these digital archives to the internet has allowed them to reach a much wider constituency of users who do not need to travel to the archive's site to view records. Moreover, the material is much easier to examine and make sense of due to the provision of powerful and easy to use curation, search and analysis tools. In addition, the provision of metadata makes it possible to link together digital records from across archives, allowing further insights to be made. In other words, the remaking of archives as digital resources has massively enhanced the reach and utility of archives and made significantly more records available for analysis (Galgano et al., 2008). Consequently, there has been major investment in building digital archives, as well as repositories that might host several archival collections, despite the fact that they are relatively expensive and challenging to construct and maintain (Borgman, 2007). This investment has been complemented by the open data movement, which has led to previously closed datasets held by public bodies being made freely available for re-use (Kitchin, 2014a).

Moreover, the internet itself is often viewed as a *de facto* archive of searchable information and a valuable source for contemporary research concerning the recent past, as well as an important resource for future historians. After all, the internet consists of hundreds of platforms, millions of apps and billions of webpages. Importantly, data from these sources form the largest collection of human testimonies ever recorded and concern the full spectrum of society and activities, including those who were previously rarely captured in traditional archives (Milligan, 2019; Nanni, 2019). Consequently, Web History has developed as a vibrant sub-field, on the one hand composed of studies focused on the historical development of internet activities, and on the other, using internet content to construct histories related to that content (Brügger, 2018); or, as Schafer and Thierry (2019: 60) put it, studies of 'the Web *in* context and the Web *as* context'. The literature often uses the terms 'internet' and 'the Web' interchangeably, though the former concerns all networked infrastructure, domains and services, and the latter typically refers to the World Wide Web and hyperlinked webpages. One of the key observations of Web historians is that while the Web is a valuable resource, it is also a fragile and unstable one. For example, webpages contain a wealth of freely accessible information about individuals, organisations and society more generally, but their lifespan is often short – 50 per cent of webpages are unrecognisable or gone within a year (Brügger, 2018). Indeed, whereas stone carvings might last several thousand years, and paper several hundred years, digital data are highly vulnerable, easily deleted or overwritten, stored on media that degrades quickly and rapidly becomes obsolete (Kitchin, 2021; Manoff, 2010). As such, digital data are more difficult to preserve as they need active maintenance and migration across media and platforms (Nanni, 2019).

The Web thus erases and forgets itself unless actively recorded. In response, a number of initiatives have sought to create Web archives that preserve web pages at particular points in time (e.g., the Internet Archive established in 1996). Unlike traditional archives that are actively curated, the artefacts in Web archives are created by the archival process itself, with the archive assembled by Web crawling bots that capture all the content and links encountered (Brügger and Milligan, 2019). The result is massive collections of material – for example, by 2016, the Internet Archive held copies of 273 billion webpages from 361 million sites, comprising 510 billion individual time-stamped digital objects (Webster, 2019). These Web archives are key sites for those researching the recent past, especially given the impact of the internet on society. As Milligan (2019: 3) notes, '[o]ne cannot write most histories of the 1990s or later without reference to web archives, or at the very least to do so would be to neglect a major medium of the period'. To aid this work, a number of tools for extracting information from these enormous archives have been produced (e.g., ArchiveSpark and the Archives Unleashed Toolkit). Given its instability, when using the web as a source it is important to create a personal archive of material (e.g., screen captures, or adding a webpage to the Internet Archive) to ensure that the evidence base can be re-accessed if required.

In addition to digital and web archives are data infrastructures used by enterprises to handle, store and make sense of the data generated in digital systems. Data infrastructures are essential resources across state bodies, companies and scientific endeavours for managing and extracting value from born-digital data. Contemporary public administration and commercial enterprise, which are highly data-driven in nature, could not function without large-scale data infrastructures capable of handling big data; that is, data that are generated in real time, are indexical in granularity (linked to individual people, objects, locations, transactions) and are exhaustive to a system (data are generated related to every single element, not a sample of them) (Kitchin, 2014a). Such data infrastructures are not intended to be digital archives in a traditional sense (there is no preservation plan to hold the data for future generations), though they nearly all perform that role, at least in the short-to-medium term; rather they are essential for managing present, and planning future, operations.

Nonetheless, data infrastructures hold significant amounts of fine-grained, extensive, longitudinal datasets that enable very detailed time-series analysis and are thus of potential interest for conducting historical analysis of events and trends that have unfolded in the recent past (especially since the millennium when such systems started to become more common). In particular, social media data is a significant reservoir of detailed historical data on the opinions, activities and memories of millions of people and enterprises (Jacobsen and Beer, 2021). The data infrastructures of data brokers similarly hold a massive amount of fine-grained personal and commercial information (Zuboff, 2019). For example, in 2019 Acxiom was thought to hold offline, online and mobile related data for 2.5 billion addressable consumers globally concerning their demographic profile and activities, including detailed consumption patterns (Melendez and Pasternack, 2019). However, both state and commercial data infrastructures are largely black-boxed enterprises, with very limited access for researchers. The closed nature of these infrastructures has been tackled through scraping and counter-archiving initiatives (Ben-David, 2020), though such practices raise ethical questions (see **Chapter 4**). Consequently, while the digital era is creating an enormous volume of data of potential historical interest, with more data openly available than ever before, access remains an issue in many cases.

Producing Historical Data

As well as sourcing data from archives, primary data about the past can be generated by researchers through conducting oral history interviews, discovering and collating artefacts, or examining or surveying material artefacts and sites. In each case, the application of digital technologies has had a significant impact on how and what data are generated and the insights that can be extracted.

Oral Histories

There is an extensive legacy of oral history and traditions in Indigenous communities for recording and passing on communal histories across generations. In Western traditions, the written document, and later photography, formed the key historical sources. It was only in the second half of the twentieth century that oral history emerged in the West as a legitimate means of recording and sharing the past. While still using documentary evidence for context, oral histories prioritise personal testimonies as a way of gathering information about a past that is within living memory (Ritchie, 2015). In part, this has enabled the exploration of issues that have been absent from the documentary record (such as how events shaped personal perceptions and experiences), and the gathering of information from populations that were minimally included in official records (such as Indigenous, immigrant and socially deprived communities). By collecting a number of personal testimonies, it becomes possible to construct 'a collective biography of a community, peopled by "real" individuals set within a context and environment'; a 'grounded history' rooted in personal experience and observation (Nyhan et al., 2015: 78). At the same time, oral history does not shy away from differences in how the past is remembered and interpreted by participants, but rather seeks to understand and account for these variances (Nylan and Flinn, 2016). Data generation consists of one-off, extended interviews or a series of interviews conducted over days or months, usually taking the form of an unstructured conversation (Ritchie, 2015).

Partly responsible for the initial growth in oral history was the development of portable microphones and tape recorders (Boyd and Larson, 2014). This was followed by tape cassettes and video recorders, which enabled the audio and visual recording of interviews. However, these materials were costly to store and to curate, and time intensive to listen to and discover useful information. Often recordings were disposed of after transcription, in the process deleting a large amount of potentially useful context such as the way something was said, pauses, laughter or tears (Boyd and Larson, 2014). The digital era has transformed the recording, archiving and analysis of oral history. Digital recorders are affordable and highly portable, and recordings can be conducted via high quality video links, supplemented by real-time transcription. Digital tools can help clean up recordings and improve sound quality. Digital recordings can be easily archived and shared across the internet, enabling users to engage with the original audio-visual content rather than transcriptions. Automatic speech recognition tools, such as Open AI's Whisper (https://openai.com/research/whisper), can be used to auto-transcribe audio recordings. Content management systems enable discovery, linking textual searches of transcripts to a correlating moment in an audio or video recording (e.g., Oral History Metadata Synchronizer) (Boyd and Larson, 2014). Additional contextual material can be easily associated with the recordings, along with detailed metadata (Schneider, 2014).

Several studies have used an oral history approach to research the development of computing, the internet and digital life, interviewing key pioneers, those working within companies and organisations, and critical commentators, theorists and artists (e.g., Anderson and Rosenfeld, 1998; Brügger and Goggin, 2022; Cullinane, 2015; Lovink, 2002; Nyhan and Flinn, 2016). The result is a rich, grounded analysis of digital innovation and adoption. Such studies, and oral history more generally, are not without their issues, however. Individuals can be unreliable witnesses, either unintentionally through weak memory, or deliberately through false testimony. The active role of the researcher influences the material generated through decisions about who is interviewed and what questions are asked, the dialogic and unfolding nature of conversation means some topics become well covered while others are skirted, and interpersonal relations and degrees of trust shape what might be disclosed (Nyhan and Flinn, 2016). Care, therefore, must be exercised in the choices and practices made in undertaking oral history research.

New Capture Technologies

A key means by which digital technologies have impacted historical research is through the provision of new kinds of evidence. A range of digital techniques, such as digital photography and processing methodologies, aerial/drone photography, photogrammetry, laser scanning, ground penetrating radar and sonar, x-ray fluorescence scanning, reflectance transformation imaging and 3D virtual rendering are providing new insights into archaeological sites, monuments, and museum and archive collections

(Vincent, 2017). For example, a terrestrial laser scanner enables a high-definition 3D model of a historical site to be produced; ground penetrating radar enables buried structures to be identified; and x-ray fluorescence scanning of old paintings enables previous layers and versions to be seen (Bruzelius, 2017; Koramaz, 2018). Rendering heritage sites as 3D virtual models, with structures restored to their original form, enables them to be experienced and explored virtually (Vincent, 2017). In all cases, what would have been difficult, time-consuming, expensive and in some cases impossible tasks can now be undertaken quickly and easily (Georgopoulos and Stathopoulou, 2017). That said, it is fair to say that many of these technologies are not cheap to purchase and maintain (though some techniques, such as 3D rendering of objects, can be undertaken using a smartphone), and they generally require some specialist knowledge to process and make sense of the resultant data. As such, some training is necessary before pursuing their use. Nonetheless, heritage and archaeological research, in particular, have been enlivened by such new forms of data generation.

Undertaking Historical Analysis

In addition to providing new means of generating and sourcing historical data, new digital tools and techniques, along with the massive expansion in the volume and interrelatedness of data, have transformed how historical analysis is performed. Indeed, new digital methods and data are having a profound effect on historiography by shifting the epistemology and methodologies of historical research. This is well illustrated by the development of the digital humanities, and computational and statistical approaches to undertaking historical research, which contrasts markedly with other established epistemologies, such as those utilised within progressive, Marxist, New Left, Annales, postmodern and poststructural historical approaches that employ alternative framings and methodologies.

Computational and statistical approaches to history making can be traced back to the late 1940s (Hockey, 2004). By the mid-1960s, quantitative approaches to history had evolved into the nascent field of Humanities Computing (Nyhan and Flinn, 2016). Research tended to consist of assembling large corpuses of text that could then be searched for patterns, or relatively simple statistical analysis of administrative data such as censuses (Graham et al., 2016). However, access to computers was limited, the work time-consuming, computing power and operations generally weak, and the questions that could be asked narrow. Moreover, the epistemological approach – which made claims to objectivity and adopting a scientific method – was rejected by most humanities scholars as being shallow, reductionist and of low utility (Galgano et al., 2008). A second wave of humanities computing took place in the 1980s and 1990s as computers became cheaper, more distributed, powerful and connected to the internet, digital archives were established, and more specialised software was developed. Rebranded as the 'digital humanities' in the 2000s, a third wave of computational approaches are presently underway due to the advent of big data and the development and application of various forms of data analytics (Graham et al., 2016).

The digital humanities is an interdisciplinary field of study that brings together scholars from across the humanities (e.g., historians, linguists, literary and media scholars) with librarians and computer, data, and information scientists (Gardiner and Musto, 2015). It seeks to apply computational methods, including statistics, analytics and graphing and mapping to digital data to extract insights (Moretti, 2005) (see **Chapter 10**). In particular, it aims to provide a distant reading and interpretation of large-scale datasets – from hundreds to millions of records – rather than a close reading of a small sample of data, as is generally practised in other humanities-based research. In other words, rather than concentrating analysis on a small selection of novels, photographs or newspaper stories, analysis is extended to entire collections to seek larger patterns and trends that cannot be identified in a narrow sample. For example, rather than examine closely the archival records of a handful of Old Bailey trials, it is now possible to analyse the 197,000 trials (127 million words) held within the digital archive as a whole (Graham et al., 2016). Similarly, with respect to recent history, it is possible to examine the content of millions of webpages and the billions of posts, photos and comments on social media (Manovich, 2020). The transformation in the scale of analysable data enables a shift from expansive historical accounts (extracting complex knowledge from small crumbs of evidence) to macroscopic accounts (knowledge is compressed from large reservoirs of evidence) (Graham et al., 2016). A multitude of methods have been developed to perform such macroscopic analysis.

The most basic of these are data management and curation tools that enable data to be easily handled, linked, searched, visualised as descriptive statistics, and shared. These have been complemented by more sophisticated analyses. For example, data might be examined using visual analytics and displayed as time-series graphics in a dashboard that reveals trends over time (Uboldi and Caviglia, 2015) (see **Chapter 10**). Or, data may be used to construct a historical GIS, in which spatial patterns can be viewed and forms of spatial analytics applied (Gregory and Ell, 2007; Gregory and Geddes, 2014). Such temporal and spatial visualisation of large datasets aids the identification of patterns that were not possible to spot previously in small samples or within the tables of database records or within massive lists of social media posts. Moreover, data can be easily combined, compared and contrasted, allowing relationships between phenomena to be observed. Such combinations can become very powerful when constructed as deep maps. Deep mapping involves creating multimedia and multi-layered temporal-spatial representations of places and communities by combining many forms of data within a system (either a GIS or a 3D virtual environment such as Unity) (Bodenhamer, 2013). The map or 3D environment acts as an interactive canvas on which data – records, texts, maps, photos, videos – are accessed and displayed. In this sense, a deep map entwines geographical, administrative and scientific data with memories, biographies, folklore, oral histories, news stories and other narratives (Harris, 2015), with the aim to combine evidence that displays multiple perspectives and can facilitate meaning making beyond patterns and trends (Bodenhamer, 2022). Such deep maps are useful for understanding the recent history of how locales have been reshaped by the embedding of digital infrastructure into the fabric of cities and processes such as gentrification caused by agglomerations of digital companies (Dawkins and Young, 2020).

In addition to methods that support interpretative analysis, several methodological approaches that seek explanation and causality have been adopted, particularly with respect to analysing longitudinal administrative and statistical data of interest for producing social, economic and political histories. These approaches involve the use of statistics, analytics and modelling techniques (see **Chapter 11**). For example, various (non)parametric tests can be used to test the strength of potential causal relationships between variables (Hudson and Ishizu, 2017). Stochastic modelling and process tracing methods can be used to identify causal mechanisms that explain historical outcomes (Buthe, 2002; Rast, 2012). Simulation models can be composed to hindcast the unfolding of events and critical junctions in their sequencing, as well as to make predictions about how events might project forward into the future under various conditions (Grzymala-Busse, 2011). Such modelling is particularly useful for assessing the strength of historical path dependencies and what we might learn from the past (Pollitt, 2008). Various forms of network analysis have been applied to historical datasets to identify the individual and collective connections between various actors and digital resources such as archives and webpages (Stevenson and Ben-David, 2019; see **Chapter 11**). The aim is to identify salient relationships between groups of actors and the evolution of these relations over time through alliances and conflicts, and how these might have affected activities. For example, network analysis has been applied to citation data to trace the evolution and diffusion of ideas over time, as well as the institutional and disciplinary collaborations of their creators and promoters (Baas et al., 2020).

Issues in Digital History Research

The digitisation of millions of historical records and artefacts, the creation of digital archives and repositories, and the rolling out of a suite of digital tools and techniques for producing and analysing historical data have undoubtedly been a boon for academic research. Moreover, it has led to a large expansion in historical research conducted beyond the academy, reflected in the growth of genealogical and local history research (Guelke and Timothy, 2008). However, while the digital transformation of historical research has been broadly positive, widening the evidence base and enhancing analysis, it also raises a number of concerns and issues that require reflection and caution.

With respect to the sourcing of data, a paradox is emerging whereby, on the one hand, there is a profusion of evidence that can be overwhelming to handle and make sense of, and on the other, an enormous amount of potentially useful data is held in private archives and state and commercial data infrastructures, which are locked from view. Moreover, there is a worry that the erosion and replacing of traditional analogue media means that important sources of information are being lost in favour of more transient media (e.g., written correspondence replaced by emails and texts, print diaries with online scheduling, print newspaper with webpages), resulting in the loss of key sources for future historians (Nanni, 2019). The digital data that are available can vary in quality and provenance, which can undermine the validity of research based on them. As noted in **Chapter 8**, there are concerns relating to the data standards of community archives, where the archivists are less likely to have formal training in selection and compiling metadata. Web archive data are what Brügger (2018) terms 'reborn data'; that is, data that have been transformed in the process of their capture (hyperlinks, images, linked files of web pages may be broken or lost), which affects what can be done with them. Moreover, there is little active curation as content gathering is automated, yet given the rapid turnover of web content, some of it might not have been captured by archiving bots (Brügger, 2018), and contextual information concerning the website's creation and operation may be absent (Ben-David and Amram, 2019).

Webpage and social media data can also contain significant amounts of faked and gamed data and disinformation and misinformation, which are designed to distort opinion rather than be valid, reliable sources (Galgano et al., 2008). The edit wars over some Wikipedia entries provide a sense of how different parties with varying intent seek to portray the same issues, places and people (Tkacz, 2015). This has led to concerns that the democratisation in access to historical data and sharing analysis has led to a 'softening' of history, creating elective histories and historical conflations, with official narratives of the past being countered by a cacophony of viewpoints (Hoskins, 2018b; Pogačar, 2018). Judging what is a reputable source is not easy, but sites run by professional bodies, universities, libraries and established archives are likely to have stronger provenance (Galgano et al., 2008). At the same time, professional archives have their own inherent biases in terms of what material has been retained, with more attention paid to elite actors in a society. In addition, much of the material recorded on various forms of social media have not been produced for archiving (as opposed to record keeping that is intentionally recorded for future re-use), raising ethical questions about their unintended re-use (see **Chapter 4**).

In epistemological terms, the digital humanities and computational approaches to history have not been universally welcomed. They have been critiqued as fostering weak, surface analysis whereby complexity, specificity, context, depth and critique are sacrificed for scale, breadth, automation and general patterns (Kitchin, 2014a). Rather than a shallow distant reading, critics argue for continued priority to be given to close readings that can adequately contextualise and identify meaning (Trumpener, 2009). Moreover, some are worried that the benefits of research in physical archives (e.g., drawing on the domain expertise of archivists and librarians and finding related records stored next to each other that a digital search would not identify) are being lost (Hoskins, 2018a). Digital humanities scholars have responded by noting that they are not seeking to replace close readings and traditional historical methods and praxis, but rather to complement them by widening the scope of analysis and enabling new questions to be asked (Manovich, 2020). While these scholars promote the benefits of digital history, they recognise that digital history takes a number of complementary forms. Ultimately, what is required is analysis that is well contextualised and strongly supported by the available evidence.

Summary

- This chapter has made the case for further historical analysis of the unfolding of digital life and the rollout of new technologies and their effects on cultural, social, political and economic relations.
- Importantly, the growing pervasiveness of digital technologies in conducting research and storing and sharing data, is leading to a transformation in historiography. Digital archives and repositories, along with new digital tools and techniques, are shifting the epistemological and methodological practices of conducting historical research by enabling new ways of asking about and making sense of the past.
- Sourcing historical data is becoming easier as old archival material is digitised and born-digital data is archived and made available through internet access. Issues of access remain, however, particularly for data held by companies.
- Digital technologies are reshaping the production of primary data about the past, facilitating the collection, processing, analysing and sharing of oral histories, the discovery and collation of new material including through crowdsourcing initiatives, and enabling new forms of evidence and analysis such as photogrammetry, laser scanning, ground penetrating radar and sonar,

x-ray fluorescence scanning, reflectance transformation imaging and 3D virtual rendering.
- In addition, new methods of data management and analysis are enabling new means of identifying relationships and trends in the past.
- These developments have led to the formation of the digital humanities, which employs an epistemology that provides a computational analysis and distant reading of many sources, in contrast to a close reading of a small sample of material.

Recommended Reading

Brügger, N., and Milligan, I. (eds) (2019) *The Sage Handbook of Web History*. Sage, London.
A comprehensive overview that details methods and issues in conducting web history, as well as providing examples of web history research.

Gardiner, E., and Musto, R.G. (2015) *The Digital Humanities: A Primer for Students and Scholars*. Cambridge University Press, Cambridge.
A broad introduction to the ideas and tools of digital humanities research.

Goggin, G., and McLelland, M. (2017) *The Routledge Companion to Global Internet Histories*. Routledge, London.
A wide-ranging collection of essays that discuss issues in researching internet histories.

Graham, S., Milligan, I., and Weingart, S. (2015) *Exploring Big Historical Data*. Imperial College Press, London.
An overarching guide to conducting digital history research in the age of big data.

10
Data Visualisation and Mapping

Overview

This chapter examines:

- what data visualisation is and how it may be incorporated as part of research projects on an array of topics about digital life;
- specific techniques for the visualisation of different kinds of digital data, including quantitative, qualitative and spatial data, respectively;
- how data visualisations figure as subjects and objects of study in research about digital life, and some methodological orientations for engaging with data visualisations as digital artefacts; and
- where to find software and programming resources for getting started with data visualisation.

Introduction

At the 1900 Paris Exposition, the famed American sociologist and civil rights activist W.E.B. Du Bois presented a series of sixty handmade 'data portraits' – including charts, graphs and maps – that captured, distilled and communicated the stark realities of systemic racial inequalities endured by African Americans in late nineteenth-century America (Du Bois, 2018). Data visualisation – the practice of turning data into graphical representations using 'abstract, geometrical forms' that stand in for data 'values and relations' (Kennedy and Engebretsen, 2020: 22) – is accordingly not a novel phenomenon unique to digital life. Yet as compared to Du Bois's handmade visualisations, current approaches to data visualisation consist largely of explicitly *computational* 'rendering practices' for visualising specifically *digital* data (Halpern, 2015: 21; Kennedy and Engebretsen, 2020). This chapter discusses data visualisation in this latter sense: computational techniques for making otherwise abstract, discrete, machine-readable units of information 'visible'. In the context of digital data visualisation, we are interested in all kinds of digital data that can be subjected to any one or combinations of 'categorization, abstraction', mapping, and other means of 'translation into graphical representation' using digital software, interfaces and techniques (Kennedy and Engbretsen, 2020: 21). This includes quantitative and qualitative data, spatial data (data with geographical co-ordinates attached), as well as digital image media (e.g., visual content posted to social media).

This chapter provides a high-level overview of a selection of techniques for visualising these different kinds of data. However, it is not a 'how to' guide for producing data visualisations – this is a task far too large to be accomplished in a single book chapter, and one that has been the subject of many dedicated volumes (see 'Recommended Reading' section). Instead, this chapter identifies which factors and characteristics of a dataset to consider in selecting a visualisation technique, and also identifies the different ways in which data visualisation may be mobilised within a research project or study. Beyond its utility for producing visual artefacts, data visualisation is also at the heart of a number of methods of analysing data about and generated as part of digital life. And, as scholars of digital life, we are also interested in the significance of the increasing pervasiveness of data visualisations *in* the spaces and practices of our everyday lives, with which we can engage via a number of approaches, including some identified later in this chapter. To provide context for these discussions, it is important to first consider the purposes of data visualisation in the context of researching digital life, as well as the kinds of themes and questions about digital life that we may be interested in engaging with through digital visualisation methods. The chapter then moves on to discussing techniques and considerations for visualising quantitative, qualitative and spatial (geographical) data, respectively. A discussion of approaches for researching data visualization artefacts concludes the chapter.

Data Visualisation and Digital Life

Why Data Visualisation Matters for Research about Digital Life

The proliferation of digital data capture technologies and practices across most aspects of our everyday lives has given rise to 'big data' (massive volumes of fine-grained data; see **Chapter 11**). This rise has been paralleled by more powerful graphics cards, interactive computer graphics, visualisation software and data visualisation libraries (Manovich, 2011; Reyes and Manovich, 2020). These computational advances allow for the visualisation of 'much larger data sets than was possible previously' (Manovich, 2011: 38), which has 'led to the increasing popularity of infographics, data visualizations, and the use of maps for representing data and communicating its significance' (Feigenbaum and Alamahoudaei, 2020: 2; Halpern, 2015; Manovich, 2011).

As scholars interested in researching digital life, these developments matter for how and what we study in three key ways. First, largely as a result of these dual developments, data visualisation is now a central feature of intertwined facets of digital life and orientations, methods and techniques for researching it. We encounter data visualisations on a routine basis. Many established media organisations now have dedicated teams of data journalists who produce the visuals that frequently accompany news reports, both analogue (print) and digital (online) (Dick, 2016; Engebretsen and Kennedy, 2020; Riche et al., 2018). Data visualisations likewise feature strongly in research outputs across the social sciences and humanities, as well as applied fields such as geographic information science, cartography and statistics.

Second, the use of computational techniques and platforms for visualisation constitute an increasingly common approach for 'making sense' of big data. Seventy per cent of the body's sensory receptors are located in the eyes, and just shy of fifty per cent of the human brain takes part in visual processing (Merieb and Hoehn, 2007). In other words, '[h]uman brains are wired for *seeing* patterns and differences, and for understanding … relationships from this' (Grant, 2019: 4; emphasis added). Data visualisation appeals directly to this visual orientation of human sensory physiology, anatomy and information processing. Visualisations can 'amplify cognition' – that is, 'the mental action or process of acquiring knowledge and understanding through thought, experience, and the senses' – by 'assisting memory (providing externalization of complex factors) and by easing comprehension (e.g., by creating representations that appropriately leverage [visual] perception)' (Riche et al., 2018: 8). And third, the proliferation of data visualisations and our increasing encounters with them in the news, research outputs, advertising and other media means that data visualisations have themselves assumed importance as unique subjects/objects of research (Engebretsen and Kennedy, 2020).

Purposes of Data Visualisation

Understood as both techniques for making data visible and as visual artefacts (objects) produced using those techniques, data visualisation serves four research objectives. First, *communication* (and *persuasion*). The goal of most research, per Friendly and Wainer (2021: 2), is to turn 'information on a topic' into 'some standard form that we can consider as evidence' and that persuades us to come to a particular 'conclusion[,] explanation' or interpretation of information, relationships, causes and effects, processes and/or dynamics (see also Tufte, 1997). Visualisations are 'often the most powerful means [of] accomplish[ing]' this transmission of information 'because [they] provide a visual framework' that allows otherwise implicit or abstract 'facts and patterns' to be conveyed 'quickly and effectively' through the use of visual representations (Friendly and Wainer, 2021: 2; Kennedy and Engebretsen, 2020: 19; Tufte, 1983; Wildbur, 1989).

Second, *analysis*. Visualisation is a powerful analysis technique that can be used to identify and render apparent relationships and patterns that would otherwise remain hidden or implied (Halpern, 2015; Reyes and Manovich, 2020; San Cornelio and Roig, 2020). Data visualisation is at the core of *exploratory data analysis* (EDA), defined by Tukey (1977: xvi) as 'graphical detective work' (see also **Chapter 11**). EDA is an informal data analysis method centred on generating visual overviews of data to identify high-level trends and patterns important for deciding which data analysis techniques to use for a particular dataset (e.g., insights such as whether a dataset is evenly or unevenly distributed, or whether a pattern is clustered or dispersed) and to inform the formulation of hypotheses that researchers may not have thought to pose before 'looking' at the data (Myatt and Johnson, 2009). EDA mobilises a range of standard quantitative data visualisation techniques, as well as a number of bespoke methods specific to the visual exploration of data covered in more detail by Tukey (1997) and, for geospatial data, by Haining (2010). Elsewhere, techniques designed specifically for the analysis of digital life – such as social network analysis (see **Chapter 11**) and cultural analytics – are at their core robust visualisation techniques.

Third, *narrative*. Closely related to data visualisation as a form of information communication, data visualisation is often mobilised not only to present facts, but also to 'tell a story'. This includes both telling stories *with* and *about* data. As defined by Riche et al. (2018: 8), a data story is a specific type of narrative that is either 'based on or contains data and incorporates this data evidence, often portrayed by data graphics, data visualizations, or data dynamics, to confirm or augment a given' explanation, account of events, conclusion, interpretation or assignation of meaning. When used to tell a story, data visualisations can frame particular understandings, interpretations of and conclusions about data for audiences through combinations of visual and textual elements, their organisation (e.g., a particular order or sequence in which graphic elements appear) and the intentional and selective deployment of techniques including but not limited to juxtaposition, contrast, subversion and inversion (see Feigenbaum and Alamahodaie, 2020). Approaches to data storytelling frequently rely on the use of multiple panels, or several data visualisations arranged together, often in a particular sequence. Multiple panels can be brought together and arranged using various narrative formats, including comic strips, magazine layouts, partitioned posters, annotated charts, slide shows, flow charts and film/video/animation (Segel and Heer, 2010). These are not data visualisation techniques *per se*, but rather conventions for and styles of organising and presenting data stories. For geospatial data, visual data narratives can be assembled using various story mapping techniques (see Song et al., 2022).

Finally, *counter-narrative*. Data visualisation can also be used to contravene, oppose or resist a dominant or hegemonic narrative by producing new visual artefacts that open onto 'spaces for action', intervention, 'and speculation' (Halpern, 2015: 21). Whereas many data visualisation techniques such as charts and graphs rely on grouped/categorical data or visually aggregate data, *counter-plots* may pursue intentional strategies of visual *disaggregation* – for instance, breaking data apart by demographic categories such as age, race, sex, etc. – to contest the elisions and obfuscations that occur with aggregation (Bowe et al., 2020). One such example is the COVID Racial Data Tracker,[1] which produced a series of race and ethnicity disaggregated data visualisations to communicate the disproportionate COVID-19 disease burden borne by Black, Indigenous and Latin communities in the United States (as discussed in Bowe et al., 2020). Elsewhere, counter-narrative data visualisation may involve the intentional use of otherwise discouraged visual techniques (D'Ignazio and Klein, 2020). One example is *occlusion* – or, in mapping terms, *overplotting* – where graphical marks and symbols are drawn over top of each other, 'obscur[ing] other important features' below (D'Ignazio and Klein, 2020: 128). An example of the strategic use of overplotting can be found in a map produced by the Anti-Eviction Mapping Project,[2] which shows a very high density of dot symbols representing evictions mapped over the entire area of San Francisco. The density of these eviction symbols is so great that the points visually obscure each other, so much so that base map features (roads, parks, etc.) cannot be seen below the dot symbols representing evictions. As described by D'Ignazio and Klein (2020: 128), this use of overplotting visualises that rather than there being any discernible spatial pattern of evictions in San Francisco, there is, in effect, no pattern of eviction; instead, 'the whole city is a pattern, and that pattern is the problem'.

Data Visualisation Basics and Design Considerations

The choice of visualisation technique begins with acknowledging the type of data to be visualised – namely, whether the data are quantitative, qualitative or spatial (contain geographical referents or metadata). This chapter discusses options for visualising each of these types of digital data separately. Before delving into these approaches, a number of data visualisation design basic premises and decisions should be considered.

---

[1] See https://covidtracking.com/race (accessed 21 August 2023).
[2] See https://antievictionmap.com/ (accessed 21 August 2023).

Data visualisations use graphical primitives including 'points … lines, curves and simple geometric shapes' to 'stand in' for real-world processes, phenomena, objects 'and the relations between them' (Kraak et al., 2020; Manovich, 2011: 38; Wildbur, 1989). These primitives may be used alone or in combination in the form of *icons* (literal graphical representations of real-world phenomenon), *symbols* (abstract representations used to stand in for real-world phenomena, where the association between the graphic element and the phenomenon being represented is provided in a visual key known as a legend), and *pictograms* (pictorial symbols; Wildbur, 1989). The use of graphical primitives to stand in for real-world complexity is inherently reductionist because it involves reducing information density through processes of *selection* (choosing which aspects of data to include versus which to exclude) and *generalisation* (removing unnecessary detail) (Kraak et al., 2020; Manovich, 2011). Graphical elements such as symbols and icons may furthermore be stylised through design choices pertaining to their aesthetic parameters, including *colour* (more accurately referred to as 'hue'), *transparency*, *saturation* (how 'true' colours appear), *value* (lightness or darkness of a colour), *texture* (of a pattern or fill, if applicable), *crispness* ('fuzziness' or discreteness of edges), *size*, and *position* (element location in the visualisation canvas and whether it appears in the foreground or background) (Kraak et al., 2020; Manovich, 2011; for best practices and conventions for working with these parameters see the work of Tufte, 1990, 1997, 2006). These parameters are often adjusted to achieve a visual hierarchy that informs the order in which different elements of the visualisation (graphics, text) are perceived, such that the most important data is visually 'read' first (Kraak et al., 2020; Yau, 2013).

In visualisations of *non*-spatial data (i.e., data without locational referents and/or where geographical metadata is not used as the organisational basis for visualisation), graphical primitives are often arranged arbitrarily on the *canvas* (a 2D representational surface, such as a computer screen, physical sheet of paper, or poster). In contrast, in geovisualisation, spatial primitives (mapped symbols) are arranged intentionally, corresponding to their real-world position on the surface of the earth in cartographic co-ordinate space (with x and y axes representing latitude and longitude, respectively). Decisions also need to be made regarding the *dynamism* and *interactivity* of the data visualisation to be produced. Dynamism describes whether the resulting data visualisation is static (a 'snapshot' of data at a single moment in time) or dynamic (the visualisation changes, e.g., series of data frames displayed in a particular sequence, such as in an animation). All visualisations rendered on a physical page (i.e., printed out on paper) will be static by nature, whereas dynamic visualisations presuppose a digital display medium (i.e., a digital screen). Interactive data visualisations enable end users to: i) reveal more about the data through actions such as clicking on graphical primitives to open detail expands, zooming in and out on portions of the visualisation canvas (display), and mouse rollovers to reveal labels for hidden or layered elements; and/or

ii) adjust the variables being displayed, the visualisation type (e.g., switching between a bar and pie chart) and perhaps even to control some of the aesthetic parameters. Interactivity likewise necessitates a digital display medium that affords the end user some control over aspects of the visualisation.

While most data visualisations are 2D, 3D visualisation is also possible, and is particularly common in geovisualisation. Digital 3D rendering – or the translation of data variables into a 3D object on a digital screen (Malizia, 2006: 13) – is also associated with *augmented reality* (AR) and *virtual reality* (VR). VR describes the production of fully immersive synthetic environments that make users feel as if they were actually in a simulated environment, including senses of '[bodily] position, movement, and balance' (Valori et al., 2020: 2; for more on the use of VR as a research method in the social sciences and humanities, see Jones et al., 2022). AR by contrast involves the layering or superimposition of digital objects over real-world space to 'enhance perception of the surrounding environment' (Valori et al., 2020: 30). Both AR and VR may be accessed using head-mounted displays, with the difference being that in a VR scenario, all that a user sees is the synthetic environment, whereas in AR, the user still sees the real-world environment in which they are actually situated, but with the addition of various kinds of computer-generated graphics superimposed over their view. Following Erickson (1993), AR can enhance data visualisation in three key ways: i) by allowing 3D data objects to be manipulated (e.g., turned around, flipped, etc.), which allows them to be seen from different perspectives; ii) by allowing multiple users to interact with a visualisation at the same time; and iii) by facilitating human interaction in the process (e.g., discussion about how to interpret data).

All these design choices – about aesthetic parameters, symbology/iconography, dynamism, interactivity, dimensionality and, to a lesser extent, the use of mixed realities (AR/VR) – should reflect and support the purpose of the visualisation and reflect the needs of the intended audience. Many data visualisation techniques assume and/or necessitate structured data – that is, 'data that has been organised and formatted in ways that make it easy to input, search, and manipulate' (Feigenbaum and Alamahodaei, 2020: 19), such as a spreadsheet or database. Yet as we will see in our discussions of media visualisation and mapping below, social media data – one of the genres of data most closely associated with digital life – is unstructured, yet may still be, and frequently is, visualised.

Visualising Quantitative Data

The bulk of data visualisations are produced using quantitative (i.e., numerical and statistical) data. Following Kennedy and Engebretsen (2020), this is for two reasons. First, quantitative as well as spatial data are more abundant than qualitative data. They are also more likely to be published as 'open' – that is, made publicly available to retrieve and use – as compared to qualitative data. And second, computational tools for visualisation – including web-based utilities, visualisation libraries, and software – are often designed with quantitative and statistical data in mind.

Methods of data visualisation for numerical data consist of techniques for generating visual representations that 'show measured quantities and categories' in 'schematic form' (Lenger and Eppler, n.d.: n.p.; Myatt and Johnson, 2009: 23). This schematic space (the canvas) is often, though not always, defined by axes (Lenger and Eppler, n.d.). One axis typically expresses quantity (this is usually the y or vertical axis), while the other axis is devoted to the measures (variables) being visualised (usually the x or horizontal axis, also sometimes referred to as the 'value axis'; Yau, 2011). In quantitative data visualisation, the choice of visualisation technique depends on a number of factors, including:

1   the number of variables to be visualised (i.e., whether the visualisation will be visualising one (*univariate*), two (*bivariate*) or more variables (*multivariate*) at a time);
2   whether the data has been categorised (grouped or aggregated) based on shared attributes/characteristics or shared measures of quantity, volume, density, intensity, ranges of values, etc.; and
3   whether the data is temporally *discrete* (representing data collected at one particular moment in time, like a snapshot) or *continuous* (representing real-world phenomena that change over time; Yau, 2011).

Evergreen (2019), Kirk (2019), Myatt and Johnson (2009) and Yau (2013) provide comprehensive overviews of the suitability of quantitative visualisation techniques based on the number of variables to be visualised, methods appropriate for visualising continuous versus discrete data, as well as approaches suitable for visualising categorical versus individual data. Particularly useful is Evergreen's (2019) 'Quantitative Chart Chooser', which not only organises quantitative visualisation techniques by the number of variables being visualised, but also by the intention of the visualisation (e.g., whether it is to show change over time, or to show similarities and/or differences between measured quantities, densities or intensities of a phenomenon).

The most common techniques for visualising quantitative data are 2D *charts* and *graphs*. The terms 'charts' and 'graphs' are often used interchangeably. However, *charts* are a more general category of quantitative visualisation techniques that includes graphs, with *graphs* referring more specifically to quantitative visualisation approaches that require the use of defined axes that determine the placement of visual primitives on the visualisation canvas.

Box plots (**Figure 10.1a**) are useful for visualising data distributions by visually summarising maximum and minimum, mean and median, and upper and lower

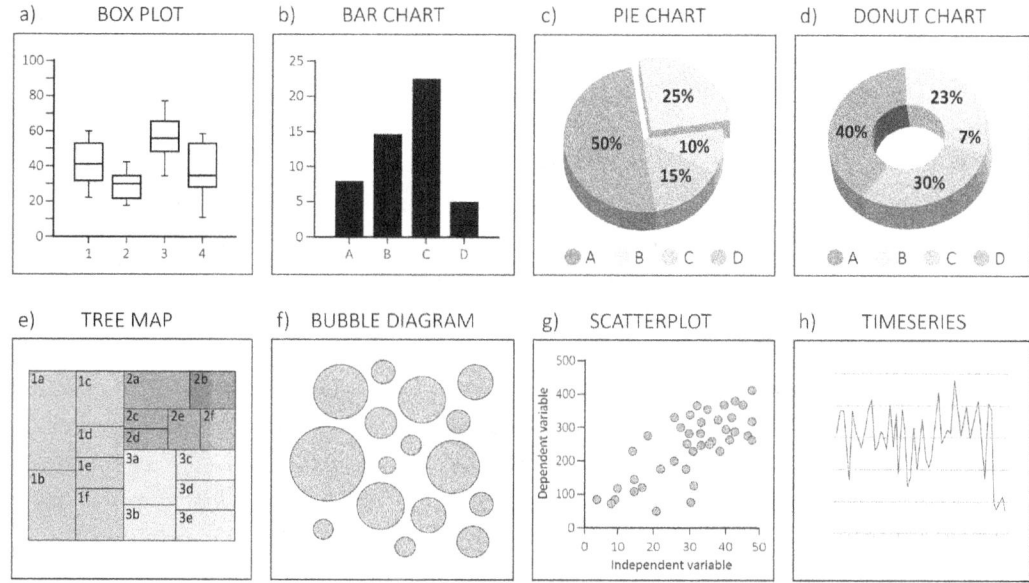

Figure 10.1 Quantitative data visualisation techniques.

quartiles of data values using a rectangle and standardised marks at key positions (Myatt and Johnson, 2009: 41). A separate technique is the *bar chart* (**Figure 10.1b**), which displays categorised data values as either horizontal or vertical 'rectangular bar[s] with a length[/height] proportional to the value it represents' (Myatt and Johnson, 2009: 36), as do *stacked bar charts* (which provide further detail about the 'composite categories that make up each bar'; The Regents of the University of California, 2019: n.p.). In charting techniques, either the horizontal or vertical axis will account for quantity (raw numerical value, percentage, etc.) of the variable being visualised, and the other axis will simply reflect the data categories. Importantly, however, the arrangement of the bars is not significant and does not need to conform to any order – for example, the categories (bars) do not need to be arranged from lowest to highest numerical values.

Other types of chart include *pie charts* (**Figure 10.1c**), which subdivide single circles into slices or wedges representing parts of a whole, as do variations of the pie chart including *donut charts* (**Figure 10.1d**), *polar charts* and *sunbursts* or *radial charts*. A *treemap* (**Figure 10.1e**) is similar to a pie chart but instead of a circle, this technique uses a bounding box that is subdivided into rectangular shapes whose different sizes reflect their share of the whole and are arranged hierarchically (grouped from largest to smallest; FlowingData, n.d.b). A *bubble diagram* (**Figure 10.1f**) is also a kind of chart, using circles whose sizes vary in proportion to the data values being visualised. However, unlike a treemap, a bubble diagram does not necessarily observe any hierarchy in the arrangement or placement of the circles (or 'bubbles') themselves.

A bubble diagram should, however, be differentiated from a *bubble chart*, which similarly uses circles of varying sizes, but the placement of the bubbles within the canvas is intentional, reflecting values of variables defined along x (independent) and y (dependent) axes (see FlowingData, n.d.a). A bubble chart, in other words, is a *graph*, and more specifically, a variation on one of the most common graph types: the *scatterplot* (**Figure 10.1g**). A scatterplot visualises individual (uncategorised) data values as dots placed in their co-ordinate locations in 2D space (Yau, 2011). Where the x axis of a scatterplot instead represents the continuous progression of time (e.g., from an earliest to latest point in time), the plot is known as a *time series* (**Figure 10.1h**). The points in the time series may be joined by a line that 'connects the dots' to better visualise trends/fluctuations in the values of the thematic variable (y axis) over time.

Beyond the instances identified here, other kinds of chart and graph – many of them much more sophisticated and complex – abound for the visualisation of numerical and statistical data. For more exhaustive inventories of these techniques, two online resources are particularly useful: the index of Chart Types on the *FlowingData* website (FlowingData, n.d.b), which links to tutorials, guides and real-world examples for each chart type; and Lenger and Eppler's (n.d.) 'Periodic Table of Visualization Methods', hosted at the visual-literacy.org website, which in addition to quantitative data visualisation types, also identifies techniques for the visualisation of qualitative data.

Visualising Qualitative Data

Qualitative data visualisation – sometimes referred to as 'information visualisation' (Knigge and Cope, 2006; Manovich, 2011; Tufte, 1997) – is 'concerned with the visual representation, exploration, and analysis of … data that is nonnumeric and nongeographic[al]' in nature (Knigge and Cope, 2006: 2027). Rather than visualising counts, percentages, rates and other numerical measures of phenomena, qualitative visualisation approaches consist of techniques for representing 'texts' – words, signs, symbols, images, sounds – and concepts (Evergreen, 2019; Henderson and Segal, 2013; Knigge and Cope, 2006; Lenger and Eppler, n.d., n.p.). While this section discusses approaches for visualising *qualitative* data, the visualisation techniques themselves may however be qualitative *or* quantitative. For instance, *word* and *tag clouds*, which are techniques for visualising the most frequently used words in textual corpora such as digital metadata (most frequently used tags) and social media posts (for instance, the content of a sample of tweets), are not actually qualitative visualisation techniques. In word/tag clouds, the size of the words in the cloud is proportional to their frequency in a dataset; the more frequent the incidence of the word, the larger it is displayed. *Frequency* is a quantitative variable; therefore, word and tag clouds may be considered a quantitative technique for the visualisation of qualitative data (texts).

Qualitative data visualisation 'reduce[s] and focus[es]' in on concepts, 'providing a structure to identify patterns[,] outliers' and relationships in order to 'introduce new levels of understanding' (Henderson and Segal, 2013: 55). Visualisation is also important for establishing the trustworthiness of qualitative data analysis findings (e.g., interpretations, assignations of meaning or importance), including dimensions of their confirmability and potential transferability (Sloane, 2009). Compared to quantitative data, qualitative datasets do not always necessarily have an innate logical structure that can be used as an organisational framework for the visualisation itself (e.g., quantities of variables that may be used to define the axes of a canvas, as in a scatter plot). Sometimes, though not always, this requires that qualitative data be subjected to some form of analysis in advance, such as qualitative coding, which may be used to interpret and organise 'raw' (non-reduced) data into thematic categories that may then form the organisational basis of a qualitative visualisation.

Matrices and Spectrum Displays

Techniques appropriate for the visualisation of thematic (coded) qualitative data include *matrices* and *spectrum displays*. A matrix (**Figure 10.2a**) is a grid-like structure subdivided into rows and columns. Each row will pertain to a theme, and each column may represent a different case, such as a respondent/participant, company, micromobility mode, or other category. Each 'box' or cell in the matrix may then be colour-coded to express presence/absence, relative importance or significance, degree of agreement/disagreement, and/or emotion/sentiment, or other set of values associated with a theme (Henderson and Segal, 2013). Conversely, a spectrum display (**Figure 10.2b**) arranges cases radially around a circle or semi-circle, with each case subdivided into rings displaying thematic categories (which must be mutually exclusive; Sloane, 2009). The thematic categories are themselves arranged such that related categories (referred to as 'factors') are visually grouped together, and values ('codes') are symbolised within the space of each ring that pertains to each individual case (Sloane, 2009). Sloane (2009) for instance uses a spectrum display to visualise online users' goals in relation to time spent in an online session, allowing for the quick visual determination of differences in key user objectives. This spectrum display shows that users engaging in shorter sessions engage in activities such as paying bills online, while users engaging in longer sessions participate in activities such as online job searches.

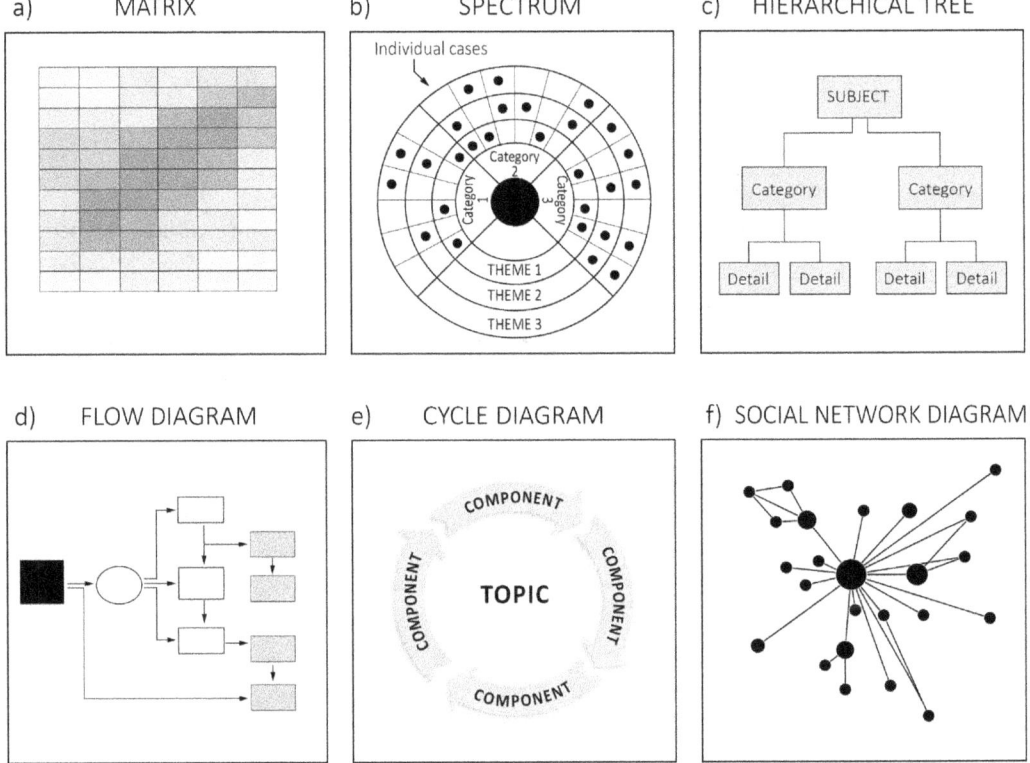

Figure 10.2 Qualitative data visualisation techniques.

Qualitative Diagrams

Where hierarchical relationships exist between qualitative themes and/or concepts, these can be visualised using approaches that include *tree diagrams* (**Figure 10.2c**) and *cone trees*, which show parent-child relationships (akin to a 'family tree' schematic) in vertical and horizontal orientations, respectively (see Lenger and Eppler, n.d.). *Mental maps* represent concepts as annotated geometric shapes connected by arrows or indicators across a canvas. *Flow diagrams* (**Figure 10.2d**) 'show the sequence of stages through a process' (Wildbur, 1989: 68). *Cycle diagrams* (**Figure 10.2e**) show processual feedback loops (Lenger and Eppler, n.d.), and are useful for the visualisation of non-hierarchical relationships.

Other quantitative visualisation techniques are highly sophisticated in nature. These include social network analysis and cultural analytics, both of which are useful for analysing social media, but for very different kinds of data (social media users and the relationships between them, and visual content posted to social media, respectively).

Social Network Diagrams

Social network analysis (SNA) is an approach for analysing 'relationships among social entities' (Wasserman and Faust, 1994: 3), such as a '"friendship" between two Facebook users, a follow relationship between two Twitter users … a reply of one user in a discussion forum to a message posted by another', and Instagram users' 'likes' of an Instagram influencer's posts (Himelboim, 2017: 1) (see also **Chapter 11**). One of the primary ways that a social network is analysed is through being visualised as a 'constellation of nodes [vertices] and links [edges]' between them (Himelboim, 2017: 1). In an SNA of social media networks, *nodes* represent social actors (such as social media accounts, typically displayed as dots, circles or other simple geometric shapes) and *links* are connectors, usually represented as lines, that establish a visual and analytic association between accounts (i.e., other nodes). This is known as a *social network diagram* or *graph* (see **Figure 10.2f**).

While SNA does analytically quantify social networks, its approach to visualising relationships is qualitative. In a schematic network space (the canvas where the social network will be visualised), node locations represent social actors' positions within a social network, rather than any quantitative variable or characteristic of the account. The result is that a 'group' of nodes with many links in common will be visually clustered together on the canvas, whereas nodes in a network that do not share many other nodes in common will be visually located further apart. As a visualisation-oriented methodology, the application of SNA to the analysis of digital networks – such as social graphs on social media platforms – allows for visual determinations of 'patterns of information flow' and 'provides context for identifying key users, and their potential influence, at different [scales] of analysis', be this a singular 'node, a link, a cluster, [or] the whole network' (Himelboim, 2017: 4).

Cultural Analytics

Cultural analytics (CA) represents a shift in analytic focus away from social media actors to digital image content, or media, shared through digital platforms such as Instagram. CA mobilises statistical and computational techniques including machine tagging to process, structure, sort and provide an organisational frame for the arrangement of image data on a visualisation canvas (Crockett, 2016). Yet as a visual-analytic methodology, CA supports the interpretation of image datasets' qualities rather than their quantities. Media visualisations generated through cultural analytics techniques 'can make visible the variability of forms in contemporary media [and] can also help to see differently elements that normally we many not notice [such as] patterns, rhythm, [and] movement traces' (Reyes and Manovich, 2020: 413).

Unlike the quantitative and qualitative visualisation techniques we have discussed so far in this chapter, CA involves 'direct visualization, or visualization without reduction' in that it does not supplant images with graphical primitives or symbols (e.g., using a geometric shape to 'stand in' for an image in a visualisation; Manovich, 2011: 41). In CA, the scaled-down thumbnails of the images themselves are the data points to be visualised. These thumbnails are referred to as *glyphs* – 'icons that carry information by way of their non-relational characteristics' (Crockett, 2016: 180). Prior to visualisation, image datasets are often structured 'using [their] metadata enriched with low-level descriptors', such as size; aesthetic variables (hue, brightness, etc.); shape (which refers to geometric features such as 'compactness, aspect ratio, rectangularity, circularity' (Reyes and Manovich, 2020: 409); and more sophisticated image features such as 'image content (objects and scenes), photo style composition, [and] texture' (Crockett, 2016: 191).

Cultural analytics offers an evolving suite of visualisation techniques or models that arrange these images 'as plot elements on large digital canvases' that constitute composite media images themselves (Crockett, 2016: 180; Reyes and Manovich, 2020). These models are predicated on and constitute variations of the *image plot*, which is the most 'general form of direct visualization for [digital] images' that arranges them on a canvas by some image property or set of properties (Crockett, 2016: 180). CA visualisation models beyond the image plot include:

- the *image montage* or *mosaic* technique, which organises images hierarchically in a matrix (row-and-column structure) by up to three variables (Manovich et al., 2014; Reyes and Manovich, 2020);
- the *image histogram* technique, which involves slicing images into equal-sized parts (segments, strips, rectangles, etc.) that may then be binned, or categorised, by some continuous variable (e.g., time, hue, brightness, saturation, etc.) (Crockett, 2016; Reyes and Manovich, 2020);
- the *radial image plot*, a polar scatterplot technique that facilitates the plotting of image glyphs by two variables (e.g., tonality and time) (Hochman and Manovich, 2014); and
- the *growing entourage plot*, which arranges image glyphs in multivariate clusters (Crockett, 2016; Manovich and Reyes, 2020).

Visualising Spatial Data

Spatial data is digital data that has geographical referents attached to it – usually, longitude and latitude. It also includes data that has a place name or spatial description associated with it, which may be converted to geographical co-ordinates. In the context of the volumes of content generated through interactions with social media platforms, these geographical referents are known as *geotags* (Crampton et al., 2013). Geotags may be produced either automatically (reflecting the real-time location of the device from which the post was made) or manually (users associate their post with a geographical place name at the time of posting, often through the affordances of the app). The distinguishing feature of spatial data, including geotagged social media data, is that spatial referents can be used as the organisational basis of visualisation, irrespective of whether the data itself is qualitative (e.g., semantics of textual content posted to Twitter, visual content posted to Instagram) or quantitative (e.g., GPS air quality metrics crowdsourced by citizen scientists using DIY sensors). In other words, spatial data are either qualitative or quantitative data that may be visualised using their spatial referents as a basis for placing those data in actual, real-world geographical co-ordinate space (where longitude = x axis and latitude = y axis) rather than the abstract space of a canvas where x and y axes represent the values of data variables.

Approaches and techniques for visualising spatial data fall under the umbrella of geovisualisation (Çöltekin et al., 2018; Dykes et al., 2005). Geovisualisation encompasses techniques for the analysis and visualisation of spatial data, and the production of visual outputs. Spatial visualisations include *maps* and *3D spatial models*, either of which may be *static* (freeze-frame snapshot view), *dynamic* (animated) or *interactive* (allow users to manipulate and/or exert some control over the geovisualisation in a digital environment). *Maps* are 2D visual representations of spatial data over a geographical expanse (portion of the surface of the earth), whereas *3D geovisualisations* involve the 'extrusion', or extension, of an *attribute* (characteristic, or variable) in the vertical dimension (z axis), be this building heights, property values, population density, broadband affordability, or density of Twitter activity over an area. To get a sense of the difference between maps and 3D geovisualisations, imagine looking at the same area in the terrain view in Google Maps, versus looking at the same area in 3D perspective in Google Earth – in the former, the Earth's surface appears 'flat', whereas in the latter, relief of the Earth's surface is visible, including changes in its depth, height and undulation, as well as concave and convex physical features (mountains, valleys, etc.). The variable that is being 'extruded' in this Google Earth example is the elevation of the Earth's surface landforms, also known as *topography*.

Types of Maps

The art and science of map-making is referred to as *cartography*. Like data visualisation, cartography and geovisualisation are expansive topics consisting of a multitude of methods and techniques that cannot fully be covered here. Instead, the focus is on *thematic mapping*, the most common approach for the geovisualisation of data about, sourced from, and/or generated in the course of everyday digital practices. Thematic mapping describes both the kinds of map outputs (visualisations) that are likely to be encountered in the domain of digital life, and also of the techniques that are likely to be the most relevant for mapping digital life. As the name implies, *thematic maps* '[depict] the variation' in, and distribution of, 'one or sometimes several geographic phenomena', or *themes*, by 'mapping location and attribute information [values of thematic variables] together' (Kraak et al., 2020: 58). An example of a theme is digital inclusion, expressed as the percentage of a population who are internet users. **Figure 10.3** presents a map of geographical differences in digital inclusion between areas in Britain produced by Blank et al. (2018). This map shows the

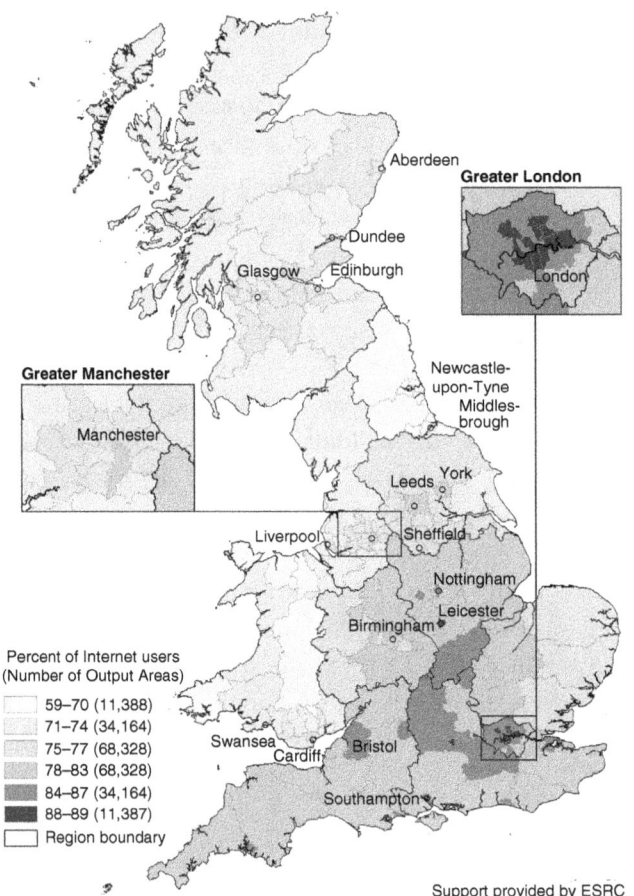

Figure 10.3 Percentage of the local area population who are internet users in England, Scotland and Wales.

Source: Blank et al. (2018). Map reproduced under terms of CC BY 4.0 licence.

percentage of the population in each local area district (LAD, a unit of administrative geography) that is 'online', showing a general pattern of *decrease* in digital inclusion as one visually moves from across the map canvas from south to north, with stark differences between the most-connected areas in the south and southeast of England (highest percentage of population online) and the least-connected areas in Wales, the north of England and Scotland (lowest percentage of the population online). Blank et al.'s (2018) map is an example of a *choropleth map*, which reports thematic variable values aggregated to enumeration areas or zones – such as the local area districts shown in **Figure 10.3** – whose boundaries (perimeters) have been established independently of the data being mapped. Choropleth maps visualise differences in thematic variables by adjusting the fill (colour, texture and/or opacity) of enumeration areas, and by using a map legend to communicate the range or category of real-world values (e.g., different bins, or categories, of percentages of the population who are online) that correspond to each fill.

Alternative thematic mapping techniques appropriate for aggregate (spatially grouped) data also include:

- *proportional symbol maps* (**Figure 10.4a**), which superimpose a symbol over each enumeration area, varying the size of the symbol in proportion to the value of the thematic attribute being mapped;
- *cartograms* (**Figure 10.4b**), which are a play on a choropleth map, with the addition that they distort the size of each enumeration area in proportion to the value of the thematic variable being mapped; and
- *dot density maps* (**Figure 10.4c**), which distribute uniformly sized dots representing a constant value of a variable (e.g., 1 dot = 2,000 persons) across an area.

Yet not all of the data that we may wish to map is categorical (spatially aggregated or enumerated). Sometimes, we need to map individual-level point event data (data defined by a single geographic co-ordinate pair), which we can do by placing a symbol for each point at its location on the map canvas – for instance, a point symbol for the location of each data centre. Other times, we are looking to represent processes, such as those associated with the movement of phenomena over space. A *flow map* uses lines to represent the movement of 'things' between locations (Steiner, 2019); for instance, data being transmitted along submarine fibre optic cables (e.g., TeleGeography's interactive Submarine Cable Map).[3] The lines can represent either abstract connections between the places to/from which phenomena flow, or actual/designated routes/paths of movement. Aesthetically, the width/weight/colour of the lines on a flow map may be adjusted to communicate the importance or dominance of particular

---

[3] See www.submarinecablemap.com (accessed 21 August 2023).

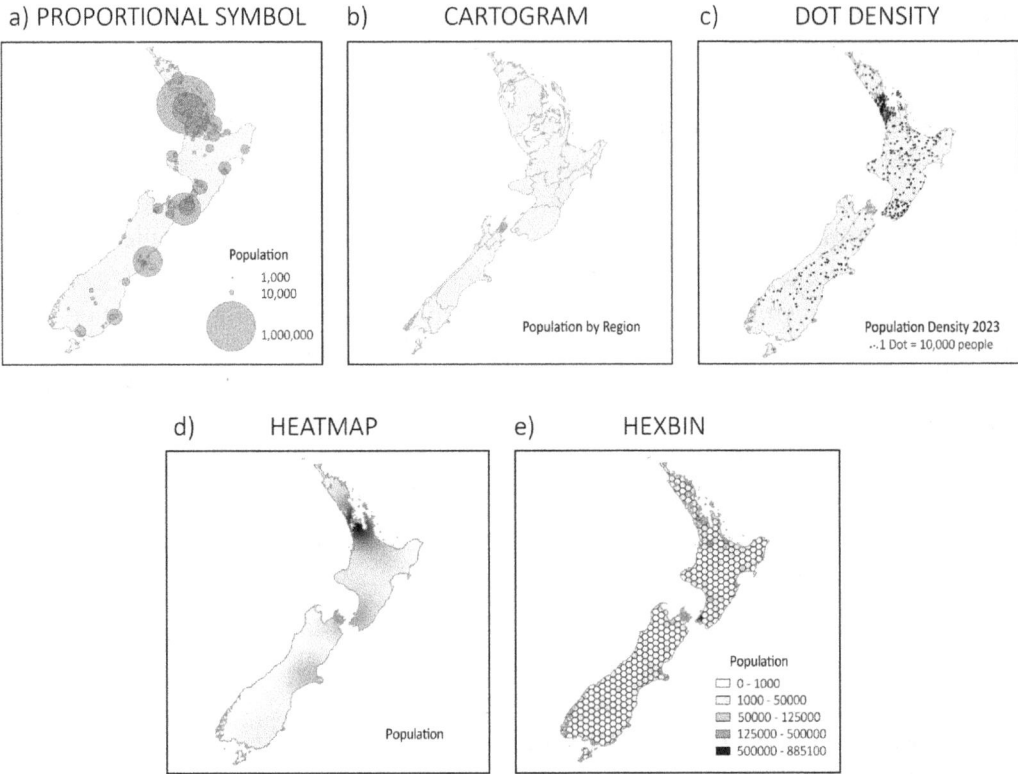

Figure 10.4 Cartographic techniques, including for mapping enumerated thematic data (a to c) and for aggregatting individual-level data (d and e).

Data sources: *Cartographic boundary files:* Tatauranga Aotearoa/Stats NZ Geographic Data Service (https://datafinder.stats.govt.nz/), licensed for reuse under the CC BY 4.0 licence. *Tabular population data:* Simple Maps, 2023 (https://simplemaps.com/data/nz-cities).

routes, and arrows can be added to the lines to visually represent the direction of movement, especially if flow is unidirectional.

Elsewhere, individual-level data may require spatial aggregation for analytic and/or visualisation purposes, even where it is not enumerated in nature (i.e., it does not make sense to think of these data as conforming to, being contained within/by, or meaningfully referring to any zone, also known as an 'enumeration area'). One reason that it may make sense to spatially group these data is that the dataset may simply be too large to meaningfully geovisualise as individual points on a map. A prime example where we may run into this situation is when working with social media data, which is produced on a continuous basis by millions – if not billions – of users around the world. Poorthuis et al. (2016) give the example of a scraped sample of natively (automatically) geotagged tweets about grits (a corn-based staple popular in the American south). Even though this data represents a limited temporal snapshot of Twitter activity, tweeting about grits during this time frame still generated a dataset of thousands of individual tweets. Mapping the tweets as individual points results in what is known as the 'overplotting problem', in which many points are drawn over the top of each other, making it impossible to get an accurate picture of the data because the map reader cannot see the points underneath, only the ones displaying on top.

Given the overplotting problem, when visualising geotagged big data, the data are customarily aggregated for both visualisation and data interpretation purposes. One approach is to mobilise a technique known as *heatmapping* (**Figure 10.4d**), which produces a density surface (a layer covering the extent of the data points) showing areas ('hotspots') where there are concentrations of comparatively more versus fewer tweets (about grits, or any other theme). Heatmapping is, however, most appropriate for *continuous* data, whereas social media posts – such as tweets about grits – are discrete (Poorthuis et al., 2016). An alternative is to produce a *hexbin map* (**Figure 10.4e**). This approach lays a hexagonal mesh of a resolution (hexbin size, or areal footprint) of the map maker's choosing, and aggregates (groups) point counts to the hexbins themselves (Poorthuis et al., 2016). The hexbins may be symbolised to report raw counts (e.g., number of tweets), but as Poorthuis et al. (2016) caution, it is advisable to normalise (i.e., standardise) raw counts by some other variable – such as population or geographical area size – to allow for more meaningful and direct comparisons between areas.

In geovisualisation, all the considerations about interactivity, dynamism, symbology, aesthetic variables (hue, saturation, value, texture, etc.) discussed above with reference to quantitative and qualitative visualisation apply to the making of maps (and 3D spatial models), as do some additional factors. These include, but are not limited to:

- the *scale* (relationship between map units and real-world distance units) at which the data is mapped (for static and dynamic visualisations), and for interactive web maps (also known as *slippy maps*), the *zoom level* (proxy for scale) at which various data layers (different themes) and annotations (e.g., labels) are visible; and
- the need to acquire *base data*, which is background map data – such as the outline of a country or continent, road networks, hydrological features (lakes, rivers), etc. – that provide geographical context for the thematic data being visualised.

Analysing Data Visualisations

Data visualisations are also something that researchers study in their own right. As Kennedy and Engebretsen (2020: 22–3) argue, data visualisations are not mere visual artefacts; they are also 'discursive resource[s]' with 'semiotic, aesthetic, and social affordances' that have the power and capacity to 'produce meanings, feeling, and engagements in their users and audiences'. Three key approaches for engaging with digital data visualisations as objects of study are *discourse analysis*, *semiotic analysis* and *multimodal analysis*. All three approaches are grounded in *visual methodologies*, a research framework that centres visual artefacts as data for researching visual – and indeed also digital – culture (Rose, 2022). More specifically:

- *Discourse analysis* accounts for the social and cultural contexts in which data visualisations are produced and put into circulation, and, in its critical variants, examining how the 'words', 'images', aesthetic choices, layout (placement of graphic elements) and symbology that comprise a data visualisation 'play a role in creating or opposing power structures and social inequalities' (Kennedy and Engebretsen, 2020: 26).
- *Semiotic analysis* examines how data visualisations make meaning by identifying visual elements of a visualisation (e.g., specific graphics, symbols or objects) to function as signs that signify (denote or connote) various social and cultural phenomena (see Aiello, 2020; Rose, 2022).
- *Multimodal analysis* focuses on how data visualisation elements (text, graphics, etc.) and the media through which they are disseminated (e.g., digital screens, posters, newspapers) work together to facilitate consistent – and intended – interpretations of data visualisations themselves (see Hippala, 2020).

Data Visualisation Resources

There are many visualisation applications to choose from, some of which are desktop based (installed on a personal computer), and others that are web based (support visualisation 'in the cloud'). Perhaps the most exhaustive inventory, and one that is updated regularly, may be found on the Resources page of Andy Kirk's *Visualizing Data*[4] website. This includes applications that do not require any coding expertise (or the desire to acquire some). These applications and utilities are organised around combinations of a graphical user interface: templates (pre-set list of the kinds of visualisation 'styles' to choose from, including many of the specific visualisation techniques that we have discussed in this chapter); and built-in functions organised under menus and toolbars that make visualising data intuitive and relatively straightforward. Some will be

---

[4]See www.visualisingdata.com (accessed 21 August 2023).

a proprietary platform (e.g., Tableau, Flourish, Carto and Mapbox); depending on the application, these may include a 'free' or 'freemium' version and a purchasable product with more sophisticated options to choose from. Others are open source (free to download and/or use), including but not limited to Gephi,[5] which is tailored to the visualisation of network data such as social network data; ImagePlot,[6] a free software tool for generating the kinds of image data visualisations identified in the discussion of cultural analytics; and QGIS,[7] an open-source digital mapping and analysis software program.

For those with some experience with programming and/or coding – or the willingness to appropriate these skills – other options for visualisation become available. One is the open-source statistical computing and graphics generation environment *R*, based on the programming language of the same name. The *FlowingData* website[8] offers tutorials for generating different kinds of quantitative visualisations using *R*; these are organised by chart type.[9] Another is the use of *JavaScript libraries*, which are collections (or 'libraries') of pre-written code that can be used to create interactive data visualisations that may be embedded in web pages and applications. Examples include *d3.js*, *WebGL* (tailored for 3D visualisation), and for web maps specifically, *Leaflet* and *OpenLayers*. If you are using the Resources page on the *Visualizing Data* website, more options are listed under the Programming tab.

Summary

- In its contemporary usage, 'data visualisation' refers to computational techniques (software and programming and scripting approaches) for making data visible in graphical and/or image form, at times supported by written text. Data visualisations refer to the visual artefacts produced through data visualisation techniques. They may be static ('freeze-frame' snapshot), dynamic (animated) or interactive (user-controllable).
- Data visualisation may be used to communicate analytic research findings and/or persuade an audience of a particular analytic interpretation; as a mode of data analysis in its own right; and to tell a story or counter a dominant narrative.
- Data visualisation techniques are specific to the type of data being visualised. Quantitative, qualitative and spatial data are visualised using different techniques.

---

[5] See https://gephi.org/ (accessed 21 August 2023).
[6] See http://lab.softwarestudies.com/p/imageplot.html (accessed 21 August 2023).
[7] See www.qgis.org (accessed 21 August 2023).
[8] See https://flowingdata.com (accessed 21 August 2023).
[9] See https://flowingdata.com/chart-types/ (accessed 21 August 2023).

- Data visualisations are also objects of study in their own right, and may be engaged via a variety of qualitative methodologies, including visual discursive, semiotic and multimodal approaches.

Recommended Reading

Abernathy, D. (2017) *Using Geodata and Geolocation in the Social Sciences: Mapping Our Connected World*. Sage, London.
A resource for mapping and visualising geotagged/spatial big data.

Engebretsen, M., and Kennedy, H. (eds) (2020) *Data Visualization in Society*. Amsterdam University Press, Amsterdam.
A collection of contributions mobilising different approaches and methods for examining the significance and social implications of data visualisation in everyday life.

Evergreen, S.D.H. (2019) *Effective Data Visualization: The Right Chart for the Right Data*, 2nd edn. Sage, London.
A how-to guide for formatting and visualising data, including a handy 'Quantitative Chart Chooser' to inform decisions about which chart style to use.

Feigenbaum, A., and Alamahodaei, A. (2020) *The Data Storytelling Workbook*. Routledge, London.
A guide to dfferent techniques for storytelling with data, supported by step-by-step examples.

Kirk, A. (2019) *Data Visualisation: A Handbook for Data Driven Design*, 2nd edn. Sage, London.
A guide to many aspects of digital data visualisation, especially for quantitative data.

Kraak, M.J., Roth, R.E., Ricker, B., Kagawa, A., and Le Sourd, G. (2020) *Mapping for a Sustainable World*. United Nations, New York.
An accessible and practical introductory guide to mapping and cartographic design, supported by plenty of examples drawn from sustainable development initiatives.

11
Data Analytics

Overview

Chapter 11 examines:

- the use of quantitative methods, data analytics and machine learning for undertaking research on digital life;
- data mining as a form of exploratory analysis to identify and extract meaningful data and insights from large datasets;
- the use of network analysis to identify and analyse the connective organisation of digital infrastructures, websites, social media and relations in big data;
- various forms of statistical analyses for establishing the salience of associations and relationships between datasets;
- the use of modelling and simulation techniques for understanding and predicting how systems work under different conditions; and
- claims that big data, data analytics and machine learning fundamentally change the epistemology of social science and humanities research.

Introduction

There is a long history of various quantitative methods, such as statistical analysis and modelling, being used in social science research. From the 1960s onwards, such methods have also become more common in humanities research (see **Chapter 9**). This chapter provides a general overview of the use of data analytics to understand digital life, placing these methods in the epistemological context of positivism (see **Chapter 2**). The latter is important since a number of claims have been made that the developments of big data and data analytics are set to fundamentally alter the epistemological and methodological bases of social sciences and humanities research through the adoption of data-driven, computational approaches. The chapter opens with an overview of data analytics and machine learning in general terms. This is then followed by more detailed discussions of methods of network analysis, statistical analysis, and modelling and simulation. The final part of the chapter examines the epistemological and methodological implications of data analytics. It provides a brief critique of quantitative and computational approaches, and details current epistemological debates, including alternative critical framings to mainstream computational social science and digital humanities research (including critical data science and radical statistics).

Data Analytics

Until recently, the analysis methods researchers used in the social sciences were generally designed to extract insight from scarce and sampled data that were generated for a specific purpose (Miller, 2010). Preferably, the data would be representative and adhere to expectations of *independence* (each variable or statistical relationship is independently delineated), *stationarity* (there is stability over time in the data's statistical properties) and *normality* (the data does not have strong biases or unusual outliers). A challenge was the data were often static, lacking temporal sequence and weakly relational, making it difficult to link datasets together. Presently, the challenge has been to make sense of big data; that is, data that are large in volume, exhaustive to a system (rather than sampled), produced in real-time, have strong relationality, and might be the product of another task (Kitchin, 2014a). In other words, the challenge has shifted from extracting insights by mining a narrow seam of data, to gaining insights by sifting through huge tracts of data (Kitchin and Lauriault, 2015). Addressing this challenge has necessitated a shift in research approach, with the solution being the development of *data analytics*. Data analytics combine new information management and storage techniques (e.g., NoSQL databases and the cloud), a range of data analysis methods that use machine learning techniques to handle and analyse big data, and novel epistemological and methodological knowledges that have been formalised as the new discipline of Data Science (Kelleher and Tierney, 2018).

Machine learning utilises the power of computation and algorithms to handle massive volumes of data and to perform calculations that would be extremely difficult and time-consuming to perform by hand. Machine learning seeks to iteratively build an autonomous understanding of a dataset, and to develop automated processes that can assess and learn from the data and their analysis (Han et al., 2011). It is a form of artificial intelligence designed to computationally mine and detect patterns and build models. Two forms of machine learning predominate: *supervised learning*, which uses training data (see discussion of algorithmic audits in **Chapter 6**), and *unsupervised learning*, which is self-organised. In supervised learning, a model is trained to match inputs to certain known outputs. It is supervised in the sense that the training data guides the learning process (Hastie et al., 2009). The model might be trained to make a prediction that matches what actually occurred in the case to which the data refer; the resulting model is then applied to other similar data. For example, a model may be fed a training dataset of images labelled as 'birds' and 'drones' as an input, learning the distinguishing features between them. Applied to a new set of images of flying objects, the model will then identify images of birds and drones. In unsupervised learning, the model seeks to teach itself to spot patterns and find structure in data without the use of training data by identifying clusters and relationships that are not known in advance (Han et al., 2011). For example, the model might learn how to identify drones by itself through spotting similar patterns of pixels across images. A model learns by applying its initial formulation to the data, and then refines itself by repeatedly using the assigned learning rules and weightings, which direct how a model is built in relation to the data until a robust model is produced (Hastie et al., 2009).

Other forms of machine learning include semi-supervised learning, which uses training data but also seeks to self-identify patterns, and active learning, which lets its implementers play an active role in directing the learning model (Han et al., 2011). While machine learning aims to perform as an automated process, the analyst remains important for setting the initial parameters, guiding its development and assessing the intermediate results (Miller, 2010). Machine learning has been employed across a range of analysis methods – data mining, pattern recognition, data visualisation, visual analytics, network analysis, statistical analysis, prediction, simulation and optimisation – to answer questions relating to *description* (what), *explanation* (why), *prediction* (future outcomes) and *prescription* (optimal outcomes) (Minelli et al., 2013). These questions can refer to scientific, business and social policy issues, and the use of data analytics is often applied in orientation seeking to address societal challenges. In addition to providing a means to make sense of big data, data analytics can also be used to examine traditional sampled datasets, such as censuses, and can be applied to sizeable volumes of qualitative data such as repositories of documents and images (see **Chapter 10**).

It is important to note that the application of data analytics requires significant preparatory work. Given that many big data datasets are repurposed for analytical work, and they are often lacking in structure and suffer from data quality issues a great deal of data pre-processing is generally needed to select and sample data of interest; remove errors and biases; account for missing fields or inconsistencies; and to structure the data into a form suitable for analysis (Miller, 2010). Such data cleaning and wrangling work might include diminishing the dimensionality of the data through transformations (e.g., smoothing, aggregation, normalisation, concept hierarchy, principal components analysis) to address data quality issues and make the data suitable for different forms of analysis, or enriching the dataset by combining the selected data with other datasets to enable further insights to be produced (Han et al., 2011). Pre-analytic and analytical tasks can be difficult to perform on real-time data (data that are continuously being produced); it is instead common to create very large samples of cleaned, reduced, restructured data for analysis. In cases where real-time analytics are desired, these samples are used to establish how best to handle, reduce, clean and make sense of the data on the fly.

Since data analytics utilises the power of computation and machine learning, it can be easy to slip into the practice of *data dredging*; that is, repeatedly analysing a dataset, altering the learning rules and weightings, until a desired result is established (e.g., finding a statistically significant result; that is, there is a high probability that the result did not occur simply by chance; see below) (Bryant et al., 2008). A related practice is using an *ensemble method*, where rather than using the most suitable method based on the dataset and knowledge of the analyst, a variety of techniques are used to build multiple models (e.g., using a series of regression, neural network, nearest neighbour and decision tree models) and then selecting the best performing model (Siegel, 2013). These practices are frowned on by many statisticians as the analysis is not being guided by theory and knowledge, but is instead fishing for an answer that confirms an analyst's belief (Taleb, 2013). Moreover, such practices do not seek to determine if what a model finds is valid, or whether the result is random and represents a false positive (Ioannidis, 2013). Care thus needs to be taken in how data analytics are practised to avoid ecological fallacies (see **Chapter 4**).

Data Mining

Data mining is a form of exploratory analysis designed to extract meaningful data from, and identify patterns within, large datasets (Manyika et al., 2011). It does so by using supervised and unsupervised machine learning to detect, classify and segment relationships, associations and trends within the dataset (Han et al., 2011). A range of techniques can be used including natural language processing, neural networks, decision trees and statistical (non-parametric and parametric) methods (see Table 11.1). The selection of data mining method varies depending on the nature of the task and the type of data (structured, unstructured or semi-structured). Unstructured data, such as texts, images and sounds raise particular data mining challenges. *Natural language processing* techniques seek to analyse human language as expressed through the written and spoken word. They use semantics and taxonomies to recognise patterns and extract information from documents, audio files, etc. Examples include *entity extraction*, which automatically extracts metadata from text by searching for particular types of text and phrasing, such as names, locations, dates, specialised terms and product

Table 11.1 Data mining tasks and techniques.

Data mining task	Description	Techniques
Segmentation or clustering	Determine a set of implicit groups within the data	Cluster analysis
Classification	Organise the data into classes	Bayesian classification Decision tree induction Neural networks
Association	Find relationships among the data; predict the value of some attribute based on the value of other attributes	Association rules Bayesian networks Social network analysis Regression
Deviations	Find data that exhibit unusual deviations from expectations	Cluster analysis Outlier detection Evolution analysis
Trends	Identify patterns that sustain over time	Regression Sequence pattern extraction
Generalisations	Determine compact descriptions of the data	Summary rules Attribute-oriented induction

Source: Adapted from Miller and Han (2009: 7).

terminology; and *entity relation extraction*, which automatically identifies the relationships between semantic entities, linking them together (e.g., person name to birth date or location, or an opinion to an item) (Kempe, 2009).

A typical application of such techniques is *sentiment analysis*, which seeks to determine the general nature and strength of opinions about an issue, for example what people are saying about an issue on social media. Detecting, classifying and extracting patterns within images – such as facial or place recognition – is not straightforward. This is being tackled through a range of new image processing, machine vision and photogrammetric techniques, including object recognition and template matching using training datasets, clustering methods, and neural networking (Ohlhorst, 2013). These techniques can be used to efficiently mine a very large number of images. For example, ImageVision (http://imagevision.com/) claims to be able to categorise 50,400 minutes of video per hour per server, using machine learning algorithms to detect certain features such as faces, objects, motion and text. Undertaking data mining on big data requires specialist skills for selecting and implementing appropriate methods and for interpreting results; it would be a folly to attempt without training.

Network Analysis

Network analysis aims to identify and analyse the interconnections between, and the form and structure of relationships among, a set of people or phenomena (such as publications or web pages). The methodology employed to analyse a network draws on *graph theory*, which establishes the relationships and structure between objects (Barabasi, 2016). This typically takes the form of a matrix that denotes connections (e.g., 'is related to', 'is friends with', 'is an acquaintance of') between objects (e.g., actors, institutions, publications) (Stevenson and Ben-David, 2019). Relationships are either directed (a hierarchical relationship between boss and employee) or undirected (two-way relationship, as in friendship). The objects and their relations can be visualised as network diagrams of nodes and lines in which different forms of connections (e.g., kinship plus friendships, or just kinship) or connections between different categories of member objects (e.g., men and women) are displayed (see **Chapter 10**). Given the complexity of mapping relationships, it is customary to use specialist software that employs a rule set to organise spatially the diagram (Barabasi, 2016). These diagrams reveal the centre and periphery of networks and the key connector nodes, as well as associated measures such as network density (the ratio between actual and potential connections in a network) and distance (the length of paths between nodes), and provide a means of comparing network structures (Barabasi, 2016; Stevenson and Ben-David, 2019).

Given that the internet is itself a network, and that it hosts large, distributed social communities, network analysis has been a key means of examining the connective organisation of infrastructure (e.g., telecom and internet service providers) (Tranos, 2013), websites (e.g., the hyperlink connections between webpages) (Park, 2003) and social networks (e.g., the friendship connections or following/followers on social media) (Park et al., 2018). It is also a key means of mapping relations within big data (e.g., citation patterns between publications as recorded in bibliographic databases) (Tang et al., 2017). While network analysis is a very useful means of making sense of the interconnections between objects, it does not reveal the nature or meaning of those relations. A network diagram may identify key nodes and clusters within a social community, but not why they exist, how the relationships between them function in practice or what it is like to be a network member (Stevenson and Ben-David, 2019). As such, additional analysis is required to establish an explanation for how a network is structured and how it operates. This might involve undertaking interviews or focus groups with network members (see **Chapter 5**), or analysing the posts, comments and sharing within a network.

Statistical Analysis

Statistics is a branch of mathematics that seeks to extract information and insight from large masses of numerical data. Over the past couple of centuries, a diverse range of statistical techniques have been developed to analyse various kinds of data and to ask and answer different kinds of questions. While some statistical techniques are relatively generic, others are more specialised, specific to the data type (e.g., spatial or temporal data), distribution (normal versus skewed), number of variables being analysed (whether one, two or more) and domain (e.g., visual analytics, photogrammetry). *Descriptive statistics* are a means of identifying the characteristics of a dataset, such as calculating the mean, median, mode, distribution and standard deviation of a variable (Holcomb, 1998; Scott Jones and Goldring, 2022). They can also include charting the data as histograms, pie charts, time-series graphs and maps (see **Chapter 10**). Such descriptive statistics are common across epistemological approaches.

The use of *inferential statistics*, in contrast, is generally limited in use to more positivist approaches (see **Chapter 2**). Inferential statistics seek to explain, not simply describe, the patterns and relationships that may exist within a dataset, and to test the strength and significance of associations between variables (MacInnes, 2022). Inferential statistics include:

- *parametric statistics* that are employed to statistically assess the salience of hypotheses using interval data (measurements along a scale with arbitrary interval and origin; e.g., temperature on the Celsius scale) and ratio data (measurements along a fixed scale that possess a zero origin; e.g., exam marks ranging from 0–100);
- *non-parametric statistics* used for testing hypotheses using nominal data (classified into categories; e.g., sensor, actuator, meter) or ordinal level data (classified into ranked categories; e.g., high, medium, low); and
- *probabilistic statistics* that determine the probability of a condition occurring.

Parametric and non-parametric statistics are used to test the significance of differences between datasets or the strength of a relationship between variables and thus whether a hypothesis can be accepted or rejected. In effect, a significance test is seeking to determine whether differences between datasets are real and thus unlikely to be the result of chance, or whether a potential relationship between variables is real and not arbitrary, and to what extent we can have confidence in the test result (Foster et al., 2015). This confidence is expressed by comparing the test result to a critical value that provides a probability estimate of the significance level of the result. The significance level is usually expressed as $p=0.05$ or $p=0.01$, meaning that we can be confident that there is only a 1 in 20, or 1 in 100, chance in making an error if the hypothesis is accepted as true.

Selecting the right statistical technique for the data and task is important (e.g., applying a parametric test to ordinal data will produce invalid results), and is best achieved by undertaking an exploratory data analysis (Spiegelhalter, 2019). This analysis, which examines the metadata and performs some descriptive statistics, is designed to identify the data type, its characteristics (e.g., whether its distribution normalised or skewed) and any data quality issues (e.g., missing values) that need addressing. If necessary, data transformations may need to be performed on the dataset, such as using a mathematical transformation (e.g., logarithmic, square root, or power function) to produce a normal distribution, or converting interval data to nominal data. Such exploratory data analysis is also necessary for big data, especially since big data might have more issues than carefully curated sampled datasets (and might in part be performed using data mining techniques). Once this transformation is undertaken, it is possible to apply statistical analysis within a data analytics framework. This analysis is not always straightforward as many statistics were designed to test differences and relationships using small, sampled data (Miller, 2010). Moreover, the massive size of the datasets mean that many of the results that have p-values above 0.05 are in fact spurious (Taleb, 2013). One means of dealing with this is to segment datasets into smaller refined samples, or to divide the dataset into random samples and see if statistical tests provide the same results across samples, or to cross-validate the results with other similar datasets (McFarland and McFarland, 2015). In addition to significance testing, statistics are routinely used in aiding data mining, prediction and optimisation. There are a large number of statistics textbooks that explain in detail how to undertake initial data analysis and correctly perform statistical analysis in the big data age.

Modelling and Simulation

Modelling is a means of explaining how systems function in practice and what might occur under different conditions. For example, we might want to model how traffic moves around a transportation network under different weather conditions or if a critical junction is closed, or see how alternative settings in an intelligent transport system might affect traffic flow. Such models are useful for informing how an organisation manages a system, plans for various contingencies and develops policy for system improvements. There is a long history of models of social and economic systems being produced. The rollout of computation in the 1960s aided the necessary and complex calculations required to produce working models and led to a rapid growth in modelling in academia and its deployment by governments and businesses, with a wide number of modelling approaches being developed. For example, models were produced to predict, simulate and/or optimise system performance relating to the siting of retail outlets, social and health services, and transportation routes (see Chorley and Haggett, 1967; Forrester, 1969).

Simulations aim to reproduce how real-world processes and systems perform within a computational model. To do so, they seek to identify key components of a system, their characteristics and interrelationships, how these act in common scenarios, and to statistically evaluate their performance in relation to real-world outcomes with a view to improving their efficiency and effectiveness (Robinson, 2003). For example, traffic forecasts are based on simulations of how traffic performs under prevalent conditions, with the actual network performance being used to further refine the model for future forecasts (Barcelo, 2010). In the case of traffic, the model used to calculate the operational decisions of an intelligent transport system is an optimisation model, designed to sequence traffic lights to provide optimal traffic flow and system performance and reduce road congestion. Optimisation models are usually used to try to reduce cost and increase efficiencies in how a system performs.

Over time, modelling has become more sophisticated and powerful. As modelling methods and techniques have improved and machine learning has been introduced, the base knowledge for models has been iterated and refined, suitable fine-grained data has become increasingly available, and the computational power to run the models has expanded enormously. In the age of big data, models are increasingly sophisticated, able to model very complex systems and process massive amounts of granular, real-time data. Modelling approaches have also diversified. These include *agent-based models*, which seek to simulate and predict how people will behave (as consumers, workers, travellers, etc.). An illustrative example is SimCity, which simulates how a city will grow and develop under different conditions based on an underlying model of known urban processes, and which has been popularised as a game (Batty, 2007). The model consists of an environment where individual features such as buildings and roads are assigned certain characteristics. This environment is then populated with agents; that is, simulated actors that are ascribed particular qualities that affect how they act. When the model is run, the agents seek to solve a task, reacting to the environment and other agents in relation to their ascribed characteristics and pre-defined rules for how they can operate. In turn, as the agents undertake their tasks, they change the environment, in this case the city they inhabit, producing a complex, emergent system (Batty, 2007).

Modelling approaches are often rooted in a metaphorical framing. For example, *genetic models* use ideas from natural selection, such as inheritance, mutation, selection and crossover to develop and evolve candidate solutions to a problem (Mitchell, 1996). Similarly, *neural networking* mimics how the human brain works, utilising highly interconnected processing elements to calculate, evaluate and solve a problem (Picton, 2000). Each modelling approach has strengths and weaknesses depending on the type and quality of data and the type of system being modelled (Seni and Elder, 2010). Since it is often difficult to prejudge which type of model and variants will perform best, an ensemble approach can be used that builds multiple models using a variety of techniques to model the same phenomena (Siegel, 2013). For example, an ensemble approach to predicting customer behaviour might construct a set of regression, neural network, nearest neighbour and decision tree models. The results from these models can be compared and combined, compensating for the weaknesses in each model (such as some being better at predicting certain kinds of consumer than others), providing a more robust prediction (Franks, 2012). At the same time, care needs to be taken not to use an ensemble approach to practise data dredging.

Critiques and Reframing of Data Analytics

Big data analytics enable complex systems to be modelled in sophisticated, computationally intensive ways, to move from static snapshots to dynamic analysis, and from coarse aggregations to fine-grained resolutions (Kitchin, 2014a). In other words, they allow scholars to undertake research that has much greater breadth, depth, scale and timeliness (Lazer et al., 2009). Moreover, big data analytics address some of the critiques of traditional positivist analysis, particularly the charges of reductionism (reduced variance in datasets due to abstraction and generalisation) and universalism (analysis being applied to wide populations rather than disaggregated groups) (Batty et al., 2012). Nonetheless, many of the critiques ranged against positivist social science from the 1960s onwards remain valid, such as their 'god's eye' (objectivist) rather than situated view (Haraway, 1988), apolitical framing and deliberate avoidance of normative and metaphysical issues (Harvey, 1972) (see **Chapter 2**).

Positivist approaches have been castigated for their seemingly apolitical framing, concentrating on the statistical analysis of facts rather than considering the contested politics of social systems (Harvey, 1972). Positivism treats people as if they are rational beings devoid of culture, ideology, history and irrationality, who act in logical, predictable ways that are straightforward to model. In this sense, positivist approaches are somewhat peopleless, in that they do not adequately account for the messy, contingent and contextual nature of peoples' beliefs, values, opinions, and feelings, and how these vary across individuals and circumstance (Buttimer, 1976). The result is a surface analysis rather than a deep understanding of complex lives and societal structures and processes. Moreover, positivist approaches focus on analysing how things are and promote the idea that social problems can be fixed by applying a set of formulaic and technical solutions. Such a framing ignores normative and ethical questions related to how society should be organised, and that solutions are rarely straightforward in practice and are necessarily infused with politics (Kitchin, 2015). At an epistemological level, this is captured by the notion that positivist approaches seek to provide a 'god's eye' (omniscient, detached and dispassionate) view of the world that is seemingly neutral and objective in nature (Haraway, 1988). This epistemological claim has been challenged by feminist critiques in particular, which argue that all science is rooted in value-laden practices of enquiry and situated within the knowledges, experience and social positionality of researchers (see **Chapter 2**). In other words, research occurs in social context and a scientist needs to acknowledge their positionality and that of any research participants (Rose, 1993).

As a number of scholars have noted, such critiques do not mean that quantitative and computational approaches should be abandoned (Kitchin, 2014b). But neither should these approaches blithely ignore such concerns and continue to be practised without considering how such concerns might be ameliorated. Over the past three decades, a number of new post-positivist epistemological positions have been developed that retain statistical and data analytics approaches, but reframe them using critical social theory. In the wake of fierce epistemological debate in the 1990s, *Critical GIS* sought to reframe GIS practice within feminist-inspired science and technology studies, acknowledging and accounting for the situated politics of mapping and recasting GIS practice through new methodological interventions such as participatory GIS and counter-mapping (Schuurman and Pratt, 2002). Challenging the ideological neutrality of positivism, the *Radical Statistics* movement has sought to use statistics explicitly within a normative framing to address social justice issues (Evans et al., 2019). *Feminist data science* promotes the situated use of data analytics and machine learning that recognises the politics of scientific practices and how data science is applied in practice (D'Ignazio and Klein, 2020). Collectively, these epistemological approaches recast data science as critical data science in which quantitative techniques, inferential statistics, modelling, simulation and visual analytics are employed, but through a framing that actively acknowledges, and seeks to compensate for, the inherent politics pervading the datasets analysed, the research conducted and the interpretations made (Kitchin, 2014b).

Summary

- This chapter has detailed the use of data analytics for researching digital life, in which machine learning and computational forms of analysis are drawn upon to explore and analyse data. Such analysis includes network analysis, statistical analysis and modelling and simulation.
- Conducting social research using a scientific epistemology borrowed from the natural sciences has a long history. The challenge of such research was to extract insights from relatively scarce and sampled data. The advent of big data provides the opposite problem – gaining insights from a massive amount of data. The solution has been machine learning and computational methods, in which algorithms are used to process and analyse data.

- Data mining uses machine-learning techniques to detect relationships, trends and patterns within a dataset that might warrant further analysis. Network analysis can identify the interconnections and structure among a large group of phenomena. Statistical analysis tests the probability of meaningful relationships between variables in a dataset and are a key means of assessing the salience of hypotheses. Modelling and simulations allow the functioning of a system to be charted and to explore what might occur in various scenarios.
- Data analytics does not necessarily need to be practised within a positivist framing. Instead, it can be applied using the ideals and practices of critical GIS, radical statistics and feminist data science.

Recommended Reading

Alvarez, R.M. (ed.) (2016) *Computational Social Science*. Cambridge University Press, Cambridge.
An overview of the approach, methods and challenges of computational social science.

Barabasi, A.-L. (2016) *Network Science*. Cambridge University Press, Cambridge.
Provides a comprehensive discussion on network analysis techniques.

D'Ignazio, C., and Klein, L.F. (2020) *Data Feminism*. MIT Press, Cambridge, MA.
Sets out a feminist epistemology and ethics for conducting critical data science.

Han, J., Kamber, M., and Pei, J. (2022) *Data Mining: Concepts and Techniques*, 4th edn. Morgan Kaufmann, Waltham, MA.
A comprehensive overview of the theory and practices of data mining.

Kitchin, R. (2022) *The Data Revolution: A Critical Analysis of Big Data, Open Data and Data Infrastructures*. 2nd edn. Sage, London.
Provides a detailed discussion of epistemological debates arising from the use of big data and data analytics.

Spiegelhalter, D. (2019) *The Art of Statistics: Learning from Data*. Pelican, London.
A lively discussion of the use of statistics in the big data age.

Part 3
Methods in Action

12
Interfaces and Apps

Overview

Chapter 12 examines:

- interfaces and apps as distinct sites of social science research into digital life;
- how interfaces and apps have been studied through walkthrough methods, tracking algorithms and code, (auto)ethnographic approaches and data visualisation and mapping;
- how different digital methods enable ways of attending to the complex interrelations between interfaces and apps.

Introduction

Digital interfaces and apps now mediate many aspects of how people engage with the world around them. At the most basic level, many people use word processor interfaces as a core part of their jobs, hundreds of millions of people spend hours every day playing video games, and a couple of billion people now own smartphones and use messaging apps such as WhatsApp to communicate with one another. Furthermore, it is common to utilise interfaces and apps to access and manage all manner of services, from self-service check-outs in supermarkets to smartphone apps that are used to pay energy bills. On a more profound level, both interfaces and apps have also transformed aspects of pre-existing practices. For instance, the way that the Google search engine interface works to order and present content fundamentally changes how people discover, access and understand knowledge. Or, in relation to apps, the Uber platform and the way that it is accessed via its app, radically transforms older services such as taxis for both the driver and rider (see **Chapter 14**). As such, it is not hyperbolic to state that interfaces and apps have fundamentally altered many aspects of social life, including work, leisure, health and romantic relationships.

However, it is important to point out that digital interfaces and apps are not the same. Digital interfaces can be broadly defined as 'the point of juncture between different bodies, hardware, software, users and what they connect to or are part of' (Cramer and Fuller, 2008: 150). From this point of view, a digital interface can be a graphical user interface (GUI) (defined as an interface based on graphical rather than textual input) on a screen, such as a word processing programme, with its particular visual layout of buttons, menus and writing space. A digital interface can also designate the functionality and capacities of the program that are accessed through the GUI and the hardware through which the GUI and the program's functions and capacities are engaged with (such as the keyboard, mouse track pad or smartphone touch screen). Or, a digital interface does not need to have a GUI and might be a simple plastic button, such as a button on a WiFi plug, which serves to wirelessly connect the plug to a router and so allow it to be controlled via third-party software or an app.

Distinct from digital interfaces, apps can be defined as 'executable pieces of software that are offered as applications, services or systems to end-users' (Ghazawneh and Henfridsson, 2013: 175). Apps are often distributed via distinct app marketplaces, which can be understood to 'offer…a venue for exchanging applications between developers and end-users belonging to a single or multiple ecosystems' (Ghazawneh and Henfridsson, 2015: 200). These app stores and the apps they sell are most commonly associated with smartphones (e.g., Apple App Store) and PC operating systems (e.g., Windows Store), but there are app stores for other types of content, such as video games (e.g., Nintendo Eshop) and specialist software (e.g., Adobe's Creative Cloud) (Morris et al., 2021).

For social scientists interested in researching digital life, it is important to understand the dense entanglements between interfaces and apps. For example, dating apps such as Tinder have GUIs that are key to both how users engage with the app and what is unique about the app (such as the swiping feature, which allows users to quickly judge and choose between a large number of potential romantic 'matches') (David and Cambre, 2016). At the same time, apps such as Tinder are not reducible to their GUI interface as there is always more going on in an app than appears in the GUI, such as algorithms that are invisible to the Tinder user, but which guide the order that potential 'matches' are shown. Furthermore, the Tinder app has multiple different versions that are platform specific. For example, the service can be accessed via specific apps for Apple and Android operating systems, which are distributed via different app marketplaces (the App Store for Apple and the Google Play store for Google). Furthermore, these different versions of the app can be used on different devices with their own distinct hardware and software interfaces (e.g., an Apple iPhone and a Google Pixel smartphone), which also have their own capacities and affordances. At the same time, Tinder also has a web interface and GUI that is distinct from, and in turn operates differently compared to, either the Apple or Android version of the app. As this example demonstrates, it is difficult to talk about Tinder as a single defined thing or as either only an app or only an interface. Recognising the complex relations between interfaces and apps, in what follows, this chapter will discuss examples of how interfaces and apps have been studied utilising app walkthrough methods (see **Chapter 6**); tracking algorithms and design patterns in interfaces and apps; ethnography (see **Chapter 5**); and visualisation and mapping techniques (see **Chapter 9**).

App Walkthroughs of Interfaces and Apps

A key method that has emerged to study the complexity of interfaces and apps and the interrelations between them is app walkthroughs (Light et al., 2018; see **Chapter 6**). A good example is MacLean and Hatcher's (2019) study, which used the app walkthrough method to understand how mental health apps such as the BEACON Rx platform implicitly communicate various ideals about what it means to be healthy. This study involved the researchers themselves conducting the walkthrough. They identified three different user profiles that could be accessed in the app – a patient-user profile, an administrator-user profile and a provider-user profile – and created a profile for each in order to understand how the app appeared differently for each type of user. To do so, the researchers also took screenshots of every distinct screen they encountered while navigating the app using the different profiles. The data was then analysed to understand both the technical aspects of how the app could be engaged with by the user, as well as the representational content of the app, including text and images within it. In this case, MacLean and Hatcher (2019) used the data collected via the app walkthrough method to understand both the ideal subject the app developer wanted to create and how the app constructed and normalised a particular notion of health, with 'good' healthy users being those who were willing to regularly submit to self-surveillance by entering updates about their mood and feelings via the app.

The app walkthrough method can be deployed as a user-led method (see **Chapter 6**), in which 'participant[s guide] the researcher through the app's features and typical interactions' (Ferris and Duguay, 2020: 494). Ferris and Duguay provide a useful example of user-led walkthroughs in action through their study of women seeking women (WSW) experiences on the dating app Tinder. The researchers interviewed twenty-seven women aged nineteen to thirty-five and with a range of sexual identities including lesbian and gay to show the researchers how they actively used Tinder and engaged with the app. Transcripts from the interviews were then coded and analysed to identify themes. Utilising the user-led walkthrough, it became clear to the researchers that WSW on Tinder actively worked around the affordances and design intentions of the interface to try to secure a safe experience where they could match with relevant people. As Ferris and Duguay (2020: 501) put it:

> The ability for users to configure Tinder's settings for 'woman seeking women' emerged as an imagined affordance, which participants perceived as allowing them to enter Gay Tinder – a space imagined as an opportunity to connect more concertedly with other women and an informational source about their potential sexual identifications. However, frequent encounters with cisgender-presenting men, predatory accounts, couples, and heterosexual women heightened the need for participants to signal their sexual identity more saliently.

These signals 'involved a fusion of digital and cultural referents, with lesbian stereotypes and tropes commonly included as highly recognizable indicators of sexual identity within Tinder's rapid swipe screen' (Ferris and Dugay, 2020: 501). In turn, the use of these signals 'were imagined to resonate with a shared community of WSW', and 'their normalization and routinization contributed to the construction of a lesbian digital imaginary that shaped participants' self-presentation and interpretation of others' profiles' (Ferris and Dugay, 2020: 501). The user-led walkthrough helped the researchers understand how different groups constructed relatively safe spaces in the app, and also raised questions about the extent to which Tinder as a platform could control or regulate its users.

App walkthroughs have also been mobilised to encourage respondents to look back at their past activity on a platform (Yang et al., 2022). Robards and Lincoln (2017) used the 'scroll back' (Møller and Robards, 2019) form of walkthrough to study memory in relation to Facebook feeds and timelines. In their study, Robards and Lincoln (2017) combined semi-structured interviews and observation of participants as they showed the researchers their Facebook feed and timelines. Data from the interviews and observation were transcribed and coded using thematic analysis. Through thematic analysis, the researchers identified that the Facebook timeline interface played an important role in shaping what the participants remembered and how they remembered it, and in turn '[gave] the young people' in their study 'a platform through which to produce and curate their own longitudinal life narratives, albeit within the confines of Facebook's own curatorial algorithmic architecture' (Robards and Lincoln, 2017: 726).

Utilising a 'designerly walkthrough' approach, Dieter and Tkacz (2020) compared the design of eight 'challenger' banking apps to identify trends in how they signed up or 'onboarded' new customers. Creating a Walkthrough Explorer tool, developed using WordPress software, Dieter and Tkacz placed the onboarding interfaces from different banking apps alongside one another to examine the visual and functional similarities and differences between them. Through a comparative analysis, where the researchers identified visual and function similarities and differences between the apps, they were able to discern patterns of interface design across different apps. In turn, this comparative data allowed the researchers to argue that the identified patterns worked to normalise practices of security verification by drawing on broader habitual practices of smartphone use (such as taking a selfie to send to the bank to confirm identity). Through the walkthrough explorer tool it therefore became possible for the researchers to speak of new patterns of finance and security that are emergent within digital life.

In all these examples, different versions of technical walkthroughs were mobilised to make sense of both how interfaces and apps appear to, and are understood to operate by, researchers, as well as how they are used and made sense of by users. In turn, these walkthrough methods provide a way of understanding how interfaces and apps alter how both researchers and users think about and relate to themselves and the world around them. At the same time, a range of methods have been used to go beyond the surface appearance of interfaces and apps to understand the algorithms and other unseen variables that influence what interfaces and apps do and how they affect human practices. As the next section details, these methods include forms of 'tracker tracking', as well as more traditional forms of interview.

Methods for Researching Algorithms and Design Patterns in Interfaces and Apps

Deville and van der Velden (2016) have studied interfaces to seek to understand the 'opaque practices' that underlie how websites appear differently to different users and 'render visible commercial forms of algorithmic calculation' (Deville and van der Velden, 2016: 94). Specifically, they developed a method called 'tracker tracking', which sought to understand how algorithms on websites work by experimenting with the interfaces through which such algorithms were accessed. In doing so, they attempted to understand the logic behind different algorithms and the variables that influenced the results an algorithm provided different users. For example, they turned to high-cost short-term credit (HCSTC) websites to try and ascertain what factors might determine how much money is offered to different website users. When logging on to sites, such as (the now defunct) Wonga.com, slider bars would indicate a minimum and maximum amount a visitor to the site might be able to borrow. However, experimentation by the researchers showed that the graphical button on the slider bar (which denoted a particular amount of British pounds) was not fixed, but actively changed depending on who was visiting the site. To understand the variables that might affect where the button appeared, the researchers experimented with a number of changes, such as altering the computer operating system they used to access Wonga.com, the time of day used to access the site and the geographical location (logged through IP address) registered when accessing the site. Recording the results of these experiments, they engaged in comparative analysis to identify trends and to see if they could isolate which exact variables might affect the amount of money offered by a loan company. Although they could not make definitive statements after their period of experimentation, their work offers a good example of how researchers can try to uncover logics of algorithmic calculation and interface design that are purposively hidden from users and which companies refuse to reveal.

Another method for researching algorithms and design patterns in interfaces are interviews. Investigating HCSTC web interfaces, Ash et al. (2018a) drew on eleven interviews with web and user experience (UX) designers who had worked on HCSTC websites, and forty interviews with people who had borrowed money using these sites. These interviews were conducted to gain insight into the same 'opaque practices' that Deville and van der Velden (2016: 91) had sought to understand. Ash et al. (2018a) focused their questions on a) the techniques that were used when designing HCSTC websites to maximise applications for loans; b) how designers used data analytics to improve applicant rates and in turn; c) how these processes were experienced by everyday users of these sites. The data from the interviews was coded and analysed through a thematic analysis. The findings of the thematic analysis demonstrated that HCSTC websites draw on a range of data about the user to actively try to 'funnel' them into applying for a loan through changing elements of their sites, including their interface design and the algorithmic forms of calculation that were not visible to the user and occurred in real time. For instance, designers of HCSTC sites would regularly trial different colours of 'apply now' button to see which colour elicited the most clicks and in turn changed the design of the website based on these analytics. Furthermore, as demonstrated in Deville and van der Velden's (2016) study discussed above, designers used algorithms to calculate the default position of the money slider depending on the user's IP address and operating system to encourage users to engage with the sliders, which increased the user's chance of applying for a loan. However, while these 'funnelling' techniques could be effective, the study also suggested that users did not simply or uncritically accept these design elements and forms of algorithmic calculation. In doing so, the research demonstrated the difficult and contested nature of attempting to influence user behaviour through digital interface design and algorithmic calculation.

Other studies have focused on the 'folklore' and assumptions that users have around the way that design patterns and algorithms work in relation to digital interfaces and apps (e.g., Huang et al., 2022; Schellewald, 2022; Swart, 2021). Bishop's (2020) study examined how algorithmic expertise on YouTube is constructed and sold to others by 'expert' users of the platform. An example of this expertise is advice on the optimal colour to use for the background of video thumbnails in order to maximise the chance of a user clicking on them. Drawing on a range of methods, including interviews and analysis of online documents such as public speeches and YouTube videos, Bishop (2020: 7) found that while presenting their advice as neutral and objective, 'experts... outputs and theories are shot through with individually and culturally informed assumptions, theories, and understandings of algorithms and audience behavior'. Regardless of its validity, Bishop used the data that the YouTube 'experts' had collected to argue that this expert information can then go on to influence the type and form of content that YouTube creators choose to create, such as the particular length of their videos or the kinds of music that they soundtrack their videos with.

What the above sets of methods demonstrate is that it is possible to study seemingly hidden algorithms and design patterns that inform what interfaces do, but it is also useful to consider how these phenomena are assumed to operate, as these assumptions can also have powerful effects. At the same time, interfaces and apps are never used or developed in a vacuum. That is to say, interfaces and apps are always experienced as part of broader spaces and times, including institutions, workplaces and public spaces that make up everyday life. Here, ethnographic approaches have provided a range of insights into interfaces and apps in relation to digital life.

Ethnographic Approaches to Interfaces and Apps

A range of studies have utilised ethnographic approaches (see **Chapter 5**) to understand both interfaces and apps and the relations between interfaces and apps. Richardson and Hjorth (2017) conducted an ethnography of mobile media interfaces drawing on re-enactments, walkthroughs (see **Chapter 6**), participant observation and diaries and interviews (see **Chapter 5**). The aim of the three-year multi-city study in Australia was to understand how mobile media devices were used within the spaces of the home, and how they might be altering social relations therein. The participants were asked to both perform and reflect on habitually used games and apps in the space-times of their homes, and to provide responses to questions from researchers. Participants were also asked to take researchers on guided visits of their homes so that the researchers could understand where digital devices were placed, and how the devices were used and linked to other social practices with other members of the household. Furthermore, participants in the research study provided media diaries that were digitally recorded, including photos and video, which the researchers would revisit with the participants in order to explore their connection between mobile media devices and the social environment of the home. In turn, this data was analysed contextually, with the researchers seeking to understand how practices of media use were informed by the spatial context of the home. Through their data analysis, Richardson and Hjorth (2017: 1660) identified that 'mobile touchscreens are transforming our embodied experience of sociality and material culture within domestic environments (i.e., our ways of "being-with-others" and "being-with-media" at home)'.

Also working in the space of the home, Bos's (2018) study of *Call of Duty* video game players drew on ethnographic methods consisting of household visits, gaming interviews and video ethnography to study war gaming interfaces. The research consisted of thirty-two participants – thirty male and two female – between the ages of eighteen and forty years old. Thirty-two semi-structured interviews were conducted, as well as fifteen gaming interviews, where the researcher played a game with the interviewee while asking questions. Five video ethnographies were also completed, in which the researcher recorded gameplay from previously interviewed participants in order to analyse what they did in-game. Bos (2018: 57) emphasises that utilising ethnographic methods enabled a shift in focus from 'what players say they do to what players actually do'. The data from the interviews and video interviews were transcribed and analysed using a descriptive approach. Through the analysis of this data, Bos discovered how players formed an embodied relationship with in-game weapons via the interface of force feedback from motors in the control pad, which worked to approximate the haptic sense of real-life weapon fire. In doing so, the ethnographic investigation demonstrated how video game interfaces could work as forms of 'symbolic geopolitical power' (Bos 2018: 61) and operate to normalise militarised violence.

Elsewhere, Ritter (2021) mixed methods of app walkthrough and participant observation into what they termed a 'fusion method', to understand how apps and interfaces shape practices of work in a Norwegian software design company. Over three months, Ritter participated in meetings, shadowed employees at the company offices and conducted thirty in-depth interviews. Data collected using these methods was analysed to understand how digital interfaces acted as sites of mediation. Through the analysis of this data, Ritter identified how the interfaces of software – such as the messaging platform Slack and online software repository GitHub – were key to how the company worked. In the case of GitHub, the internal metrics of the software were used to chart and analyse employee performance. As 'units of analysis', how the GitHub interface displayed metrics of work in terms of graphs and charts was key to how the productivity of employees was understood. As Ritter (2021: 928) puts it:

> the skilled practices in which software developers engaged on this platform underwent a process of datafication and were constantly displayed in ordinal rankings and classifications ... [T]he number of commits per user [the number of changes they had made to files] ... generated a ranking system of the firm's software developers and assigned meanings to individual work performances.

Ritter's findings demonstrate that the way data was collected and presented via the GitHub interface changed social relationships among employees and their managers, with the culture of ranking working to organise activities and relationships within the office environment and beyond. As this ethnographic approach to interfaces demonstrates, interfaces and apps are both made sense of within particular contexts, such as the workplace, but can also change these contexts and the social relationships therein.

Visualising and Mapping Interfaces and Apps

Alongside app walkthroughs, researching algorithms and design patterns that underlie interfaces and apps, and ethnographies of interfaces and apps, other studies have used visualisation and mapping methods (see **Chapter 10**) to understand and chart the proliferation of interfaces, app platforms and app marketplaces and economies (Jia et al., 2022). In particular, work from the field of 'app studies' (Dieter et al., 2019) has sought to understand how apps are distributed across different platforms using quantitative methods (also see Dieter et al., 2018; van der Vlist and Helmond, 2021). Dieter et al. (2021) for example focus on how COVID-19 apps were distributed across two key app stores: Google Play and Apple's App Store. In doing so, they drew:

> attention to how platform governance is layered across different dimensions. Specifically, this includes: the algorithmic sorting of COVID-19 apps; the kinds of actors involved in app development; the types of app responses; the geographic distribution of the apps; the responsivity of their development (i.e., how quickly apps are released or updated); how developers frame their apps and address their users; and the technical composition of the apps themselves. (Dieter et al., 2021: 4)

Utilising scraping and searching techniques (see **Chapters 3** and **6**) of the Google Play and Apple app stores they examined, a) app source sets; b) actor types behind COVID-19 apps; c) geographical distribution of COVID-19 related apps by country and region; d) the type of app (e.g., contact tracing, educational etc); and e) developer responsivity in updating the app, among other variables. They presented this data through a range of visualisation techniques, including bar charts, heat maps and Venn diagrams. For example, a Venn diagram visualisation was used to identify which apps were available in either the Apple or Google Play app stores or both. The apps were visualised using colour-coded circles within the Venn diagram sets to denote which actors had produced these apps (e.g., government, civil society, the private sector, etc.). Through the production and analysis of this visualisation the researchers discovered that many COVID-19 apps were only available on either Google Play or the Apple App Store, not both. In their words, 'about 70% (N=134) of government apps within the Google Play editorial set do not have an iOS equivalent in the App Store' (Dieter et al., 2021: 9).

A timeline graph was also produced, which visualised when COVID-19 apps were released in different countries and when they were updated on the Google Play store, with countries presented on the X axis, and time in years and months on the Y axis. Circles on the timeline denoted the initial release of apps and squares denoted updates of these apps, with the size of the squares scaled relative to the number of releases within a specific period. Through the production and analysis of this visualisation, in concert with pre-existing data on app updating (McIlroy et al., 2016), the researchers found that in comparison to other types of app, COVID-19 apps were regularly updated on the Google Play app store. These kinds of finding are important to help contextualise studies of apps that might be based on more individual engagements with interfaces and apps, or ethnographic studies of interfaces and apps based in particular settings. For example, Dieter et al.'s (2021) findings suggest that it cannot be assumed that an interface or app is available to all users of a device (in this case a smartphone, such as an Apple iPhone or a Google Pixel), which might not be made apparent through an app walkthrough or ethnographic study. Furthermore, this type of large-scale study emphasises the fact that apps (and the interfaces within these apps) are not universal or stable things, but are regularly updated, or withdrawn and abandoned. As such, researchers interested in studying interfaces and apps should be aware of the fact that the app they study may be specific to the hardware or operating system they are using. Furthermore, the app they are using today may not be the same app that is available tomorrow, or crucially may not be the same version of the app that is being used by the participants in their research.

Summary

- Interfaces are points of contact between software and hardware and a range of different people. Apps are distributable pieces of software that are often made available via particular app stores or platforms. When studying interfaces and apps, it is important that digital researchers are aware of the differences and interrelations between the two and how they might overlap in complex ways.
- Walkthrough methods are some of the most common ways that interfaces and apps have been studied by social scientists.
- Methods such as 'tracker tracking' can be used to attempt to understand the underlying or hidden code and algorithms that inform how interfaces and apps appear and operate.
- Ethnographic approaches to interfaces and apps have sought to contextualise these phenomena in relation to a range of settings in everyday life, including the home and workplace.

- Techniques of visualisation and mapping can be employed to understand the interrelations between interfaces and apps and broader app marketplace and platform economies.

Recommended Reading

Deville, J., and Velden, L. (2016) 'Seeing the invisible algorithm: The practical politics of tracking the credit trackers', in Amoore, L. and Piotukh, V. (eds) *Algorithmic Life: Calculative Devices in the Age of Big Data.* Routledge, London, pp. 87–106.
Details how the 'tracker tracking' approach can be used to study the operation of website interfaces.

Dieter, M., Helmond, A., Tkacz, N., van der Vlist, F., et al. (2021) 'Pandemic platform governance: Mapping the global ecosystem of COVID-19 response apps', *Internet Policy Review* 10(3): 1–27.
An article that demonstrates how apps can be mapped using a range of visualisation techniques.

MacLean, S., and Hatcher, S. (2019) 'Constructing the (healthy) neoliberal citizen: Using the walkthrough method to "do" critical health communication research', *Frontiers in Communication*, 4, https://doi.org/10.3389/fcomm.2019.00052.
A helpful article that illustrates the app walkthrough method in practice.

Ritter, C.S. (2021) 'Rethinking digital ethnography: A qualitative approach to understanding interfaces', *Qualitative Research*, 22(6): 916–32.
Demonstrates how multiple interface methods can be drawn on in a digital ethnography to understand the role interfaces play in the function of workplaces.

Robards, B., and Lincoln, S. (2017) 'Uncovering longitudinal life narratives: Scrolling back on Facebook', *Qualitative Research,* 17(6): 715–30.
An article that uses the 'scroll back' method as a form of app walkthrough to understand the Facebook timeline interface.

13
Social and Locative Media

Overview

Chapter 13 examines:

- the relationship between social and locative media and why investigating these topics are important for understanding digital life;
- how social and locative media has been studied through interviews and ethnography to understand the ways that people's understandings are shaped through their use of such media; and
- how researchers use data from social and locative media to make sense of other social phenomena.

Introduction

Social and locative media are intertwined phenomena. Social media can be defined as '[i]nternet-based channels that allow users to opportunistically interact and selectively self-present, either in real-time or asynchronously, with both broad and narrow audiences who derive value from user-generated content and the perception of interaction with others' (Carr and Hayes, 2015: 50). Social media include social networking platforms such as Twitter/X and Facebook, video sharing platforms like YouTube, image-sharing platforms such as Instagram, and short-form video platforms like TikTok. Locative media on the other hand may be broadly defined as platforms and digital devices that communicate their location to other digital devices and infrastructures. As Zeffiro et al. (2020: 19) put it:

> Something as straightforward as an IP (internet protocol) address that connects with a specific Wi-Fi hotspot is locative in many cases because the location of the Wi-Fi router is known by the system. Closed-circuit television (CCTV) is locative in the sense that it captures data traces of where bodies are at a

given moment. And with the emergence of the Internet of Things, more and more objects will communicate their locations to infrastructure in new ways. In cases where those objects are attached in some way to a person's identity (e.g., through credit-card data), those objects become locative media.

Brantner (2018) identifies five forms of locative media, which utilise the locative functionality of digital devices and infrastructures in different ways, three of which are also social media. These are:

- *map services* such as Google Maps or Apple Maps, where location is used to position users and plan routes;
- *user-generated digital maps* such as crowdsourced maps developed in disaster response efforts using a range of services, including OpenStreetMap;
- *location-based services* such as dating apps including Tinder and Grindr, where location is used to connect potential matches;
- *location-based augmented reality* (AR) applications such as AR games like Ingress or Pokémon Go, where game elements are overlaid onto map services and players move through space to access different parts of the game and its features; and
- *social media with location-based features* such as Facebook or Twitter/X, where users can check in to locations, or post their location alongside other forms of textual and image-based content.

Locational data refers to 'codified (digital) content that includes spatial referents … such as longitude and latitude', or some other digital association with a place, such as a geotag[1] (Leszczynski, 2020b: 101). These data can be contributed voluntarily by users. For example, users can choose to provide a location when posting to social media platforms such as Twitter/X (a post may be marked up with precise co-ordinates of where it was generated from) or Instagram (a post may be annotated with a 'place') (Budge, 2020). Alternatively, social media can draw on users' locative data without their explicit awareness (Leszczynski, 2017b). For instance, social media websites and apps might install cookies on a user's device that then allows that social media platform to track the location and activity of a user beyond their explicit engagement with that website or app (Smith, 2019b). At the same time, many social media apps can function without the user actively or passively providing locative data about themselves. As Kitchin et al. (2017: 1–2) suggest, 'social media apps such as Twitter and Facebook enable users to georeference tweets/posts creating a rich set of geosocial data, but the apps work as intended without such georeferencing'. As such, social media can be locative and

---

[1] A geotag can be a place-based descriptor (e.g., a place name associated with geographical co-ordinates).

locative media can operate across and around social media platforms, with data about location flowing in and out of these platforms to a number of other digital devices and infrastructures in a variety of ways (Smith, 2019a).

As Kitchin et al. (2017) suggest, social and locative media can: a) modify the spatial behaviour of users; b) create new products and markets for those products; c) transform governance; d) enable and enhance political openness and transparency; while simultaneously; e) increasing levels of surveillance and control through regimes of spatial sorting, profiling and prediction of what people do in ways that transform what privacy is and how it is understood. To make sense of these transformations, this chapter focuses on two key areas of digital research into social and locative media. First, it examines how surveys, interviews and ethnographic methods (see **Chapter 5**) and walking methodologies (see **Chapter 6**) have been utilised to study how people use social and locative media, their experiences of interacting with these media, and the significances and roles of these media practice in digital life. Second, the chapter details how researchers collect data from social and locative media to make sense of other social phenomena, drawing on methods of visualisation and mapping (see **Chapter 10**) and data analytics (see **Chapter 11**).

Interview, Observation, Survey and Ethnographic Methods for Studying Social and Locative Media

Studies utilising a variety of methods have investigated how social and locative media have transformed a number of different aspects of everyday life. In terms of navigation, map apps running on smartphones have been shown to be key in altering how people relate to the environment around them. Laurier et al. (2016) utilised ethnographic video methods to record fifteen participants in the cities of Stockholm and London walking while using map apps on smartphones and completing wayfinding tasks set by the researchers. The study analysed the captured data using ethnomethodology and conversation analysis and demonstrated that smartphone maps reorientated users' experiences around the 'dot' that represented where the user was on the digital map interface. In turn, users 'walked the dot' and as a result often prioritised the information on the app over their own existing spatial experience and knowledge of the environment. For example, people using the map app might fail to notice obvious shortcuts such as unmarked footpaths or fail to deviate from the route the app provided, even when an easier route could be observed in the environment (also see Farman, 2014).

Likewise, Wilmott (2016) utilised participant led video-recorded walking interviews in Sydney, Australia and Hong Kong to study how people navigated and made sense of these postcolonial cities via digital map apps. The data collected through this method was then analysed using Foucault's (2002) 'archaeological method', where 'words, occurrences, documents and events' (Wilmott, 2016: 3) were read alongside one another to identify recurring themes that revealed power relations in these cities. In doing so, it became clear that the digital mapping of space and individualised route finding produced via smartphone navigation apps worked to cover over the Indigenous histories and knowledges of these spaces, as well as exposing the limitations of access to different parts of the cities under study. As such, not only do mapping apps change navigational capacities, but they can also change how people relate to the histories and geographies of the cities that they move through.

Elsewhere, Smith et al. (2020) investigated navigational practices in the *Bannau Brycheiniog* ('Brecon Beacons') National Park in Wales using video cameras worn by participants. They studied how eight groups, consisting of two to four participants, used a smartphone app visitor guide called Walking with Romans to navigate a 6-kilometre walking trail. In turn, the data was analysed using ethnomethodology and conversation analysis, where the sequential organisation of practices from the video recordings were described. In doing so, the researchers came to understand that rather than simply leading to a loss of knowledge or skill in navigation, the emptied and sterilised space of the app's representation of the ground and terrain of the national park (which presented the ground as a series of flat colours) required users to become highly attuned to the physical surfaces of the landscape to navigate it successfully.

Turning the focus from navigation to dating apps, work on these latter phenomena has demonstrated how social and locative media has a direct impact on relationships and sexual practices. Yeo and Fung (2018) studied how gay dating apps Grindr and Jack'd were used among seventy-four gay and bisexual men between the ages of eighteen to twenty-six in Hong Kong. The research drew on thirty in-depth interviews and eight focus groups consisting of five to six participants, with the data being analysed through a grounded theory approach using open, axial and theoretical coding. Through the analysis of the data, their work identified how the locative functions of these apps altered understandings and expectations around the types of encounter that could occur. For instance, Yeo and Fung (2018) argued that these apps enabled instantaneous meeting and so changed the temporal dynamics of dating, encouraging 'hook ups' (on the temporal dynamics of dating apps, see also Blackwell et al., 2015). Also studying Grindr, Bonner-Thompson (2019) drew on interviews with thirty men who used the app in Newcastle upon Tyne in the northeast of England, and analysed the interview transcripts using coding via NVivo software. Bonner-Thompson argued that the visual centric nature of dating apps results in users creating expectations around how potential dates would move and sound; and, if these expectations were not met, this could significantly alter users' desire towards one another. Both Yeo and Fung's (2018) and Bonner-Thompson's (2019) research shows that social and locative media can alter both the spaces and times of encounter in everyday life, as well as the expectations that are brought to these encounters (see also Bonner-Thompson, 2021; Brubaker et al., 2016; Hobbs et al., 2017; Weltevrede and Jansen, 2019).

Research shows that mobile and AR games that use social and locative functions – known as location-based games – also work to transform experiences and understandings of space, place and encounter. A number of studies have examined the AR game Pokémon Go and how it relates to complex issues around surveillance (de Souza e Silva, 2017; Hjorth and de Souza e Silva, 2023), place (Evans and Saker, 2019), embodiment (Apperley and Moore, 2019) and gamification (Woods, 2020). Using an online survey of 375 Pokémon Go players from around the world, Evans and Saker (2019) found that Pokémon Go encouraged people to experience the environment around them in a new way. In their words:

> 79% of respondents (n = 295) reported that playing Pokémon Go had impacted upon their day-to-day movements; 93% (n = 347) reported that Pokémon Go had led to them exploring their environment more than they would before playing the game; 89.5% (n = 333) reported that Pokémon Go play had led them to going to new or novel places; and 86% (n = 321) reported that Pokémon Go play had changed the routes or pathways they used to move around their environments. (Evans and Saker, 2019: 237)

Here, the conventional structure of the survey and its sample size provided a reasonable degree of representativeness as to views across players. Elsewhere, Woods (2021) conducted twenty-two in-depth interviews with Pokémon Go players from Singapore, with the interview transcripts being analysed thematically using open coding. Through their analysis of the data, Woods (2021) argued that players' game-supported spatial exploration was also competitive and had the potential to give rise to territorial tensions as Pokémon Go players formed teams to try and control different 'gyms' (battle arenas where players fight other players' Pokémon) that were distributed in distinct public spaces. As Woods (2021: 406) suggested, '(dis)assembling of power through the playing of Pokémon Go … encourages players to territorialize, counter-territorialize and re-territorialize public space in ways that cause it to become an increasingly contested construct'.

Work is another important area of life where social and locative media have had a transformative effect. Social and locative media can become new sites of work, but also change understandings of spaces and places in relation to work. Repenning (2022), for example, discussed the ways that Berlin-based fashion designers refer to the city of Berlin in Germany through posting images and captions on Instagram and how posting these images is an important form of labour to build their fashion brands. Repenning's study was based on ten semi-structured interviews with Berlin-based fashion professionals (e.g., fashion journalists) and nine interviews with independent Berlin-based fashion designers. Repenning also followed the Instagram profiles of the interviewees and other Instagram profiles that were recommended to them and documented their posts, creating a series of 647 screenshots. Analysing this data using qualitative content analysis, Repenning argued that by posting images of Berlin and referring to these images as inspiration for their fashion designs, alongside the use of hashtags (e.g., #berlinstyle) and geotags (e.g., Berlin Alexanderplatz), platforms such as Instagram become 'a hybrid of … visual and … spatial media as it visualises daily design practices, forms fashion aesthetics, and connects these to localities' (Repenning, 2022: 216). Such forms of fashion labour then also fed back into how the city is understood, providing 'digital shadows of locations in the city as well as of the city's atmosphere' (Repenning, 2022: 220; see also Zasina, 2018).

Analytics, Mapping and Visualisation of Data from Social and Locative Media

Data derived from social and locative media can also be used to inform understandings of a range of other issues, as well as allowing further critical reflection on social and locative platforms themselves. As the next section will outline, these issues are as diverse as disaster management, tracking virus outbreaks, understanding the agenda setting effects of social media platforms and studying the spatial distribution of different lifestyles in cities.

Utilising geolocative data harvested from platforms such as Twitter/X and user-generated digital mapping platforms, a number of studies have demonstrated the importance of social and locative media for detecting and responding to different disaster events. For instance, Crooks et al. (2013) show that sites like Twitter can be used as a kind of distributed sensor system for monitoring earthquakes. Examining a 5.8 magnitude earthquake that occurred on the east coast of the United States in 2011, the researchers collected data using the Twitter application programming interface (API) to understand how the event was reported. Specifically, they harvested a 1 per cent random sample of Twitter posts from within the contiguous forty-eight states of the United States over a timespan of eight hours after the quake, using the Twitter API. They mined the data to identify geolocated tweets with references to the earthquake through keywords (such as 'earthquake', or 'earth' and 'quake') and hashtags (e.g., #earthquake or #quake), resulting in 144,892 tweets collected. The location of tweets were derived through a) the geolocation that was directly provided by the user when tweeting or b) deduced via the IP address from where the tweet was sent.

The researchers then visualised this data through a variety of graphs, including histograms that compared factors such as distance from the epicentre of the quake to the precise location of the geolocated tweet and the time between the quake's occurrence and the timestamp of tweets about the quake. In doing so, Crooks et al. (2013) found that social and locative media platforms such as Twitter can act as early warning systems to those in locations outside of the epicentre of future earthquakes. In their words:

> information dissemination through Twitter can travel faster than the physical event to distant locations ... This is a very critical observation supporting the use of social media in general, and Twitter in particular, for providing novel geographic information and thus acting as an early warning system for large-scale incidents. (Crooks et al., 2013: 144)

Beyond utilising geotagged tweets, Grace (2021) drew on toponym data (place names from within the content of tweets) to understand how social and locative media can be used in disaster response and management. Through a study of tweets that were posted in relation to a significant storm in the northeast United States, Grace harvested tweets using the Twitter API based on location, using a geographical bounding box to collect only tweets from within the storm epicentre for six hours before and after the storm; keyword filtering to collect only tweets that used local places names; and network filtering to 'ground truth' results by examining who was following the accounts that were posting about the storm to ensure they were tweeting from within the storm area. This resulted in 22,343 unique tweets, which were then manually qualitatively coded for their relevance to the storm event and the types of information they reported during the storm. In turn, the tweets were manually coded in relation to their use of toponyms, and the relationship between toponym usage and locality to the storm. These coded tweets were then analysed for toponym usage (where tweets were distinguished according to whether they used specific or generic toponyms from tweets without toponyms), relation (whether tweets referred to local, remote or generic places) and granularity (whether tweets referred to hyper-local place names). The result of this analysis demonstrated that:

> toponym granularity varies by crisis-related information: reports of infrastructure damage and service disruption are more likely to include hyperlocal toponyms, as well as additional municipal and regional contextual markers, than other crisis-related information such as warnings, forecasts, and personal experiences. (Grace, 2021: 8)

As such, this study attests to the importance of going 'beyond the geotag' (Crampton et al., 2013) in methods that utilise data from social and locative media; that is, to complement the analysis with additional contextual and analytical data to reveal associations, relationships and patterns that remain hidden if the data remain isolated. Focusing on the content of social media posts in terms of toponyms enabled a more complex and fine-grained picture of how discussions of place happen on social media in relation to disaster, which would not have been possible if the study had used only geotags to collect data from Twitter (on studies using data from social and locative media in relation to disaster, see also Suwaileh et al., 2022; De Longueville et al., 2009; Earle et al., 2011; Zook et al., 2010).

Data from social and locative media can also be used to study issues around health. Hagen et al. (2018) provide a useful example of how network analysis (see **Chapter 10**) of social and locative media was used in relation to the 2015–16 Zika outbreak in the United States (a virus transmitted to humans through mosquitos) and how the virus was discussed on Twitter. Their research analysed how communities on Twitter formed around discussion of the virus, and identified which accounts on Twitter were most effective in connecting different individual users on the platform. Using the Twitter Streaming API, the researchers harvested 359,043 tweets with the keyword 'Zika' during a survey window of 25 August to 5 September 2016, when reports on outbreaks of Zika in the United States began to increase. In turn, they worked to identify edges (or connections) between different nodes (Twitter accounts). To do this, they defined an edge or connection whenever a tweet was retweeted. This resulted in 112,165 nodes and 150,324 edges. Gephi visualisation software supported the identification of how different communities (sets of edges) formed around different discussion points, such as US Congress, scientific information about the disease, and US government analysis of Zika. Subsequently, manual content analysis of tweets was conducted to identify and name different categories of content within tweets. The process of network graphing and content analysis allowed the researchers to understand how specific Twitter users became influential in these communities based on attributes such as their connectivity, popularity and authority. As a result of their network and content analysis, Hagen et al. (2018) found that, contrary to popular opinion, Twitter users were keen to share verified scientific information about the disease, and experts from medical science became influential and trusted points for the communication and spread of this information (for other examples of how health can be studied using social and locative media, see Brambilla and Pedrielli, 2020 and Rana et al., 2015 on environmental noise mapping using smartphones; and Ghosh and Guha, 2013 on spatial patterns of discussion of obesity using Twitter).

In relation to issues surrounding politics, Instagram has been studied to examine the agenda setting effect of Instagram posts on mainstream newspaper coverage of the 2016 US presidential primary (Towner and Muñoz, 2020). A visual intelligence platform[2] 'Beautifeye' was used to harvest images, videos, captions and tags from US

---

[2] Defined as a service that uses image recognition and machine learning to identify and code the content of images and video.

citizens made during the period of the presidential primary that referred to the primary, such as #hillaryclinton, #hillary2016 and #rubio2016, resulting in a sample of 638,977 posts. To compare Instagram discussion of the primary with US newspaper coverage, four national US newspapers were sampled during the same period, with all articles referring to the 'primaries' or 'caucuses' collected. This resulted in a sample of 724 articles. In turn, the content of both samples was qualitatively coded to identify the range of election issues that were discussed and the frequency with which these issues appeared. The range and frequency of issues were then quantitively ranked and compared to one another. Through an analysis of this data, the authors found 'minimal evidence for an intermedia agenda-setting relationship between newspapers and Instagram posters' issue agendas' (Towner and Muñoz, 2020: 9). As such, the study establishes the importance of data scraping techniques for understanding the relationship between social and locative media and traditional media, and the extent to which information from one might affect the other. In this case, the research highlighted that it is important not to assume that newer forms of social and locative media will necessarily affect other forms of legacy mass media, and that just because platforms have large user bases, this does not mean that information from these platforms will necessarily travel beyond them (on other studies that use social and locative data to analyse politics, see Baik, 2020; Bonilla and Rosa, 2015; Hemsley and Eckert, 2014).

In relation to studying cities, Boy and Uitermark (2020) drew on geotagged data from Instagram to study lifestyle enclaves in different parts of Amsterdam, the Netherlands. To do this, they collected a corpus of 709,348 posts geotagged with Amsterdam from Instagram, using the Instagram API. The researchers' sampling strategy was to include all posts from a six-month period that included 'posts by users with at least two geotagged posts at least four weeks apart' (Boy and Uitermark, 2020: 3). This resulted in their corpus containing 78,207 Instagram users, which is the equivalent to a tenth of the Amsterdam population. Qualitatively coding individual Instagram posts from the sample according to particular displays of interest and status (e.g., pictures of coffee or running), the researchers created groups of users, such as 'city consumers', 'hedonists' and 'fitness enthusiasts'. Utilising the 'like' feature of Instagram, where users can 'like' images others have posted, they sought to understand how social media are part of the emergence of subcultures and social divisions in the city. Specifically, they identified reciprocal liking of posts to identity affinity between users and then 'zoned' these users according to geotags in their posts. In their words:

> when users within the same clusters use places as staging grounds for their status displays, we assume a link between those places; the more links between places, the more likely they are part of the same zone. We construct[ed] a proximity matrix of places based on how frequently they are tagged by people in the same cluster. (Boy and Uitermark, 2020: 4)

Through these methods, Boy and Uitermark (2020: 8) point to the ways that social and locative media like Instagram can operate as 'vehicles of integration rather than fragmentation' in cities such as Amsterdam, and so question notions of 'algorithmically fortified divisions' that social and locative media are sometimes assumed to create.

A good example of how cultural analytics (see **Chapter 10**) have been used to study cities is Tifentale and Manovich's (2015) SELFIECITY project (see selfiecity.net). The project partnered with the data service provider gnip.com, which provided images of people from Instagram to understand practices and trends in self photography in different cities, including Bangkok, Berlin, Moscow, New York and Sao Paulo. In turn, Mechanical Turk Workers (digital workers who are paid money to complete large numbers of small, often repetitive tasks through the Amazon.com website; see **Chapter 3**) identified whether the image of a person was a selfie or not. Facial analysis software was then used to measure twenty aspects of faces in the images, such as smiling, whether glasses were being worn and whether eyes were open or closed. One way that this data was analysed was through the production of a graph using the software ImagePlot (see **Chapter 10**), which allowed all the selfies collected to be visualised through a 'histogram type visualization' (Tifentale and Manovich, 2015: 113). The histogram visualisation enabled the researchers to identify clusters and patterns of images that shared various traits with one another, such as 'distributions of genders, ages and smiles in different cities' (Tifentale and Manovich, 2015: 113) and to generate a range of insights. One finding of the research was that, contrary to popular understanding, '[p]eople take fewer selfies than often assumed' and '[d]epending on the city, only 3–5% of images we analysed were actually selfies' (Tifentale and Manovich, 2015: 115). Furthermore, comparison between cities highlighted trends that were specific to different places, such as people being more likely to smile in photos from Bangkok and less likely to smile in photos from Moscow. Here, cultural analytics provided insight into trends across the platform of Instagram; and, in being sensitive to geographic locality, demonstrated how Instagram was used differently across a range of national contexts and cultures.

Summary

- Social and locative media describe a range of devices, platforms and services, which include mapping and user generated geodata, location-based services, location-based AR and social media with location-based features and affordances.
- Various forms of social and locative media have been studied through a range of interview and ethnographic methods to understand how they shape various aspects of the social world.

- Social and locative media also provide an important source of data to research other social issues. This data can include geolocation as well as the content of social and locative media posts, which can be used to study disasters, health, politics and cities, among many other topics.

Recommended Reading

Evans, L., and Saker, M. (2019) 'The playeur and Pokémon Go: Examining the effects of locative play on spatiality and sociability', *Mobile Media & Communication*, 7(2): 232–47.
A survey-based study that examines how the AR game Pokémon Go changes users' route taking decisions and navigation.

Hagen, L., Keller, T., Neely, S., et al. (2018) 'Crisis communications in the age of social media: A network analysis of Zika-related tweets', *Social Science Computer Review*, 36(5): 523–41.
Demonstrates the use of social network analysis to understand how knowledge about the Zika virus was distributed across Twitter.

Tifentale, A., and Manovich, L. (2015) 'Selfiecity: Exploring photography and self-fashioning in social media', in Berry, D., and Dieter, M. (eds) *Postdigital Aesthetics*. Palgrave Macmillan, London, pp. 109–22.
A study that uses scraping techniques to gain locative data on Instagram to identify trends in self-photography practices in different cities around the world.

Wilmott, C. (2016) 'Small moments in spatial big data: Calculability, authority and interoperability in everyday mobile mapping', *Big Data & Society*, 3(2): 1–16.
Uses ethnographic and walking interview methods to examine how mobile mapping creates disjunctions between users' expectations of spaces and the spaces themselves.

Yeo, T.E.D., and Fung, T.H. (2018) '"Mr Right Now": Temporality of relationship formation on gay mobile dating apps', *Mobile Media & Communication*, 6(1): 3–18.
An insightful paper that demonstrates how locative dating apps alter the temporality of dating through the use of focus group and interview data.

14
Mobilities

Overview

This chapter examines:

- the concept of digital mobilities and different forms of digitally mediated mobilities;
- how digital mobilities have been studied using ethnography and audits; and
- how transport models using smart sensor and third-party data are used to investigate mobilities in a range of environments.

Introduction

Mobilities can be defined as the movement and circulation of people, goods and information through time and space. Mobilities consist of technologies and practices of movement, which are longstanding, intertwined and have significant societal implications. For example, Harvey (1989) suggested that technologies of mobility – such as the telegraph and steam ship – led to 'time-space compression', understood as 'a significant shrinkage in the time taken to traverse and connect across space, making the world seem smaller and [more] interconnected' (Kitchin, 2023: 29). The effects of time-space compression are highly uneven and ongoing, with the same networks of transport and communication that make some places more accessible, making other places seem relatively less accessible. For instance, networks of international airports and airlines have developed around a range of hubs that make travelling between some places by air much faster than others, even when the metrical distance between them is greater (e.g., Los Angeles is geographically further away from London than Kisumu in Kenya, but it is generally cheaper and faster to travel between Los Angeles and London than it is between London and Kisumu). Or, in terms of information and communication, the laying of multiple undersea high-speed internet cables between places such as London and New York ensures the dominance of these locations in global stock exchange and finance networks, where the speed of trading is key, which puts other places at a disadvantage (Starosielski, 2015). As Warf (2011: 153) puts it:

> [w]aves of time-space compressions always simultaneously empower and disempower different social groups. Often the process accentuates existing social inequalities, as when, for example, the wealthy deploy new technologies that leave the poor further behind. Because time and space are always saturated with relations of power and inequality, time-space compression for some may be time-space expansion for others.

Recognising the longstanding relationship between technology and mobility, and the uneven effects that these relations can generate, digital mobilities refer to a broad set of practices and processes wherein existing mobilities are mediated and augmented by digital technologies. Digital technologies can both modify existing mobilities and transform these mobilities into new socio-technical forms. For instance, much mobility could now be understood as digitally mediated, such as computationally managed traffic-light systems on many roads (Coletta and Kitchin, 2017), digital timetables at bus stops that provide real-time updates on bus arrivals (Heaphy, 2019), GPS-enabled travel apps that provide location aware information on potential routes and real-time information on present road conditions (Bissell, 2018), and people who use smart watches to measure the number of steps they have walked (Lupton, 2020).

At the same time, digital technologies modify and transform mobilities. An example is ride-hailing services such as Uber or Lyft. While taxis have long driven passengers around, and combustion engine cars have long pre-existed digital computation, it is the advent and widespread adoption of smartphones and apps that have made it possible for Uber, Lyft and other transportation network companies (TNCs) to reorganise how on-request, single-occupancy vehicle transportation services operate for both drivers and passengers (Cetin, 2017). This in turn has altered what mobility is and means for both parties; for instance, such apps have been important players in enabling new forms of digital labour to emerge as the gig economy; see **Chapter 16**). Or, drawing on a different example, the development of digital sensors enables the production of autonomous functionality by vehicles and drones (Herrmann et al., 2018). Furthermore, on a global scale, digital mobilities reconfigure the complex organisation of logistical chains and how they function (Kitchin, 2023). As Lyster (2016) details in relation to the global shipping corporation FedEx, the corporation uses digitally automated sorting and tracking systems run via large digitally controlled centres to move and deliver packages at speeds that would be impossible otherwise. As she details, FedEx's systems enable it to quickly move tens of thousands of items daily, with its distribution centre in Memphis handling the cargo of 150 aeroplanes between midnight and 3 a.m. daily, with no package stationary for more than thirty minutes, and no domestic items being in the facility for more than ninety minutes.

Recognising the complex and overlapping nature of digital mobilities and the uneven forms of movement and practice that they augment and enable, this chapter can discuss only a small number of methods that might be helpful to study these phenomena. These are: interviews, observations and ethnography of digital mobilities; audits; and transport models that use digital technologies to track and analyse movement.

Interviews, Observations and Ethnography of Digital Mobilities

Interviews, observation and performing ethnographies have been a key means of examining digital mobilities as they enable insights from key actors to be gleaned and for thoughts, practices and processes to be closely monitored in situ. In relation to ride-hailing, Mosseri (2022) used observation and interview methods as part of an ethnographic study on trust, work and ride-hailing platforms in New York City. Periodic observations of Uber drivers were carried out across four work settings, including: a) Taxi and Limousine Commission meetings relevant to ride-hailing drivers; b) visits to driver hubs that were run by ride-hailing companies; c) informal conversations with local ride-hailing experts; and d) spending time with drivers waiting for work at New York City airports over a period of fourteen months. One hundred and twenty-two in-person, in-depth interviews with drivers were conducted. The interviews were analysed using an interpretive approach, with an emphasis on open and closed coding. Through an analysis of eighteen in-depth interviews drawn from this larger interview dataset and nine months of observation across the four work settings outlined above, it became clear that seemingly micro changes in drivers' reputational scores had big effects on their being potentially locked out or temporarily deactivated from the Uber platform, meaning they were unable to work. For example, even one or two journeys resulting in scores of fewer than five stars from riders might drop a driver's reputational ranking in a substantial way (perhaps from 4.7 to 4.3 out of 5). In particular, Mosseri (2022) identified that the sensitivity of the reputational system on ride-hailing apps caused considerable stress for drivers, and that driver scoring by passengers was often felt to be racially motivated.

Also in relation to ride hailing, Rosenblat and Stark (2016: 3759) engaged in real-time analysis of posts from five online message boards used by Uber drivers in the United States to understand 'how Uber drivers experience labor under a specific regime of automated and algorithmic management'. Through further analysis of 1,300 archived posts on these forums and seven semi-structured interviews with Uber drivers conducted between 2014 and 2015, they identified themes within the posts around the automated management of Uber drivers and techniques of soft control (on digital observation and ethnography, see **Chapter 5**). Specifically, by analysing the archived posts and interviews, the researchers identified key differences between what Uber promises drivers (freedom and flexibility to drive when they want) and how Uber actually treat drivers (using soft power tactics on the app – e.g., activating 'surge pricing', where the driver could earn more money when the driver was about to log off from the app – to try and encourage drivers to keep driving even when they want to stop). In doing so, Rosenblat and Stark (2016) argued that Uber drivers experience strong asymmetries in power *vis-à-vis* Uber's largely automated employment systems, and identified that it was the digitally mediated nature of drivers' work that was key to Uber establishing and maintaining this asymmetry. Alongside methods of observation, Shapiro's (2020) ethnographic study on working as a bike courier for the food-delivery platform Caviar in San Francisco, conducted as part of a broader project on control in smart cities, demonstrated how participant observation approaches can be utilised to understand experiences of platform work (see also **Chapter 16**). Writing field notes after each shift, Shapiro (2020: 96) found that working as a bike courier involved navigating a complex interface between the demands of the Caviar platform and its smartphone interface and the 'lived experience of the city and all its uneven surfaces – traffic jams, potholes, high-rise apartments … often thanklessly and without much support'. Here, the method of participant observation helped Shapiro understand the embodied materiality of the labour involved in working for these platforms and so further emphasised the exploitative nature of this labour in ways that could not be accounted for by interviews or observation alone (for another participant observation study of food-delivery platforms such as Deliveroo, see Richardson, 2020).

Observation and interviews have also been used as methods to study digital mobilities in relation to the control and management of movement in cities. For example, Coletta and Kitchin (2017) drew on observations and interviews related to a traffic-control centre in Dublin to study an intelligent digital transport system called Sydney Co-ordinated Adaptive Traffic System (SCATS), which was used to monitor and manage traffic flows in real time. According to Coletta and Kitchin (2017: 5–6), SCATS used real-time data:

> from a fixed network of 380 CCTV cameras, 800 sensors (induction loops), a small number of Traffic Cams (traffic sensing cameras) used when induction loops are faulty or the road surface is not suitable for them, a mobile network of approximately 1,000 bus transponders (controllers can also directly contact drivers if needed), phone calls and messages by the public to radio stations and the operators, and social media posts.

In turn, the SCATs system could automatically synchronise the timing of traffic light signals at different junctions to maximise the flow of vehicles and minimise congestion in Dublin. These interviews were from a larger set of seventy-seven interviews conducted on smart city initiatives in Dublin. Through a thematic analysis of their observations and interviews, Coletta and Kitchin (2017) argued that the SCATs system constituted a form of 'algorhythmic governance', where the system, and those that operated it, attempted to record and track different temporal rhythms of mobility in the city, as well as creating new rhythms. An example of how SCATs recorded and monitored rhythms was through the comparison of traffic flows at junctions on different days of the week. An example of how SCATs created rhythms was through the setting of temporal cycles of waiting times at pedestrian crossings, which would change depending on the amount of traffic on the road system. As a result of their study, Coletta and Kitchin argued that managers of digital traffic systems need to be mindful of the rhythms of mobility that digital systems such as SCAT can contribute to, as well as the accountability of these systems, which are often black-boxed to the road users and pedestrians whose mobility is managed by them.

Another project that sought to understand the use of control rooms in the digital governance of mobility is Anderson and Gordon's (2017) study of motorway management. This work used methods of observation over a period of six months in seven Highway Agency Regional Control Rooms across England. These control rooms gathered data from the motorway incident detection and signalling (MidAS) system, a series of inductive loops beneath the motorway road surface that register the flow of traffic. Data from these sensors was then processed and automatically presented to control room operators on digital screens to highlight congestion and other road-based events. For example, once a particular number of induction loops were occupied on a stretch in the road, a Q alert was sent to the control room operator to indicate the potential presence of traffic congestion. The control centres also involved human monitoring of live streamed video images from CCTV cameras placed around the motorway network and the recording of calls from motorway emergency phones and eyewitness reports from motorway users.

Utilising 'ethnomethodological principles' (Anderson and Gordon, 2017: 175) and analysis of field note extracts, the researchers discussed a range of events that took place in the control room, including how MidAS Q alerts were detected, made sense of and responded to. For example, one such event was whether the building of road congestion highlighted by the automatic MidAS Q alerts required human operator intervention, such as setting warning signs on overhead gantries or adjusting the speed limit on the road. Through an analysis of a range of events that took place in different control rooms, the study demonstrated that human operators played a crucial role in digital control rooms by working to delineate events that required action from those that did not.

In this digital system, the management of mobility was not automatic, with human judgement required to make sense of often ambiguous events according to what was deemed normal or abnormal by operators based on their prior experience.

Audits of Digital Mobilities

Audit methods (see **Chapter 6**) have also been employed to study digital mobilities. A good example of an audit study is Brown's (2019a) research on riders' experiences of racial discrimination when using the ride-hailing apps Uber and Lyft in Los Angeles, and comparing these to racial discrimination experienced when using taxis. Brown performed an in-person audit using a team of eighteen participants recruited as auditors. The auditors were of different genders (male and female) and ethnic/racial background (white, Hispanic, Asian and Black), but were otherwise similar (all were between twenty and thirty years of age, all had ratings as riders with these TNCs of 4.5 stars or higher, and all dressed plainly for the audits). The auditors were instructed to request rides at different times of the day and on different days of the week from two sites in Los Angeles, and they rotated between requesting Lyft, Uber and taxis. The auditors were trained to identify characteristics of the driver, including age and race/ethnicity. In turn, the auditors recorded different aspects of the time that they waited for each of the rides to arrive, including 1) the time that it took for the app to assign a driver; 2) the time it took for the car to arrive; and 3) the total wait time. Racial discrimination was defined as ethnic minoritised (non-white) riders either waiting longer for their rides or outright cancellation of trips when the driver or dispatcher inferred that the rider was a member of an ethnic/racial minority group.

Brown (2023) analysed the data collected by the auditors using three estimated logistic regression models and nine estimated linear regression models. In doing so, Brown discovered that Black riders were significantly discriminated against compared to other riders when booking regular taxis. While Black riders were also discriminated against when using ride-hailing services, this discrimination was less pronounced. In Brown's (2023: 278) words:

> [t]axis failed to pick up [B]lack riders for more than one-quarter of their trip hails (26.3%), compared with about one-fifth of trips hailed by Asian and Hispanic rider (19.9%) and one-seventh (14.4%) of trips hailed by white riders. By contrast, ride-hail services dramatically reduced the differences across rider characteristics. On taxis, [B]lack riders waited 10.5 minutes (52%) longer than white riders; by comparison, [B]lack riders waited less than a minute (fifty-four seconds, 15%) longer for ride-hail services than white riders.

Brown's audit study identified that digital mobilities are both informed by pre-existing forms of discrimination but can also alter these forms of discrimination. This can be seen in the study's findings, which 'suggest that while ride-hailing does not eliminate discrimination against [B]lack riders, it dramatically narrows the gap between riders' (Brown, 2023: 273).

Other audit methods have utilised digital tools to study existing forms of mobility in a new way. For example, 'virtual audits' (Clarke et al., 2010; Griew et al., 2013; Phillips et al., 2017) involve the use of satellite imagery accessed via platforms such as Google Street View to study a range of phenomena. Virtual auditing tools are often checklists used to identify and record features, such as pavement width and continuity or the number of benches present on a street. In turn, these checklists can be used to analyse some aspect of an environment and how it might relate to a social issue. For instance, Brookfield and Tilley (2016) used the virtual audit method to investigate the walkability of routes chosen by older adults in Edinburgh (Scotland). The researchers asked nineteen adults aged sixty-five and over to choose and complete walks in Edinburgh using a GPS tracking application (Google My Tracks) to measure the route, speed and distance the participants walked. In turn, the researchers then audited the routes that were walked using Google Street View and the FASTVIEW auditing tool, developed by Griew et al. (2013). The FASTVIEW tool focuses on nine different categories of environmental characteristics that inform the walkability of an environment, such as lighting, road permeability and pavement surface quality, which are scored from negative to positive. Analysing the routes that participants walked, the researchers found that, perhaps predictably, older adults preferred to walk on routes that scored more highly on the FASTVIEW tool. Simultaneously, while older adults in the study preferred walking close to green environments, there were significant gender differences in route choice. For instance, women were more willing to walk in poorly scored environments compared to men, although the study could not provide evidence to explain why this was the case.

Mooney et al. (2016) used virtual audits in concert with publicly available collision data to investigate the relationship between the built environment and the likelihood of pedestrian injury in New York City. Specifically, they sampled 532 intersections across the city to identify the presence or absence of a number of objects and factors that are associated with pedestrian injury, such as crosswalks, bus stops and the condition of roads, using the Computer Assisted Neighbourhood Visual Assessment System. Through comparison between collision data from the public databases CrashStat and Crash-Mapper and the audit data, the researchers discovered that, in line with other pedestrian collision and injury studies, certain objects and factors increased and decreased the number of collisions that occurred. For example, marked crossings could actually increase the risk of collision, as pedestrians felt secure on marked crossings and so did not pay as much attention as when crossing at unmarked junctions.

Finally, Verhoeven et al. (2018) developed a virtual audit to study adolescent cycling route choice in Ghent, Belgium. Drawing on a convenience sample from schools in the area, the study recruited 238 adolescents to wear GPS devices for a four to five-day period. From this data, the researchers identified cycling journeys and calculated the shortest distance routes for each of these journeys. For each journey that did not follow the shortest distance route, an audit was conducted of both the shortest distance route calculated and the route that was actively travelled by the participant. This was done using the Environmental Google Street View Based Audit-Cycling tool, which was used alongside questionnaires and semi-structured interviews. While more than 70 per cent of trips cycled followed the shortest route, other trips using longer routes favoured residential streets and avoided larger arterial roads, even when there were no cycling lanes present on these more indirect routes. As such, the research demonstrated the different perceptions of adolescent cyclists and their cycling preferences and suggested that future policy might create cycle routes that are not accessible to motorised traffic.

Transport Models for Understanding Digitally Mediated Mobility

There is a long history of computational transportation models and modelling going back to the 1950s (Wise et al., 2017). Before the advent of big data, transport models were built using data from 1) actual recorded trips and counts of journeys; 2) travel surveys; and 3) simulated data. Data were often limited in sample and granularity (collected occasionally and aggregated). The models on the one hand sought to replicate and explain mobility patterns, and on the other hand to predict what might occur under different scenarios and to determine optimal solutions. While some models were descriptive in nature, more often they sought to determine cause and effect, and the aim was to generate computational tools for managing and planning transport systems and infrastructure, with key models becoming central to the everyday operations of travel services (Hensher and Button, 2008).

Now, 'new Big Data sources such as mobile phone call data records, smart card data and geo-coded social media records allow us to observe and understand mobility behaviour on an unprecedented level of detail' (Anda et al., 2017: 20). These new big data sources include the movement of digital devices captured using Wi-Fi probes, consisting of hardware that collects packets of data that are sent out by mobile devices (such as smartphones) when the device comes into range of the sensor; automatic number-plate recognition (ANPR) cameras that can track the movement of vehicles (Coletta and Kitchin, 2017); and the use of facial recognition cameras to track passenger movements (Luo and Guo, 2021). Importantly, granularity is often at the scale of the individual and for whole populations (e.g., an ANPR camera tracks every vehicle, not a sample of vehicles), and the sampling is in real time and continuous. Such rich data enables comparisons across different periods to understand temporal patterns of use and movement across and between different spaces.

Big data are now routinely used to inform and develop a range of models, though gaining access to such data is often not straightforward given the legal implications of sharing highly resolute and identifiable data and the fact that they are generated by companies and states (see **Chapter 3**). These data are used to model a wide variety of transportation issues. For example, models can be used to minimise traffic congestion by continually recalibrating traffic light systems (Zhang and Su, 2021); prediction models can be used to forecast what will happen to traffic if a new shopping mall or road is built (Lana et al., 2018); and rostering models can calculate how to get aeroplane crews and aircraft back into the right pattern during or after major disruption (Novak et al., 2020).

A number of different modelling approaches can be applied to mobility issues. For example, the *Handbook of Transport Modelling* (Hensher and Button, 2008) details numerous model types including demand modelling (forecasting future trip demand and route and destination choice); network modelling (estimating flows and capacities across transport networks); congestion modelling (calculating how to resolve congestion); performance modelling (estimating optimal productivity and timeliness); and econometric modelling (calculating the cost-benefit of transportation options). Each of these can be performed using a variety of statistical and computational techniques (e.g., multivariate analysis, Markov chains, Monte-Carlo methods, regression, neural networks, random trees, agent-based models), with the modeller selecting the modelling technique deemed most suitable to achieving a functioning and valid model (see **Chapter 11**).

To take one such technique, agent-based models (ABMs) are now used widely in mobility research. Agent-based transport models are defined as 'models providing a microscopic representation of travel decisions of individuals as they move from place to place' (Kagho et al., 2020: 727). Importantly, ABMs have granularity in that they allow the tracking of individual agents and movements, rather than aggregate groups and flows. Furthermore, the agents can have varying behaviours rather than being uniform in character, and ABMs can be dynamic, unfolding iteratively in relation to emerging patterns and context. Within the model, agents 'interact with one another and with their environment based on their own individual attributes and behavioural rules' (Wise et al., 2017: 133). As such, in ABMs, the mobility phenomena modelled emerges from the interaction of many heterogeneous agents. For the past two decades, Michael Batty and colleagues have developed agent-based urban models, including of transportation. In one of their early studies, they used an agent-based model to study the movement of people at the Notting Hill Carnival, London, and how the small-scale movement of pedestrians can form crowds (Batty et al., 2003). Boavida-Portugal et al. (2015) used ABMs to explore and predict tourist decision-making processes, imbuing the agents with motivations based on survey data and simulating the sharing of information on social networking sites. An ABM was used by Wang et al. (2016) to run a simulation model for a tsunami evacuation, exploring how information communication and decision time, choice of transport (e.g., walking or car) and the availability of high ground impacts on casualties and mortality.

Woodcock et al. (2014) demonstrated how data from the London cycle hire scheme was used to model the health impacts of bike sharing. The scheme comprised twenty-four hours a day, 365 days a year access to 8,000 bikes located in 571 docking stations throughout London. The study used data provided by Transport for London for all 'cycle hire trips made between 30 July 2010 and 31 March 2012, including trip level data for the final twelve months. This trip level data included a unique ID for each user and the start and end time and location of each trip. It also included the sex and area of residence of registered users' (Woodcock et al., 2014: 2). Utilising a health impact monitoring tool, the study sought to understand whether the cycle scheme could be shown to increase 'lifelong change in non-discounted, non-age weighted disability adjusted life years (DALYs), calculated as the sum of years of life lost owing to premature mortality (YLL) and years of healthy life lost due to disability (YLD)' (Woodcock et al., 2014: 2). Using trip level data derived from actual journeys, the research demonstrated the positive effect of bike sharing on the health of users and no increased risk of injury in using a bike-sharing scheme as compared to owned-bike travel (for other uses of big data to study cycling, see Zaltz et al., 2013 on network and spatial analysis of bike sharing and Kon et al., 2022 on the analysis of mobility flows in bike sharing).

Finally, Pieroni et al. (2021) used smart card data from bus systems in São Paulo, Brazil, to investigate travel patterns of low-income groups that live in precarious forms of settlement. Eighty-five per cent of public transport is paid for by smart card, which provided a large dataset for analysis. Data from journeys was based on the swipe card being logged as users entered the system (users do not swipe to exit the system when using smart cards) and included the stops where users entered the public transport; GPS data; and the public transport structure of the region where the user was travelling. Data from individual swipes included the date and time of transaction; anonymised card ID; the route number and direction of travel; and the ID of the vehicle the user travelled on. Over a window of eleven weeks, 803 million smart card transactions were recorded, representing the use of 9.5 million smart cards. Low-income and middle/higher-income passenger groups were then identified from this data using a variety of methods, including semantic enrichment and k-means clustering. In turn, cluster analysis of the data was employed to identify people who used the transport system for commuting and in turn, where they travelled to and when they left and returned. The results of the analysis informed insight into the differences in mobility patterns between low-income residents housed in precarious housing and other residents of São Paulo. In particular, it became clear that there were different temporal patterns of travel between these groups, with the precariously housed beginning their travels earlier in the day (between 5 a.m. and 7 a.m.), compared to middle and high-income groups, who began to travel later (between 7 a.m. and 9 a.m.).

The above research point to only some of the ways that big data can be used to study mobilities and many other methods and types of transport models are possible. For instance, Bao et al. (2021) use data from a range of sources, including Twitter, to discuss traffic crashes in New York; Liao (2021) uses geo-locative data from ride-hailing platforms to understand the relationship between public transport and ride hailing in China; and Adam et al. (2021) use GPS traces to monitor road freight transit in Belgium.

Summary

- Digital mobilities refers to a broad set of practices and processes wherein existing mobilities are mediated and augmented by digital technologies. In turn, digital technologies can both modify existing mobilities and transform these mobilities into new socio-technical forms.
- Methods such as observation and ethnography provide a way of studying how digital mobilities alter a range of practices, including around work and the management of cities.
- Audits can be used to understand how digital mobilities reinforce or challenge existing forms of social problems, such as discrimination.
- Data drawn from digital devices can be used to develop new forms of transport models, including agent-based transport models, which can be used to track and anticipate the flow of people through different spaces.

Recommended Reading

Brown, A.E. (2023) 'Prevalence and mechanisms of discrimination: Evidence from the ride-hail and taxi industries', *Journal of Planning Education and Research*, 43(2): 268–80.
An important study that demonstrates how the in-person audit method can be used to examine discrimination in digital mobilities.

Coletta, C., and Kitchin, R. (2017) 'Algorhythmic governance: Regulating the "heartbeat" of a city using the Internet of Things', *Big Data & Society*, 4(2): 1–16.
A study that utilises ethnographic observation and interviews to understand how digital control rooms work to manage urban spaces.

Mosseri, S. (2022) 'Being watched and being seen: Negotiating visibility in the NYC ride-hail circuit', *New Media & Society*, 24(3): 600–20.
An investigation of ride-hailing platforms using observation, interviews and analysis of web forum archives.

Pieroni, C., Giannotti, M., Alves, B.B., et al. (2021) 'Big data for big issues: Revealing travel patterns of low-income population based on smart card data mining in a global south unequal city', *Journal of Transport Geography*, 96: 1–12.
A study that uses data from smart cards to analyse transit users' travel patterns.

15
Smart Cities

Overview

Chapter 15 examines:

- the concept of the smart city and reasons for why it is a prominent subject of research about digital life;
- how smart cities and aspects of digital life in 'smart' urban environments have been studied using walking methodologies, visualisation (cultural analytics), and sensory prototyping and participatory sensing; and
- how the mobilisation of different methodological approaches and research techniques opens onto engagements with different aspects of smart cities, including smart infrastructures, the urban aesthetics of smartness, smart city space and smart city breakdowns, workarounds and ruins.

Introduction

While there is no formal or singular, agreed-upon definition of a 'smart city', the term generally refers to the proliferation of networked digital technologies across urban environments – including sensors and connected objects (the internet of things); communications infrastructures such as 5G cells and Wi-Fi access points; and apps and interfaces that capture, enrol and share data – and how they may 'improve economic and political efficiency and enable social, cultural and urban development' (Batty, 2020; Hollands, 2008: 307; Houston et al., 2019). Proponents claim that these improvements are realised through the adoption of 'data-driven' approaches to governing cities via the processing of real-time data to automate, optimise, and increase the efficiency of city operations (e.g., street lighting) and urban flows (e.g., motor vehicle traffic) (e.g., Halegoua, 2020a; Leszczynski, 2016).

Yet social scientists have also critiqued the concept of the smart city as constituting a falsely utopian vision rather than an 'actually existing' or even fully attainable urban reality (see e.g., Green, 2019; Halegoua, 2020a, 2020b; Marvin et al., 2016; Mattern, 2021). Researchers have raised concerns about how smart city initiatives heighten urban inequalities (e.g., Caragliu and Del Bo, 2022; Datta, 2020); reduce meaningful opportunities for urban citizenship and participation (e.g., Cardullo and Kitchin, 2019a, 2019b); and erode privacy and heighten ethical concerns with respect to surveillance (e.g., Galdon-Clavell, 2013; Halegoua, 2020a; Melgaço and van Brakel, 2021). These critiques notwithstanding, smart cities and related conceptual frameworks of platform urbanism (Barns, 2020) and computational cities (Luque-Ayala and Marvin, 2020; Mattern, 2021) figure as important foci of research about digital life. This is because cities loom large in questions about the 'where' of digital life. When thinking about the kinds of places where digital life happens and takes place, cities immediately come to mind. This is because cities concentrate people, digital devices (e.g., smartphones), 'smart' objects (e.g., autonomous vehicles), and technological infrastructures (e.g., 5G masts, Wi-Fi hotspots, and fibre-optic cable networks) that support the everyday digital practices, logistics, encounters, spatialities and representations that comprise facets of digital life.

Smart cities have been researched using many of the methods profiled in Part 2 of this book, including but not limited to the use of digital ethnography to examine the gendered dimensions of life on the urban margins of the smart city (e.g., Datta and Thomas, 2022); focus groups convened to solicit people's perceptions of surveillance and datafication in smart cities (e.g., Jameson et al., 2019); interviews conducted with key stakeholders to gauge cities' expectations for citizen involvement in smart urban development (Granier and Kudo, 2016); and the design of location-based games to foster citizen participation in the smart city (Innocent, 2018). This chapter profiles a selection of studies that have used walking methodologies, image data visualisation, and sensor prototyping and participatory sensing to engage with different facets of life in smart cities. As is shown through a detailed engagement with these studies, the methods mobilised open onto distinct yet related dimensions of smart cities, including smart urban infrastructures and their ruins; smart city aesthetics; and breakdowns and workarounds that characterise the rollout and implementation of 'smart' technologies across cityscapes.

Walking and the Smart City

In studies of smart cities, walking methodologies (see **Chapter 6**) have been used to investigate the affective and sensory dimensions of smart urban environments, informing researchers' scholarly considerations of how and where smart objects, infrastructures, and developments are encountered, perceived and experienced.

Walking methodologies have also been mobilised to identify the kinds of response that smart city infrastructures, architectures and other material objects provoke in research participants and researchers alike.

Fraser and Wilmott (2020) mobilised a methodology of walking-with to investigate how 'smartness' had actually materialised in and around two sites in the Greater Manchester, UK area: Manchester's 'smart' Oxford Road Corridor, designated a technology innovation district; and abandoned post-industrial wastelands ('brownfields') in the Pomona district. Walking-with represents a specific walking methodologies approach developed by Springgay and Truman (2018), which is predicated on the physical act of movement as a mechanism of attuning to non-human materialities and beings in space. Walking-with sensitises researchers and participants to their surroundings while simultaneously inviting observation, reflection and affective responses to what is encountered, where and how. In Fraser and Wilmott's (2020) project, they walked-with the non-human 'smart' objects of Greater Manchester alongside the traces of natural rewilding observable along a number of mapped routes over a series of walks, taking more than 800 photos while they walked.

'Walking-with' the ecological natures and digitally mediated objects of the Greater Manchester cityscape attuned Fraser and Wilmott (2020) to what they term the 'ruins' of smart cities: the discarded and abandoned non-human smart city detritus, and the resurgent force of nature that is always trying to 'take back' and reclaim the (smart) city. For instance, along the Oxford Road Corridor, they encountered a 'smart' solar powered pod light embedded in the cycleway that, covered in blades of dead grass, was 'gradual[ly] ero[ding]' away (Fraser and Wilmott, 2020: 359). Elsewhere, they encountered a shared bike – a material object of 'smart', platformised mobility infrastructure – that had been retrieved from the canal after being tossed into the waterway following the bicycle having been stripped of its 'digital GPS tracker and locking mechanism' (Fraser and Wilmott, 2020: 364).

By attuning to smart city ruins and encroachments of nature in the process of walking-with, Fraser and Wilmott (2020) identified the smart city to comprise a complex visual regime of contrasts between the urban 'push for' digital innovation, the 'messiness of everyday life' and the 'perpetually overlooked organic transformations and recuperative strategies' of nature (362). Fraser and Wilmott's interpretation of photographs, observations and reflections collected along their walks informed their understanding of the mismatch between aspirational visions for pristine smart city developments and the messy reality of what 'smartness' looks like on the ground in cities. Their findings further capture that smart urban innovation is continuously negotiated and/or rejected by urban citizens who may, for instance, toss components of smart mobility infrastructure (such as a shared e-bike) into waterways – not an uncommon occurrence (see, e.g., CBC Radio, 2019).

Leszczynski and Kong (2022) similarly mobilised an approach of walking-with to inform their examination of how material components of Vancouver's docked bike-sharing system functioned aesthetically within a broader visual ecology of the built environment. Leszczynski and Kong's (2022) study was part of a broader project that involved traversing a sample of neighbourhoods, mostly on foot, to inventory visible traces of platformisation in three Canadian cities: Toronto, Vancouver and Montreal. In the process of conducting this inventory in Vancouver, the researchers repeatedly encountered bike-sharing stations across their selection of neighbourhoods. As they came across shared bike docks in the course of their walk, they began to visually attune to bike-sharing stations' immediate built environment surrounds. By paying attention to what else was materially and visually coincident with these smart urban infrastructures – including types of building, the kinds of places they housed and their architectural design forms – Leszczynski and Kong (2022) developed an inductive analysis of these smart mobility infrastructures increasingly figuring alongside other aesthetic referents of the visual 'aesthetics of gentrification' in the city, including cube-style miminalist architecture, boutique retail venues, third-wave coffee shops and design flourishes like exposed brick. Based on the interpretation of their walking data, Leszczynski and Kong (2022: 16) theorised that bike-sharing stations are one of the ways in which smartness is (re)shaping 'imaginaries of what gentrification "looks like" in place', with platformised mobility infrastructures increasingly figuring as an anticipated and even expected component of these visual tableaux of the smart city.

Visualising the Smart City

A different approach to researching smart city aesthetics is Rose and Willis's (2019) cultural analytics (see **Chapter 10**) study of smart city images circulated via Twitter. In this study, the researchers were interested in how smart cities were aesthetically represented in images shared through social media platforms. Rose and Willis (2019) collected smart-city related tweets generated over a seventeen-day period (20 November to 6 December 2016) via the Twitter streaming data service. The tweets were captured if they included the use of nine different hashtags – including #smartcities, #smartcity, #smartcitizen, #smartlighting, and similar others – in the text of the tweet. Post filtering, the dataset consisted of 9,030 tweeted images. Rose and Willis (2019) analysed this image media dataset using ImagePlot[1] to determine the *hue* (conventionally referred to as 'colour') and *brightness* (illumination/reflectance value) for each pixel in the

---

[1] See http://lab.softwarestudies.com/p/imageplot.html (accessed 21 August 2023).

images, using the software to arrange thumbnails of the tweeted smart city images in a radial plot, with median brightness and hue as the x and y canvas axes. The researchers subsequently engaged with the data at both the scale of the resulting radial image plot, as well as the scale of the individual image thumbnails that could be zoomed into on the resulting visualisation canvas. At the scale of the radial image plot itself, they identified two dominant colour schemes of the smart city imagery: those with median hues in the yellow-orange-brown spectrum, as well as images with median hues in the azure-blue-teal range. One of the researchers (Rose) then investigated a subset of these images at a regular interval of every tenth image by zooming into their thumbnails. In the process of zooming into and examining this subset of images, Rose developed an inductive theorisation of what these images were doing in terms of their impact on the viewing social media user. She determined that the images actualised three distinct affects or ways of 'being smart', corresponding to the colour zones of the radial image plot: participating in smart cities (yellow-orange-brown), anticipating smart cities (azure-blue-teal) and learning about smart cities (diverse hues) (Rose and Willis, 2019: 413).

Using a cultural analytics approach to visualise digital smart city images circulated via social media opened onto a structured exploratory, inductive analysis of the image data for Rose and Willis (2019). Their approach to data analysis informed two important research outcomes: i) an understanding of how smart cities are represented in digital imagery circulated on social media; and ii) how these images disseminate, naturalise and build up excitement – and ultimately consumer and urban citizen 'buy in' – for the concept of smart cities. Elsewhere, other studies have gone beyond examining the discursive construction of smart cities by instead investigating whether and how the celebratory rhetoric of smart cities aligns with the reality of how smartness is rolled out and operationalised across 'actually existing' smart city initiatives (Shelton et al., 2015). These include studies that mobilise the prototyping of sensors and participatory sensing approaches to inform empirical understandings of how 'smart' urban initiatives unfold in cities, becoming part and parcel of everyday, digitally mediated urban spaces and practices.

Sensor Prototyping and Participatory Sensing of the Smart City

Houde and Hill (1997: 369) define a prototype as 'any representation of a design idea, regardless of medium'. In the context of digital and digitally mediated phenomena (code, software, hardware, etc.), a prototype may be a foam or 3D printed model of the physical dimensions of a robot, a computer simulation model or a preliminary version of an interactive technology such as a digital sensor placed in an urban environment. What is distinctive about prototype artefacts is their design, in that they may be comprised of entirely original building blocks, but may also equally be assembled from pre-existing components. Prototype artefacts are further characterised by their relationship to consumer products, representing either pre-production, refinable versions of things along the way of their development to commercial products (Coutts et al., 2019); or, they are not destined for mass production and/or consumption at all.

As Wensveen and Matthews (2015) describe, designing and operationalising prototypes constitutes a distinct practice-based research methodology. Oriented around the 'conception, development and realisation of new forms, functions, systems and interactions', prototyping can be mobilised as something akin to a research 'kit' that supports answering an array of questions at the heart of research about digital life (Wensveen and Matthews, 2015: 263), including about how digital technologies are made in terms of the kinds of values and compromises that inform their design; how they are received and/or adopted (or not) by communities; and how they are actually used, negotiated, maintained and intervened in in the course of everyday life practices. This chapter profiles two projects centred on sensor prototyping as a smart city research design approach: a participatory 'civic tech' (see **Chapter 8**) air quality sensing initiative in the United Kingdom, and a top-down, researcher-led sensor prototyping experiment in Sweden.

As part of a project with residents engaged in documenting air quality degradation arising from increased traffic congestion and construction activity in the Deptford neighbourhood of Southeast London, UK, Houston et al. (2019) designed a prototype sensing infrastructure to 'augment' these smart (though largely analogue) urban citizen science practices already underway (p. 853). This infrastructure consisted of a number of integrated components: a prototype 3D printed optical sensor device, named the *Dustbox*, for detecting concentrations of particulate matter 2.5 (PM 2.5), a hazardous pollutant, in the air; a database for receiving and storing the digitally transmitted sensor data; and a publicly accessible data analysis platform named *Airsift* for 'analyzing and visualizing sensor data' from the database (Houston et al., 2019: 854). Houston et al. (2019) brought together residents, health researchers and local politicians in a series of meetings to initiate and organise the deployment of the *Dustboxes* within the neighbourhood. They likewise put on workshops that involved walking to locations of pollutant emission concern, offered support in setting up the *Dustboxes* across a number of sensing sites in the community, and held drop-in data analysis workshops for participants.

In the course of these activities, Houston et al.'s (2019) participatory sensing methodology (see **Chapter 8**) shed light on how this smart air quality sensor infrastructure was actually operationalised, negotiated and maintained in place and in practice.

Specifically, they identified that the roll-out of their prototype sensor kit prompted the development of a number of 'workarounds' to actually get, and keep, the sensor infrastructure functioning, including protecting the *Dustboxes* from inclement weather, finding ways to restore network connectivity to the sensors, and increasing the size of the database such that it could store more data when it was identified that the database had stopped working. Houston et al. (2019) then used these identified workarounds to speak back to idealised, hegemonic conceptions of the 'smart city' in two key ways. First, their findings inform a more nuanced and expansive picture of what it means to be a citizen in the smart city, pushing back against 'narrow [narratives] of citizen-participation-as-data-collection' (p. 849) by showing that citizens in their study took an active role in the data collection technologies themselves by 'maintaining and repairing' them (p. 845). And second, their hybrid sensor prototyping/participatory sensing methodology reveals that narratives of smart cities as 'large-scale and monolithic ... urban systems' that function as intended '[break] down in practice' once component technologies are rolled out across the fabric of the city, and spatially and temporally contingent constellations of 'sensors, cities, and people' necessarily 'exceed the systems in place to anticipate or react to disorder', where such systems ever exist (pp. 843–4; 864).

In a separate sensor prototyping study, Enlund et al. (2022: 2) designed and deployed a bespoke sensor infrastructure for 'collecting data on air quality, sound, and mobility in a smart city testbed' along Kungsgatan, a central street in the city of Norrköping, Sweden. This study differs from Houston et al.'s (2019) project in that its design is not participatory, as it does not engage members of the public in the prototyping, deployment and maintenance of the sensors, nor in the collection and analysis of the sensor data. Rather, the project was carried out by an interdisciplinary team of researchers who prototyped combining a number of different kinds of sensor – including those for monitoring and recording 'traffic volume, sound level, particulate matter ... temperature, and humidity' (p. 4) – within a lightweight weatherproof box that was affixed to elements of public infrastructure (namely, lamp-posts) at five locations in the testbed site. As the project developed, team members had numerous discussions about the design and configuration of sensors within the boxes, their placement in the city and the kinds of data that the sensors captured. In the course of the team's discussions, it became apparent that the design of the sensor boxes, including the arrangement of sensors within the boxes, operational decisions about their deployment in the testbed, and citizens' speculated-on engagements with the sensors (e.g., suspected tampering) were influencing the sensor readings, and thereby the nature and quality of the data collected. These discussions, in turn, raised questions not only about how glitches or obstacles in sensor design and deployment may be 'worked around', as in Houston et al.'s (2019) study, but also about how sensor technologies actively produce smart city spaces.

To answer this question about how sensors produce the smart city, Enlund et al. devised a matrix whose axes were defined by intersections of Henri Lefebvre's tripartite of perceived (directly encountered), conceived (imagined) and lived (habituated) social space (*columns*) with David Harvey's distinction between absolute (measurable), relative (contingent) and relational (space-time) space (*rows*). The researchers then populated the matrix with their observations, recollections of experiences and reflections on the design and roll-out of their sensing infrastructure. For instance, the sensor boxes were ultimately affixed to lamp-posts because the boxes could be connected to the electrical power source that also powered the streetlights. However, because of the long days of the Swedish summer, the lights themselves were powered for only a short time, which was not long enough for the sensor box battery to sustain a sufficient enough charge to continue collecting data over a full twenty-four hours. Here, the relational perceived space of the sensor-box-lamp-post interactions meant that the data captured by these sensors was 'producing' Kungsgatan only at night during the summer months.

Enlund et al.'s (2022) matrix-centred analytic methodology informed a key insight about the nature of urban data captured through smart sensor infrastructures: that smart city data does not accurately 'mirror' real-time urban processes (pollution emissions and dispersal, mobility, noise production), but rather codifies what is going on with the sensors themselves. In other words, '[w]hile [the] sensors [were] meant to capture an accurate "map" of the street and what [was] going on along it' (Enlund et al., 2022: 1), interactions between sensor components within the box, sensor interactions with other elements of urban infrastructure, and (suspected) human-sensor interactions on the street are what actually 'influence[d] the "map"' of the smart city 'that the sensor boxes produce[d]' (Enlund et al., 2022: 2).

Summary

- Walking methodologies, image data visualisation and sensor prototype design and participatory sensing are some approaches that have been used to study smart cities and their infrastructures.
- Sensor prototyping and participatory sensing have also been used to research how smart city sensor technologies are configured, deployed, maintained and troubleshooted in smart cities.
- Walking methodologies and image data visualisation have been used to study the aesthetics of smart cities.

Recommended Reading

D'Ignazio, C., Gordon, E., and Christoferotti, E. (2019) 'Sensors and civics: Toward a community-centered smart city', in Cardullo, P., Di Deliciantonio, C., and Kitchin, R. (eds) *The Right to the Smart City*. Emerald Publishing, Bingley, pp. 113–24.
Uses sensor prototyping as an approach for studying smart cities, with a particular focus on feedbacks between sensors and smart citizens.

Fraser, E., and Wilmott, C. (2020) 'Ruins of the smart city: A visual intervention', *Visual Communication*, 19(3): 353–68.
An exemplar of the use of walking methodologies for researching the material landscapes and built environments of smart cities through an engagement with abandoned smart urban initiatives in Manchester and Salford.

Gabrys, J., Pritchard, H., and Barratt, B. (2016) 'Just good enough data: Figuring data citizenships through air pollution sensing and data stories', *Big Data & Society*, 3(2): 1–14.
A detailed account of a robust participatory action research study centred on prototyping and deploying community digital air quality sensing infrastructure in London.

Mahajan, S., Gabrys, J., and Armitage, J. (2021) '*AirKit*: A Citizen-Sensing Toolkit for Monitoring Air Quality', *Sensors*, 21, 4044: 1–19.
A description of *AirKit* as a 'research kit', with a discussion of how it may be mobilised for citizen science urban air-quality sensing initiatives.

Rose, G., and Willis, A. (2018) 'Seeing the smart city on Twitter: Colour and the affective territories of becoming smart', *Environment and Planning D: Society and Space*, 37(3): 411–27.
An example of a cultural analytics approach to researching smart cities through an examination of image-based representations of smart cities circulated on the social media platform Twitter.

16
Digital Labour

Overview

Chapter 16 examines:

- the concept of 'digital labour' as a distinct form of work, and how and why it has emerged as an urgent subject of research about digital life;
- the kinds of research question that social science studies of digital labour have aimed to answer; and
- how digital labour has been studied using interviews and ethnography, data visualisation and digital mapping, and participatory and action research approaches.

Introduction

Many jobs now involve the use of digital technologies – computers, digital screens, digital devices, software – for some aspect of the work involved. This of course includes research and scholarly work, as we now rely on digital tools to capture, manage and analyse research data, and also to write papers, generate data visualisations and put together scholarly presentations. While acknowledging the incursion of digital technologies and processes into workplaces and work processes, job-related tasks 'that have been *reshaped* by [digital] media systems' – such as responding to email – are distinct from types of work that have been termed 'digital labour' (Jarrett, 2022: 8; emphasis added). 'Digital labour' specifically refers to work within, for, and shaped directly by the 'digital media industries': sectors of the economy 'involved with software, websites, platforms, apps, [and] the creation of content or data for these systems' (Jarrett, 2022: 11–12).

At one end of the spectrum of digital labour are the kinds of work done by salaried, stably employed coders, software engineers and app developers, digital hardware designers and even full-time content moderators who work for big digital media companies, including social media platforms (e.g., Meta), search engines (e.g., Google), cloud computing services (e.g., Amazon Web Services), content (e.g., Netflix), digital product titans (e.g., Apple), and e-tailers (e.g., Amazon). At the other end of the spectrum of digital labour exist highly *un*stable, piecemeal (task-based), 'casual and non-permanent' forms of 'gig work' consisting of unsalaried 'independent contracting that happens through, via, and on digital platforms' (Woodcock and Graham, 2020: 3). Platforms are digital intermediaries – a company website or an app – that brokers work by bringing together workers, clients and tasks, as in the case of a ride-hailing app matching drivers with riders, or a microtasking website listing jobs needing completion (worker-end interface) and/or participating workers (client-end interface). As detailed by James (2022: 3), types of platform-based gig work:

> [range] from on-demand urban service delivery (food, personal transport, courier services); to remote crowdsourced microtasks (often menial and monotonous [work] requiring some sort of judgement beyond AI capability, such as image categorisation, tagging, content moderation, information finding); to remote crowdsourcing of more complex white-collar tasks, or 'cloudworking' (for example, web and software development, sales and marketing, HR, legal work, social media management, graphic design, writing and translation, clerical data entry, and accounting).

While some gig workers such as software developers or computer programmers engaged in cloudwork produce digital products and engage directly in digital media work, others such as ride-hail drivers or on-demand delivery couriers do not. Yet workers in this second group are still classified as 'digital labourers' because 'the mechanisms that create the labor relationship' – such as ranking and dispatch algorithms – 'rely on [the existence]' of digital platforms (Jarrett, 2022: 11). Forms of digital work also come in two spatial forms: 'geographically tethered' jobs that require a worker to be in a specific place (e.g., driving for a ride-hail platform in a specific city), and delocalised forms of cloud-based work ('cloudwork') in which workers can complete digital tasks from anywhere in the world (Woodcock and Graham, 2020).

Labour and work have long been at the forefront of social science research agendas. *Digital* labour has emerged as a pressing and highly urgent subject of interdisciplinary social science scholarship because of the profound ways in which it is informed by and is driving profound transformations in societies around the world, often resulting in the deepening precarity of an increasingly globalised digital labour force engaged in task-based work (Graham and Anwar, 2019). This chapter explores select examples of how digital labour has been researched by social scientists via approaches centred on the use of interviews and ethnography (see **Chapter 5**); visualisation and mapping (see **Chapter 10**); and participatory and action research (see **Chapter 8**). In exploring how these methods have been used, this chapter attends to the kinds of research question that these techniques have been used to answer about digital labour, as well as the research aims and objectives that these methods have been used to satisfy across a selection of studies.

Interviews and Ethnography of Digital Labour

To date, the most common approaches to researching the gig economy have involved the mobilisation of interviews and ethnography (see **Chapter 5**). These techniques have been used to study salaried, stable forms of gig work in the context of gainful employment with digital technology/media companies, as well as highly precaritised forms of gig work brokered via digital platforms. Studies of digital work based on interviews and ethnography have been used to answer three broad categories of research question:

- questions about the nature of digital work, including about how it is structured, organised, arranged and executed;
- questions about workers' encounters with and experiences of digital media industries and the gig economy, their digital labour practices and how they navigate, negotiate and respond to digital work, digital work arrangements and digital labour employers (e.g., platforms); and
- questions about the effects and consequences of digital labour for individual workers, the working class and society at large.

Importantly, these questions are not mutually exclusive. Rather, they are often interlinked, as for example when considering the role of algorithms in the gig economy. This prompts simultaneous questions about how algorithms arrange or 'broker' digital labour (make digital work possible) and about how they structure the ways in which workers encounter, experience, navigate and respond to platform entities in the course of their work.

In addressing and answering these questions, scholars have mobilised a variety of interview and ethnographic approaches. These include more traditional forms of these methodologies that are themselves non-digital in nature, as well as explicitly digital ethnographic techniques. Examples of studies using traditional (non-digital) ethnographic and interview approaches to studying the gig economy are plentiful. Over an eight-year period, Roberts (2019) conducted in-depth interviews with key stakeholders in the digital content moderation sector, including current and former content moderators and representatives of content moderation companies across the United States, Mexico and the Philippines. Her study sheds light on the heavy psychological toll of repeated exposure to hateful and harmful content on both gig and permanently employed moderators paid to screen videos, images, text and audio posted online. Shifting from digital content moderation to the labour of fulfilling on-demand deliveries, Gregory (2021) conducted twenty-five in-depth interviews with both current and former meal delivery couriers in Edinburgh to identify how they perceived, experienced, understood and negotiated various risks associated with platform-mediated gig work.

Elsewhere, James (2022) interviewed forty-nine women microtaskers recruited through popular crowdwork platforms in the United Kingdom. The purpose of these interviews was to identify the unique challenges experienced by women cloudworkers, who have largely been ignored in digital labour research. These challenges include gender discrimination leading to fewer task requests and reviews; and gendered constraints on temporal flexibility (ability to respond to requests promptly, be ubiquitously available, etc.) associated with childcare responsibilities, resulting in lower rankings – and thereby less visibility – of women on job marketplace platforms (James, 2022). Likewise, problematising the absence of gender considerations from digital labour research, Dattani (2021) conducted twenty-two interviews and two focus groups with low-income Indian women domestic workers to identify why attempts to 'Uberise' domestic labour (i.e., to digitally incorporate domestic work as a gig economy service) failed in the Delhi metropolitan region. The reasons for the failures of attempts to platformise domestic work included not contending with low-income women's lack of access to and ownership of digital devices; their resulting lower levels of digital literacy; and limitations on their spatial mobilities, whereby these women tend to travel by the slowest modes of transport and are unlikely to work far from home due to social norms and codes (Dattani, 2021).

Scholars have also used digital ethnography alongside conventional interviews to research digital labour. Siriano (2021) for instance combined interviews with fifty-one stakeholders in the Philippines cloudwork sector (workers, coaches, agencies and platform owners) with observations of Filipino digital freelancer Facebook groups to identify how remote digital work is brokered in the Philippines. This study found that in addition to cloudwork platforms themselves brokering connections between gig workers and clients, significant roles were also played by coaches (successful cloudworkers providing training to aspiring digital workers) and platform agencies (a model whereby cloudworkers sub-contract portions of large projects to other gig workers). Digital ethnography has also been used as a standalone method for researching digital labour, as in a study of gig worker identity and collective mobilisation among on-demand delivery couriers in Thailand conducted by Mieruch and McFarlane (2022). Here, the researchers spent seven months observing interactions and posts on courier-managed Facebook pages mobilising gig workers to participate in a series of on-demand-worker protests against poor working conditions held in Bangkok in 2020. Mieruch and McFarlane

(2022) used their personal social media accounts to conduct non-participant observation of a selection of these public pages, subjecting the collected posts to qualitative coding using a narrative analysis approach. Their analysis identified that couriers espoused a 'hero' narrative of delivery work propagated by the on-demand platforms as a means of recruiting gig workers, while simultaneously contesting and rejecting this narrative by speaking out about the unfair working conditions they experienced, which led to collective organising for on-demand delivery couriers' labour rights (Mieruch and McFarlane, 2022).

While ethnographic methods and interviews help inform understandings of digital labour as an organising structure, logic and set of situated everyday life practices at a localised scale, they are not oriented towards painting the 'big picture' of digital labour. To research digital labour at a large (national, regional and even global) scale, scholars have turned to techniques including data visualisation and mapping.

Visualising and Mapping Digital Labour

Although the dramatic reconfigurations of work driven by the rise of platforms and the digital gig economy are experienced locally, the sweeping transformations of labour markets and societies wrought by the rapid expansion of digital work are global in scale and scope (Graham and Anwar, 2019). To ascertain the extent, geography and nature of these transformations, researchers have turned to the use of data visualisation and digital mapping (see **Chapter 10**) to capture both quantitative and qualitative aspects of digital labour markets. The leading example of such efforts are the data visualisations and maps of digital labour indicators produced by the Online Labour Observatory,[1] an information and data 'hub for researchers, policy makers, and the public interested in global online labour markets' (Lehdonvirta et al., n.d.: n.p.). Among the interactive data visualisations produced by the observatory are those associated with the Observatory's Online Labour Index (OLI). Focusing on digital labour marketplaces,[2] the OLI is an 'economic indicator' that 'measures the utilization of online labour platforms over time and across countries and occupations' (Kässi and Lehdonvirta, 2018: 241).

---

[1] See http://onlinelabourobservatory.org/ (accessed 21 August 2023).
[2] The OLI captures metrics about activity on labour platforms that list jobs for which the 'result of the work is delivered digitally', such as software development, graphic design and data entry, among others (Kässi and Lehdonvirta, 2018: 243). This excludes labour platforms such as ride hailing and on-demand delivery, where the nature of the work is digitally mediated but the work product is a physical service or object (e.g., a ride in a vehicle, a delivered meal) (Kässi and Lehdonvirta, 2018: 243).

The OLI releases autonomously updating data sourced predominantly via the scraping of a selection of English, Spanish and Russian-language cloudwork platforms.

The OLI's indicators are published for both the supply (digital workers) and demand (buyers of digital work) sides of digital labour markets. The visualisation of supply-side metrics includes an interactive, world-scale choropleth map (see **Chapter 10**) that communicates the top digital labour occupations in each country.[3] An interactive slider allows users to toggle the data on the map to show changes in the dominance top digital labour force occupations in each country over time, from 2017 to the present. The OLI's visualisations of digital labour demand-side dynamics include interactive charts and graphs that facilitate different views of metrics about the sources demand for digital labour by country.[4] For instance, viewing online labour demand metrics by countries and occupations allows users to switch between two different horizontally oriented stacked bar charts: a view of the 'within country share' of demand for different types of digital work (by occupation) for six countries (the United States, the United Kingdom, India, Canada, Australia and Germany), with the bars showing the distribution of what percentage of total digital labour demand in each country is represented by different categories of digital work (see Figure 16.1); and a view of the 'global market share' of demand for each category of digital work (i.e., each occupation) accounted for by each of the six countries (see Figure 16.2).

The OLI's data visualisations and web maps serve two important purposes for research about digital labour. First, they visually summarise and facilitate interaction with big datasets that cover a continuously expanding temporal range as more data is autonomously added to the index. This allows for the effective communication (see **Chapter 10**) of global-scale digital labour market trends in a visual format that supports the quick and efficient interpretation of information. And second, the OLI's interactive visualisations support the exploratory analysis (**Chapters 10** and **11**) of its continuously updated data, which is published as open data by the Digital Labour Observatory (Stephany et al., n.d.). This allows researchers to preview the data, which may inform decisions about which datasets to download for purposes of their own studies.

Participatory and Action Approaches to Digital Labour

Ethnography and data visualisation and mapping represent approaches for studying digital workers, workplaces and work practices as objects of research. These studies

---

[3]See http://onlinelabourobservatory.org/oli-supply/ (accessed 21 August 2023).
[4]See http://onlinelabourobservatory.org/oli-demand/ (accessed 21 August 2023).

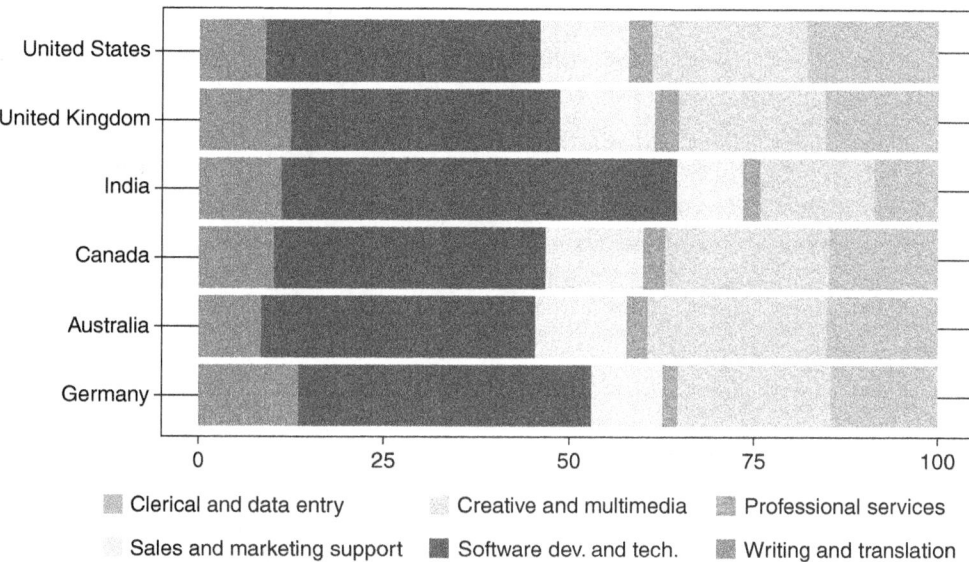

Figure 16.1 Online labour demand: within-country share of demand by occupation.

Source: Online Labour Index 2020, http://onlinelabourobservatory.org/oli-demand/. Produced by Stephany et al. (n.d.) as part of the Online Labour Observatory. Chart reproduced under terms of CC BY 4.0 licence.

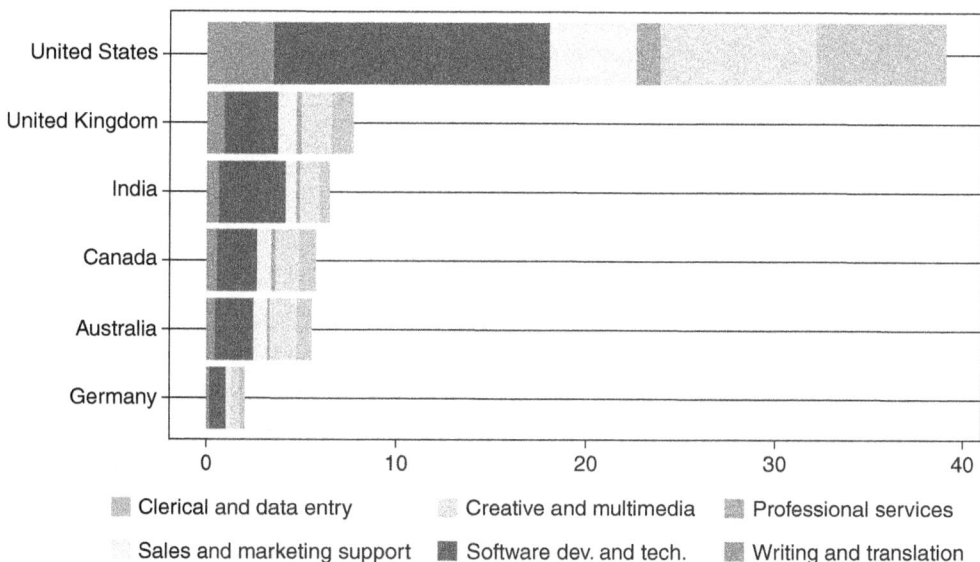

Figure 16.2 Online labour demand: global market share of demand for digital work by occupation.

Source: Online Labour Index 2020, http://onlinelabourobservatory.org/oli-demand/. Produced by Stephany et al. (n.d.) as part of the Online Labour Observatory. Chart reproduced under terms of CC BY 4.0 licence.

advance understandings of how work is being transformed by digital technologies such as platforms, and what it means to work as a digital labourer. However, these studies do not typically involve researchers actively working to improve labour conditions for digital workers. Yet researchers of digital labour have also been heavily invested in research as a political project of actively transforming the power assymetries between digital work platforms, clients (buyers of digital work) and digital labourers. Two specific participatory and action research methods have been used to study digital labour: workers' enquiry and the rating of platform fairness.

Workers' Enquiry

Workers' enquiry is a participatory approach to knowledge production – sometimes referred to as 'co-research' – where research is worker-led or engages with workers as researchers (Brown and Quan-Haase, 2012; Evangelinidis and Lazaris, 2014; Figiel et al., 2014; Wellbrook, 2014). The objective of a workers' enquiry is to ascertain workers' own experiences of precarity and exploitation, and to identify opportunities for organising and agitating against capitalist entities (e.g., corporations) with the goal of actively transforming labour relations and working conditions in the process (Figiel et al., 2014; Wellbrook, 2014; Woodcock, 2014). Workers' enquiry is motivated by a conviction that workers' organising and resistance against unfair labour conditions is an organic process that needs to be 'discovered' by workers *in* their places of work, rather than being informed by 'abstract generalizations' that prescribe pathways for class struggle (Cant, 2020: 136). Concerned with labour consciousness and class relations, workers' enquiry is deeply inflected by a historical materialist[5] worldview, or ontology (see **Chapter 2**), and has been most commonly conducted by sociologists.

Workers' enquiry is not a singular method, but rather an approach that understands labour-related research as a political project aimed at changing unequal power relations between workers and capital (Figiel et al., 2014). As such, workers' enquiry may draw from and even 'mix' (combine) a range of methods for data collection, including ethnography and autoethnography, in-depth interviews, qualitative questionnaires, quantitative surveys and the collection and analysis of social media posts, conversation threads on messaging apps, and blogs (Brown and Quan-Haase, 2012; Cant, 2020; Evangelinidis and Lazaris, 2014; Woodcock, 2014, 2021). Workers' enquiries

---

[5] Historical materialism is an ontological commitment to understanding history – and thereby societies – as the outcome of class struggle and unequal power relations that have crystallised over time.

may also involve labourers engaging in readings of classic socialist texts to identify possibilities 'for resistance against new forms of capitalist organization' (Woodcock, 2014: 499), as well as the worker-led writing, publication and circulation of 'proletarian documentary literature', including newspapers and bulletins (Cant, 2020: 139).

An example of a workers' enquiry of digital labour is found in Cant's participant ethnography of the development of resistance among gig workers delivering meals for the Deliveroo on-demand delivery platform in Brighton, England. Cant's (2020) worker enquiry centred on an extended case study that included the researcher engaging as a Deliveroo platform worker over an eight month period between September 2016 and May 2017. As part of the workers' enquiry, Cant (2019) actively intervened 'to support worker self-organisation with the goal of engag[ing] in a process of "coresearch"' with other Deliveroo couriers. This included Cant's participation in generating and distributing the *Rebel Roo*, a Deliveroo worker-published and worker-circulated bulletin, as well as participating in and observing how Deliveroo couriers organised to improve their working conditions and pay. Cant's (2022: 151) worker enquiry informed the development of an 'analysis of worker self-organization and resistance within platform capitalism'. Focusing on how and where Deliveroo courier resistance emerged, Cant (2019) identified three key contributing factors: the role of 'zone centres' (sites where couriers congregate waiting to be dispatched to their next delivery) as meeting points where couriers would air grievances related to working for the platform as they waited for their next gig; numerous Deliveroo worker groups being active on messaging app WhatsApp, which captured 'an estimated 50% of the workforce' and allowed workers' discussions and organising efforts to go beyond zone centres (p. 148); and the circulation of the *Rebel Roo*.

Following a number of labour actions, including strikes that reduced order volumes at participating restaurants and 'flying pickets' consisting of couriers 'mov[ing] along key roads ... disrupt[ing] the circulation of commodities in the city', Brighton-area Deliveroo couriers saw improvements in their pay (Cant, 2020: 151). Two of the Deliveroo worker's trade union demands were also met: a freeze on new recruitment (which diluted the pool of available deliveries per gig worker); and that couriers who participated in the strikes to not be 'victimized' (Cant, 2020: 140–1).

Rating Platform Fairness

A distinct action research approach to studying and intervening in the platform economy is provided by the ongoing work of the Fairwork Foundation (FF).[6] The FF is a

---

[6] See https://fair.work/ (accessed 21 August 2023).

digital labour research initiative of the Oxford Internet Institute[7] that is 'developing an intervention around the quality of work on digital labour platforms' by evaluating and rating the fairness of platforms' labour conditions for gig workers (Graham et al., 2020: 100). Fairwork's main focus is on assessing working conditions at geographically tethered platforms, but it also evaluates cloudwork platforms (Oxford Internet Institute, 2023d). The objectives of the FF's action research project are to 'foster more transparency about working conditions', including making differences in conditions of working for different platforms transparent to gig workers, and 'ultimately to encourage fairer working conditions' in the global platform economy (Graham et al., 2020: 100).

The FF fosters this transparency by assessing conditions of working for a platform company according to five principles of fairness:

- *fair pay* (pay rates, pay terms and the meeting of workers' costs);
- *fair conditions* (risks of work are mitigated and/or there are improvements to health and safety);
- *fair contracts* (terms and conditions of work are transparent and accessible to workers and documents reflect workers' actual engagement with a platform);
- *fair management* (fairness of any disciplinary practices, established lines of communication between workers and platform representatives, transparency in decision-making processes, absence of discrimination, and fair and transparent use of data); and
- *fair representation* (fair dispute resolution, workers' rights of association and access to collective bargaining)

(Graham et al., 2020; Oxford Internet Institute, 2023a, 2023c).

Each of these principles is defined by two thresholds of fairness, which serve as metrics against which platforms' working conditions may be evaluated: a first threshold that constitutes a 'floor' of fairness below which working conditions are unfair, and a second threshold that demonstrates active improvement above the floor. For instance, for the fair-pay principle, the first fairness threshold is met if the rate of pay is above the local minimum wage, and exceeded if pay rates remain above the local minimum wage once workers' costs are accounted for (Graham et al., 2020). These fairness principles and thresholds were co-developed through the participation of a range of platform economy stakeholders – including 'workers, unions, platforms, labour lawyers, academics, government and third sector organisations' – at a number of international workshops (Graham et al., 2020: 100). The FF uses these principles and thresholds of fairness to rate major platforms according to the fairness of working for any one platform. Each platform that is rated is given a fairness score out of ten, with a maximum of two points

---

[7] See www.oii.ox.ac.uk (accessed 21 August 2023).

awarded per principle: two points if the principle's initial threshold is met, two if it is exceeded, and zero if the fairness floor is not met (Graham et al., 2020; Oxford Internet Institute, 2023b).

The FF develops platform ratings geographically by country, recognising that while many platform companies are global, others operate uniquely in one or only a few national markets. When assessing platform fairness country by country, all major platforms operating in that market are subjected to and given a score to allow for 'comparing fairness of work across platforms' (Graham et al., 2020: 102). The cross-platform comparison enabled by the ratings is key to how Fairwork actualises its action agenda to improve platform working conditions. Platform comparison raises public awareness about differences in how different platforms treat their workers (Rakheja, 2022), informs platform operators how they measure up against their competitors, and provides platform companies with actionable criteria for improving conditions for their workers (Graham et al., 2020).

To assess and develop ratings for a platform company, Fairwork uses a tripartite methodological approach that begins with 'desk research', which includes 'analys[ing] a wide range of documents including contracts, terms and conditions, and published policies and procedures, as well as digital interfaces and website/app functionality' (Oxford Internet Institute, 2023b: n.p.). Once appropriate data collection instruments are developed for each national/regional/local context, Fairwork project researchers conduct interviews with platform company managers[8] and also conduct surveys and interviews with gig workers recruited through a number of approaches that include hiring gig workers for jobs through platforms, approaching workers in places they are known to congregate, posting to social media and online forums, and referral sampling (Oxford Research Institute, 2023b). This diversified approach allows for the triangulation of platforms' working conditions (e.g., how well a platform company's claims of fairness 'stack up' against workers' own experiences of working for the platform) and informs each platform's ratings.

The Fairwork project began by rating the labour fairness of platform companies in India and South Africa; at the time of writing, this has expanded to include platform ratings for twenty-two additional countries, including Egypt, Ecuador, Tanzania, Serbia, Indonesia, Ghana and the Philippines amongst others (Oxford Internet Institute, 2023d). Twenty-four cloudwork platforms have also been evaluated and rated (Oxford Internet Institute, 2023d). As reported by Graham et al. (2020), a number of platform companies have agreed to improve their conditoins for their workers in accordance with Fairwork's five principles.

---

[8]Not all platform companies make their representatives available for interviews. Platforms that opt-out of participating in interviews still receive a rating (Graham et al., 2020).

Summary

- 'Digital labour' describes different types of work carried out for large technology enterprises (e.g., content moderation for social media platforms), as well as forms of piecemeal – or task-based – gig-style work brokered by digital platforms (e.g., ride hailing, on-demand delivery, microtasking and cloudwork).
- Interviews and ethnography – including digital ethnography – constitute the most common approaches to researching digital labour in the social sciences and humanities.
- Data visualisation and mapping of digital labour data capture and communicate digital labour market dynamics at national and global scales, and also support exploratory analysis of digital labour datasets.
- Participatory and action research approaches to studying digital labour – including workers' enquiry and rating the fairness of platform work – have sought to improve digital labourers' working conditions.

Recommended Reading

Anwar, M.A., and Graham, M. (2022) *The Digital Continent: Placing Africa in Planetary Networks of Work.* Oxford University Press, Oxford.
A detailed account of Africa as a key player in the growth of the global digital labour market.

Cant, C. (2019) *Riding for Deliveroo: Resistance in the New Economy.* Polity Press, Cambridge.
An ethnography and workers' enquiry of worker resistance by Deliveroo platform workers.

Graham, M., Woodcock, J., Heeks, R., Mungai, P., Van Belle, J.P., du Toit, D., Fredman, S., Osiki, A., van der Spuy, A., and Silberman, S.M. (2020) 'The Fairwork Foundation: Strategies for improving platform work in a global context', *Geoforum*, 112: 100–3.
A comprehensive account of an interventionist research initiative – the Fairwork Foundation – centred on rating the fairness of labour conditions specific to individual platform operators and digital labour marketplaces.

Kässi, O., and Lehdonvirta, V. (2018) 'Online labour index: Measuring the online gig economy for policy and research', *Technological Forecasting & Social Change*, 137: 241–8.
An overview of the kinds of digital labour metrics that are tracked and made available for research by the OLI.

Spilda, F. U., Howson, K., Johnston, H., Bertolini, A., Feuerstein, P., Bezuidenhout, L., Alyanak, O., and Graham, M. (2022) 'Is anonymity dead? Doing critical research on digital labour platforms through platform interfaces', *Work Organisation, Labour & Globalisation*, 16(1): 82–7.

A consideration of the ethical and other methodological challenges of studying digital labour platforms, including the challenges of using these interfaces to recruit research participants.

Part 4
Conclusion

17
Final Thoughts

The digital is having a profound effect on society and economy across scales from the local to global, reshaping social, spatial and temporal relations and altering the organisation and operations of production, consumption, mobility, leisure, education, health and every other facet of humanity. Digital technologies are reconfiguring what it means to be human, mediating how we interface with others, how we perform tasks and how we reflect on and understand ourselves. It is not an understatement to assert that the digital is *the key* mediator of how everyday life now unfolds. Making sense of digital life then is a critical endeavour.

Our aim in this book has been to introduce a range of methods for researching how the digital is affecting everyday life in a multitude of ways and how such research is framed, formulated and applied in practice to make sense of phenomena. We have not sought to document all possible methods of data generation and analysis, or to detail exhaustively associated issues of research design, implementation and ethics. Documenting the full range of methods and issues used across the social sciences and humanities to make sense of digital life would be a sizeable task; one that would require several volumes. Indeed, there are whole books focused solely on the methods examined in each of our chapters, and, in many cases, sections of these chapters. And these books are themselves inexhaustive in scope. In other words, *Researching Digital Life* provides a starting point for considering how to approach and implement a research study. It is not a substitute for developing deep domain knowledge about specific methods or for how other researchers have sought to answer particular questions. As such, while this book provides a guide to salient methods and issues, a wider engagement with the empirical and methodological literature is essential for evaluating the most appropriate means of researching a particular phenomenon.

Keeping up with developments in domain knowledge and methods can be a challenge. Innovation is central to all aspects of digital life. Just as the digital seeks to disrupt different domains, digital technologies are themselves constantly being reconfigured and superseded by new developments in fast paced cycles of what Schumpeter (1942) termed 'creative destruction'. Through innovation and competition, it seems that digital products and systems are quickly rendered obsolete and ceaselessly replaced with new ones. As a result, the digital is never static, but always in a process of unfolding. Indeed, over the past fifty years there have been waves of digital innovations, each hailed as having profound effects for society: the internet, the personal computer, relational databases, telematics, the World Wide Web, the Internet of Things, Web 2.0, big data, smartphones, AI, virtual reality and 5G, among others. Those interested in digital life are never then short of topical issues to be investigated or of research questions to be answered. Indeed, the opposite is often the case – there is a super-abundance of interesting issues and questions to investigate, and the problem is deciding on how to narrow down the scope of a study to a manageable project in terms of the specific questions to be researched and empirical cases to be examined. Such narrowing though is necessary, as researchers are generally seeking to provide an in-depth understanding of a phenomenon rather than a shallow, superficial explanation. A key challenge then is to be able to identify a *specific* critical question or hypothesis to examine and to hone and concentrate the investigation to make the project manageable, while maintaining sufficient representativeness so that the findings are applicable in other cases and have wider relevance. For novice researchers, finding such a balance might involve some trial and error, and undertaking pilot scoping and implementation studies is a useful strategy.

Just as there is ceaseless novelty in how the digital is inflecting all facets of everyday life, researchers of the digital need to be mindful that digital technologies and systems are also changing the conduct of research in three key ways. First, by producing new data and enabling access to older datasets; second, by facilitating the creation of new methods; and third, by fostering new epistemologies.

As a result of the digital era, we live in an age of data abundance. In 2012, IBM contended that '90% of the data in the world today has been created in the last two years alone' (IBM, 2012). Since then, as more and more systems produce ever-greater amounts of big data, the volume of data has continued to expand exponentially. These data are born digital and, importantly, they are often highly granular in attribute, spatial and temporal terms, providing very detailed, longitudinal records. Some of these data have been made open access, though much of them are locked inside commercial enterprises or state bodies. Nonetheless, they constitute valuable data sources for research if access can be negotiated. Alongside mass datafication, there has been a move to digitise archives of existing analogue data and to assemble them in new data infrastructures accessible across the internet. Never before have researchers had such easy access to large volumes of historical and contemporary data. It is important then to be aware of what potential new datasets are available for researching an issue that mitigate the need to produce primary data or which can supplement such data.

As we have detailed throughout the book, digital technologies have had a marked effect on the methods employed in research. Older, more traditional methods of data generation and analysis have been recast through digital mediation. For example, interviews are mediated via online chat, social media channels or video calls, with these media enabling recording and, in the latter case, automatic transcription (see **Chapter 5**). Data visualisation has become easier to perform, more sophisticated in its techniques and interactive in its delivery, allowing viewers to 'play' with the data and its presentation (see **Chapter 10**). Statistical analysis and modelling have been transformed through the use of machine learning, enabling complex calculations on ever-larger datasets (see **Chapter 11**). Calculations that used to take days or hours are now performed in milliseconds. In addition, a range of new digital methods have been invented that are entirely digital in their conception and application, such as data scraping, crowdsourcing data across digital platforms, participatory GIS, generating data via laser scanning, x-ray fluorescence scanning, reflectance transformation imaging, interactive 3D virtual rendering and various forms of multidimensional visualisation. And just as traditional analogue methods require certain knowledge and skills to deploy, the same is true of digitally mediated methods that may require the use of specialist software and coding. Developing these skills can be a challenge, but digital media also provides help through the numerous online forums and YouTube videos dedicated to sharing advice about using specific software and techniques for crafting code.

Digital technologies and tools have had a profound impact on the epistemology and methodology of the social sciences and humanities (see **Chapter 2**). As detailed in **Chapter 9**, the mass digitisation of historical records, the creation of digital archives and repositories, and the creation of new data about the past enabled by new technologies such as aerial/drone photography, photogrammetry, ground penetrating radar and sonar is having a profound effect on how history is practised. The digital humanities is founded on a new means to make sense of the past, based not on a close, analogue reading of a relatively small sample of data, but a digitally mediated analysis of potentially millions of records. Similarly, as examined in **Chapter 11**, a broad set of data analytic techniques that utilise machine learning, along with the availability of big datasets, has reconfigured and extended quantitative approaches used in the social sciences. The granularity of big data, coupled with automated processes that are capable of learning from these data, has led to a resurgence in statistical analyses and the development of the computational social sciences. As we detailed in **Chapter 2**, in a well-conceived and designed study there is a strong alignment of epistemology, methodology and methods. It is important then to be aware of unfolding debates concerning these facets of research and to reflect on their appeal and salience with respect to one's own approach to research. There is no requirement to always move with emerging trends; indeed, one might believe that new conceptual developments are ill-conceived and ill-judged. Both cases – re-orienting or maintaining one's approach – however, must be based on an informed decision.

Regardless of conceptual fortitude, researching digital life is an exercise in seeking to identify and aim focused attention at a quickly transitioning target. The methods of data generation and analysis used to make sense of these evolving phenomena are likewise evolving through digital mediation. Perhaps then, the greatest skills that a researcher interested in understanding and explaining digital life needs to hone and apply are adaptability, creativity and endurance. In this book, we have provided a baseline set of concepts and methods to help provide workable starting points for research design and application, but these need to be reformulated in imaginative and contingent ways to make them suitable for the context of a study. This, we feel, is the most difficult challenge for researchers – to keep abreast of domain knowledge and methodological advances, and to be able to tailor existing methods or invent new ones that are capable of revealing the difference the digital makes. Our final message is to wish you luck in addressing this challenge and to be mindful that undertaking research is rarely easy. While careful planning is essential, research also involves trial, error and perseverance. The insights gained, however, are worth the effort.

References

Abbate, J. (1999) *Inventing the Internet*. MIT Press, Cambridge, MA.
Abbate, J. (2012) *Recoding Gender: Women's Changing Participation in Computing*. MIT Press, Cambridge, MA.
Abernathy, D. (2017) *Using Geodata and Geolocation in the Social Sciences: Mapping Our Connected World*. Sage, London.
Abidin, C., and de Seta, G. (2020) 'Private messages from the field: Confessions on digital ethnography and its discomforts', *Journal of Digital Social Research*, 2(1): 1–19.
Adam, A., Finance, O., and Thomas, I. (2021) 'Monitoring trucks to reveal Belgian geographical structures and dynamics: From GPS traces to spatial interactions', *Journal of Transport Geography*, 91: 102977.
Adams, C., and Thompson, T.L. (2016) *Researching a Posthuman World: Interviews with Digital Objects*. Palgrave Macmillan, London.
Afzalan, N., Sanchez, T.W., and Evans-Cowley, J. (2017) 'Creating smarter cities: Considerations for selecting online participatory tools', *Cities*, 67: 21–30.
Agar, J. (2003) *The Government Machine: A Revolutionary History of the Computer*. MIT Press, Cambridge, MA.
Ahmed, S. (2006) *Queer Phenomenology*. Duke University Press, Durham, NC.
Aiello, G. (2020) 'Inventorizing, situating, transforming: Social semiotics and data visualization', in Engebretsen, M., and Kennedy, H. (eds) *Data Visualization in Society*. Amsterdam University Press, Amsterdam, pp. 49–62.
Aiello, G., and Parry, K. (2020) *Visual Communication: Understanding Images in Media Culture*. Sage, London.
Akkerman, S., Admiraal, W., Brekelmans, M., and Oost, H. (2008) 'Auditing quality of research in social sciences', *Quality and Quantity*, 42: 257–74.
Alderson, P. and Morrow, V. (2020) *The Ethics of Research with Children and Young People: A Practical Handbook*, 2nd edn. Sage, London.
Allen, C. (2011) 'Against dialogue: Why being critical means taking sides rather than learning how to play the "policy research" game', *Dialogues in Human Geography*, 1(2): 223–7.
Alshenqeeti, H. (2014) 'Interviewing as a data collection method: A critical review', *English Linguistics Research*, 3(1): 39–45.
Alvarez, R.M. (ed.) (2016) *Computational Social Science*. Cambridge University Press, Cambridge.
Amaturo, A., and Aragona, B. (2022) 'Epistemology of the digital', in Punziano, G., and Delli, P.A. (eds) *Handbook of Research on Advances Research Methodologies for a Digital Society*. IGI Global, Hershey, PA, pp. 1–10.

Amon, K.L., Campbell, A.J., Hawke, C., and Steinbeck, K. (2014) 'Facebook as a recruitment tool for adolescent health research: a systematic review', *Academic Pediatrics*, 14(5): 439–47.

Anda, C., Erath, A., and Fourie, P.J. (2017) 'Transport modelling in the age of big data', *International Journal of Urban Sciences*, 21(sup1): 19–42.

Anderson, B., and Gordon, R. (2017) 'Government and (non)event: The promise of control', *Social & Cultural Geography*, 18(2): 158–77.

Anderson, B., and Harrison, P. (2012) *Taking-Place: Non-Representational Theories and Geography*. Ashgate, Farnham.

Anderson, B., Langley, P., Ash, J., and Gordon, R. (2020) 'Affective life and cultural economy: Payday loans and the everyday space-times of credit-debt in the UK', *Transactions of the Institute of British Geographers*, 45(2): 420–33.

Anderson, J. (2004) 'Talking whilst walking: A geographical archaeology of knowledge', *Area*, 36(3): 254–61.

Anderson, J.A., and Rosenfeld, E. (eds) (1998) *Talking Nets: An Oral History of Neural Networks*. MIT Press, Cambridge, MA.

Andrade, C. (2020) 'The Limitations of Online Surveys', *Indian Journal of Psychological Medicine*, 42(6): 575–6.

Angrosino, M. (2007) *Doing Ethnographic and Observational Research*. Sage, London.

Angwin, J., Larson, J., Mattu, S., and Kirchner, L. (2016) 'Machine bias', *ProPublica*, 23 May. https://www.propublica.org/article/machine-bias-risk-assessments-in-criminal-sentencing (accessed 2 March 2023).

Anttiroiko, A.-V. (2021) 'Digital urban planning platforms: The interplay of digital and local embeddedness in urban planning', *International Journal of E-Planning Research*, 10(3): 1–15.

Anwar, M.A., and Graham, M. (2022) *The Digital Continent: Placing Africa in Planetary Networks of Work*. Oxford University Press, Oxford.

Apperley, T., and Moore, K. (2019) 'Haptic ambience: Ambient play, the haptic effect and co-presence in Pokémon GO', *Convergence*, 25(1): 6–17.

Arafat, S.M.Y., Alradie-Mohamed, A., Kar, S.K., Sharma, P., and Kabir, R. (2020) 'Does COVID-19 pandemic affect sexual behaviour? A cross-sectional, cross-national online survey', *Psychiatry Research*, 289: 113050.

Ash, J. (2012) 'Technology, technicity, and emerging practices of temporal sensitivity in videogames', *Environment and Planning A*, 44(1): 187–203.

Ash, J. (2015) 'Sensation, networks, and the GIF: Toward an allotropic account of affect', in Hillis, K., Paasonen, S., and Petit, M. (eds) *Networked Affect*. MIT Press, Cambridge, MA, pp. 119–35.

Ash, J. (2017) *Phase Media: Space, Time and the Politics of Smart Objects*. Bloomsbury, London.

Ash, J., Anderson, B., Gordon, R., and Langley, P. (2018a) 'Digital interface design and power: Friction, threshold, transition', *Environment and Planning D: Society and Space*, 36(6): 1136–53.

Ash, J., Anderson, B., Gordon, R., and Langley, P. (2018b) 'Unit, tone, vibration: a post-phenomenological method for studying digital interfaces', *Cultural Geographies*, 25(1): 165–81.

Ash, J., Kitchin, R., and Leszczynski, A. (eds) (2018a) *Digital Geographies*. Sage, London.

Ash, J., Kitchin, R., and Leszczynski, A. (2018b) 'Digital turn, digital geographies?', *Progress in Human Geography*, 42(1): 25–43.

Baas, J., Schotten, M., Plume, A., Côté, G., and Karimi, R. (2020) 'Scopus as a curated, high-quality bibliometric data source for academic research in quantitative science studies', *Quantitative Science Studies*, 1(1): 377–86.

Baik, J. (2020) 'The geotagging counterpublic: The case of Facebook remote check-ins to Standing Rock', *International Journal of Communication*, 14: 2057–77.

Balbi, G., and Magaudda, P. (2018) *A History of Digital Media: An Intermedia and Global Perspective*. Routledge, London.

Baldacchino, J. (2012) 'Preface: Scholarship and art's ambiguous objects', in Daichendt, G.J. *Artist Scholar: Reflections on Writing and Research*. Intellect, Bristol, pp. xi–xxiii.

Bao, J., Yang, Z., Zeng, W., and Shi, X. (2021) 'Exploring the spatial impacts of human activities on urban traffic crashes using multi-source big data', *Journal of Transport Geography*, 94: 103118.

Barabasi, A.-L. (2016) *Network Science*. Cambridge University Press, Cambridge.

Barcelo, J. (ed.) (2010) *Fundamentals of Traffic Simulation*. Springer, Cham.

Barns, S. (2020) *Platform Urbanism: Negotiating Platform Ecosystems in Connected Cities*. Palgrave Macmillan, Singapore.

Baron, L.F., and Gomez, R. (2016) 'The associations between technologies and societies: The utility of actor-network theory', *Science, Technology and Society*, 21(2): 129–48.

Bashe, C.J., Johnson, R.L., Palmer, J.H., and Pugh, E.W. (1985) *IBM's Early Computers*. MIT Press, Cambridge, MA.

Bastow, S., Dunleavy, P., and Tinkler, J. (2014) *The Impact of the Social Sciences: How Academics and Their Research Make a Difference*. Sage, London.

Batty, M. (2007) *Cities and Complexity: Understanding Cities with Cellular Automata, Agent Based Models, and Fractals*. MIT Press, Cambridge, MA.

Batty, M. (2020) 'The smart city', in LeGates, R.T., and Stout, F. (eds) *The City Reader*, 7th edn. London, Routledge, pp. 503–15.

Batty, M., Axhausen, K.W., Giannotti, F., Pozdnoukhov, A., Bazzani, A., Wachowicz, M., Ouzounis, G., and Portugali, Y. (2012) 'Smart cities of the future', *European Physical Journal Special Topics*, 214: 481–518.

Batty, M., Desyllas, J., and Duxbury, E. (2003) 'Safety in numbers? Modelling crowds and designing control for the Notting Hill Carnival', *Urban Studies*, 40(8): 1573–90.

BCD (Building City Dashboards) (2018) *Building City Dashboards Data Art Exhibition*, www.maynoothuniversity.ie/library/events/building-city-dashboards-data-exhibition (last accessed 12 June 2023).

BCD (Building City Dashboards) (2020) *Virtual exhibition*, https://dashboards.maynoothuniversity.ie/exhibition/ (last accessed 12 June 2023).

Bechmann, A., and Zevenbergen, B. (2020) *AI and Machine Learning: Internet Research Ethics Guidelines, IRE 3.0 Companion 6.1*. Association of Internet Researchers, https://aoir.org/reports/ethics3.pdf (last accessed 12 June 2023).

Ben-David, A. (2020) 'Counter-archiving Facebook', *European Journal of Communication*, 35(3): 249–64.

Ben-David, A., and Amram, A. (2019) 'Computational Methods for Web History', in Brugger, N., and Milligan, I. (eds) *The Sage Handbook of Web History*. Sage, London, pp. 153–67.

Benedict, C., Hahn, A.L., Diefenbach, M.A., and Ford, J.S. (2019) 'Recruitment via social media: Advantages and potential biases', *Digital Health*, 5, https://doi.org/10.1177/2055207619867223.

Benjamin, R. (2019) *Race After Technology: Abolitionist Tools for the New Jim Code*. Polity Press, Cambridge.

Bennett, J. (2009) *Vibrant Matter: A Political Ecology of Things*. Duke University Press, Durham, NC.

Berry, D. (2017) 'The post-archival constellation: The archive under the technical conditions of computational media', in Blom, I., Lundemo, T., and Røssaak, E. (eds) *Memory in Motion: Archives, Technology and the Social*. Amsterdam University Press, Amsterdam, pp. 103–25.

Bhaskar, R. (1989) *Reclaiming Reality: A Critical Introduction to Contemporary Philosophy*. Verso, London.

Bhaskar, R. (2007) 'Theorising ontology', in Lawson, C., Lasis, J., and Martins, N. (eds) *Contributions to Social Ontology*. Routledge, New York, pp. 192–204.

Bishop, S. (2020) 'Algorithmic experts: Selling algorithmic lore on YouTube', *Social Media + Society*, 6(1): 1–11.

Bissell, D. (2018) *Transit Life: How Commuting Is Transforming Our Cities*. MIT Press, Cambridge, MA.

Blackwell, C., Birnholtz, J., and Abbott, C. (2015) 'Seeing and being seen: Co-situation and impression formation using Grindr, a location-aware gay dating app', *New Media & Society*, 17(7): 1117–36.

Blaikie, N. (2000) *Designing Social Research: The Logic of Anticipation*. Polity, Cambridge.

Blaikie, N., and Priest, J. (2019) *Designing Social Research*. 3rd edn. Polity Books, Cambridge.

Blank, G., Graham, M., and Calvino, C. (2018) 'Local geographies of digital inequality', *Social Science Computer Review*, 36(1): 82–102.

Bluteau, J.M. (2021) 'Legitimising digital anthropology through immersive cohabitation: Becoming an observing participant in a blended digital landscape', *Ethnography*, 22(2): 267–85.

Boavida-Portugal, I., Ferreira, C.C., and Rocha, J. (2015) 'Where to vacation? An agent-based approach to modelling tourist decision-making process', *Current Issues in Tourism*, 20(15): 1557–74.

Bodenhamer, D.J. (2013) 'Beyond GIS: Geospatial technologies and the future of history', in von Lunen, A., and Travis, C. (eds) *History and GIS: Epistemologies, Considerations and Reflections*. Springer, Dordrecht, pp. 1–14.

Bodenhamer, D.J. (2022) 'The varieties of deep maps', in Bodenhamer, D.J., Corrigan, J., and Harris, T.M. (eds) *Making Deep Maps: Foundations, Approaches, and Methods*. Routledge, London, pp. 1–16.

Boellstorff, T. (2015) *Coming of Age in Second Life: An Anthropologist Explores the Virtually Human*. Princeton University Press, Princeton, NJ.

Boellstorff, T., Nardi, B., Pearce, C., and Taylor, T.L. (2012) *Ethnography and Virtual Worlds: A Handbook of Method.* Princeton University Press, Princeton, NJ.

Bonilla, Y., and Rosa, J. (2015) '#Ferguson: Digital protest, hashtag ethnography, and the racial politics of social media in the United States', *American Ethnologist*, 42(1): 4–17.

Bonner-Thompson, C. (2019) '"I didn't think you were going to sound like that": Sensory geographies of Grindr encounters in public spaces in Newcastle-upon-Tyne, UK', in Nash, C.J., and Gorman-Murray, A. (eds) *The Geographies of Digital Sexuality*. Springer Nature, Singapore, pp. 159–79.

Bonner-Thompson, C. (2021) 'Anticipating touch: Haptic geographies of Grindr encounters in Newcastle-upon-Tyne, UK', *Transactions of the Institute of British Geographers*, 46(2): 449–63.

Bonney, R., Ballard, H., Jordan, R., McCallie, E., Phillips, T., Shirk, J., and Wilderman, C.C. (2009) *Public Participation in Scientific Research: Defining the Field and Assessing Its Potential for Informal Science Education*, Center for Advancement of Informal Science Education, Washington, DC. https://files.eric.ed.gov/fulltext/ED519688.pdf (accessed 1 December 2020).

Borgdorff, H. (2020) 'Cataloguing Artistic Research: The Passage from Documented Work to Published Research', in Borgdorff, H., Peters, P., and Pinch, T. (eds) *Dialogues Between Artistic Research and Science and Technology Studies*. Routledge, London, pp. 19–30.

Borgman, C.L. (2007) *Scholarship in the Digital Age*. MIT Press, Cambridge, MA.

Borgman, C.L. (2015) *Big Data, Little Data, No Data: Scholarship in the Networked World*. MIT Press, Cambridge, MA.

Bos, D. (2018) 'Answering the Call of Duty: Everyday encounters with the popular geopolitics of military-themed videogames', *Political Geography*, 63: 54–64.

Boulamwini, J., and Gebru, T. (2018) 'Gender shades: Intersectional accuracy in disparities in commercial gender classification', *Proceedings of Machine Learning Research*, 81(1): 1–15.

Bowe, E., Simmons, E., and Mattern, S. (2020) 'Learning from lines: Critical COVID visualizations and the quarantine quotidian', *Big Data & Society*, 7(2): 1–13.

Bowker, G. (2005) *Memory Practices in the Sciences*. MIT Press, Cambridge, MA.

Boy, J.D., and Uitermark, J. (2020) 'Lifestyle enclaves in the Instagram city?', *Social Media + Society* 6(3): 1–10.

boyd, D., and Crawford, K. (2012) 'Critical questions for big data', *Information, Communication and Society*, 15(5): 662–79.

Boyd, D.A., and Larson, M.A. (2014) 'Introduction', in Boyd, D.A., and Larson, M.A. (eds) *Oral History and the Digital Humanities*. Palgrave Macmillan, New York, pp. 1–18.

Brambilla, G., and Pedrielli, F. (2020) 'Smartphone-based participatory soundscape mapping for a more sustainable acoustic environment', *Sustainability*, 12(19): 7899.

Brantner, C. (2018) 'New visualities of space and place: Mapping theories, concepts and methodology of visual communication research on locative media and geomedia', *Westminster Papers in Communication and Culture*, 13(2): 14–30.

Braun, V., and Clarke, V. (2021) *Thematic Analysis: A Practical Guide*. Sage, London.

Brookfield, K., and Tilley, S. (2016) 'Using virtual street audits to understand the walkability of older adults' route choices by gender and age', *International Journal of Environmental Research and Public Health*, 13(11): 1061.

Brown, A.E. (2023) 'Prevalence and mechanisms of discrimination: Evidence from the ride-hail and taxi industries', *Journal of Planning Education and Research*, 43(2): 268–80.

Brown, A.E. (2019) 'Redefining car access: Ride-hail travel and use in Los Angeles', *Journal of the American Planning Association*, 85(2): 83–95.

Brown, B.A., and Quan-Haase, A. (2012) 'A worker's inquiry 2.0: An ethnographic method for the study of produsage in social media contexts', *triple*, 10(2): 488–508.

Brown, S. (2021) *Evidence and Absence in the Archives: A Study of the Irish Refugee Appeals Tribunal Archive to Assess the State Practice of Determining Asylum in Ireland*. PhD thesis, Maynooth University, Maynooth.

Brubaker, J.R., Ananny, M., and Crawford, K. (2016) 'Departing glances: A sociotechnical account of "leaving" Grindr', *New Media & Society*, 18(3): 373–90.

Brugger, N. (2018) *The Archived Web: Doing History in the Digital Age*. MIT Press, Cambridge, MA.

Brugger, N., and Goggin, G. (2022) 'Oral histories of the Internet and the Web: An introduction', in Brugger, N., and Goggin, G. (eds) *Oral Histories of the Internet and the Web*. Routledge, London, pp. 1–8.

Brugger, N., and Milligan, I. (eds) (2019) *The Sage Handbook of Web History*. Sage, London.

Brugger, N., and Schroeder, R. (eds) (2017) *The Web as History*. UCL Press, London.

Bruzelius, C. (2017) 'Digital technologies and new evidence in Architectural History', *Journal of the Society of Architectural Historians*, 76(4): 436–9.

Bryant, R., Katz, R.H., and Lazowska, E.D. (2008) *Big-Data Computing: Creating Revolutionary Breakthroughs in Commerce, Science and Society*, Computing Community Consortium, www.cra.org/ccc/docs/init/Big_Data.pdf (accessed 1 December 2020).

Bryman, A., and Bell, E. (2019) *Social Research Methods*. 5th edn. Oxford University Press, Oxford.

Buchanan, E. (2017) 'Considering the ethics of big data research: A case of Twitter and ISIS/ISIL', *PLoS ONE*, 12(12): e0187155.

Bucher, T. (2012) '"Want to be on the top?" Algorithmic power and the threat of invisibility on Facebook', *New Media and Society*, 14(7): 1164–80.

Budge, K. (2020) 'Visually imagining place: Museum visitors, Instagram, and the city', *Journal of Urban Technology*, 27(2): 61–79.

Burgum, S. (2022) 'This city is an archive: Squatting history and urban authority', *Journal of Urban History*, 48(3): 504–22.

Burke, C., and Byrne, B. (eds) (2021) *Social Research and Disability: Developing Inclusive Research Spaces for Disabled Researchers*. Routledge, Abingdon.

Burke, J.A., Estrin, D., Hansen, M., Parker, A., Ramanathan, N., Reddy, S., and Srivastava, M.B. (2006) 'Participatory sensing', in *Proceedings of the Workshop on World-Sensor Web*. ACM Sensys, Conference on Embedded Network Sensor Systems, Boulder, CO, pp. 117–34.

Burkholder, G.J., Cox, K.A., Crawford, L.M., and Hitchcock, J.H. (eds) (2019) *Research Design and Methods: An Applied Guide for the Scholar-Practitioner*. Sage, London.

Buthe, T. (2002) 'Taking temporarility seriously: Modeling history and the use of narratives as evidence', *American Political Science Review*, 96(3): 481–93.

Buttimer, A. (1976) 'Grasping the dynamism of lifeworld', *Annals of the Association of American Geographers*, 66: 277–92.

Butz, D., and Besio, K. (2009) 'Autoethnography', *Geography Compass*, 3(5): 1660–74.

Campbell-Kelly, M. (2003) *From Airline Reservations to Sonic the Hedgehog: A History of the Software Industry*. MIT Press, Cambridge, MA.

Cant, C. (2019) *Riding for Deliveroo: Resistance in the New Economy*. Polity Press, Cambridge.

Cant, C. (2020) 'The warehouse without walls: A workers' inquiry at Deliveroo', *Ephemera: Theory & Politics in Organization*, 20(4): 131–61.

Caragliu, A., and Del Bo, C.F. (2022) 'Smart cities and urban inequality', *Regional Studies*, 56(7): 1097–112.

Cardullo, P. (2017) 'Gentrification in the mesh? An ethnography of Open Wireless Network (OWN) in Deptford', *City*, 21(3–4): 405–19.

Cardullo, P., and Kitchin, R. (2019a) 'Being a "citizen" in the smart city: Up and down the scaffold of smart citizen participation in Dublin, Ireland', *GeoJournal*, 84: 1–13.

Cardullo, P., and Kitchin, R. (2019b) 'Smart urbanism and smart citizenship: The neoliberal logic of "citizen-focussed" smart cities in Europe', *Environment and Planning C: Politics and Space*, 37(5): 813–30.

Carpiano, R.M. (2009) 'Come take a walk with me: The "Go-Along" interview as a novel method for studying the implications of place for health and well-being', *Health & Place*, 15(1): 263–72.

Carr, C.T., and Hayes, R.A. (2015) 'Social media: Defining, developing, and divining', *Atlantic Journal of Communication*, 23(1): 46–65.

Carr, N.G. (2007) 'The ignorance of crowds', *Strategy + Business Magazine*, 47: 1–5.

Carroll, S.R., Herczog, E., Hudson, M., Russell, K., and Stall, S. (2021) 'Operationalizing the CARE and FAIR Principles for Indigenous data futures', *Nature: Scientific Data*, 8: 108.

Carter, D. (2004) 'Living in virtual communities: Making friends online', *Journal of Urban Technology*, 11(3): 109–25.

Carter, D. (2005) 'Living in virtual communities: An ethnography of human relationships in cyberspace', *Information, Community & Society*, 8(2): 148–67.

Caswell, M., Migoni, A., Geraci, N., and Cifor, M. (2017) '"To be able to imagine otherwise": Community archives and the importance of representation', *Archives and Records*, 38(1): 5–26.

Cater, J.K. (2011) 'Skype a cost-effective method for qualitative research', *Rehabilitation Counselors & Educators Journal*, 4(2): 10–17.

CBC Radio (2019) 'Why are people throwing electric scooters in the water?', *Spark* [podcast], 11 January, www.cbc.ca/radio/spark/spark-421-1.4973383/why-are-people-throwing-electric-scooters-in-the-water-1.4973388 (accessed 10 November 2022).

Ceruzzi, P.E. (1998) *A History of Modern Computing*. MIT Press, Cambridge, MA.

Cetin, T. (2017) 'The rise of ride sharing in urban transport: Threat or opportunity', in Yaghoubi, H. (ed.) *Urban Transport Systems*. InTech Open, pp. 191–202.

Chamorro-Padial, J., Cozzo, E., and Calleja-Lopez, A. (2023) *Decidim.Viz: A data dashboard prototype for a digital democracy platform*. Working paper, SSRN, http://dx.doi.org/10.2139/ssrn.4427708.

Chenou, J.-M., and Cepeda-Másmela, C. (2019) '#NiUnaMenos: Data activism from the Global South', *Television & New Media*, 20(4): 396–411.

Cherry, F., and Bendick Jr, M. (2018) 'Making it count: Discrimination auditing and the activist scholar tradition', in Gaddis, M.S. (ed.) *Audit Studies: Behind the Scenes with Theory, Method, and Nuance*. Springer, Cham, pp. 45–62.

Chorley, R.J., and Haggett, P. (eds) (1967) *Models in Geography*. Methuen, London.

Ciesielska, M., Boström, K.W., and Öhlander, M. (2018) 'Observation methods', in Ciesielska, M., and Jemielniak, D. (eds) *Qualitative Methodologies in Organization Studies: Volume II: Methods and Possibilities*. Springer, Cham, pp. 33–52.

Cifor, M., Caswell, M., Migoni, A., and Geraci, A. (2018) '"What we do crosses over to activism": The politics and practice of community archives', *Archives and Public History*, 40(2): 69–95.

Cinnamon, J. (2020) 'Attack the data: Agency, power, and technopolitics in South African data activism', *Annals of the American Association of Geographers*, 110(3): 623–39.

Cizek, K. (2015) *Highrise – Universe Within*. National Film Board, Canada, www.nfb.ca/interactive/highrise_universe_within_en/ (accessed 11 June 2023).

Clark, A., and Emmel, N. (2010) 'Using walking interviews', *Realities Toolkit #13*. ESRC National Centre for Research Methods, https://eprints.ncrm.ac.uk/id/eprint/1323/ (accessed 26 August 2022).

Clarke, P., Ailshire, J., Melendez, R., Bader, M., and Morenoff, J. (2010) 'Using Google Earth to conduct a neighborhood audit: Reliability of a virtual audit instrument', *Health & Place*, 16(6): 1224–9.

Coleman, B. (2016) 'Let's get lost: Poetic city meets data city', in Gordon, E., and Mihailidis, P. (eds) *Civic Media: Technology, Design and Practice*. MIT Press, Cambridge. pp. 267–94.

Coletta, C., and Kitchin, R. (2017) 'Algorhythmic governance: Regulating the "heartbeat" of a city using the Internet of Things', *Big Data & Society*, 4(2): 1–16.

Collins, N., Schedel, M., and Wilson, S. (2013) *Electronic Music*. Cambridge University Press, Cambridge.

Collister, L.B. (2014) 'Surveillance and community: Language policing and empowerment in a World of Warcraft guild', *Surveillance & Society*, 12(3): 337–48.

Colom, A. (2022) 'Using WhatsApp for focus group discussions: Ecological validity, inclusion and deliberation', *Qualitative Research*, 22(3): 452–67.

Çöltekin, A., Janetzko, H., and Fabrikant, S.I. (2018) 'Geovisualization', in Wilson, J.P. (ed.) *The Geographic Information Science & Technology Body of Knowledge* (2nd quarter 2018 edn). https://doi.org/10.22224/gistbok/2018.2.6 (accessed 22 August 2023).

Consolvo, S., Bentley, F.B., Hekler, E.B., and Phatek, S.S. (2017) *Mobile User Research. A Practical Guide*. Morgan & Claypool, San Rafael, CA.

Coole, D., and Frost, S. (2010) *New Materialisms: Ontology, Agency, and Politics*. Duke University Press, Durham, NC.

Cope, M., and Kurtz, H. (2016) 'Organizing, coding and analyzing qualitative data', in Clifford, N., Cope, M., Gillespie, T., and French, S. (eds) *Key Methods in Geography*, 3rd edn. Sage, London, pp. 647–64.

Corti, L., van den Eynden, V., Bishop, L., and Woollard, M. (2014) *Managing and Sharing Research Data: A Guide to Good Practice*. Sage, London.

Costello, S. (2020) 'The sensors that make the iPhone so cool', *Lifewire*, 4 February, www.lifewire.com/sensors-that-make-iphone-so-cool-2000370 (accessed 12 June 2023).

Cotrin, P., Moura, W., Gambardela-Tkacz, C.M., et al. (2020) 'Healthcare workers in Brazil during the COVID-19 pandemic: A cross-sectional online survey', *INQUIRY: The Journal of Health Care Organization, Provision, and Financing*, 57, https://doi.org/10.1177/0046958020963711 (accessed 22 August 2023).

Coulson, S., Woods, M., Scott, M., and Hemment, D. (2018a) 'Making sense: Empowering participatory sensing with transformation design', *The Design Journal*, 21(6): 813–33.

Coulson, S., Woods, M., Scott, M., Hemment, D., and Balestrini, M. (2018b) 'Stop the noise! Enhancing meaningfulness in participatory sensing with community level indicators', in *Proceedings of Designing Interactive Systems*, 18. Association for Computing Machinery (ACM), pp. 1183–92.

Coutts, E.R., Wodehouse, A., and Robertson, J. (2019) 'A Comparison of Contemporary Prototyping Methods', in *Proceedings of the 22nd International Conference on Engineering Design (ICED19)*, Delft, The Netherlands, 5–8 August 2019, The Design Society, pp. 1313–21.

Cowen, D., Mitchell, A., Paradis, E., and Story, B. (eds) (2020) *Digital Lives in the Global City: Contesting Infrastructures*. University of British Columbia Press: Vancouver, BC.

Crain, M. (2019) 'A critical political economy of Web advertising history', in Brugger, N., and Milligan, I. (eds) *The Sage Handbook of Web History*. Sage, London, pp. 330–43.

Cramer, F., and Fuller, M. (2008) 'Interface', in Fuller, M. (ed.) *Software Studies: A Lexicon*. MIT Press, Cambridge, MA, pp. 149–53.

Crampton, J.W., Graham, M., Poorthuis, A., et al. (2013) 'Beyond the geotag: Situating "big data" and leveraging the potential of the geoweb', *Cartography and Geographic Information Science*, 40(2): 130–9.

Crawford, K. (2021) *Atlas of AI: Power, Politics, and the Planetary Costs of Artificial Intelligence*. Yale University Press, New Haven, CT.

Crawford, S.P., and Walters, D. (2013) *Citizen-centered governance: The Mayor's Office of New Urban Mechanics and the evolution of CRM in Boston*. Berkman Center Research Publication, 17, Harvard University, Cambridge, MA.

Cresswell, J.W., and Cresswell, J.D. (2018) *Research Design: Qualitative, Quantitative, and Mixed Methods Approaches*. 5th edn. Sage, London.

Crockett, D. (2016) 'Direct visualization techniques for the analysis of image data: The slice histogram and the growing entourage plot', *International Journal for Digital Art History*, 2 (October): 178–97.

Crockford, K. (2020) *How is facial recognition surveillance technology racist?* American Civil Liberties Union, 16 June. www.aclu.org/news/privacy-technology/how-is-face-recognition-surveillance-technology-racist (accessed 3 March 2023).

Crooks, A., Croitoru, A., Stefanidis, A., and Radzikowski, J. (2013) '#Earthquake: Twitter as a distributed sensor system', *Transactions in GIS*, 17(1): 124–47.

Crutcher, M., and Zook, M. (2009) 'Placemarks and waterlines: Racialized cyberscapes in post-Katrina Google Earth', *Geoforum*, 40(4): 523–34.

Cullinane, J. (2015) *Smarter Than Their Machines: Oral Histories of Pioneers in Interactive Computing*. ACM Books/Morgan & Claypool Publishers.

Currie, M., Paris, B.S., Pasquetto, I., and Pierre, J. (2016) 'The conundrum of police officer involved homicides: Counter-data in Los Angeles County', *Big Data & Society*, 3(2): 1–14.

Curtis, V. (2018) *Online Citizen Science and the Widening of Academia: Distributed Engagement with Research and Knowledge Production*. Palgrave Macmillan, London.

D'Ignazio, C., and Klein, L.F. (2020) *Data Feminism*. MIT Press, Cambridge, MA.

D'Ignazio, C., Gordon, E., and Christoferotti, E. (2019) 'Sensors and civics: Toward a community-centered smart city', in Cardullo, P., Di Feliciantonio, C., and Kitchin, R. (eds) *The Right to the Smart City*. Emerald Publishing, Bingley, pp. 113–24.

DataWalking.org (n.d.) *Data Walkshops – data walking for social research*, www.datawalking.org/ (accessed 23 December 2019).

Datta, A. (2020) 'The "smart safe city": Gendered time, speed, and violence in the margins of India's urban age', *Annals of the American Association of Geographers*, 110(5): 1318–34.

Datta, A., and Thomas, A. (2021) 'Curating #AanaJaana [#ComingGoing]: Gendered authorship in the "contact zone" of Delhi's digital and urban margins', *Cultural Geographies*, 29(2): 233–52.

Dattani, K. (2021) '"Platform 'glitch as surprise": The on-demand domestic work sector in Delhi's National Capital Region', *City*, 25(3–4): 376–95.

Dattani, K. (2022) *A Suitable Swipe: Leisure, Pleasure and Dating Apps in Mumbai*. PhD thesis, School of Geography, Queen Mary, University of London, London.

David, G., and Cambre, C. (2016) 'Screened intimacies: Tinder and the swipe logic', *Social Media + Society*, 2(2): 1–11, https://doi.org/10.1177/2056305116641976 (accessed 22 August 2023).

Davies, T., Walker, S., Rubinstein, M., and Perini, F. (eds) (2019) *The State of Open Data: Histories and Horizons*. African Minds and International Development Research Centre, Cape Town and Ottawa.

Dawkins, O., and Young, G.W. (2020) 'Engaging place with mixed realities: Sharing multisensory experiences of place through community-generated digital content and multimodal interaction', in Chen, J.Y.C., and Fragomeni, G. (eds) *HCII 2020: Virtual, Augmented and Mixed Reality. Industrial and Everyday Life Applications*, LNCS 12191, Springer, Cham, pp. 199–218.

DCTP (n.d.) *Our story*, Detroit Community Technology Project, https://detroitcommunitytech.org/?q=story (accessed 1 December 2020).

DDJC (n.d.) *About*, Detroit Digital Justice Coalition, http://detroitdjc.org/about/story/ (accessed 1 December 2020).

De Leeuw, S., Parkes, M.W., Morgan, V.S., Christensen, J., Lindsay, N., Mitchell-Foster, K., and Jozkow, J.R. (2017) 'Going unscripted: A call to critically engage storytelling methods and methodologies in geography and the medical-health sciences', *Canadian Geographer*, 61(2): 152–64.

De Longueville, B., Smith, R.S., and Luraschi, G. (2009) '"OMG, from here, I can see the flames!": A use case of mining location based social networks to acquire spatio-temporal data on forest fires', in *Proceedings of the 2009 International Workshop on Location Based Social Networks*. ACM, Seattle, WA, 3 November 2009, pp. 73–80.

de Souza e Silva, A. (2017) 'Pokémon Go as an HRG: Mobility, sociability, and surveillance in hybrid spaces', *Mobile Media & Communication*, 5(1): 20–3.

Deakin, H., and Wakefield, K. (2014) Skype interviewing: Reflections of two PhD researchers', *Qualitative Research*, 14(5): 603–16.

DeLyser, D., and Sui, D. (2014) 'Crossing the qualitative-quantitative chasm III: Enduring methods, open geography, participatory research, and the fourth paradigm', *Progress in Human Geography*, 38(2): 294–307.

Desjardins, A., and Tihanyi, T. (2019) 'ListeningCups: A case of data tactility and data stories', in *Proceedings of the 2019 Designing Interactive Systems Conference*. ACM, Vancouver, pp. 147–60.

Deville, J., and van der Velden, L. (2016) 'Seeing the invisible algorithm: The practical politics of tracking the credit trackers', in Amoore, L., and Piotukh, V. (eds) *Algorithmic Life: Calculative Devices in the Age of Big Data*. Routledge, London, pp. 87–106.

Dewaele, J.-M. (2018) 'Online questionnaires', in Phakiti, A., De Costa, P., Plonsky, L., et al. (eds) *The Palgrave Handbook of Applied Linguistics Research Methodology*. Palgrave Macmillan, London, pp. 269–86.

Diakopoulos, N. (2013). *Algorithmic Accountability Reporting: On the Investigation of Black Boxes*. A Tow/Knight Brief. Tow Center for Digital Journalism, Columbia Journalism School, http://towcenter.org/algorithmic-accountability-2/ (accessed 22 August 2023).

Dibb, S., Rushmer, A., and Stern, P. (2001) 'New survey medium: Collecting marketing data with e-mail and the World Wide Web', *Journal of Targeting, Measurement and Analysis for Marketing,* 10(1): 17–25.

Dick, M. (2016) 'Developments in infographics', in Franklin, B., and Eldridge, S.A. (eds) *The Routledge Companion to Digital Journalism Studies*. Routledge, London. pp. 498–508.

Dickinson, G., and Aiello, G. (2016) 'Being through there matters: Materiality, bodies, and movement in urban communication research', *International Journal of Communication*, 10: 1294–308.

Dieter, M., and Tkacz, N. (2020) 'The patterning of finance/security: A designerly walkthrough of challenger banking apps', *Computational Culture*, (7): 1–34.

Dieter, M., Gerlitz, C., Helmond, A., et al. (2018) 'Store, interface, package, connection', *SFB 1187 Medien der Kooperation-Working Paper Series* (4): 1–16, https://doi.org/10.25969/mediarep/3795 (accessed 22 August 2023).

Dieter, M., Gerlitz, C., Helmond, A., et al. (2019) 'Multi-situated app studies: Methods and propositions', *Social Media+ Society*, 5(2): 1–15.

Dieter, M., Helmond, A., Tkacz, N., van der Vlist, F., et al. (2021) 'Pandemic platform governance: Mapping the global ecosystem of COVID-19 response apps', *Internet Policy Review*, 10(3): 1–27.

Digital Curation Centre (2013) *Checklist for a Data Management Plan*, www.dcc.ac.uk/DMPs/Checklist (accessed 7 March 2022).

DiSalvo, C., and Anderson, K. (2016) 'Case study: Hackathons as a site for civic IoT – Initial insights', in Gordon, E., and Mihailidis, P. (eds) *Civic Media: Technology, Design and Practice*. MIT Press, Cambridge, MA, pp. 605–8.

Dodge, M., and Kitchin, R. (2013) 'Crowdsourced cartography: Mapping experience and knowledge', *Environment and Planning A*, 45(1): 19–36.

Donnelly, M. (2012) 'Data management plans and planning', in Pryor, G. (ed.) *Managing Research Data*. Facet Publishing, London, pp. 83–104.

Dreyfus, H.L. (1991) *Being-in-the-World: A Commentary on Heidegger's Being and Time, División I*. MIT Press, Cambridge, MA.

Du Bois, W.E.B., with Battle Baptiste, W., and Rusert, B. (eds) (2018) *W.E.B. Du Bois' Data Portraits: Visualizing Black America*. Princeton Architectural Press, Hudson, NY.

Duarte, M.E., Vigil-Hayes, M., Littletree, S., and Belarde-Lewis, M. (2019) '"Of course, data can never fully represent reality": Assessing the relationship between "Indigenous Data" and "Indigenous Knowledge", "Traditional Ecological Knowledge", and "Traditional Knowledge"', *Human Biology*, 91(3): 163–78.

Duggan, M. (2017) 'Questioning "digital ethnography" in an era of ubiquitous computing', *Geography Compass*, 11(5): e12313.

Dykes, J., MacEachren, A.M., and Kraak, M.J. (eds) (2005) *Exploring Geovisualization*. Elsevier, Amsterdam.

Earle, P.S., Bowden, D., and Guy, M. (2011) 'Twitter earthquake detection: Earthquake monitoring in a social world', *Annals of Geophysics*, 54(6): 708–15.

Eitzel, M.V., et al. (2017) 'Citizen science terminology matters: Exploring key terms', *Citizen Science: Theory and Practice*, 2(1): 1–20.

Elwood, S., and Ghose, R. (2001) 'PPGIS in community development planning: Framing the organizational context', *Cartographica*, 38(3–4): 19–33.

Elwood, S., and Leszczynski, A. (2018) 'Feminist digital geographies', *Gender, Place & Culture*, 25(5): 629–44.

Engebretsen, M., and Kennedy, H. (eds) (2020) *Data Visualization in Society*. Amsterdam University Press, Amsterdam.

England, K. (1994) 'Getting personal: Reflexivity, positionality, and feminist research', *The Professional Geographer*, 46(1): 80–9.

Enlund, D., Harrison, K., Ringdahl, R., Börütecene, A., Löwgren, J., and Angelakis, V. (2022) 'The role of sensors in the production of smart city spaces', *Big Data & Society*, 9(2): 1–13.

Erde, J. (2014) 'Constructing archives of the Occupy movement', *Archives & Records*, 35(2): 77–92.

Erickson, T. (1993) 'Artificial realities as data visualization environments: Problems and prospects', in Wexelblat, A. (ed.) *Virtual Reality: Applications and Explorations*. Academic Press, Cambridge, MA, pp. 3–22.

Ernwein, M. (2020) 'Filmic geographies: Audio-visual, embodied-material', *Social & Cultural Geography*, 23(6): 779–96.

Estrada-Jaramillo, A., Michael, M., and Farrimond. H. (2022) 'Absence, multiplicity and the boundaries of research? Reflections on online asynchronous focus groups', *Qualitative Research*, https://doi.org/10.1177/14687941221110169.

Eugster, M.J.A. (2011) *R Package benchmark*, https://benchmark.r-forge.r-project.org/ (accessed 4 March 2023).

Evangelinidis, A., and Lazaris, D. (2014) 'Workers' inquiry in praxis', *Ephemera: Theory & Politics in Organization*, 20(4): 411–27.

Evans, J., and Jones, P. (2011) 'The walking interview: Methodology, mobility and place', *Applied Geography*, 31: 849–58.

Evans, J.R., and Mathur, A. (2018) 'The value of online surveys: A look back and a look ahead', *Internet Research*, 28(4): 854–87.

Evans, J., Ruane, S., and Southall, H. (eds) (2019) *Data in Society: Challenging Statistics in an Age of Globalisation*. Policy Press, Bristol.

Evans, L., and Saker, M. (2019) 'The playeur and Pokémon Go: Examining the effects of locative play on spatiality and sociability', *Mobile Media & Communication*, 7(2): 232–47.

Evergreen, S.D.H. (2019) *Effective Data Visualization: The Right Chart for the Right Data*, 2nd edn. Sage, London.

Fagan, M.E. (1986) 'Design and code inspections to reduce errors in program development', *IBM Systems Journal*, 15(3): 182–211.

Farman, J. (2014) 'Map interfaces and the production of locative media space', in Wilken, R., and Goggin, G. (eds) *Locative Media*. Routledge, London, pp. 83–93.

Feigenbaum, A., and Alamahodaei, A. (2020) *The Data Storytelling Workbook*. Routledge, London.

Ferdinand, S. (2018) 'Cartography at ground level: Spectrality and streets in Jeremy Wood's My Ghost and Meridians', in Dibazar, P., and Naeff, J.A. (eds) *Visualizing the Street: New Practices of Documenting, Navigating and Imagining the City*. Amsterdam University Press, Amsterdam, pp. 137–58.

Ferris, L., and Duguay, S. (2020) 'Tinder's lesbian digital imaginary: Investigating (im)permeable boundaries of sexual identity on a popular dating app', *New Media & Society*, 22(3): 489–506.

Figiel, J., Shukaitis, S., and Walker, A. (2014) 'The politics of workers' inquiry', *Ephemera: Theory & Politics in Organization*, 14(3): 307–14.

Fink, J. (2012) 'Walking the neighbourhood, seeing the small details of community life: Reflections from a photography walking tour', *Critical Social Policy*, 32(1): 31–50.

FlowingData (n.d.a) *Bubble Chart*, https://flowingdata.com/charttype/bubble-chart (accessed 26 September 2022).

FlowingData (n.d.b) *Treemap*, https://flowingdata.com/charttype/treemap/ (accessed 26 September 2022).

Foley, J. (2016) *inreach: A Choreographic process of transversality*. Unpublished PhD, Trinity College Dublin, Dublin.

Foley, J. (2019) 'EF#1.19 How do I Love Thee, Let me Count/Map the Ways …', *Engineering Fictions*, https://engineeringfictions.org/2019/03/02/ef1-19-how-do-i-love-thee-let-me-count-map-the-ways/ (accessed 22 August 2023).

Foley, J. (2021) *Fastidious Inquiry, Weird Compliance: A Corona of Sonnets by Anonymous*. Humanities Commons, http://dx.doi.org/10.17613/qbg4-6b33 (accessed 22 August 2023).

Forrester, J.W. (1969) *Urban Dynamics*. MIT Press, Cambridge, MA.

Foster, L., Diamond, I., and Jeffries, J. (2015) *Beginning Statistics: An Introduction for Social Scientists*. Sage, London.

Fotopoulou, A., and Beavon, C. (2020) '104 days later: A lockdown data story', Art/Data/Health Project, Brighton, www.artdatahealth.org/104-days-later-a-lockdown-data-story/ (accessed 19 June 2021).

Foucault, M. (2002) *The Archaeology of Knowledge*. Routledge, London.

Fox, F.E., Morris, M., and Rumsey, N. (2007) 'Doing synchronous online focus groups with young people: Methodological reflections', *Qualitative Health Research*, 17(4): 539–47.

Franks, B. (2012) *Taming the Big Data Tidal Wave: Finding Opportunities in Huge Data Streams with Advanced Analytics*. John Wiley & Sons, Hoboken, NJ.

franzke, a.s., Bechmann, A., Zimmer, M., Ess, C., and the Association of Internet Researchers (2020) *Internet Research: Ethical Guidelines 3.0*, https://aoir.org/reports/ethics3.pdf (accessed 16 August 2023).

Fraser, A. (2019) 'Curating digital geographies in an era of data colonialism', *Geoforum*, 104: 193–200.

Fraser, E., and Wilmott, C. (2020) 'Ruins of the smart city: A visual intervention', *Visual Communication*, 19(3): 353–68.

Friendly, M., and Wainer, H. (2021) *A History of Data Visualization and Graphic Communication*. Harvard University Press, Cambridge, MA.

Fuller, D., and Kitchin, R. (eds) (2004) *Radical Theory, Critical Praxis: Making a Difference Beyond the Academy?* Praxis E-Press. https://kitchin.org/wp-content/uploads/2020/05/RTCP_Whole.pdf

Gabrys, J., Pritchard, H., and Barratt, B. (2016) 'Just good enough data: Figuring data citizenships through air pollution sensing and data stories', *Big Data & Society*, 3(2): 1–14.

Gaddis, M.S. (ed.) (2018a) *Audit Studies: Behind the Scenes with Theory, Method, and Nuance*. Springer, Cham.

Gaddis, M.S. (2018b) 'An introduction to audit studies in the social sciences', in Gaddis, M. S. (eds) *Audit Studies: Behind the Scenes with Theory, Method, and Nuance*. Springer, Cham, pp. 3–44.

Gal, M., and Rubinfeld, D.L. (2019) 'Data standardization', *NYU Law Review*, 94(4): 737–70.

Galdon-Clavell, G. (2013) '(Not so) smart cities? The drivers, impacts and risks of surveillance-enabled smart environments', *Science and Public Policy*, 40(6): 717–23.

Galgano, M.J., Arndt, J.C., and Hyser, R.M. (2008) *Doing History: Research and Writing in the Digital Age*. Thomson Wadsworth, Boston, MA.

García, B., Welford, J., and Smith, B. (2016) 'Using a smartphone app in qualitative research: the good, the bad and the ugly', *Qualitative Research*, 16(5): 508–25.

Gardiner, E., and Musto, R.G. (2015) *The Digital Humanities: A Primer for Students and Scholars*. Cambridge University Press, Cambridge.

Garnett, E. (2016) 'Developing a feeling for error: Practices of monitoring and modelling air pollution data', *Big Data & Society*, 3(2): 1–12.

Garrett, B. (2011) 'Videographic geographies: Using digital video for geographic research', *Progress in Human Geography*, 35 (2011): 521–41.

Geckoboard (2020) *Data fallacies*, www.geckoboard.com/best-practice/statistical-fallacies/ (accessed 2 December 2020).

Geertz, C. (1998) 'Deep hanging out', *New York Review of Books*, 45(16): 69–72.

Gelinas, L., Pierce, R., Winkler, S., et al. (2017) 'Using social media as a research recruitment tool: Ethical issues and recommendations', *The American Journal of Bioethics*, 17(3): 3–14.

Georgopoulos, A., and Stathopoulou, E.K. (2017) 'Data acquisition for 3D geometric recording: State of the art and recent innovations', in Vincent, M.L., et al. (eds) *Heritage and Archaeology in the Digital Age: Acquisition, Curation, and Dissemination of Spatial Cultural Heritage Data*. Springer, Cham, pp. 1–26.

Ghazawneh, A., and Henfridsson, O. (2013) 'Balancing platform control and external contribution in third-party development: The boundary resources model', *Information Systems Journal*, 23(2): 173–92.

Ghazawneh, A., and Henfridsson, O. (2015) 'A paradigmatic analysis of digital application marketplaces', *Journal of Information Technology*, 30(3): 198–208.

Ghosh, D., and Guha, R. (2013) 'What are we "tweeting" about obesity? Mapping tweets with topic modeling and Geographic Information System', *Cartography and Geographic Information Science*, 40(2): 90–102.

Giaccardi, E., Speed, C., Cila, N., and Caldwell, M. (2016) 'Things as co-ethnographers', in Smith, R.C., Tang Vangkilde, K., Kjaersgaard, M.G., Otto, T., Halse, J., and Binder, T. (eds) *Design Anthropological Futures*. Routledge, London, pp. 235–48.

Gibson, K. (2022) 'Bridging the digital divide: Reflections on using WhatsApp instant messenger interviews in youth research', *Qualitative Research in Psychology*, 19(3): 611–31.

GIDA (Global Indigenous Data Alliance) (2019) 'CARE principles for indigenous data governance', www.gida-global.org/care (accessed 1 December 2020).

Gill, P., and Baillie, J. (2018) 'Interviews and focus groups in qualitative research: An update for the digital age', *British Dental Journal*, 225(7): 668–72.

Goggin, G., and McLelland, M. (2017) *The Routledge Companion to Global Internet Histories*. Routledge, London.

Golledge, R., and Stimson, R. (1997) *Spatial Behaviour*. Guildford, New York.

Goodchild, M.F. (2007) 'Citizens as sensors: the world of volunteered geography', *GeoJournal*, 69: 211–21.

Gordon, A.R., Calzo, J.P., Eiduson, R., et al. (2021) 'Asynchronous online focus groups for health research: Case study and lessons learned', *International Journal of Qualitative Methods*, 20, https://doi.org/10.1177/1609406921990489 (accessed 22 August 2023).

Gordon, E., and Mihailidis, P. (2016) 'Introduction', in Gordon, E., and Mihailidis, P. (eds) *Civic Media: Technology, Design and Practice*. MIT Press, Cambridge, MA, pp. 1–26.

Gordon, E. and Walter, S. (2016) 'Meaningful Inefficiencies: Resisting the Logic of Technological Efficiency in the Design of Civic Systems', in Gordon, E. and Mihailidis, P. (eds) *Civic Media: Technology, Design and Practice*. MIT Press, Cambridge, MA, pp. 243–66.

Grace, R. (2021) 'Toponym usage in social media in emergencies', *International Journal of Disaster Risk Reduction*, 52: 101923.

Grady, C. (2019) 'The continued complexities of paying research participants', *The American Journal of Bioethics*, 19(9): 5–7.

Graham, M., and Anwar, A.M. (2019) 'The global gig economy: Towards a planetary labour market?', *First Monday*, 24(4), https://doi.org/10.5210/fm.v24i4.9913 (accessed 22 August 2023).

Graham, M., Straumann, R.K., and Hogan, B. (2015) 'Digital divisions of labor and informational magnetism: Mapping participation and Wikipedia', *Annals of the Association of American Geographers*, 105(6): 1158–78.

Graham, M., Kitchin, R., Mattern, S., and Shaw, J. (eds) (2019) *How to Run a City Like Amazon, and Other Fables*. Meatspace Press, Oxford.

Graham, M., Woodcock, J., Heeks, R., Mungai, P., Van Belle, J.P., du Toit, D., Fredman, S., Osiki, A., van der Spuy, A., and Silberman, S.M. (2020) 'The Fairwork Foundation: Strategies for improving platform work in a global context', *Geoforum*, 112: 100–3.

Graham, S., Milligan, I., and Weingart, S. (2016) *Exploring Big Historical Data: The Historian's Macroscope*. Imperial College Press, London.

Granier, B., and Kudo, H. (2016) 'How are citizens involved in smart cities? Analysing citizen participation in Japanese "Smart Communities"', *Information Polity*, 21(1): 61–76.

Grant, R. (2019) *Data Visualization: Charts, Maps, and Interactive Graphics*. CRC Press, London.

Gray, L.M., Wong-Wylie, G., Rempel, G.R., and Cook, K. (2020) 'Expanding qualitative research interviewing strategies: Zoom video communications', *The Qualitative Report*, 25(5): 1292–301.

Grbich, C. (2013) *Qualitative Data Analysis: An Introduction*. Sage, London.

Green, B. (2019) *The Smart Enough City: Putting Technology in Its Place to Reclaim Our Urban Future*. MIT Press, Cambridge, MA and London.

Green, B., Cunningham, G., Ekblaw, A., Kominers, P., Linzer, A., and Crawford, S. (2017) *Open Data Privacy*, The Berkman Klein Center for Internet & Society Research Publication, 2017–1. Harvard University, Cambridge, MA. https://ssrn.com/abstract=2924751 (accessed 22 August 2023).

Gregory, I.N., and Ell, P.S. (2007) *Historical GIS: Technologies, Methodologies and Scholarship*. Cambridge University Press, Cambridge.

Gregory, I.N., and Geddes, A. (eds) (2014) *Towards Spatial Humanities: Historical GIS and Spatial History*. Indiana University Press, Bloomington.

Gregory, K. (2021) '"My life is more valuable than this": Understanding risk among on-demand food couriers in Edinburgh', *Work, Employment and Society*, 35(2): 316–31.

Griew, P., Hillsdon, M., Foster, C., Jones, A., and Wilkinson, P. (2013) 'Developing and testing a street audit tool using Google Street View to measure environmental supportiveness for physical activity', *International Journal of Behavioral Nutrition and Physical Activity*, 10: 103.

Grincheva, N. (2017) 'Museum ethnography in the digital age', in Zimmer, M., and Kinder-Kurlanda, K. (eds) *Internet Research Ethics for the Social Age: New Challenges, Cases, and Contexts*. Peter Lang, New York, pp. 187–94.

Grzymala-Busse, A. (2011) 'Time will tell? Temporality and the analysis of causal mechanisms and processes', *Comparative Political Studies*, 44(9): 1267–97.

Guelke, J.K., and Timothy, D.J. (2008) *Geography and Genealogy: Locating Personal Pasts*. Routledge, London.

Guest, G., Namey, E., Taylor, J., Eley, N., and McKenna, K. (2017) 'Comparing focus groups and individual interviews: Findings from a randomized study', *International Journal of Social Research Methodology*, 20(6): 693–708.

Gugerell, K., Funovits, P., and Ampatzidou, C. (2019) 'Daredevil or socialiser? Exploring the relations between intrinsic motivation, game experience and player types in serious games with environmental narratives', in Devisch, O., Huybrechts, L., and de Ridder, R. (eds) *Participatory Design Theory: Using Technology and Social Media to Foster Civic Engagement*. Routledge, London, pp. 157–78.

Guillory, J., Wiant, K.F., Farrelly, M., et al. (2018) 'Recruiting hard-to-reach populations for survey research: Using Facebook and Instagram advertisements and in-person intercept in LGBT Bars and Nightclubs to recruit LGBT young adults', *Journal of Medical Internet Research*, 20(6): e9461.

Gunkel, D.J. (2018) *Robot Rights*. MIT Press, Cambridge, MA.

Guthrie, G. (2010) *Basic Research Methods: An Entry to Social Science Research*. Sage, London.

Gutiérrez, M. (2018) *Data Activism and Social Change*. Palgrave, London.

Hagen, L., Keller, T., Neely, S., dePaula, N., and Robert-Cooperman, C. (2018) 'Crisis communications in the age of social media: A network analysis of Zika-related tweets', *Social Science Computer Review*, 36(5): 523–41.

Haigh, T. (2019) 'Introducing the early digital', in Haigh, T. (ed.) *Exploring the Early Digital*. Springer, Cham, pp. 1–18.

Haining, R. (2010) *Spatial Data Analysis: Theory and Practice*. Cambridge University Press, Cambridge.

Haklay, M. (2013) 'Citizen Science and Volunteered Geographic Information – overview and typology of participation', in Sui, D.Z., Elwood, S., and Goodchild, M.F. (eds) *Crowdsourcing Geographic Knowledge: Volunteered Geographic Information (VGI) in Theory and Practice*. Springer, Berlin, pp. 105–22.

Haklay, M. (2018) 'Participatory citizen science', in Hecker, S., Haklay, M., Bowser, A., Makuch, Z., Vogel, J., and Bonn, A. (eds) *Citizen Science: Innovation in Open Science, Society and Policy*. UCL Press, London, pp. 52–62.

Halegoua, G.R. (2020a) *Smart Cities*. MIT Press, Cambridge, MA.

Halegoua, G.R. (2020b) *The Digital City: Media and the Social Production of Place*. New York University Press, New York.

Hallam, K.F. (2022) 'Moving on from trials and errors: A discussion on the use of a forum as an online focus group in qualitative research', *International Journal of Social Research Methodology*, 25(4): 429–39.

Halpern, O. (2015) *Beautiful Data: A History of Vision and Reason Since 1945*. Duke University Press, Durham, NC.

Han, J., Kamber, M., and Pei, J. (2011) *Data Mining: Concepts and Techniques*, 3rd edn. Morgan Kaufmann, Waltham, MA.

Haraway, D. (1988) 'Situated knowledges: The science question in feminism and the privileges of partial perspective', *Feminist Studies*, 14(3): 575–99.

Haraway, D.J. (1991) *Simians, Cyborgs, and Women: The Reinvention of Nature*. Routledge, New York.

Hård af Segerstad, Y., Kasperowski, D., Kullenberg, C., and Howes, C. (2017) 'Studying closed communities online: Digital methods and ethical considerations beyond informed consent and anonymity', in Zimmer, M., and Kinder-Kurlanda, K. (eds) *Internet Research Ethics for the Social Age: New Challenges, Cases, and Contexts*. Peter Lang, New York, pp. 213–25.

Harris, T.M. (2015) 'Deep geography — deep mapping: Spatial storytelling and a sense of place', in Bodenhamer, D.J., Corrigan, J., and Harris, T.M. (eds). *Deep Maps and Spatial Narratives*. Indiana University Press, Bloomington, IN, pp. 28–53.

Harrison, C. (2003) 'Visual social semiotics: Understanding how still images make meaning', *Technical Communication*, 50(1): 46–60.

Harvey, D. (1972) *Social Justice and the City*. Blackwell, Oxford.

Harvey, D. (1989) *The Condition of Postmodernity: An Enquiry into the Origins of Cultural Change*. John Wiley & Sons, Chichester.

Hastie, T., Tibshirani, R., and Friedman, J. (2009) *The Elements of Statistical Learning: Data Mining, Inference, and Prediction*. 2nd edn. Springer, Cham.

Hawkins, H. (2011) 'Dialogues and doings: Sketching the relationships between Geography and Art', *Geography Compass*, 5(7): 464–78.

Hawkins, H. (2015) 'Creative geographic methods: Knowing, representing, intervening. On composing place and page', *Cultural Geographies*, 22(2): 247–68.

Hawkins, H. (2021) *Geography, Art, Research: Artistic Research in the GeoHumanities*. Routledge, London.

Hay-Gibson, N.V. (2009) 'Interviews via VoIP: Benefits and disadvantages within a PhD study of SMEs', *Library and Information Research*, 33(105): 39–50.

Head, E. (2009) 'The ethics and implications of paying participants in qualitative research', *International Journal of Social Research Methodology*, 12(4): 335–44.

Heaphy, L. (2019) 'Data ratcheting and data-driven organisational change in transport', *Big Data and Society*, 6(2): 1–12.

Hecker, S., Haklay, M., Bowser, A., Makuch, Z., Vogel, J., and Bonn, A. (2018) 'Innovation in open science, society and policy – setting the agenda for citizen science', in Hecker, S., Haklay, M., Bowser, A., Makuch, Z., Vogel, J., and Bonn, A. (eds) *Citizen Science: Innovation in Open Science, Society and Policy*. UCL Press, London, pp. 1–23.

Hein, J.R., Evans, J., and Jones, P. (2008) 'Mobile methodologies: Theory, technology and practice', *Geography Compass*, 2(5): 1266–85.

Hemsley, J.J., and Eckert, J. (2014) 'Examining the role of "place" in Twitter networks through the lens of contentious politics', in *The Proceedings of the 47th Hawaii International Conference on System Sciences*, pp. 1844–53.

Henderson, S., and Segal, E.H. (2013) 'Visualizing qualitative data in evaluation research', *New Directions for Evaluation*, 139: 53–71.

Hennink, M., and Kaiser, B.N. (2022) 'Sample sizes for saturation in qualitative research: A systematic review of empirical tests', *Social Science & Medicine*, 292: 114523.

Henry, E., and Pene, H. (2001) '*Kaupapa Maori*: Locating Indigenous Ontology, Epistemology and Methodology in the Academy', *Organization*, 8(2): 234–42.

Hensher, D.A., and Button, K.J. (2008) *Handbook of Transport Modelling*. 2nd edn. Emerald, Bingley.

Herbert, S. (2000) 'For ethnography', *Progress in Human Geography*, 24(4): 550–68.

Hermann, A., Brenner, W., and Stadler, R. (2018) *Autonomous Driving: How the Driverless Revolution Will Change the World*. Emerald, Bingley.

Hewson, C. (2016) 'Ethical issues in digital methods research', in Snee, H., Hine, C., Morey, Y., Roberts, S., and Watson, H. (eds) *Digital Methods for Social Sciences: An Interdisciplinary Guide to Research Innovation*. Palgrave Macmillan, New York, pp. 206–21.

Highfield, T. (2017) 'Histories of blogging', in Goggin, G., and McLelland, M. (eds) *The Routledge Companion to Global Internet Histories*. Routledge, London, pp. 331–42.

Hill, K. (2020) 'Wrongfully accused by an algorithm', *The New York Times*, 3 August. www.nytimes.com/2020/06/24/technology/facial-recognition-arrest.html (accessed 3 March 2023).

Himelboim, I. (2017) 'Social Network Analysis (Social Media)', in Matthes, H., Davis, C.S., and Potter, R.F. (eds) *The International Encyclopedia of Communication Research Methods*. John Wiley & Sons, Chichester, pp. 1–15.

Hine, C. (2000) *Virtual Ethnography*. London, Sage.

Hippala, T. (2020) 'A multimodal perspective on data visualization', in Engebretsen, M., and Kennedy, H. (eds) *Data Visualization in Society*. Amsterdam University Press, Amsterdam. pp. 277–93.

Hjorth, L., and de Souza e Silva, A. (2023) 'Playing with place: Location-based mobile games in post-pandemic public spaces', *Mobile Media & Communication*, 11(1): 52–8.

Hobbs, M., Owen, S., and Gerber, L. (2017) 'Liquid love? Dating apps, sex, relationships and the digital transformation of intimacy', *Journal of Sociology*, 53(2): 271284.

Hochman, N., and Manovich, L. (2014) 'A view from above: Exploratory visualizations of the Thomas Walther collection', in Abbaspour, M., Daffner, L.A., and Morris Hambourg, M. (eds) *Object: Photo. Modern Photographs: The Thomas Walther Collection 1909–1949*. The Museum of Modern Art, New York, www.moma.org/interactives/objectphoto/assets/essays/Manovich_Hochman.pdf (accessed 30 September 2022).

Hockey, S. (2004) 'The history of Humanities Computing', in Schreibman, S., Siemens, R., and Unsworth, J. (eds) *Companion to Digital Humanities*. Blackwell, Oxford, pp. 3–19.

Hoffman, A.L., and Jonas, A. (2017) 'Recasting justice for Internet and online industry research ethics', in Zimmer, M., and Kinder-Kurlanda, K. (eds) *Internet Research Ethics for the Social Age: New Challenges, Cases, and Contexts*. Peter Lang, New York, pp. 3–18.

Holcomb, Z.C. (1998) *Fundamentals of Descriptive Statistics*. Routledge, London.

Hollands, R.G. (2008) 'Will the real smart city please stand up? Intelligent, progressive or entrepreneurial?', *City*, 12(3): 303–20.

Horst, H.A., and Miller, D. (2012) *Digital Anthropology*. Bloomsbury, London.

Hoskins, A. (2018a) 'The restless past: an introduction to digital memory and media', in Hoskins, A. (ed.) *Digital Memory Studies*. Routledge, New York, pp. 1–24.

Hoskins, A. (2018b) 'Memory of the multitude: The end of collective memory', in Hoskins, A. (ed.) *Digital Memory Studies*. Routledge, New York, pp. 85–109.

Houde, S., and Hill, C. (1997) 'What do prototypes prototype?', in Helander, M., Landauer, T.K., and Prabhu, P. (eds) *Handbook of Human-Computer Interaction*, 2nd edn. Elsevier, Amsterdam, pp. 367–81.

Housley, W., Edwards, A., Beneito-Montagut, R., and Fitzgerald, R. (eds) (2022) *The Sage Handbook of Digital Society*. Sage, London.

Houston, L., Gabrys, J., and Pritchard, H. (2019) 'Breakdown in the smart city: Exploring workarounds with urban-sensing practices and technologies', *Science, Technology & Human Values*, 44(5): 843–70.

Hovhannisyan, I., and Sougari, A.-M. (2014) 'Reconsidering the impact of gender on learners' motivation to learn English', in Tsantila, N., Mandalios, J., and Melpomeni, I. (eds) *ELF: Pedagogical and Interdisciplinary Perspectives*. Deree, The American College of Greece, Athens, pp. 359–67.

Howlett, M. (2022) 'Looking at the "field" through a Zoom lens: Methodological reflections on conducting online research during a global pandemic', *Qualitative Research*, 22(3): 387–402.

Huang, S.A., Hancock, J., and Tong, S.T. (2022) 'Folk theories of online dating: Exploring people's beliefs about the online dating process and online dating algorithms', *Social Media + Society*, 8(2): 1–12.

Hudson, P., and Ishizu, M. (2017) *History by Numbers: An Introduction to Quantitative Approaches*. Bloomsbury, London.

Huff, D. (1993) *How to Lie with Statistics*. W.W. Norton & Company, New York.

Hugel, S., and Davies, A.R. (2022) 'Playing for keeps: Designing serious games for climate adaptation planning education with young people', *Urban Planning*, 7(2): 306–20.

Huhtamo, E., and Parikka, J. (2011) *Media Archaeology: Approaches, Applications and Implications*. University of California Press, Berkeley, CA.

Hunter, D. (2019) *Data Walking*. Ravensbourne, Greenwich.

Hutchinson, J., Martin, F., and Sinpeng, A. (2017) 'Chasing ISIS: Network power, distributed ethics and responsible social media research', in Zimmer, M., and Kinder-Kurlanda, K. (eds) *Internet Research Ethics for the Social Age: New Challenges, Cases, and Contexts*. Peter Lang, New York, pp. 57–71.

IBM (2012) *What is Big Data?*, https://web.archive.org/web/20120707193145/http://www-01.ibm.com/software/data/bigdata/ (last accessed 21 March 2023).

Innocent, T. (2018) 'Play about place: Placemaking in location-based game design', in Fatah gen Schieck, A., Colangelo, D., and Zhigang, C. (eds) *MAB18: Proceedings of the 4th Media Architecture Biennale Conference*. Association for Computing Machinery, New York, pp. 137–43.

Inside Airbnb (n.d.) http://insideairbnb.com/about/ (accessed 8 December 2022).

Ioannidis, J.P.A. (2013) 'Informed consent, big data, and the oxymoron of research that is not research', *American Journal of Bioethics*, 13(4): 40–2.

Irani, L. (2015) 'Hackathons and the making of entrepreneurial citizenship', *Science, Technology and Human Values*, 40(5): 799–824.

Irwin, A. (1995) *Citizen Science: A Study of People, Expertise and Sustainable Development*. Routledge, London.

Ison, N.L. (2009) 'Having their say: Email interviews for research data collection with people who have verbal communication impairment', *International Journal of Social Research Methodology,* 12(2): 161–72.

Israel, M. and Hay, I. (2006) *Research Ethics for Social Scientists.* Sage, London.

Jacobsen, B.N., and Beer, D. (2021) *Social Media and the Automatic Production of Memory.* Bristol University Press, Bristol.

James, A. (2022) 'Women in the gig economy: Feminising "digital labour"', *Work in the Global Economy,* 2(1): 2–26.

Jameson, S., Richter, C., and Taylor, L. (2019) 'People's strategies for perceived surveillance in Amsterdam Smart City', *Urban Geography,* 40(10): 1467–84.

Janghorban, R., Roudsari, R.L., and Taghipour, A. (2014) 'Skype interviewing: The new generation of online synchronous interview in qualitative research', *International Journal of Qualitative Studies on Health and Well-Being,* 9(1): 24152.

Jann, B., and Hinz, T. (2016) *The Sage Handbook of Survey Methodology.* Sage, London.

Jansen, Y., Dragicevic, P., Isenberg, P., Alexander, J., Karnik, A., Kildal, J., Subramanian, S., and Hornbaek, K. (2015) 'Opportunities and challenges for data physicalization', *Proceedings of the ACM Conference on Human Factors in Computing Systems (CHI).* ACM, New York.

Jarke, J. (2019) 'Open government for all? Co-creating digital public services for older adults through data walks', *Online Information Review,* 43(6): 1003–20.

Jarrett, K. (2022) *Digital Labor.* Polity Press, Cambridge, MA.

Jensen, K.B. (2012) 'Lost, found, and made', in Volkmer, I. (ed.) *The Handbook of Global Media Research.* Wiley-Blackwell, Oxford, pp. 433–50.

Jia, L., Nieborg, D.B., and Poell, T. (2022) 'On super apps and app stores: Digital media logics in China's app economy', *Media, Culture & Society,* 44(8): 1437–53.

Johnson, D.R., Scheitle, C.P., and Ecklund, E.H. (2021) 'Beyond the in-person interview? How interview quality varies across in-person, telephone, and Skype interviews', *Social Science Computer Review,* 39(6): 1142–58.

Johnson, K. (2023) 'Face recognition software led to his arrest. It was dead wrong', *Wired,* 28 February. www.wired.com/story/face-recognition-software-led-to-his-arrest-it-was-dead-wrong/ (accessed 3 March 2023).

Jones, P., Osborne, T., Sullivan-Drage, C., Keen, N., and Gadsby, E. (2022) *Virtual Reality Methods: A Guide for Researchers in the Social Sciences and Humanities.* Policy Press, Bristol.

Jones, R., and Pitt, N. (1999) 'Health surveys in the workplace: Comparison of postal, email and World Wide Web methods', *Occupational Medicine,* 49(8): 556–8.

Kagho, G.O., Balac, M., and Axhausen, K.W. (2020) 'Agent-based models in transport planning: Current state, issues, and expectations', *Procedia Computer Science,* 170: 726–32, https://doi.org/10.1016/j.procs.2020.03.164 (accessed 22 August 2023).

Kanhere, S.S. (2013) 'Participatory sensing: Crowdsourcing data from mobile smartphones in urban spaces', in Hota, C., and Srimani, P.K. (eds) *Distributed Computing and Internet Technology.* ICDCIT 2013. Lecture Notes in Computer Science, vol. 7753. Springer, Berlin, pp. 19–26.

Kara, H. (2015) *Creative Research Methods in the Social Sciences.* Policy Press, Bristol.

Kässi, O., and Lehdonvirta, V. (2018) 'Online labour index: Measuring the online gig economy for policy and research', *Technological Forecasting & Social Change,* 137: 241–8.

Kaufmann, K., and Peil, C. (2020) 'The mobile instant messaging interview (MIMI): Using WhatsApp to enhance self-reporting and explore media usage in situ', *Mobile Media & Communication*, 8(2): 229–46.

Kaur-Gill, S., and Dutta, M. (2017) 'Digital ethnography', in Matthes, J., Davis, C.S., and Potter, R.F. (eds) *The International Encyclopaedia of Communication Research Methods*. Wiley-Blackwell, Oxford, pp. 1–10.

Kelleher, J.D., and Tierney, B. (2018) *Data Science*. MIT Press, Cambridge, MA.

Kember, S., and Zylinska, J. (2012) *Life after New Media: Mediation as a Vital Process*. MIT Press, Cambridge MA.

Kempe, S. (2009) 'Entity extraction and the semantic web', *Dataversity*, 12 January, www.dataversity.net/entity-extraction-and-the-semantic-web/ (accessed 12 June 2023).

Kennedy, H., and Engebretsen, M. (2020) 'Introduction: The relationships between graphs, charts, maps, and meanings, feelings, engagements', in Engebretsen, M., and Kennedy, H. (eds) *Data Visualization in Society*. Amsterdam University Press, Amsterdam, pp. 19–31.

Khot, R.A., Lee, J., Hjorth, L., and Mueller, F. (2015) 'TastyBeats: Celebrating heart rate data with a drinkable spectacle', in *Proceedings of the Ninth International Conference on Tangible, Embedded, and Embodied Interaction*. ACM, New York, pp. 229–32.

Kidd, D. (2019) 'Extra-activism: Counter-mapping and data justice', *Information, Communication & Society*, 22(7): 954–70.

Kidder, L.H. (1981) *Research Methods in Social Relations*. Harcourt Brace, London.

Kindon, S., Pain, R., and Kesby, M. (2007) *Participatory Action Research Approaches and Methods*. Routledge, Abingdon.

Kirk, A. (2019) *Data Visualisation: A Handbook for Data Driven Design*, 2nd edn. Sage, London.

Kitchin, R. (1996) 'Methodological convergence in cognitive mapping research: investigating configurational knowledge', *Journal of Environmental Psychology*, 16(3): 163–85.

Kitchin, R. (2000) 'The researched opinions on research: Disabled people and disability research', *Disability and Society*, 15(1): 25–48.

Kitchin, R. (2014a) *The Data Revolution: Big Data, Open Data, Data Infrastructures and Their Consequences*. Sage, London.

Kitchin, R. (2014b) 'Big data, new epistemologies and paradigm shifts', *Big Data and Society*, 1(1): 1–12.

Kitchin, R. (2014c) 'Engaging publics: Writing as praxis', *Cultural Geographies*, 21(1): 153–7.

Kitchin, R. (2015) 'Positivistic geography', in Aitken, S., and Valentine, G. (eds) *Approaches to Human Geography*, 2nd edn. Sage, London, pp. 23–34.

Kitchin, R. (2017) 'Thinking critically about and researching algorithms', *Information, Communication and Society*, 20(1): 14–29.

Kitchin, R. (2021) *Data Lives*. Bristol University Press, Bristol.

Kitchin, R. (2022) *The Data Revolution: A Critical Analysis to Big Data, Open Data and Data Infrastructures*. 2nd edn. Sage, London.

Kitchin, R. (2023) *Digital Timescapes: Technology, Temporality and Society*. Polity, Cambridge.

Kitchin, R., and Dodge, M. (2011) *Code/Space: Software and Everyday Life*. MIT Press Cambridge, MA.

Kitchin, R., and Fotheringham, A.S. (1997) 'Aggregation issues in cognitive mapping research', *Professional Geographer*, 49(3): 269–80.

Kitchin, R., and Lauriault, T. (2015) 'Small data in the era of big data', *GeoJournal*, 80(4): 463–75.

Kitchin, R., and Stehle, S. (2021) 'Can smart city data be used to create new official statistics?', *Journal of Official Statistics*, 37(1): 121–47.

Kitchin, R., Collins, S., and Frost, D. (2015) 'Funding models for open access digital data repositories', *Online Information Review*, 39(5): 664–81.

Kitchin, R., Lauriault, T.P., and Wilson, M.W. (eds) (2017) *Understanding Spatial Media*. Sage, London.

Klykken, F.H. (2022) 'Implementing continuous consent in qualitative research', *Qualitative Research*, 22(5): 795–810.

Knigge, L., and Cope, M. (2006) 'Grounded visualization: Integrating the analysis of qualitative and quantitative data through grounded theory and visualization', *Environment and Planning A*, 38(11): 2021–37.

Kon, F., Ferreira, É.C., de Souza, H.A., et al. (2022) 'Abstracting mobility flows from bike-sharing systems', *Public Transport*, 14(3): 545–81.

Koramaz, T.K. (2018) 'Digital representation of urban history and notes from an exhibition, Urban Intermedia: City, Archive, Narrative', *Disegnare.Con*, 11(21): 1–6.

Kraak, M.J., Roth, R.E., Ricker, B., Kagawa, A., and Le Sourd, G. (2020) *Mapping For a Sustainable World*. United Nations, New York.

Kruger, L.J., Rodgers, R.F., Long, S.J., et al. (2019) 'Individual interviews or focus groups? Interview format and women's self-disclosure', *International Journal of Social Research Methodology*, 22(3): 245–55.

Kuhn, T. (1962) *The Structure of Scientific Revolutions*. University of Chicago Press, Chicago, IL.

Kukutai, T., and Taylor, J. (2016) 'Data sovereignty for indigenous peoples: Current practice and future needs', in Kukutai, T., and Taylor, J. (eds) *Indigenous Data Sovereignty: Towards an Agenda*. Australian National University Press, Canberra, pp. 1–22.

Kullman, K. (2013) 'Geographies of experiment/experimental geographies. A rough guide', *Geography Compass*, 7(12): 879–94.

Kumar, K., and Naik, L. (2016) 'How to create an online survey using google forms', *International Journal of Library and Information Studies*, 6(3): 118–26.

Kwan, M.-P. (2007) 'Affecting geospatial technologies: Toward a feminist Politics of Emotion', *The Professional Geographer*, 59(1): 22–34.

Lana, I., Del Ser, J., Velez, M., & Vlahogianni, E. I. (2018) 'Road traffic forecasting: Recent advances and new challenges', *IEEE Intelligent Transportation Systems Magazine*, 10(2): 93–109.

Lauriault, T.P., and Wood, J. (2009) 'GPS tracings – Personal cartographies', *The Cartographic Journal*, 46(4): 360–5.

Lauriault, T.P., Craig, B.L., Taylor, D.R.F., and Pulsifier, P.L. (2007) 'Today's data are part of tomorrow's research: Archival issues in the sciences', *Archivaria*, 64: 123–79.

Laurier, E., Brown, B., and McGregor, M. (2016) 'Mediated pedestrian mobility: Walking and the map app', *Mobilities*, 11(1): 117–34.

Lawrence, L. (2022) 'Conducting cross-cultural qualitative interviews with mainland Chinese participants during COVID: Lessons from the field', *Qualitative Research*, 22(1): 154–65.

Lazer, D., Pentland, A., Adamic, L., et al. (2009) 'Computational social science', *Science*, 323: 721–33.

Leavy, P. (2015) *Method Meets Art: Arts-Based Research Practice*, 2nd edn. Guildford Press, New York.

Leavy, P. (2017) *Research Design: Quantitative, Qualitative, Mixed Methods, Arts-Based, and Community-Based Participatory Research Approaches*. Guildford Press, New York.

Lecher, C., and Varner, M. (2021) 'NYC's algorithms cement segregation. This data show how', *The Markup*, 26 May. https://themarkup.org/machine-learning/2021/05/26/nycs-school-algorithms-cement-segregation-this-data-shows-how (accessed 2 March 2023).

Lee, C.S. (2019) 'Datafication, dataveillance, and the social credit system as China's new normal', *Online Information Review*, 43(6): 952–70.

Lee, M.H., Son, O., and Nam, T.J. (2016) 'Patina-inspired personalization: personalizing products with traces of daily use', in *Proceedings of the 2016 ACM conference on designing interactive systems*. ACM, Brisbane, pp. 251–63.

Lehdonvirta, V., Rani, U., Stephany, F., et al. (n.d.) *Online Labour Observatory*, http://onlinelabourobservatory.org/ (accessed 24 January 2023).

Lemon, L.L., and Hayes, J. (2020) 'Enhancing trustworthiness of qualitative findings', *The Qualitative Report*, 25(3): 604–14.

Lenger, R., and Eppler, M.J. (n.d.) *A Periodic Table of Visualization Methods*, version 1.5, www.visual-literacy.org/periodic_table/periodic_table.html (accessed 13 September 2022).

Leonelli, S. (2016) 'Locating ethics in data science: Responsibility and accountability in global and distributed knowledge production systems', *Philosophical Transactions of the Royal Society A*, 374: 20160122.

Leszczynski, A. (2016) 'Speculative futures: Cities, data, and governance beyond smart urbanism', *Environment and Planning A*, 48(9): 1691–708.

Lesczynski, A. (2017a) 'Epistemological critiques', in Wilson, J.P. (ed.) *The Geographic Information Science & Technology Body of Knowledge* (4th quarter 2017 edn), https://doi.org/10.22224/gistbok/2017.4.1 (accessed 22 August 2023).

Leszczynski, A. (2017b) 'Geoprivacy', in Kitchin, R., Lauriault, T., and Wilson, M.W. (eds) *Understanding Spatial Media*. Sage, London, pp. 235–44.

Leszczynski, A. (2020a) 'Digital methods III: The digital mundane', *Progress in Human Geography*, 44(6): 1194–201.

Leszczynski, A. (2020b) 'Geolocation', in Kobayashi, A. (ed.) *International Encyclopedia of Human Geography*, vol. 6, 2nd edn. Elsevier, Oxford, pp. 101–6.

Leszczynski, A., and Kong, V. (2022) 'Walking (with) the platform: Bikesharing and the aesthetics of gentrification in Vancouver', *Urban Geography*, https://doi.org/10.1080/02723638.2022.2036926 (accessed 22 August 2023).

Liao, Y. (2021) 'Ride-sourcing compared to its public-transit alternative using big trip data', *Journal of Transport Geography*, 95: 103135.

Light, B., Burgess, J., and Duguay, S. (2018) 'The walkthrough method: An approach to the study of apps', *New Media & Society*, 20(3): 881–900.

Lin, W. (2013) 'Situating performative neogeography: Tracing, mapping, and performing Everyone's East Lake', *Environment and Planning A*, 45(1): 37–54.

Linabary, J.R., and Hamel, S.A. (2017) 'Feminist online interviewing: Engaging issues of power, resistance and reflexivity in practice', *Feminist Review*, 115(1): 97–113.

Lobe, B. (2017) 'Best practices for synchronous online focus groups', in Barbour, R.S., and Morgan, D.L. (eds) *A New Era in Focus Group Research: Challenges, Innovation and Practice*. Palgrave Macmillan, London, pp. 227–50.

Lomberg, S. (2019) 'Ethical considerations for Web archives and Web history research', in Brugger, N., and Milligan, I. (eds) *The Sage Handbook of Web History*. Sage, London. pp. 99–111.

Longhurst, R. (2013) 'Using Skype to mother: Bodies, emotions, visuality, and screens', *Environment and Planning D: Society and Space*, 31(4): 664–79.

Loveless, N. (2019) *How to Make Art at the End of the World: A Manifesto for Research-Creation*. Duke University Press, Durham, NC.

Lovink, G. (2002) *Uncanny Networks: Dialogues with the Virtual Intelligentsia*. MIT Press, Cambridge, MA.

Lunenfeld, P. (1999) *The Digital Dialectic: New Essays on New Media*. MIT Press, Cambridge, MA.

Luo, Y., and Guo, R. (2021) 'Facial recognition in China: Current status, comparative approach and the road ahead', *University of Pennsylvania Journal of Law and Social Change*, 25(2): 153–79.

Lupton, D. (2014) *Digital Sociology*. Routledge, London.

Lupton, D. (2020) *Data Selves*. Polity Press, Cambridge.

Lupton, D., and Watson, A. (2021) 'Towards more-than-human digital data studies: Developing research-creation methods', *Qualitative Research*, 21(4): 463–80.

Luque-Ayala, A., and Marvin, S. (2020) *Urban Operating Systems: Producing the Computational City*. MIT Press, Cambridge, MA.

Lurie, E. (2023) 'Comparing platform research API requirements', *Tech Policy Press*, 22 March, https://techpolicy.press/comparing-platform-research-api-requirements/ (accessed 22 August 2023).

Lyster, C. (2016) *Learning from Logistics: How Networks Change Our Cities*. Birkhauser, Basel.

Maalsen, S. (2020) 'Revising the smart home as assemblage', *Housing Studies*, 35(9): 1534–49.

Maalsen, S. (2023) 'Algorithmic epistemologies and methodologies: Algorithmic harm, algorithmic care and situated algorithmic knowledges', *Progress in Human Geography*, https://doi.org/10.1177/03091325221149439 (accessed 22 August 2023).

MacInnes, J. (2022) *Statistical Inference and Probability*. Sage, London.

MacLean, S., and Hatcher, S. (2019) 'Constructing the (healthy) neoliberal citizen: Using the walkthrough method "do" critical health communication research', *Frontiers in*

Communication, 4, https://doi.org/10.3389/fcomm.2019.00052 (accessed 22 August 2023).

MacNamara, N., Mackle, D., Trew, J.D., et al. (2021) 'Reflecting on asynchronous internet mediated focus groups for researching culturally sensitive issues', *International Journal of Social Research Methodology*, 24(5): 553–65.

Mahajan, S., Gabrys, J., and Armitage, J. (2021) 'AirKit: A citizen-sensing toolkit for monitoring air quality', *Sensors*, 21, 4044: 1–19.

Malizia, A. (2006) *Mobile 3D Graphics*. Springer-Verlag, London.

Mann, M., and Daly, A. (2019) '(Big) data and the north-in-south: Australia's informational imperialism and digital colonialism', *Television & New Media*, 20(4): 379–95.

Manoff, M. (2010) 'Archive and database as metaphor: Theorizing the historical record', *Portal: Libraries and the Academy*, 10(4): 385–98.

Manovich, L. (2011) 'What is visualisation?', *Visual Studies*, 26(1): 36–49.

Manovich, L. (2013) *Software Takes Command: Extending the Language of New Media*. Bloomsbury, London.

Manovich, L. (2020) *Cultural Analytics*. MIT Press, Cambridge, MA.

Manovich, L., Giachino, M., and Chow, J. (2014) *Image Montage*, https://imagej.nih.gov/ij/plugins/image-montage/index.html (accessed 30 September 2022).

Manyika, J., Chiu, M., Brown, B., Bughin, J., Dobbs, R., Roxburgh, C., and Hung Byers, A. (2011) *Big Data: The Next Frontier for Innovation, Competition, and Productivity*. McKinsey Global Institute, Amsterdam.

Markham, A. (2013) 'Remix culture, remix methods: Reframing qualitative inquiry for social media contexts', in Denzin, N.K., and Giardina, M.D. (eds) *Global Dimensions of Qualitative Inquiry*. Left Coast Press, Walnut Creek, CA, pp. 63–81.

Markham, A. (2018) 'Bricolage', in Navas, E., Gallagher, O., and Burrough, X. (eds) *Keywords in Remix Studies*. Routledge, London, pp. 43–55.

Markham, A.N., and Buchanan, E. (2015) 'Ethical considerations in digital research contexts', in Wright, J.D. (ed.) *Encyclopedia for Social & Behavioral Sciences*. Elsevier, Waltham, MA, pp. 606–13.

Markham, A., and Pereira, G. (2019a) 'Analyzing public interventions through the lens of experimentalism: The case of the Museum of Random Memory', *Digital Creativity*, 30(4): 235–56.

Markham, A., and Pereira, G. (2019b) 'Experimenting with algorithmic memory-making: Lived experience and future-oriented ethics in critical data science', *Frontiers in Big Data*, 2, www.frontiersin.org/articles/10.3389/fdata.2019.00035/full (accessed 22 August 2023).

Markham, A.N., Tiidenberg, K., and Herman, A. (2018) 'Ethics as methods: Doing ethics in the era of big data research – Introduction', *Social Media + Society*, 4(3): 1–9.

Marsden, E. (2019) 'Methodological transparency and its consequences for the quality and scope of research', in McKinley, J., and Rose, H. (eds) *The Routledge Handbook of Research Methods in Applied Linguistics*. Routledge, London, pp. 15–28.

Marshall, C., and Rossman, G.B. (1995) *Designing Qualitative Research*. 2nd edn. Sage, London.

Marston, S.A., and De Leeuw, S. (2013) 'Creativity and Geography: Toward a Politicized Intervention', *Geographical Review*, 103(2): iii–xxvi.

Martinez, E., and Kirchner, L. (2021) 'The secret bias hidden in mortgage-approval algorithms', *The Markup*, 25 August, https://themarkup.org/denied/2021/08/25/the-secret-bias-hidden-in-mortgage-approval-algorithms (accessed 2 March 2023).

Marvin, S., Luque-Ayala, A., and McFarlane, C. (eds) (2016) *Smart Urbanism: Utopian Vision or False Dawn?* Routledge, Abingdon and New York.

Massey, D. (2005) *For Space.* Sage, London.

Mattern, S. (2021) *A City is Not a Computer: Other Urban Intelligences.* Princeton University Press, Princeton, NJ.

May, J., and Thrift, N. (2001) 'Introduction', in May, J., and Thrift, N. (eds) *Timespace: Geographies of Temporality.* Routledge, London, pp. 1–46.

Mayer-Schonberger, V., and Cukier, K. (2013) *Big Data: A Revolution that will Change How We Live, Work and Think.* John Murray, London.

McArdle, G., and Kitchin, R. (2016) 'Improving the veracity of open and real-time urban data', *Built Environment*, 42(3): 446–62.

McFarland, D.A., and McFarland, H.R. (2015) 'Big Data and the danger of being precisely inaccurate', *Big Data & Society*, 2(2): 1–4.

McGrath, J. (2019) 'Memes', in Brugger, N. and Milligan, I. (eds) *The Sage Handbook of Web History.* Sage, London, pp. 505–19.

McIlroy, S., Ali, N., and Hassan, A.E. (2016) 'Fresh apps: An empirical study of frequently-updated mobile apps in the Google Play store', *Empirical Software Engineering*, 21(3): 1346–70.

McLean, J. (2020) *Changing Digital Geographies: Technologies, Environments and People.* Palgrave Macmillan, London.

Melendez, S., and Pasternack, A. (2019) 'Here are the data brokers quietly buying and selling your personal information', *The Fast Company*, 2 March, www.fastcompany.com/90310803/here-are-the-data-brokers-quietly-buying-and-selling-your-personalinformation (accessed 1 December 2020).

Melgaço, L., and van Brakel, R. (2021) 'Smart cities as surveillance theatre', *Surveillance & Society*, 19(2): 244–9.

Meltzer, B.N., Petras, J.W., and Reynolds, L.T. (1975) *Symbolic Interactionism: Genesis, Varieties, and Criticism.* Routledge & Kegan Paul, London.

Meng, A., and DiSalvo, C. (2018) 'Grassroots resource mobilization through counter-data action', *Big Data & Society*, 5(2): 1–12.

Merieb, E.N., and Hoehn, K. (2007) *Human Anatomy & Physiology*, 7th edn. Pearson Benjamin Cummings, San Francisco, CA.

Merolli, M., Martin-Sanchez, F., and Gray, K. (2014) 'Social media and online survey: Tools for knowledge management in health research', *Proceedings of the Seventh Australasian Workshop on Health Informatics and Knowledge Management (HIKM 2014)*, Auckland, 153: 21.

Metcalf, J., and Crawford, K. (2016) 'Where are human subjects in Big Data research? The emerging ethics divide', *Big Data & Society*, 3(1): 1–14.

Michaelidou, N., and Dibb, S. (2006) 'Using email questionnaires for research: Good practice in tackling non-response', *Journal of Targeting, Measurement and Analysis for Marketing*, 14(4): 289–96.

Middleton, J. (2010) 'Sense and the city: Exploring the embodied geographies of urban walking', *Social & Cultural Geography*, 11(6): 575–96.

Middleton, J. (2011) 'Walking in the city: The geographies of everyday pedestrian practices', *Geography Compass*, 5(2): 90–105.

Mieruch, Y., and McFarlane, D. (2022) 'Gig economy riders on social media in Thailand: Contested identities and emergent civil society organizations', *Voluntas*, https://doi.org/10.1007/s11266-022-00547-7 (accessed 22 August 2023).

Milan, S., and van der Velden, L. (2016) 'The alternative epistemologies of data activism', *Digital Culture & Society*, 2(2): 57–74.

Miller, H.J. (2010) 'The data avalanche is here: Shouldn't we be digging?', *Journal of Regional Science*, 50(1): 181–201.

Miller, H.J., and Han, J. (2009) 'Geographic data mining and knowledge discovery: An overview', in Miller, H.J., and Han, J. (eds), *Geographic Data Mining and Knowledge Discovery*. Taylor and Francis, London, pp. 3–32.

Milligan, I. (2019) 'Historiography and the Web', in Brugger, N. and Milligan, I. (eds) *The Sage Handbook of Web History*. Sage, London, pp. 3–15.

Minelli, M., Chambers, M., and Dhiraj, A. (2013) *Big Data, Big Analytics*. John Wiley & Sons, Hoboken, NJ.

Mitchell, M. (1996) *An Introduction to Genetic Algorithms*. MIT Press, Cambridge, MA.

Mitchell, W.J.T., and Hansen, M.B.N. (2010) *Critical Terms for Media Studies*. University of Chicago Press, Chicago, IL.

Mohamed, S., Png, M.T., and Isaac, W. (2020) 'Decolonial AI: Decolonial theory as sociotechnical foresight in artificial intelligence', *Philosophy & Technology*, 33: 659–84.

Møller, K., and Robards, B. (2019) 'Walking through, going along and scrolling back: Ephemeral mobilities in digital ethnography', *Nordicom Review*, 40(s1): 95–109.

Monaghan, L.F., O'Dwyer, M., and Gabe, J. (2013) 'Seeking university research ethics committee approval: The emotional vicissitudes of a "rationalised" process', *International Journal of Social Research Methodology*, 16(1): 65–80.

Mondal, H., Mondal, S., Ghosal, T., and Mondal, S. (2018) 'Using Google forms for medical survey: A technical note', *International Journal of Clinical and Experimental Physiology*, 5(4): 216–18.

Monmonier, M. (1996) *How to Lie with Maps*. 2nd edn. University of Chicago Press, Chicago, IL.

Monson, A. (2013) 'Text adventure', in Singer, M., and Walker, N. (eds) *Bending Genre: Essays on Creative Non-Fiction*. Bloomsbury, London, pp. 81–90.

Mooney, S.J., DiMaggio, C.J., Lovasi, G.S., et al. (2016) 'Use of Google Street View to assess environmental contributions to pedestrian injury', *American Journal of Public Health*, 106(3): 462–9.

Moraes, R.R., Correa, M.B., Daneris, Â., et al. (2021) 'Email vs. Instagram recruitment strategies for online survey research', *Brazilian Dental Journal*, 32: 67–77.

Moretti, F. (2005) *Graphs, Maps, Trees: Abstract Models for a Literary History*. Verso, London.

Morris, J.W., Prey, R., and Nieborg, D.B. (2021) 'Engineering culture: Logics of optimization in music, games, and apps', *Review of Communication*, 21(2): 161–75.

Mosseri, S. (2022) 'Being watched and being seen: Negotiating visibility in the NYC ride-hail circuit', *New Media & Society*, 24(3): 600–20.

Mullan, P.C. (2016) *A History of Digital Currency in the United States: New Technology in an Unregulated Market*. Palgrave, London.

Murthy, D. (2008) 'Digital ethnography: An examination of the use of new technologies for social research', *Sociology*, 42(5): 837–55.

Myatt, G.J., and Johnson, W.P. (2009) *Making Sense of Data II: A Practical Guide to Data Visualization, Advanced Data Mining Methods, and Applications*. John Wiley & Sons, Hoboken, NJ.

Nagar, R. (2013) 'Storytelling and co-authorship in feminist alliance work: Reflections from a journey', *Gender, Place and Culture*, 20(1): 1–18.

Nanni, F. (2019) 'Collecting primary sources from Web archives: A tale of scarcity and abundance', in Brugger, N., and Milligan, I. (eds) *The Sage Handbook of Web History*. Sage, London, pp. 112–24.

Nardi, B. (2010) *My Life as a Night Elf Priest: An Anthropological Account of World of Warcraft*. University of Michigan Press, Michigan.

NASEM (National Academies of Sciences, Engineering, and Medicine) (2019) *Reproducibility and Replicability in Science*. The National Academies Press, Washington DC.

Nicholas, D.B., Lach, L., King, G., et al. (2010) 'Contrasting Internet and face-to-face focus groups for children with chronic health conditions: Outcomes and participant experiences', *International Journal of Qualitative Methods*, 9(1): 105–21.

NISO (National Information Standards Organization) (2004) *Understanding Metadata*. Bethesda, MD, www.niso.org/publications/press/UnderstandingMetadata.pdf (accessed 1 December 2020).

Nissenbaum, H. (2010) *Privacy in Context: Technology, Policy, and the Integrity of Social Life*. Stanford University Press, Stanford, CA.

Noble, S.U., and Roberts, S.T. (2019) 'Technological elites, the meritocracy, and postracial myths in Silicon Valley', in Mukherjee, R., Banet-Weiser, S., and Gray, H. (eds) *Racism Postrace*. Duke University Press, Durham, NC, pp. 113–29.

Nold, C. (2009) *Emotional Cartography: Technologies of the Self*, http://emotionalcartography.net/EmotionalCartographyLow.pdf (accessed 12 June 2023).

Novak, A., Badanik, B., Brezonakova, A., and Lusiak, T. (2020) 'Implications of crew rostering on airline operations', *Transportation Research Procedia*, 44: 2–7.

Nyhan, J., and Flinn, A. (2016) *Computation and the Humanities: Toward an Oral History of Digital Humanities*. Springer Open, Cham.

Nyhan, J., Flinn, A., and Walsh, A. (2015) 'Oral history and the Hidden Histories project: Towards histories of computing in the humanities', *Digital Scholarship in the Humanities*, 30(1): 71–85.

O'Connor, H., and Madge, C. (2023) *The Sage Handbook of Online Research Methods*. Sage, London.

O'Neill, M., and Roberts, B. (2020) *Walking Methods: Research on the Move*. Routledge, London.

OECD (1980) *OECD Guidelines on the Protection of Privacy and Transborder Flows of Personal Data*. OECD, Paris, www.oecd.org/sti/ieconomy/

oecdguidelinesontheprotectionofprivacyandtransborderflowsofpersonaldata.htm (accessed 2 December 2020).

OECD (2011) *Quality Framework and Guidelines for OECD Statistical Activities*. OECD, Paris, www.oecd.org/sdd/qualityframeworkforoecdstatisticalactivities.htm (accessed February 2021).

OECD (2019) *OECD AI Principles overview*. OECD, Paris, https://oecd.ai/en/ai-principles (accessed 3 March 2023).

OED (Oxford English Dictionary) (2022) *Citizen Science*. Oxford University Press, Oxford.

Offenhuber, D. (2020) 'What we talk about when we talk about data physicality', *IEEE Computer Graphics and Applications*, 40(6): 25–37.

Ohlhorst, F.J. (2013) *Big Data Analytics: Turning Big Data into Big Money*. John Wiley & Sons, New York.

Oliver, M. (1992) 'Changing the social relations of research production', *Disability and Society*, 7(2): 101–14.

Opara, V., Spangsdorf, S., and Ryan, M.K. (2021) 'Reflecting on the use of Google Docs for online interviews: Innovation in qualitative data collection', *Qualitative Research*, https://doi.org/10.1177/14687941211045192 (accessed 22 August 2023).

Osborne, T., Warner, E., Jones, P.I., and Resch, B. (2019) 'Performing social media: Artistic approaches to analyzing big data', *GeoHumanities*, 5(1): 282–94.

Oxford Internet Institute (2023a) *Fairwork*, https://fair.work/en/fw/homepage/ (accessed 28 January 2023).

Oxford Internet Institute (2023b) *Methodology*, https://fair.work/en/fw/methodology/ (accessed 28 January 2023).

Oxford Internet Institute (2023c) *Principles*, https://fair.work/en/fw/principles/ (accessed 28 January 2023).

Oxford Internet Institute (2023d) *Ratings*, https://fair.work/en/fw/ratings/ (accessed 28 January 2023).

Paasonen, S. (2019) 'Online Pornography', in Brugger, N., and Milligan, I. (eds) *The Sage Handbook of Web History*. Sage, London, pp. 551–63.

Park, E.J.W. (1999) 'Racial ideology and hiring decision in Silicon Valley', *Qualitative Sociology*, 22(3): 223–33.

Park, H.W. (2003) 'Hyperlink network analysis: A new method for the study of social structure on the web', *Connections*, 25(1): 49–61.

Park, P.S., Blumenstock, J.E., and Macy, M.W. (2018) 'The strength of long-range ties in population-scale social networks', *Science*, 362(6421): 1410–13.

Parker, A. and Tritter, J. (2006) 'Focus group method and methodology: current practice and recent debate', *International Journal of Research & Method in Education*, 29(1): 23–37.

Pasquale, F. (2015) *The Black Box Society*. Harvard University Press, Cambridge, MA.

Patton, M.Q. (1999) 'Enhancing the quality and credibility of qualitative analysis', *Health Services Research*, 35(5 pt 2): 1189–208.

Pedwell, C. (2016) 'Transforming habit: Revolution, routine and social change', *Cultural Studies*, 31(1): 1–28.

Pedwell, C. (2017) 'Mediated habits: images, networked affect and social change', *Subjectivity*, 10: 147–69.

Perng, S., and Kitchin, R. (2018) 'Solutions and frictions in civic hacking: Collaboratively designing and building a queuing app for an immigration office', *Social and Cultural Geography*, 19(1): 1–20.

Perng, S.-Y., Kitchin, R., and MacDonncha, D. (2018) 'Hackathons, entrepreneurship and the making of smart cities', *Geoforum*, 97: 189–97.

Petrelli, D., Marshall, M.T., O'Brien, S., McEntaggart, P., and Gwilt, I. (2017) 'Tangible data souvenirs as a bridge between a physical museum visit and online digital experience', *Personal and Ubiquitous Computing*, 21(2): 281–95.

Petty, T., Saba, M., Lewis, T., Gangadharan, S.P., and Eubanks, V. (2016) *Our Data Bodies: Reclaiming Our Data*. Our Data Bodies Project, www.odbproject.org/wp-content/uploads/2016/12/ODB.InterimReport.FINAL_.7.16.2018.pdf (accessed 22 August 2023).

Philips, R., and Kara, H. (2021) *Creative Writing for Social Sciences: A Practical Guide*. Sage, London.

Phillips, C.B., Engelberg, J.K., Geremia, C.M., et al. (2017) 'Online versus in-person comparison of Microscale Audit of Pedestrian Streetscapes (MAPS) assessments: reliability of alternate methods', *International Journal of Health Geographics*, 16(1): 27.

Picton, P.D. (2000) *Neural Networks*, 2nd edn. Palgrave Macmillan, Basingstoke.

Pieroni, C., Giannotti, M., Alves, B.B., et al. (2021) 'Big data for big issues: Revealing travel patterns of low-income population based on smart card data mining in a global south unequal city', *Journal of Transport Geography*, 96: 103203.

Piirto, J. (2009) 'The question of quality and qualifications: Writing inferior poems as qualitative research', in Prendergast, M., Leggo, C., and Sameshima, P. (eds) *Poetic Inquiry: Vibrant Voices in the Social Sciences*. Sense Publishers, Rotterdam, pp. 83–100.

Pink, S. (2007) 'Walking with video', *Visual Studies*, 22(3): 240–52.

Pink, S. (2015) *Doing Sensory Ethnography*. Sage, London.

Pink, S., and Mackley, K.L. (2012) 'Video and a Sense of the Invisible: Approaching Domestic Energy Consumption through the Sensory Home', *Sociological Research Online*, 17(1): 87–105.

Pink, S., Horst, H., Postill, J., Hjorth, L., Lewis, T., and Tacchi, J. (2015) *Digital Ethnography: Principles and Practice*. Sage, London.

Pink, S., Sinanan, J., Hjorth, L., and Horst, H. (2016) 'Tactile digital ethnography: Researching mobile media through the hand', *Mobile Media & Communication* 4(2): 237–51.

Pink, S., Sumartojo, S., Lupton, D., and Heyes La Bond, C. (2017) 'Mundane data: The routines, contingencies and accomplishments of digital living', *Big Data & Society*, 4(1): 1–12.

Pittman, M., and Sheehan, K. (2017) 'Ethics of using online commercial crowdsourcing sites for academic research: The case of Amazon's Mechanical Turk', in Zimmer, M., and Kinder-Kurlanda, K. (eds) *Internet Research Ethics for the Social Age: New Challenges, Cases, and Contexts*. Peter Lang, New York, pp. 177–86.

Pogacar, M. (2018) 'Culture of the past: Digital connectivity and dispotentiated futures', in Hoskins, A. (ed.) *Digital Memory Studies*. Routledge, New York, pp. 27–48.

Pollitt, C. (2008) *Time, Policy, Management: Governing with the Past*. Oxford University Press, Oxford.

Polson, P.G., Lewis, C., Reimat, J., and Wharton, C. (1992) 'Cognitive walkthroughs: A method for theory-based evaluation of user interfaces', *International Journal of Man-Machine Studies*, 36: 741–73.

Pool, I. (2016) 'Colonialism's and postcolonialism's fellow traveller: The collection, use and misuse of data on indigenous people', in Kukutai, T., and Taylor, J. (eds), *Indigenous Data Sovereignty: Towards an Agenda*. Australian National University Press, Canberra, pp. 57–76.

Poor, N. (2017) 'The ethics of using hacked data: Patreon's data hack and academic data standards', in Zimmer, M., and Kinder-Kurlanda, K. (eds) *Internet Research Ethics for the Social Age: New Challenges, Cases, and Contexts*. Peter Lang, New York, pp. 277–80.

Poorthuis, A., Zook, M., Shelton, T., and Stephens, M. (2016) 'Using geotagged digital social data in geographic research', in Clifford, N., Cope, M., Gillespie, T., and French, S. (eds) *Key Methods in Geography*. Sage, London, pp. 248–69.

Powell, A. (2008) 'Wifi publics: Producing community and technology', *Information, Communication & Society*, 11(8): 1068–88.

Powell, A. (2018a) 'Alison Powell on data walking', *TMG Journal for Media History*, 21(2): 146–50.

Powell, A. (2018b) 'The data walkshop and radical bottom-up data knowledge', in Knox, H., and Nafus, D. (eds) *Ethnography for a Data-Saturated World*. Manchester University Press, Manchester, pp. 212–32.

Propen, A. (2009) 'Cartographic representation and the construction of lived worlds: Understanding cartographic practice as embodied knowledge', in Dodge, M., Kitchin, R., and Perkins, C. (eds) *Rethinking Maps*. Routledge, London, pp. 113–30.

Quillian, L., Pager, D., Hexel, O., and Midtbøen, A.H. (2017) 'Meta-analysis of field experiments shows no change in racial discrimination in hiring over time', *Proceedings of the National Academy of Sciences*, 114(41): 10870–5.

Rainie, S.C., Kukutai, T., Walter, M., Figueroa-Rodríguez, O.L., Walker, J., and Axelsson, P. (2019) 'Issues in open data: Indigenous data sovereignty', in Davies, T., Walker, S., Rubinstein, M., and Perini, F. (eds) *The State of Open Data: Histories and Horizons*. African Minds and International Development Research Centre, Cape Town and Ottawa, pp. 300–19.

Rakheja, H. (2022) 'Is the Fairwork ratings on gig workers' conditon a wake-up call?', *Business Standard*, 10 January, www.business-standard.com/podcast/companies/is-the-fairwork-ratings-on-gig-workers-condition-a-wake-up-call-122011000073_1.html (accessed 28 January 2023).

Ramsden, H. (2017) 'Walking & talking: Making strange encounters within the familiar', *Social & Cultural Geography*, 18(1): 53–77.

Rana, R., Chou, C.T., Bulusu, N., et al. (2015) 'Ear-Phone: A context-aware noise mapping using smart phones', *Pervasive and Mobile Computing*, 17(A): 1–22.

Ranieri, V., Kennedy, E., Walmsley, M., et al. (2019) 'Rare but heard: Using asynchronous virtual focus groups, interviews and roundtable discussions to create a personalised psychological intervention for primary sclerosing cholangitis: a protocol', *BMJ Open*, 9(10): e031417.

Rast, J. (2012) 'Why history (still) matters: Time and temporality in urban political analysis', *Urban Affairs Review*, 48(1): 3–36.

Reddy, S., Estrin, D., and Srivastava, M. (2010) 'Recruitment framework for participatory sensing data collections', in *Proceedings of the 2010 International Conference on Pervasive Computing*, Lecture Notes in Computer Science, vol 6030. Springer, Berlin, pp. 138–55.

Redmond, K.C., and Smith, T.M. (2000) *From Whirlwind to MITRE: The R&D Story of the SAGE Air Defense Computer*. MIT Press, Cambridge, MA.

Regmi, P.R., Waithaka, E., Paudyal, A., et al. (2016) 'Guide to the design and application of online questionnaire surveys', *Nepal Journal of Epidemiology*, 6(4): 640–4.

Reisner, S.L., Randazzo, R.K., White Hughto, J.M., et al. (2018) 'Sensitive health topics with underserved patient populations: Methodological considerations for online focus group discussions', *Qualitative Health Research*, 28(10): 1658–73.

Repenning, A. (2022) 'Workspaces of mediation: How digital platforms shape practices, spaces and places of creative work', *Tijdschrift voor Economische en Sociale Geografie*, 113(2): 211–24.

Restuccia, F., Das, S.K., and Payton, J. (2016) 'Incentive mechanisms for participatory sensing: Survey and research challenges', *ACM Transactions on Sensor Networks*, 12(2), Article 13: 1–40.

Reyes, E., and Manovich, L. (2020) 'Cultural viz: An aesthetic approach to cultural analytics', *Leonardo*, 53(4): 408–14.

Richardson, I., and Hjorth, L. (2017) 'Mobile media, domestic play and haptic ethnography', *New Media & Society*, 19(10): 1653–67.

Richardson, J., Godfrey, B., and Walklate, S. (2021) 'Rapid, remote and responsive research during COVID-19', *Methodological Innovations*, 14(1), https://doi.org/10.1177/20597991211008581 (accessed 22 August 2023).

Richardson, L. (2020) 'Platforms, markets, and contingent calculation: The flexible arrangement of the delivered meal', *Antipode*, 52(3): 619–36.

Riche, N.H., Hurter, C., Diakopoulos, N., and Carpendale, S. (2018) 'Introduction', in Riche N.H., Hurter, C., Diakopoulos, N., and Carpendale, S. (eds) *Data Driven Storytelling*. CRC Press, London, pp. 1–15.

Ritchie, D.A. (2015) *Doing Oral History*. 3rd edn. Oxford University Press, Oxford.

Ritter, C.S. (2021) 'Rethinking digital ethnography: A qualitative approach to understanding interfaces', *Qualitative Research*, 22(6): 916–32.

Rivera, I. (2023) 'Undoing settler imaginaries: (Re)imagining digital knowledge politics', *Progress in Human Geography*, https://doi.org/10.1177/03091325231154873 (accessed 22 August 2023).

Robards, B., and Lincoln, S. (2017) 'Uncovering longitudinal life narratives: Scrolling back on Facebook', *Qualitative Research*, 17(6): 715–30.

Roberts, S.T. (2019) *Behind the Screen*. Yale University Press, London.

Roberts, T. (2014) 'From things to events: Whitehead and the materiality of process', *Environment and Planning D: Society and Space*, 32(6), 968–83.

Robinson, S. (2003) *Simulation: The Practice of Model Development and Use*. John Wiley & Sons, Chichester.

Rochefort, A. (2020) 'Regulating social media platforms: A comparative policy analysis', *Communication Law and Policy*, 25(2): 225–60.

Rodgers, S., and Moore, S. (2018) 'Platform urbanism: An introduction', *Mediapolis*, 23(4), www.mediapolisjournal.com/2018/10/platform-urbanism-an-introduction/ (accessed 10 May 2023).

Rogers, R. (2013) *Digital Methods*. MIT Press, Cambridge, MA.

Rose, G. (1993) *Feminism and Geography*. Cambridge University Press, Cambridge.

Rose, G. (1997) 'Situating knowledges: Positionality, reflexivities and other tactics', *Progress in Human Geography*, 21(3): 305–20.

Rose, G. (2022) *Visual Methodologies: An Introduction to Researching with Visual Materials*, 5th edn. Sage, London.

Rose, G., and Willis, A. (2019) 'Seeing the smart city on Twitter: Colour and the affective territories of becoming smart', *Environment and Planning D: Society and Space*, 37(3): 411–27.

Rosenblat, A., and Stark, L. (2016) 'Algorithmic labor and information asymmetries: A case study of Uber's drivers', *International Journal of Communication*, 10: 27.

Rowlands, T. (2012) *Video Game Worlds: Working at Play in the Culture of EverQuest*. Left Coast Press, Walnut Creek, CA.

Rzeszewski, M., and Kotus, J. (2019) 'Usability and usefulness of internet mapping platforms in participatory spatial planning', *Applied Geography*, 103: 56–69.

Rzeszewski, M., and Naji, J. (2022) 'Literary placemaking and narrative immersion in extended reality virtual geographic environments', *International Journal of Digital Earth*, 15(1): 853–86.

Salganik, M.J. (2018) *Bit by Bit: Social Research in the Digital Age*. Princeton University Press, Princeton, NJ.

San Cornelio, G., and Roig, A. (2020) 'Mixed methods on Instagram research: Methodological challenges in data analysis and visualization', *Convergence*, 26(5–6): 1125–43.

Sandvig, C., Hamilton, K., Karahalios, K., and Langbort, C. (2014) 'Auditing algorithms: Research methods for detecting discrimination on Internet Platforms'. Paper presented to 'Data and Discrimination: Converting Critical Concerns into Productive Inquiry' workshop, May 22, Seattle, WA, ai.equineteurope.org/library/auditing-algorithms-research-methods-detecting-discrimination-internet-platforms (accessed 2 March 2023).

Scassa, T. (2019) 'Ownership and control over publicly accessible platform data', *Online Information Review*, 43(6): 986–1002.

Schafer, V., and Thierry, B.G. (2019) 'Web history in context', in Brugger, N., and Milligan, I. (eds) *The Sage Handbook of Web History*. Sage, London, pp. 59–73.

Schatzki, T.R., Knorr-Cetina, K., and von Savigny, E. (2001) *The Practice Turn in Contemporary Theory*. Routledge London.

Schellewald, A. (2022) 'Theorizing "stories about algorithms" as a mechanism in the formation and maintenance of algorithmic imaginaries', *Social Media + Society*, 8(1), https://doi.org/10.1177/20563051221077025 (accessed 22 August 2023).

Schiek, D., and Ullrich, C.G. (2017) 'Using asynchronous written online communications for qualitative inquiries: A research note', *Qualitative Research*, 17(5): 589–97.

Schneider, W. (2014) 'Oral history in the age of digital possibilities', in Boyd, D.A., and Larson, M.A. (eds) *Oral History and the Digital Humanities*. Palgrave Macmillan, New York, pp. 19–34.

Schrock, A.R. (2016) 'Case study: Code for America – Scaling civic engagement through open data and software design', in Gordon, E., and Mihailidis, P. (eds) *Civic Media: Technology, Design, Practice*. MIT Press, Cambridge, MA, pp. 217–19.

Schroeder, P. (1996) 'Report on Public Participation GIS Workshop', in Harris, T., and Weiner, D. (eds) *GIS and Society: The Social Implications of How People, Space, and Environment Are Represented in GIS*. Scientific Report for the Initiative 19 Specialist Meeting, National Centre for Geographic Information, March 2–5, South Haven, MN.

Schrock, A. (2018) *Civic Tech: Making Technology Work for People*. Rogue Academic Press, Los Angeles, CA.

Schumpeter, J. (1942) *Capitalism, Socialism and Democracy*. Taylor and Francis, London.

Schuurman, N. (2020) 'Epistemology', in Wilson J.P. (ed.) *The Geographic Information Science & Technology Body of Knowledge* (1st quarter 2020 edn), https://doi.org/10.22224/gistbok/2020.1.3 (accessed 22 August 2023).

Schuurman, N., and Pratt, G. (2002) 'Care of the subject: Feminism and critiques of GIS', *Gender, Place & Culture*, 9(3): 291–9.

Scotland, J. (2012) 'Exploring the philosophical underpinnings of research: Relating ontology and epistemology to the methodology and methods of the scientific, interpretive, and critical research paradigms', *English Language Teaching*, 5(9): 9–16.

Scott Jones, J., and Goldring, J. (2022) *Exploratory and Descriptive Statistics*. Sage, London.

Searle, J.R. (1995) *The Construction of Social Reality*. Free Press, New York.

Searle, J.R. (2010) *Making the Social World: The Structure of Human Civilization*. Oxford University Press, Oxford.

Seaver, N. (2013) 'Knowing algorithms', *Media in Transition 8*, Cambridge, MA, digitalsts.net/wp-content/uploads/2019/11/26_digitalSTS_Knowing-Algorithms.pdf.

Segel, E., and Heer, J. (2010) 'Narrative visualization: Telling stories with data', *IEEE Transactions on Visualization and Computer Graphics*, 16(6): 1139–48.

Seitz, S. (2016) 'Pixilated partnerships, overcoming obstacles in qualitative interviews via Skype: A research note', *Qualitative Research*, 16(2): 229–35.

Seni, G., and Elder, J. (2010) *Ensemble Methods in Data Mining: Improving Accuracy Through Combining Predictions*. Morgan and Claypool, San Rafael, CA.

Sewell, W.H. (2005) *Logics of History: Social Theory and Social Transformation*. University of Chicago Press, Chicago, IL.

Shapiro, A. (2020) *Design, Control, Predict: Logistical Governance in the Smart City*. University of Minnesota Press, Minneapolis, MN.

Shelton, T., Zook, M., and Wiig, A. (2015) 'The 'actually existing smart city'', *Cambridge Journal of Regions, Economy and Society*, 8(1): 13–25.

Shi, W., Fisher, P., and Goodchild, M.F. (2003) *Spatial Data Quality*. CRC Press, London.

Shirk, J.L., Ballard H.L., Wilderman, C.C., et al. (2012) 'Public Participation in Scientific Research: A Framework for Deliberate Design', *Ecology and Society*, 17(2): 29.

Sieber, R. (2006) 'Public Participation Geographic Information Systems: A Literature Review and Framework', *Annals of the Association of American Geographers*, 96(3): 491–507.

Siegel, E. (2013) *Predictive Analytics*. John Wiley & Sons, Hoboken, NJ.

Silver, N. (2012) *The Signal and The Noise: The Art and Science of Prediction*. Penguin, London.

Silvertown, J. (2009) 'A new dawn for citizen science', *Trends in Ecology & Evolution*, 24(9): 467–71.

Singer, M. (2013) 'On convention', in Singer, M., and Walker, N. (eds) *Bending Genre: Essays on Creative Non-Fiction*. Bloomsbury, London, pp. 141–49.

Singer, M., and Walker, N. (2013a) 'Introduction', in Singer, M., and Walker, N. (eds) *Bending Genre: Essays on Creative Non-Fiction*. Bloomsbury, London, pp. 1–7.

Singer, M., and Walker, N. (2013b) 'Unconvention', in Singer, M., and Walker, N. (eds) *Bending Genre: Essays on Creative Non-Fiction*. Bloomsbury, London, p. 139.

Singh, S.S. (2022) *Screening Surveillance*. Surveillance Studies Centre, University of Ottawa, www.surveillance-studies.ca/projects/screening-surveillance (accessed 22 August 2023).

Siriano, C.R.R. (2021) 'Digital labour in the Philippines: Emerging forms of brokerage', *Media International Australia*, 179(1): 23–37.

Sloane, D.J. (2009) 'Visualizing qualitative information', *The Qualitative Report*, 14(3): 489–97.

Smith, A., and Martín, A.P. (2021) 'Going beyond the smart city? Implementing technopolitical platforms for urban democracy in Madrid and Barcelona', *Journal of Urban Technology*, 28(1–2): 311–30.

Smith, H. (2019a) 'Metrics, locations, and lift: Mobile location analytics and the production of second-order geodemographics', *Information, Communication & Society*, 22(8): 1044–61.

Smith, H. (2019b) 'People-based marketing and the cultural economies of attribution metrics', *Journal of Cultural Economy*, 12(3): 201–14.

Smith, L.T. (2012) *Decolonizing Methodologies: Research and Indigenous Peoples*. Zed Books, London.

Smith, L.T., Maxwell, T.K., Puke, H., and Temara, P. (2016) 'Indigenous knowledge, methodology and mayhem: What is the role of methodology in producing Indigenous insights? A discussion from Mātauranga Māori', *Knowledge Cultures*, 4(3): 131–56.

Smith, T.A., Laurier, E., Reeves, S., et al. (2020) '"Off the beaten map": Navigating with digital maps on moorland', *Transactions of the Institute of British Geographers*, 45(1): 223–40.

Solove, D. (2013) 'Privacy management and the consent dilemma', *Harvard Law Review*, 126: 1880–903.

Song, Z., Roth, R.E., and Houtman, L. (2022) 'Visual storytelling with maps: An empirical study on story map themes and narrative elements, visual storytelling genres and tropes, and individual audience differences', *Cartographic Perspectives*, https://doi.org/10.14714/CP100.1759 (accessed 22 August 2023).

Speed, C., and Luger, E. (2019) 'Sensing data in the home', in Schnädelbach, H., and Kirk, D. (eds) *People, Personal Data and the Built Environment*. Springer, Cham, pp. 123–42.

Spiegelhalter, D. (2019) *The Art of Statistics: Learning from Data*. Pelican, London.

Spilda, F. U., Howson, K., Johnston, H., Bertolini, A., Feuerstein, P., Bezuidenhout, L., Alyanak, O., and Graham, M. (2022) 'Is anonymity dead? Doing critical research on digital labour platforms through platform interfaces', *Work Organisation, Labour & Globalisation*, 16(1): 82–7.

Springgay, S., and Truman, S.E. (2018) *Walking Methodologies in a More-than-Human World: WalkingLab*. Routledge, London.

Stanley, L., and Wise, S. (1993) *Breaking Out Again: Feminist Ontology and Epistemology*. Routledge, London.

Stark, L. (2014) 'Come on feel the data (and smell it)', *The Atlantic*, 19 May, www.theatlantic.com/technology/archive/2014/05/data-visceralization/370899/ (accessed 22 August 2023).

Starosielski, N. (2015) *The Undersea Network*. Duke University Press, Durham, NC.

Steiner, E. (2019) 'Flow maps', in Wilson, J.P. (ed.) *The Geographic Information Science & Technology Body of Knowledge* (4th quarter 2019 edn), https://doi.org/10.22224/gistbok/2019.4.10 (accessed 22 August 2023).

Stephany, S., Kässi, O., and Lehdonvirta, V. (n.d.) *Online Labour Index 2020*, http://onlinelabourobservatory.org/oli-demand/ (accessed 24 January 2023).

Stevenson, M., and Ben-David, A. (2019) 'Network analysis for Web history', in Brugger, N. and Milligan, I. (eds) *The Sage Handbook of Web History*. Sage, London, pp. 125–37.

Stewart, D.W., and Shamdasani, P. (2017) 'Online focus groups', *Journal of Advertising*, 46(1): 48–60.

Strasser, B.J., Baudry, J., Mahr, D., Sanchez, G., and Tancoigne, E. (2019) '"Citizen science"? Rethinking science and public participation', *Science and Technology Sciences*, 32(2): 52–76.

Sui, D., Goodchild, M., and Elwood, S. (2013) 'Volunteered Geographic Information, the Exaflood, and the Growing Digital Divide', in Sui, D.Z., Elwood, S., and Goodchild, M.F. (eds) *Crowdsourcing Geographic Knowledge: Volunteered Geographic Information (VGI) in Theory and Practice*. Springer, Berlin, pp. 1–12.

Sullivan, J.R. (2012) 'Skype: An appropriate method of data collection for qualitative interviews?', *The Hilltop Review*, 6(1): 54–60.

Suwaileh, R., Elsayed, T., Imran, M., et al. (2022) 'When a disaster happens, we are ready: Location mention recognition from crisis tweets', *International Journal of Disaster Risk Reduction*, 78: 1037.

Swart, J. (2021) 'Experiencing algorithms: How young people understand, feel about, and engage with algorithmic news selection on social media', *Social Media + Society*, 7(2): 1–11.

Szanto, D., and Sicotte, G. (2022) 'Research-creation about and with food: Diffraction, pluralism, and knowing', *Journal for Artistic Research*, 26, www.jar-online.net/en/exposition/abstract/research-creation-about-and-food-diffraction-pluralism-and-knowing (accessed 22 August 2023).

Tacchi, J., and Chandola, T. (2015) 'Complicating connectivity: Women's negotiations with smartphones in an Indian slum', in Hjorth, L., and Khoo, O. (eds) *Routledge Handbook of New Media in Asia*. Routledge, London, pp. 179–88.

Taleb, N. (2013) 'Beware the big errors of "big data"', *Wired*, 2 February, www.wired.com/2013/02/big-data-means-big-errors-people/ (accessed 2 December 2020).

Tang, M.C., Cheng, Y.J., and Chen, K.H. (2017) 'A longitudinal study of intellectual cohesion in digital humanities using bibliometric analyses', *Scientometrics*, 113: 985–1008.

Tarr, J., Gonzalez-Polledo, E., and Cornish, F. (2018) 'On liveness: Using arts workshops as a research method', *Qualitative Research*, 18(1): 36–52.

Taylor, L., Floridi, L., and van der Sloot, B. (eds) (2017) *Group Privacy: New Challenges of Data Technologies*. Springer, Cham.

Tene, O., and Polonetsky, J. (2012) 'Big data for all: Privacy and user control in the age of analytics', *Northwestern Journal of Technology and Intellectual Property*, 11(5): 240–73.

Thacker, E. (2010) *After Life*. University of Chicago Press, Chicago, IL.

Thatcher, J. (2014) 'Living on fumes: Digital footprints, data fumes, and the limitations of spatial big data', *International Journal of Communication*, 8: 1765–83.

The Regents of the University of California (2019) *Visualizing Data: A Guide to Chart Types*. Berkeley Graduate School of Journalism Advanced Media Institute, https://guides.lib.berkeley.edu/data-visualization/type (accessed 26 September 2022).

Thornton, P. (2018) 'A critique of linguistic capitalism: Provocation/intervention', *GeoHumanities*, 4(2): 417–37.

Tifentale, A., and Manovich, L. (2015) 'Selfiecity: Exploring photography and self-fashioning in social media', in Berry, D., and Dieter, M. (eds) *Postdigital Aesthetics*. Palgrave Macmillan, London. pp. 109–22.

Tiidenberg, K. (2018) 'Ethics in digital research', in Flick, U. (ed.) *The Sage Handbook of Qualitative Data Collection*. Sage, London, pp. 466–79.

Tkacz, N. (2015) *Wikipedia and the Politics of Openness*. University of Chicago Press, Chicago, IL.

Tomás, L., and Bidet, O. (2023) 'Conducting qualitative interviews via VoIP technologies: Reflections on rapport, technology, digital exclusion, and ethics', *International Journal of Social Research Methodology*, https://doi.org/10.1080/13645579.2023.2183007 (accessed 22 August 2023).

Towner, T., and Muñoz, C.L. (2020) 'Instagramming issues: Agenda setting during the 2016 Presidential campaign', *Social Media + Society*, 6(3): 1–13.

Tranos, E. (2013) *The Geography of the Internet: Cities, Regions and Internet Infrastructure*. Edward Elgar, Cheltenham.

Troeger, J., and Bock, A. (2022) 'The sociotechnical walkthrough – a methodological approach for platform studies', *Studies in Communication Sciences*, 22(1): 43–52.

Truman, S. (2021) *Feminist Speculations and the Practice of Research-Creation: Writing Pedagogies and Intertextual Affects*. Routledge, London.

Trumpener, K. (2009) 'Critical response I. Paratext and genre system: A response to Franco Moretti', *Critical Inquiry*, 36(1): 159–71.

Tuck, E., and Yang, K.W. (2012) 'Decolonization is not a metaphor', *Decolonization: Indigeneity, Education & Society*, 1(1): 1–40.

Tufte, E.R. (1983) *The Visual Display of Quantitative Information*. Graphics Press, Cheshire, CT.
Tufte, E.R. (1990) *Envisioning Information*. Graphics Press, Cheshire, CT.
Tufte, E.R. (1997) *Visual Explanations: Images and Quantities, Evidence and Narrative*. Graphics Press, Cheshire, CT.
Tufte, E.R. (2006) *Beautiful Evidence*. Graphics Press, Cheshire, CT.
Tukey, J.W. (1977) *Exploratory Data Analysis*. Addison-Wesley, Reading, MA.
Tuttas, C.A. (2015) 'Lessons learned using Web conference technology for online focus group interviews', *Qualitative Health Research*, 25(1): 122–33.
Uboldi, G., and Caviglia, G. (2015) 'Information visualizations and interfaces in the Humanities', in Bihanic, D. (ed.) *New Challenges for Data Design*. Springer, Cham, pp. 207–81.
UNECE (2014) *A Suggested Framework for the Quality of Big Data*. United Nations Economic Commission for Europe, https://statswiki.unece.org/download/attachments/108102944/Big%20Data%20Quality%20Framework%20-%20final-%20Jan08-2015.pdf (accessed February 2021).
University of California Curation Centre (2022) *Data Management General Guidance*, https://dmptool.org/general_guidance (accessed 7 March 2022).
Urban Praxis (2017) *O'Hair Park Campaign*, https://urbanpraxis.org/research/ (accessed 2 December 2020).
Utrecht Data School (n.d.) *Data Ethics Decision Aid for Researchers*, https://deda.dataschool.nl/en/.
Valentine, G. (1997) 'Tell me about …: using interviews as a research methodology', in Flowerdew, R., and Martin, D. (eds) *Methods in Human Geography*, 2nd edn. Routledge, London, pp. 110–27.
Valori, I., McKenna-Plumley, P.E., Bayramova, R., Zandonella Callegher, C., Altoè, G., and Farroni, T. (2020) 'Proprioceptive accuracy in immersive virtual reality: A developmental perspective', *PLoS ONE*, 15(1): e0222253.
van der Vlist, F.N., and Helmond, A. (2021) 'How partners mediate platform power: Mapping business and data partnerships in the social media ecosystem', *Big Data & Society*, 8(1): 1–16.
van Dijck, J. (2014) 'Datafication, dataism and dataveillance: Big Data between scientific paradigm and ideology', *Surveillance & Society*, 12(2): 197–208.
van Doorn, N. (2013) 'Assembling the affective field: How smartphone technology impacts ethnographic research practice', *Qualitative Inquiry*, 19(5): 385–96.
van Es, K., and de Lange, M. (2020) 'Data with its boots on the ground: Datawalking as research method', *European Journal of Communication*, 35(3): 278–89.
van Selm, M. and Jankowski, N.W. (2006) 'Conducting online surveys', *Quality and Quantity*, 40(3): 435–56.
van Zeeland, I., van den Broeck, W., Boonen, M., et al. (2021) 'Effects of digital mediation and familiarity in online video interviews between peers', *Methodological Innovations*, 14(3): 1–15.
Vaughan, L. (2014) *Beginning Ethics: An Introduction to Moral Philosophy*. W.W. Norton, New York.

Vehovar, V., and Manfreda, K.L. (2017) *The Sage Handbook of Online Research Methods.* Sage, London.

Verhoeven, H., van Hecke, L., van Dyck, D., et al. (2018) 'Differences in physical environmental characteristics between adolescents' actual and shortest cycling routes: A study using a Google Street View-based audit', *International Journal of Health Geographics*, 17(1): 16.

Vincent, M. (2017) 'Crowdsourced data for cultural heritage', in Vincent, M.L. et al. (eds) *Heritage and Archaeology in the Digital Age: Acquisition, Curation, and Dissemination of Spatial Cultural Heritage Data.* Springer, Cham, pp. 1–26.

Waclawski, E. (2012) 'How I use it: Survey Monkey', *Occupational Medicine*, 62(6): 477.

Wagner, A.J. (2018) 'Do not click "Like" when somebody has died: The role of norms for mourning practices in social media', *Social Media+ Society*, 4(1): 1–11.

Wagner, B. (2018) 'Ethics as an escape from regulation: From ethics-washing to ethicsshopping?', in Hildebrandt, M. (ed.) *Being Profiling. Cogitas ergo sum.* Amsterdam University Press, Amsterdam, pp. 84–9.

Walter, M., and Andersen, C. (2013) *Indigenous Statistics: A Quantitative Research Methodology.* Left Coast Press, Walnut Creek, CA.

Walter-Herrmann, J., and Buching, C. (2013) *FabLab: Of Machines, Makers and Inventors.* Transcript Verlag, Bielefeld.

Wang, H., Mostafizi, A., Cramer, L.A., Cox, D., and Park, H. (2016) 'An agent-based model of a multimodal near-field tsunami evacuation: Decision-making and life safety', *Transportation Research Part C: Emerging Technologies*, 64(1): 86–100.

Warf, B. (2011) 'Teaching time-space compression', *Journal of Geography in Higher Education*, 35(2): 143–61.

Wasserman, S., and Faust, K. (1994) *Social Network Analysis: Methods and Applications.* Cambridge University Press, Cambridge.

Watson, A. (2020) 'Methods braiding: A technique for arts-based and mixed-methods research', *Sociological Research Online*, 25(1): 66–83.

Watson, A., Clark, M., Southerton, C., et al. (2021) 'Fieldwork at your fingertips: Creative methods for social research under lockdown', *Nature*, 3 March. www.nature.com/articles/d41586-021-00566-2 (accessed 12 June 2023).

Webster, D. (2021) *Beyond the click: Interventions in digital adspace.* PhD thesis, Queens University Belfast. https://pure.qub.ac.uk/en/studentTheses/beyond-the-click (accessed 22 August 2023).

Webster, P. (2019) 'Existing Web archives', in Brugger, N., and Milligan, I. (eds) *The Sage Handbook of Web History.* Sage, London, pp. 30–41.

Weinberg, T. (n.d.) *About the woven climate datascapes*, www.taliweinberg.com/datascapes (accessed 22 August 2023).

Wellbrook, C. (2014) 'A workers' inquiry or an inquiry of workers?', *Ephemera: Theory & Politics in Organization*, 14(3): 357–54.

Weller, S. (2017) 'Using internet video calls in qualitative (longitudinal) interviews: Some implications for rapport', *International Journal of Social Research Methodology*, 20(6): 613–25.

Weltevrede, E., and Jansen, F. (2019) 'Infrastructures of intimate data: Mapping the inbound and outbound data flows of dating apps', *Computational Culture*, 7: 1–41.

Wensveen, S., and Matthews, B. (2015) 'Prototypes and prototyping in design research', in Rodgers, P.A., and Yee, J. (eds) *Routledge Companion to Design Research*. Routledge, London, pp. 262–76.

White House Office of Science and Technology Policy (2022a) *Blueprint for an AI Bill of Rights: Making Automated Systems Work for the American People*, www.whitehouse.gov/ostp/ai-bill-of-rights/ (accessed 3 March 2023).

White House Office of Science and Technology Policy (2022b) Blueprint for an AI Bill of Rights: Making Automated Systems Work for the American People., www.whitehouse.gov/wp-content/uploads/2022/10/Blueprint-for-an-AI-Bill-of-Rights.pdf (accessed 12 January 2024).

Whitson, R. (2017) 'Painting pictures of ourselves: Researcher subjectivity in the practice of feminist reflexivity', *The Professional Geographer*, 69(2): 299–306.

Wildbur, P. (1989) *Information Graphics: A Survey of Typographic, Diagrammatic, and Cartographic Communication*. Van Nostrand Reinhold Company, New York.

Wilkinson, M.D. et al. (2016) 'The FAIR Guiding Principles for scientific data management and stewardship', *Scientific Data*, 3: 160018.

Wilkinson, S. (1998) 'Focus group methodology: A review', *International Journal of Social Research Methodology*, 1(3): 181–203.

Willcox, M.G., and Hickey-Moody, A.C. (2020) 'Queer materialities and the Instagram live interviewing: Community Entanglements', *AoIR Selected Papers of Internet Research*, https://doi.org/10.5210/spir.v2020i0.11363 (accessed 22 August 2023).

Willemsen, R.F., Aardoom, J.J., Chavannes, N.H., et al. (2022) 'Online synchronous focus group interviews: Practical considerations', *Qualitative Research*, https://doi.org/10.1177/14687941221110161 (accessed 22 August 2023).

Williams, A. (2017) *History of Digital Games: Developments in Art, Design and Interaction*. CRC Press, London.

Williams, M., Bagwell, J., and Zozus, M.N. (2017) 'Data management plans: The missing perspective', *Journal of Biomedical Informatics*, 71(July): 130–42.

Williams, S. (2016) 'Data visualizations break down knowledge barriers in public engagement', in Gordon, E., and Mihailidis, P. (eds) *Civic Media: Technology, Design and Practice*. MIT Press, Cambridge, pp. 165–98.

Wilmott, C. (2016) 'Small moments in Spatial Big Data: Calculability, authority and interoperability in everyday mobile mapping', *Big Data & Society*, 3(2): 1–16.

Wise, S., Crooks, A., and Batty, M. (2017) 'Transportation in agent-based urban modelling', in Namazi-Rad, M.-R., Padgham, L., Perez, P., Nagel, K., and Bazzan, A. (eds) *Agent Based Modelling of Urban Systems*. Springer, Cham, pp. 129–48.

Wood, J. (2022) GPS Drawing. http://www.gpsdrawing.com/.

Woodcock, J. (2014) 'The workers' inquiry from Trotskyism to *Operaismo*: A political methodology for investigating the workplace', *Ephemera: Theory & Politics in Organization*, 14(3): 493–513.

Woodcock, J. (2021) 'Towards a digital workerism: Workers' inquiry, methods, and technologies', *NanoEthics*, 15: 87–98.

Woodcock, J., and Graham, M. (2020) *The Gig Economy: A Critical Introduction*. Polity Press, Cambridge.

Woodcock, J., Tainio, M., Cheshire, J., et al. (2014) 'Health effects of the London bicycle sharing system: Health impact modelling study', *BMJ*, 348: 1–14.

Woods, O. (2020) 'Gamifying place, reimagining publicness: The heterotopic inscriptions of Pokémon Go', *Media, Culture & Society*, 42(6): 1003–18.

Woods, O. (2021) 'The territoriality of teams: Assembling power through the playing of Pokémon Go', *Mobile Media & Communication*, 9(3): 405–21.

Wynn, J. (2017) *Citizen Science in the Digital Age: Rhetoric, Science and Public Engagement*. University of Alabama Press, Tuscaloosa, AL.

Yang, F., Heemsbergern, L., and Marshall, D.P. (2022) 'Studying WeChat official accounts with novel 'backend-in' and 'traceback' methods: Walking through platforms back-to-front and past-to-present', *Media International Australia*, 184(1): 63–78.

Yau, N. (2011) *Visualize This: The FlowingData Guide to Design, Visualization, and Statistics*. John Wiley & Sons, Indianapolis, IN.

Yau, N. (2013) *Data Points: Visualization That Means Something*. John Wiley & Sons, Indianapolis, IN.

Yeo, T.E.D., and Fung, T.H. (2018) '"Mr Right Now": Temporality of relationship formation on gay mobile dating apps', *Mobile Media & Communication*, 6(1): 3–18.

Zaltz, A.M., O'Brien, O., Strano, E., et al. (2013) 'The structure of spatial networks and communities in bicycle sharing systems', *PloS One*, 8(9): e74685.

Zasina, J. (2018) 'The Instagram image of the city: Insights from Lodz, Poland', *Bulletin of Geography, Socio-economic Series*, (42): 213–25.

Zeffiro, A., Hildebrand, J.M., Frith, J., et al. (2020) 'Locative-media ethics: A call for protocols to guide interactions of people, place, and technologies', *Journalism & Mass Communication Quarterly*, 97(1): 13–29.

Zhang, Y., and Su, R. (2021) 'An optimization model and traffic light control scheme for heterogeneous traffic systems', *Transportation Research Part C: Emerging Technologies*, 124: 102911.

Zimmer, M. (2018) 'Addressing conceptual gaps in big data research ethics: An application of contextual integrity', *Social Media + Society*, 4(3): 1–11.

Zimmer, M., and Kinder-Kurlanda, K. (2017a) 'Introduction', in Zimmer, M., and Kinder-Kurlanda, K. (eds) *Internet Research Ethics for the Social Age: New Challenges, Cases, and Contexts*. Peter Lang, New York, pp. ix–xxvii.

Zimmer, M., and Kinder-Kurlanda, K. (eds) (2017b) *Internet Research Ethics for the Social Age: New Challenges, Cases, and Contexts*. Peter Lang, New York.

Zook, M., Graham, M., Shelton, T., et al. (2010) 'Volunteered geographic information and crowdsourcing disaster relief: A case study of the Haitian earthquake', *World Medical and Health Policy*, 2(2): 7–33.

Zook, M., and Poorthuis, A. (2015) 'Small stories in big data: Gaining insights from large spatial point pattern datasets', *Cityscape: A Journal of Policy Development and Research*, 17(1): 151–60.

Zuboff, S. (2019) *The Age of Surveillance Capitalism: The Fight for the Future at the New Frontier of Power.* Profile Books, New York.

Zwaanswijk, M., and van Dulmen, S. (2014) 'Advantages of asynchronous online focus groups and face-to-face focus groups as perceived by child, adolescent and adult participants: A survey study', *BMC Research Notes*, 7: 756.

Index

3D
    model 134, 151, 153, 163, 171, 175
    geovisualisation 121, 171, 177
    printed model 119, 223
5G 5, 229, 230, 256

access 29, 30, 31, 32, 35, 36–7, 43, 48, 54, 57, 58, 59, 60, 62, 65, 66, 72, 76, 121, 129, 131, 132, 136, 146–9, 225, 256
accountability 48, 55, 57, 64, 123, 221
agency 5
agent-based model 38, 187, 225–6
aggregation 37, 41, 131, 161, 164, 174, 175, 181, 188, 224
Airbnb 60, 137
algorithm 5, 12, 21, 22, 29, 36, 58, 64, 93, 96, 102–6, 180, 183, 193–203, 219, 240
    audit 103–6
anonymisation 36, 48, 59, 80, 93
APIs 29, 37, 59, 60, 86, 104, 131, 134, 210, 211, 213
Apple Maps 206
appropriation 52
archives 36–7, 43, 61, 64–5, 136, 137, 144, 146–9, 152, 153–5, 219, 220, 256
    community 137, 154
artificial intelligence (AI) 5, 10, 22, 93, 102, 103, 104–6, 150, 240, 256
arts-based methods 109–24
artistic practice 17, 110, 117–8, 123
audits 101–6, 222–4
augmented reality 119, 163, 200
autoethnography 12, 83, 87–8, 98, 116, 246
automated facial recognition *see facial recognition*
automatic speech recognition 150
autonomy 5, 22, 48, 50, 51, 57, 65, 180, 218, 230, 244

bar chart 165, 202, 244
beneficence 48, 61
benchmarking 105–6
bias 9, 24, 25, 34, 38, 19, 40, 41, 42, 52, 64, 81, 92, 101, 102, 105, 106, 154, 180, 181
biographies 117, 145, 149–50, 153,

black-boxed 8, 12, 29, 36, 103, 104, 148, 221
boxplot 164–5
budget 33

calibration 39, 40
CARE principles 43
cartography 159, 171
children 51, 116, 242
citizen science 40, 128–30, 132, 135, 139, 171, 234
civic
    engagement 132–3
    hacking 137–8
    media 137–8
    tech 234–5
classification 105, 129, 182, 183, 185, 200
coercion 63
completeness 38, 40
computational social science 24, 180, 257
confidentiality 37, 43, 48, 58–9, 61, 65, 79
consent 47, 48, 49, 51, 52, 54, 55, 57, 58, 59–60, 61, 62, 63–4, 65, 88
consistency 38, 39, 40, 41, 123, 129
constructivist 18, 19, 20, 21, 24, 26
content analysis 10, 210, 212
contextual integrity 49, 50–1, 55
control room 221
counter
    archiving 128, 136, 137
    data action 130
    data visualisation 161
coverage 30, 34, 38, 40
covert research 62–3, 83
Covid-19 121, 161, 201, 202
creative
    non-fiction 116, 120–1
    writing 109, 115–7, 120–1, 123
credibility 40–1, 123
critical GIS 189, 190
crowdsourcing 40, 104, 129–31, 171, 206, 240, 257
    commercial 63–4
cultural analytics 160, 169–70, 177, 214, 232–3

data
    activism 136
    analytics 24, 37, 64, 129, 152, 179–90, 198, 257
    big 34, 37, 40, 42, 58, 59, 61, 148, 152, 158, 159, 175, 179, 180, 181, 184, 186, 187, 188, 224, 225, 256
    aggregated *see aggregation*
    broker 148–9
    derived 34, 36, 37–8, 42, 43, 60
    dredging 41, 42, 182, 188
    feminism 25, 189
    geographical *see spatial data*
    historical 61
    management plan 42–44, 59
    minimisation 58, 59–60, 65
    mining 182–3, 186
    physicalisation 119
    primary 33–6, 61–66, 149–51, 256
    protection 43, 53, 59, 65
    qualitative 10, 17, 65, 97, 166–8, 171
    quality 30, 38–41, 42, 43, 54, 129, 140, 141, 181–2
    quantitative 10, 16, 40–1, 65, 80, 97, 158, 163, 164, 166–70, 181
    reborn 154
    re-use 30, 43, 59, 64–5, 147, 155
    secondary 36–7, 38, 49, 53, 57–61
    sharing 6, 39, 42, 43, 49, 53, 58, 60, 65, 129, 130, 131, 144, 146–50, 152, 154, 205, 225
    simulated 33, 37–8, 224
    sovereignty 43, 52
    spatial 127, 131, 157–8, 162, 170–1
    stories 119, 161
    tertiary 36, 37–8, 43, 53
    training 22, 38, 42, 105, 180–1, 183
    transformation 37, 39, 42, 43, 181, 186
    wrangling 38–9, 42, 43, 181
datafication 25, 37, 95, 98, 122, 136, 200, 230, 256
decolonialism 19–21, 52, 111
deduction 16, 17, 25, 31, 34
deidentification 58–9, 60, 65
Deliveroo 247–248
democracy 130, 134, 135, 154
digital
    ethnographies, *see* ethnographies, digital
    life 3–4, 8–11, 13, 21, 233
    humanities 145, 151–3, 155, 180, 257
    methods 29, 30, 33–4, 151, 257
digital, the xv, 4–6, 255–7
digitality 4, 5–6, 7, 9, 21, 143
digitisation 143, 146, 153, 257
disability 51, 52, 74, 78, 102, 137
disaggregation 161, 188

discourse 5, 7, 8, 92, 93
discourse analysis 11, 116, 176
drones 150, 218

ecological fallacy 41–2, 182
embodiment 6, 24, 25, 84, 85, 92, 93, 95, 111, 199, 200, 209, 220
empiricism 23
ensemble method 42, 182, 187–8
epistemology 15–6, 20, 22–5, 26, 29, 30, 33, 56, 93, 106, 111, 114, 124, 127, 145, 151, 155, 179, 180, 185, 188–9, 256, 257
error 38, 39, 40, 42, 181, 185
ethics 20, 25, 30, 43, 47–66, 76, 104, 112, 134, 141, 149, 155, 188, 230
ethnography 10, 12, 62, 82–7, 199–201, 202, 207, 219–20, 241–3, 246, 247
    covert 83
    digital 13, 29, 83, 84–7, 230
    video 84, 85, 200, 207
    virtual 83–4
ethnomethodology 207–8, 221
exhibition 122
exploratory data analysis 160

fabrication 48
Facebook 63, 75, 76, 86, 137, 169, 196, 205, 206, 242
facial recognition 105–6, 183, 214, 224
fair information practice principles 37, 53, 54–5, 59
FAIR principles 43
false positives 42, 182
feminism 6, 8, 9, 12, 17, 24–5, 26, 50, 56, 111, 188–9
feminist data science 25, 189
film 85, 110, 121–2, 160
flow diagram 168
focus group 33, 35, 76–9, 134, 208, 230, 242

Gantt chart 32, 33
GDPR 43, 53, 59, 65
gender 6, 19, 24, 51, 59, 77, 78, 86, 100, 101, 102, 103, 105, 106, 136, 196, 214, 222, 223, 230, 242
geographic information science 159
Geographic Information Systems (GIS) 12, 44, 133, 152, 153, 177
geotag 95, 118, 171, 174, 175, 206, 210, 211, 212, 213
geovisualisation 171–5
glyphs 121, 170
gig
    economy 218, 241, 242, 243
    work 19, 240, 241–3, 247, 248, 249

GitHub 25, 34, 200
Google 25, 37, 73, 76, 77, 80, 81, 88, 117, 118, 131, 171, 193, 194, 201, 202, 206, 223, 224, 240
Google Maps 118, 131, 206
GPS 96, 117, 129, 131, 171, 218, 223, 224, 226, 227, 231
Grindr 206, 208
graphs 41, 164–5, 169, 185, 202, 210, 214, 244

hackathon 132, 138, 139, 140
historical methods 143–56
historiography 144, 148, 151–3
humanities computing 151–2
hypothesis 16, 17, 23, 24, 110, 160, 185, 190, 256

induction 16, 25, 31, 232, 233
image plot 170, 233
Indigenous knowledge 19, 20–1, 43, 50, 52, 149, 161, 208
integrity 140–1
Instagram 37, 73, 82, 169, 171, 205, 206, 209, 210, 212, 213–4
Institutional Review Board (IRB) 49, 50, 51, 53, 55, 61, 63, 66
intellectual property 21, 37, 43, 60
interface 5, 8, 22, 58, 73, 85, 87, 92, 99, 100, 103, 119, 158, 193–203, 207, 220, 229, 240, 249
interpretivism 20, 24
interview 11, 33, 35, 36, 37, 40, 62, 72–6, 77, 78, 79, 80, 84, 85, 86, 87, 97–8, 100, 117 195, 196, 198, 200, 208, 209, 210, 219–22, 241–3, 249
   gaming 200
   mobile instant messaging 74, 78
   online 73–5
   oral history 149–50
   semi-structured 72, 84
   structured 72, 79
   unstructured 72
   text-based 75
   video 62, 73, 74, 75, 76, 77, 257
   walking 97–8, 207–8
irreducible 4, 5, 9, 13

justice 43, 48, 61, 111, 116, 189

labour 7, 13, 19, 25, 63, 209, 210, 218, 220, 239–49
locative media 117, 119, 205–14
logistics 131, 218–9, 230
longitudinal analysis 60, 83, 148, 153, 196, 256
lurking 62–3

machine learning 22, 42, 64, 103, 105, 180–3, 187, 189

mapping
   agencies 131
   applications 132, 201–2, 207
   cartographic 84, 96, 133, 145, 152, 158, 161, 171–5, 189, 207–8
   community 118
   counter 136, 161
   deep 152–3
   historical 152
   inequality 136, 161, 172
   linguistic 116
   maps 41, 42, 89, 95, 131, 117, 153, 159, 171–5
   mashups 131
   mental/mind 113, 115, 168
   practices 96, 132, 171–5
   platforms 210
   services 206
   sound 119, 212
   story 161
   thematic 171–5
   web 131, 175, 177
   user-generated 206
Marxism 7, 17, 19, 151
materialism 8–9, 21, 22, 246
matrices 167
Mechanical Turk 63, 214
mediation 7, 8, 9, 12, 13, 22, 33, 36, 56, 58, 62, 71, 72, 76, 77, 92, 93, 96, 97, 98, 101, 102, 120, 130, 133, 138–9, 146–9, 200, 218, 220, 231, 255, 257, 258
metadata 38, 39–40, 43, 129, 131, 140, 146–7, 150, 154, 161, 162, 166, 182, 185
metaphysics 23, 188
methodology 9–10, 11, 12, 15, 16–7, 19, 25, 26, 30, 31, 32, 33, 52, 56, 127, 142, 151, 153, 180, 255, 257, 258
mixed methods 32, 200
models 24, 37, 38, 39, 42, 64, 103, 105–6, 145, 153, 170, 180–1, 182, 186–8, 222, 224–7, 234
moral philosophy 49, 65
more-than-human 3, 116
multimodal 107, 176, 178

natural language processing 182–3
non-human 3, 5, 6, 7, 9, 20, 86, 231
non-representational theory 6
normative 23, 53, 55, 188, 189

objectivity 9, 21, 23–4, 25, 55, 56, 101, 123, 151, 188, 199, 206, 223, 229, 230, 231
objects 5, 6, 17, 18, 21–2, 58, 82, 85–6, 92, 93, 96, 99, 151, 163, 183, 184
observation 18, 82–3, 84, 94–5, 96, 97, 98, 100, 103, 196, 200, 219–21, 242

open
    access 37, 256
    data 37, 58, 59, 136, 147, 244
OpenStreetMap 34, 131, 140, 206
Online Labour Observatory 243–4, 245
online participation tools 133–4, 140
ontology 7, 15–6, 17–22, 23, 24, 25–6, 29, 30, 111, 146, 246
oral history 149–50
overfitting 42
overplotting 161, 175

panel companies 63–4
paradigm 16, 19, 21
participatory
    action research 130, 135–8
    methods 12, 13, 53, 96, 118, 124, 127–41, 189, 233–6, 244–7
    sensing 130–1, 132, 136, 140, 233–6,
payment 63–4
performance art 109, 113, 117, 118, 119
photogrammetry 150, 183, 185
photography, digital 23, 36, 37, 39, 57, 65, 77, 85, 85, 86, 87, 95, 96, 97, 107, 115, 118, 149, 150, 152, 153, 170 199, 214, 231
pie chart 163, 165, 185
pilot studies 32, 79, 256
plagiarism 48
platforms 6, 10, 12, 19, 25, 31, 34, 35, 36, 56, 57, 58, 59, 60, 61, 62–3, 66, 73, 75, 76, 77, 78, 80–1, 86, 87, 92, 99, 103, 104, 129, 131, 134, 137, 138, 147, 169, 194, 195, 196, 198, 200, 201, 205, 206, 210, 211, 213, 214, 219, 220, 223, 227, 232, 240, 241, 242, 243, 244, 246, 247–9
positionality 18, 24–5, 26, 56, 115, 189
positivism 20, 23–4, 26, 179, 185, 188–9
postcolonial 17, 52, 207
power 6, 11, 19, 20, 22, 49, 51–3, 55, 56, 79, 111, 118, 122, 137, 176, 208, 209, 218, 220, 246
practices 4, 6, 9, 12, 13, 18, 19, 20, 22, 24, 30, 33, 38, 42, 43, 71, 82, 8405, 87, 88, 92, 93, 95, 98, 99, 101, 102, 111, 158, 200, 218, 291, 230, 234, 243
pragmatism 6
prediction 31, 105, 135, 153, 181, 187, 188, 225
privacy 37, 43, 48, 49, 53, 57, 58–9, 63, 65, 76, 80, 86, 207, 230
    group 59
prototyping 230, 233–5
public participation GIS (PPGIS) 133

QGIS 177
qualitative coding 10, 213
questionnaire 12, 79–82, 134, 224, 246

race 19, 22, 24, 51, 101–3, 161, 222
ratings 79, 222, 247–9
realism 18, 23, 24
    critical 19, 24, 26
real-time 21, 74, 119, 131, 132, 134, 150, 171, 180, 182, 187, 205, 218, 219, 220
recruitment 35–6, 63, 74, 75, 76, 81, 82, 129, 139
redaction 65
reductionist 151, 163, 188
reflexivity 25, 49, 55–6, 114, 115, 120, 134
relativism 18, 19, 236
relational 8, 20–1, 56, 58, 112, 236
relevance 39, 40
reliability 39, 40, 54, 64, 105, 123, 140, 141, 150, 154
replication 23, 64, 65
representativeness 30, 34, 35, 39, 40, 41, 44, 56, 79, 81, 123, 140, 180, 209, 256
reproducibility 39, 43, 64, 65, 123
research
    creation 110–9, 123–4
    design 16, 26, 29, 30–3, 34, 47, 48, 50, 51–2, 56, 83, 110, 111, 112, 114, 129, 133, 135, 139
resourcing 32, 35, 43, 114, 140

sampling 30, 34–5, 38, 39, 40, 41, 44, 58, 63, 74, 81, 104, 123, 131, 139, 152, 180, 186, 209, 213, 225, 149
saturation point 35
scraping 29, 37, 49, 57, 58, 60–1, 104, 137, 149, 174, 201, 213, 244, 257
selfie 62, 197, 214
semiotic analysis 11, 100, 176
sensors 40, 96, 118, 130–1, 132, 171, 218, 220, 221, 224, 233–6
sentiment analysis 37, 183
serious games 134–5
sexuality 51, 80, 100, 195–6, 208
significance test 185, 186
simulation 12, 130, 134, 153, 163, 181, 186–8, 226, 234
situated knowledge 24–5, 56
situational ethics 55–6
smart
    card 224, 226
    city 13, 31, 117, 122, 132, 134, 135, 220, 221, 229–36
    watch 130, 218
smartphones 5, 86–7, 130, 151, 193, 104, 197, 202, 207–8, 212, 218, 220, 230, 256

social media 5, 6, 12, 30, 36, 37, 39, 40, 53, 57, 58, 59, 61, 62, 73, 75–6, 81, 82, 85, 111, 114, 118, 122, 129, 131, 134, 139, 144, 148, 152, 154, 163, 166, 168, 169, 171, 175, 183, 184, 205–14, 224, 232–3, 240, 243, 246, 249, 257
social network
    analysis 169, 183–4
    diagram 169
space-times 3, 7–8, 13, 199, 236
spectrum display 167
standardisation 38, 40, 42, 43, 50, 72, 79, 123, 129, 175
statistics 16, 34, 42, 52, 151, 152, 155, 159, 169, 177, 180, 184–6, 187, 188, 189, 257
    descriptive 152, 185
    inferential 185, 189
    radical 189
subjective 6, 18, 19, 24–5, 56, 88, 96, 123
surveillance 58, 95, 117, 122, 124, 207, 209, 230
survey 4, 33, 62, 72, 74, 79–82, 122, 134, 209, 224, 226

technicity 5, 22
temporality 4, 7–8, 18, 37, 38, 61, 96, 152, 175, 208, 221, 225, 227, 235, 242, 256
TikTok 37, 60
timeliness 39, 188
Tinder 194–5, 196
traffic management 220–22
transcription 73, 75, 150, 195, 208, 257
trust 36, 40, 41, 48, 50, 59, 63, 64, 76, 101, 117, 123, 139, 141, 150, 167
Twitter/X 75, 116, 118, 137, 169, 171, 175, 205, 206, 210, 211, 212, 2227, 232

Uber 8, 193, 218, 219–20, 222, 242
universalism 18, 50, 188

validity 31, 38, 39, 41, 56, 81, 154
veracity 38, 39, 40, 127
video 17, 37, 57, 65, 74, 77, 87, 95, 153, 160, 199
    conferencing 62, 73, 74, 75, 76
    ethnography, see ethnography, video
    interview, see interview, video
    recording 85, 86, 95, 100, 150, 207, 208
virtual
    audit 223–4
    ethnography, see ethnography,
    reality 119, 120, 122, 150, 151, 153, 163
    world 57, 83–4
visual methods 11, 176
visualisation 97, 122, 132, 152, 157–70, 175–7, 181, 200–2, 207, 210–4, 232–3, 243–4, 257
    quantitative data 10, 16, 40, 160, 163–66, 167, 171
voice over internet protocol (VOIP) 73, 74
volunteered geographic information (VGI) 130, 131, 132

walking methods 73, 91–8, 116, 223, 230–2, 234
walkthrough methods 73, 85, 98–101, 195–7, 200–2, 207–8
Web History 147–8
Whatsapp 73, 74, 77, 78, 80, 86, 87, 122, 193, 247
WiFi 5, 130, 205, 224, 229, 230
Wikipedia 34, 129, 140, 154
word cloud 119, 166
workers enquiry 246–7

Youtube 60, 198, 199, 205, 257

www.ingramcontent.com/pod-product-compliance
Lightning Source LLC
Chambersburg PA
CBHW080213040426
42333CB00044B/2650